OFFICE OF POPULATION

The Government Social Survey

A History

Louis Moss

London: HMSO

© Crown copyright 1991
First published 1991

ISBN 0 11 691302 9

Contents

	Page
List of abbreviations	iv
List of tables	v
Foreword	vii

Part one
1	Government, public concerns and public enquiry	1
2	1941–52: A new beginning	5
3	1952–57: Climbing back	26
4	1958–67: On a rising tide	40
5	1967–70: A government social survey department	59
6	1971–81: The research expansion and after	75

Part two: The Survey's contribution to government
7	Housing design, housing statistics, noise, mobility	109
8	Health and social services	127
9	Jobs, productivity and industrial relations	164
10	Income, expenditure and social security	193
11	Education, children and the family	201
12	Criminal justice and the law	217
13	Operational surveys	231
14	Institutions and scrutiny	247
15	An appraisal	255

Appendix A Paper for Estimates Committee, March 1966	269
Appendix B Government Social Survey Department: note by the Treasury	273
Appendix C Statement by senior staff on the announcement of the new office	277
Appendix D Summary of main topics included in the GHS questionnaires 1971 to 1981	279
Index	291

Abbreviations

AMSO	Association of Market Survey Organisations
BBC	British Broadcasting Corporation
BMA	British Medical Association
BRS/BRE	Building Research Station/Establishment
BSA	British Statistical Association
COI	Central Office of Information
CPRS	Central Policy Review Staff
CSO	Central Statistical Office
CSSR	Committee on Social Science Research
DHSS	Department of Health and Social Security
DSIR	Department of Scientific and Industrial Research
EEC	European Economic Community
FES	Family Expenditure Survey
FPA	Family Planning Association
GHS	General Household Survey
GPs	General Practitioners
GRO	General Register Office
GSSD	Government Social Survey Department
IMF	International Monetary Fund
IPCS	Institution of Professional Civil Servants
IPS	International Passenger Survey
LSE	London School of Economics
MOI	Ministry of Information
MRC	Medical Research Council
NAAS	National Agricultural Advisory Service
NCCOP	National Corporation for the Care of Old People
NHS	National Health Service
NIESR	National Institute of Economic and Social Research
OME	Office of Manpower Economics
OPCS	Office of Population Censuses and Surveys
PEP	Political and Economic Planning
RSS	Royal Statistical Society
SSRC	Social Science Research Council
WTSS	Wartime Social Survey

Tables

Table 1	Items in suggested 1954–5 programme	32
Table 2	Review of sponsored surveys	53
Table 3	Proposed programme and costs 1968–9	68
Table 4	Social Survey costs 1962–3 to 1968–9: percentage of total	69
Table 5	Continuous and ad hoc surveys: percentage of operational expenditure	69
Table 6	Resources 1970–71 to 1981–82	86
Table 7	Staffing 1971–81	86
Table 8	The main heating appliance of the main living room – postwar Local Authority sample	110
Table 9	Scottish miners: 'What occupation would you like for your son?	112
Table 10	1957 and 1959 net rents paid for unfurnished non-service tenants (1959)	115
Table 11	Housing Survey 1960	116
Table 12	Privately rented accommodation in London (1961)	117
Table 13	Attitudes to letting (1976)	120
Table 14	Distribution over noise levels of the total population and the 'annoyed' section of the population	122
Table 15	International migration: occupation, 1971–1980	125
Table 16	Milk consumption (1942)	129
Table 17	Consumption of eggs (1942)	130
Table 18	Average intake for one week of nutrients by food expenditure groups (1943)	131
Table 19	Average intake for one week of nutrients by age of child (1943)	132
Table 20	Cigarette smoking by sex (1982)	137
Table 21	Home help survey 1967	144
Table 22	Type of household in which elderly people live (1976)	146
Table 23	Personal mobility of elderly people (1976)	147
Table 24	Proportion of people with different degrees of handicap who are on the Local Authority register (1968)	148
Table 25	Proportion of handicapped people with different degrees of handicap benefiting from various health and welfare services (1968)	149

Table 26	Whether worker directors would affect managerial authority (1976) 181
Table 27	Informant's view on what worker participation should involve (1976) 182
Table 28	Composition of the labour force, 1975–1982 188
Table 29	Young school leavers (1966) 206
Table 30	Socio-economic group of father/head of household by type of school attended, by age of child (1973) 211
Table 31	The Police and the public (1960) 219
Table 32	Committee on the Management of Local Government (1965) 249
Table 33	Government Social Survey: Staff in post 1946–83 262
Table 34	Survey vote, actual and deflated 1941–2 to 1981–2 265

Foreword

THIS IS A HISTORY of a survey research unit which for over forty years has worked in and for government. It is therefore an account of applications of the sample survey method in a particular situation. The situation determined those applications and shaped the organisation created to deal with them. The social survey method originated many years before it came to be applied in the ways described here, but it was used intermittently, as concerned individuals sought to throw light on particular social problems. With one or two exceptions the method was not used officially in Britain before the last war, but in the 1930s it was used increasingly for commercial purposes, and for early exercises in the study of public opinion. The history of a public institution over such a long period must necessarily be affected by the changes in government purposes and organisation. Part of the story must therefore be an account of how the fortunes of the Survey reflected the changes in government. This history follows two main paths – a description of changes in the position of the Survey as part of government, and a description of the main subject areas to which the Survey contributed and how these changed over time.

Part One describes changes in the situations in government which provided the framework within which, under 12 different administrations, the Survey gradually grew, developed its structure and found its limitations. The sources for this historical account were the files of the Ministry of Information (MOI) located in the Public Record Office, files of the Central Office of Information (COI), the Government Social Survey Department (GSSD – a short-lived incarnation) and of the Office of Population Censuses and Surveys (OPCS). The early files were not in good order. Details of staffing and funding under different administrations were not necessarily presented consistently and some persistence was needed to produce a continuous account. What is given here seems reasonably consistent over time and is in agreement with the judgments of people personally acquainted with the data in some periods. In these early chapters the emphasis is on changes in the direction of government and the accompanying changes of sentiment, especially concerning the use of research, and the public setting in which the Survey grew in scope and capacity.

Part Two turns to the Survey's contribution to government: the main subject areas in which work was done, how these changed over time, and innovations in methods as they were developed to cope with the Survey's changing work programme. The sources for this discussion were mainly published reports of work done, supplemented by files on individual surveys in the customer departments, the COI and OPCS. It seems to me that the contribution and limitations of the work should be readily apparent in the findings, conclusions and analyses set against the descriptions of methods used which are presented in the published reports. Part Two therefore concentrates on such a display of work done. The final chapter assesses the role of the Survey as an institution – part of government in Britain – and also as a kind of mirror which reflects some aspects of government organisation.

The report mainly refers to forty years continuous work and development from mid-1941. However, some events occurred in the years just after this period which either materially affected the situation of the Survey or extended in subsequent years its contribution in particular subject areas. It was thought useful to make some mention of these events.

I wish to thank all those individuals who gave me time to talk about the topics dealt with out of their own experience. The National Institute of Economic and Social Research kindly allowed me to read some of their records which illuminated a very early stage in the Survey's history. Especially I wish to thank the many public librarians who have found the useful documents and files without which very little could have been done.

Where particular persons made a special contribution to the work I have described this in the body of the text or made reference to the relevant methodological papers.

I must acknowledge the editorial help given by Tess Wright of HMSO and Pat Broad of OPCS and the support of former colleagues especially Bob Barnes, the present Director of the Social Survey Division of OPCS. I should like to stress, though, that any views expressed are mine and not necessarily shared by OPCS. My thanks also to Marjorie Goldschmidt who produced a useful typescript from an unwieldy manuscript.

The work was funded by the Social and Economic Research Council. I am grateful for the council's patience and support.

PART ONE

1  Government, public concerns and public enquiry

THE APPROPRIATE STARTING DATE is 1832 – the year the Reform Bill was passed, the first government statistical department was created, the first professional statistical society was set up, and also the year Bentham, who had argued for more rational approaches to public affairs, died.

The Reform Bill was the starting point for the long process of widening the franchise, which gradually led to many things becoming public business for the first time. As wider sections of the population gained the vote, greater responsibility was accepted by government for dealing with their economic and social concerns. But change was slow. After the Bill became law, only about one in seven adult males had the vote. It did, however, open the door to the influence of new social classes. The proportion of adult males with the vote more than doubled as a result of the second Reform Bill in 1867, but still only 16% of all adults could vote. After the 1884 Bill, about a third of all adults and perhaps 60% of adult males had the vote, and a further generation passed before the next major change, in 1918, which enfranchised all adult males, and females over the age of 30.

These changes were reflected in the creation of public services and institutions, designed to ameliorate the unfavourable living conditions that multiplied with the growth of large urban populations and threatened their very existence. Attention was focused on these problems by enquiries conducted by new groupings of professional people who accumulated and analysed evidence and proposed solutions. Edwin Chadwick stands out as an energetic promoter of such studies. The new statistical societies and, later, bodies like the British Association for the Advancement of Science and the National Association for the Promotion of Social Science provided public platforms for these endeavours. Another arena emerged in the royal commissions set up to review social problems and to make recommendations.

Towards the middle of the 19th century the increasing use of royal commissions for these enquiries reached its peak. There was a flow of legislation to authorise appropriate administrative functions intended to deal with some of the unsatisfactory circumstances of parts of the population. Concrete results did not come quickly, but as the new organisations multiplied, many of the professionals associated with the accompanying enquiries moved into them as public officials and ensured that the data the enquiries produced were used to throw light on situations where there was now a public responsibility to act. Between 1840 and 1870 change was piecemeal. It did not lead to an integrated system of public action but rather to an uncoordinated multiplication of independent bodies set up to perform particular functions. The information produced was similarly disjointed, but greatly increased the available descriptive data. This information became indispensable for future public enquiry.

After 1870 the process which resulted eventually in a more organised pattern of government began. Changes followed in local government, including its acquisition of responsibility for education. Towards the end of the century there was a major new political impulse, prompting a new surge of social enquiry associated with public debate about the urgent need for a widening of government responsibility in particular problem areas – health insurance, old age pensions and other issues. As public responsibility widened, official statistics became more and more inadequate for the new policies appropriate to new and changing circumstances. It began to become clear that 'the official statistics obtained as by-products were often conditioned by legislation or other limitations arising from the way the administrative arrangements of a department operated in practice'.[1] So a new feature of enquiry around the turn of the century was the study of the social and economic circumstances of individuals in the classic social surveys. They mainly used census-type enquiry methods covering all the households in selected urban areas and were consequently laborious – so much so that many years elapsed between the fieldwork involved and the reports with conclusions for action. But their purpose was to throw light on new, or rather newly recognised, problems for which data derived from past legislation would not serve. It was during the first world war that Arthur Bowley showed how sampling methods could be used to collect dependable information on a more economical scale.

The new interest in living conditions was also reflected in some of the activities of the Board of Trade, which sheltered many of the functions later to become the province of separate departments. It set up a Labour Department which towards the end of the 19th century initiated the public study of prices and incomes, including the collection of data on household budgets. While Bowley's work had shown how such studies could be more efficiently organised, it was not until the eve of the second world war that official studies were made based on probability sampling. Indeed, until the war, very little official use was made of surveys based on adequate samples despite the accumulating social and economic problems of the years between the wars. The methods were available and, as was shown subsequently on most problems of public concern, could make a contribution to description and understanding. As Lord Kennet emphasised in his paper to the Royal Statistical Society (RSS) in 1937, 'The means of making enquiries are there. The Government has but to ask for them to have them made. If our political action is fortuitous it is not for lack of the means'.[2]

The pressures of war provided the necessary will. The government announced its decision to mobilise all resources for what was seen as a struggle for national survival. Available information on human resources, behaviour, opinions and circumstances was very limited. After the war, Lord Woolton said 'Those who found themselves in 1939 responsible for the conduct of the country in the rapidly changing conditions of war – when facts were more important than precedents – had very little to help them'.[3] The organisation of rationing systems, the deployment of men and women and the mobilisation of voluntary activity for many purposes required information previously not thought relevant to government. It could only come from studies based on a direct approach to individuals, and was needed to facilitate operational decisions made under pressure as the wartime administration tried to cope with a rapidly changing environment. The sample survey method was seen as an appropriate instrument and, as use of the method showed what it could contribute, it became acceptable and used over a widening field.

It was in these circumstances that a government survey organisation came into being, after several false starts. In his book *Ministry of Morale* Ian McLaine[4] examines the work of the Ministry of Information (MOI) during the war. He shows how the ministry provided a matrix in which the idea of the survey and what it could contribute to wartime needs developed. This was a complicated process and the end result, described in later chapters, was very different from earlier proposals.

Pre-war discussions appear not to have seen any systematic study of social circumstances or opinion as relevant to the war effort. It was assumed that customary sources of information through the Home Office and other official networks would provide what was necessary. Given the pre-war state of social research in Britain these notions are not surprising. However, some of the officials appointed early in the war had clearer ideas. Among them was John Hilton who, with Bowley's encouragement, had applied sampling methods to departmental data during his work at the Ministry of Labour. He strongly pressed for the revival of the Home Intelligence Division of the MOI and the appointment of Mrs Mary Adams of the BBC as its head.

A division with this title had been set up at the outbreak of war but it was eliminated rather quickly in one of the ministry's numerous purges and reconstructions. Mrs Adams produced proposals for a new Home Intelligence Division which she saw as necessary to guide publicity and to assess morale. Other departments expressed interest in the possibility of using any organisation set up: clearly, the pressure of war had rapidly demonstrated that effective action demanded more information than was usually available from the government apparatus. A group of academics from the London School of Economics (LSE) were invited to set up an organisation on market research lines under the auspices of the National Institute of Economic and Social Research (NIESR), to be called Wartime Social Survey (WTSS).

These developments were interrupted by a newspaper campaign attacking the MOI's home intelligence activities, particularly the surveys. Duff Cooper, the Minister, was selected for the main criticism and the Survey's interviewers were pilloried as 'Cooper's Snoopers'. The motivation for these attacks is not clear. A robust defence was mounted, including a strong ministerial statement in the House of Commons, but the Ministry's senior officials were alarmed. Home

Intelligence Division was instructed to stop any work on morale and to concentrate its efforts on the needs of other departments. The NIESR, meanwhile, had decided that morale studies would have taken it out of the research area in which it felt competent and that their connection with the WTSS should end. The MOI had already decided that since the scope of the Survey was to be limited now to the work for other departments there was no longer any point in sponsorship. The Survey staff were upset by this decision. Their view of the work they were doing required some assurance of independence, which they saw as the purpose of NIESR's sponsorship. It was a view that related to academic research rather than the customer–contractor system that the MOI (which provided all the available resources) had now decided should be the future basis of the work. Most of the staff had been recruited with some kind of morale research in mind, but it was clear that had the proposals for morale studies been implemented, the NIESR would not have wanted to sponsor.

Mrs Adams left the MOI in early 1941, and Dr Stephen Taylor became the new head of Home Intelligence Division. His views of the division's work differed from those of Mrs Adams. He approached me while I was working at the Gallup Poll on the BBC audience research continuing survey, and asked me to examine the Survey's procedures and output. This upset the staff even more and they did not take kindly to the resulting proposals for developing the work. Dr Taylor, however, took the view that my proposals should be implemented. At this point the small staff resigned, and put their case to senior officials of the MOI. It was not accepted, and I was asked to set up a new organisation and implement the decision to provide a survey research service for other departments. The new organisation began work in the middle of 1941, and the following chapters describe what was done.

Notes

[1] *Government Statistical Services*, HMSO, 1962.
[2] Lord Kennet, President's Inaugural Address, *Journal of the Royal Statistical Society*, Part 1, 1937.
[3] Lord Woolton, Presidential Address, *Journal of the Royal Statistical Society*, 1945.
[4] Ian McLaine, *Ministry of Morale*, Allen and Unwin, 1979.

2   1941–52: A new beginning

IT WAS NOT TO BE EXPECTED that the old WTSS staff would help in the reconstruction – rather the reverse. And so the third attempt to create a government survey research unit had to start from scratch, and use what skills and experience were available. I was formally appointed in May 1941 as Superintendent (changed later to Director) of the WTSS, and this can be taken as the starting date. My experience included time as research officer on the Marketing Survey of the United Kingdom, participation in the organisation of the new BBC continuing Survey of Listening, and work for the British Institute of Public Opinion. The other staff included Dennis Chapman, who came from work on the second Rowntree survey of York; W E Franklin, a market researcher, and, very soon after, Kathleen Box and Geoffrey Thomas from Mass Observation. Helen Brooks, who had been a member of Home Intelligence, came across as business manager and played an indispensable role in organising WTSS finances and, above all, interviewer recruitment. A Scientific Advisory Committee, consisting of well-known practitioners in the fields of statistics, psychology, sociology, psychiatry, medicine and social welfare was set up to review the work, and received all Survey reports for comment. Work began speedily, and by the end of 1941 six surveys had been carried out. They varied in length and detail. One study for the Ministry of Food embraced five separate topics all covered in rather summary fashion. Another survey dealt in some detail with women's attitudes to the new Auxiliary Territorial Service, which was finding recruitment difficult.

As more staff became available the range and number of surveys expanded. Provision was available for six researchers, but it took some months to fill the posts. There were to be two separate groups of interviewers. One was located permanently in specific towns and its function was to carry out short, quick studies. A second group were to be mobile and to work in areas selected as specially relevant to particular topics. There were to be 50 interviewers in all, and by the end of 1941 around this number had started work. They were all full-time appointments.

The methods used reflected the mixed experience of the new staff. At that stage the emphasis was on producing reports quickly and trying to ensure that they met the needs of the customer departments. The new reports were based on some attempt at nationally representative samples. All the former Survey's customer departments came to the new organisation, and within a year surveys had been done for all of these and some new ones. The first surveys were mainly done for officials at the Board of Trade and the Ministry of Food, concerned with consumer needs and shortages, but the Ministry of Labour was also an early customer.

An early test for the new organisation was the public acceptability of its methods. All surveys face a public test. They have to achieve a satisfactory level of cooperation from the individuals in their sample or they fail. A publicly funded body, however, has also to survive a scrutiny by the controlling organs of central government and by Parliament. Public reception of the early surveys was favourable. Refusals to participate were negligible – under one per cent. The topics covered were, in the main, easily comprehensible; the wartime situation favoured a high degree of public cooperation with government actions; most people wanted to do whatever they could to help, and did not need much persuasion to discuss the way government actions impinged on their daily lives. In fact many of the early surveys focused on such matters. Some surveys asked interviewers to record the reception given to their enquiries and, in response to a request from the Ministry of Food in August 1942, an analysis of these recorded judgments showed that 73% of respondents were 'interested and cooperative', 12% were 'doubtful but cooperative', 12% were 'uninterested but cooperative' and 3% were 'doubtful or uninterested and not cooperative'.

Such responses, of course, contradict the presentations in the press at the time of the 'Cooper's Snoopers' campaign two years previously, which were designed to hinder work. Much more serious was the examination of WTSS by the parliamentary Select Committee on National Expenditure, in March 1942. The committee heard evidence from MOI officials, officials of customer departments, and 'other witnesses connected with its work in earlier stages'.[1] The committee's report describes the history of the unit and notes that the original intention was that its work should be 'on the same lines as various Market Research organizations'. The early decision to keep its existence and the reasons for it secret, contrary to the views of those who were to be put in charge, 'was largely responsible for much of the later trouble'. On the latter point the reports says 'it appears to your Committee that the case against the Survey's work was much exaggerated. They find little evidence of objection on the part of the public to being interviewed'. The reorganisation of summer 1941 took place 'in order that the work should be done more rapidly and more efficiently'. No details are given of the changes made to achieve this.

The report notes that 'in the early days the machinery of the Survey was sometimes used to assess morale though this practice has now been abandoned. Your Committee has no hesitation in recommending that no such enquiries should be made. Enquiries should be factual and used to guide a Ministry on some particular policy ... occasionally a questionnaire must contain a question or two the answers to which entail an expression of opinion'. And finally, the committee expressed the view that 'much of the past trouble might have been avoided if the survey had not been controlled by the Ministry of Information ... the storm over the Survey in 1940 was part of the general flood of criticism to which the Ministry as a whole was being subjected ... when a service is common to more than one Department it is desirable that if possible it should not be connected with any one of them'. They therefore recommend that the Survey should rather be 'under the direct authority of a member of the War Cabinet . . . the Lord President of the Council sprang to mind as most suitable since he is already responsible for scientific matters'. The committee concluded that 'the Wartime Social Survey is an essential service performing useful work and that on the whole the lessons of past experience have been learned'.

In responding to the committee the MOI accepted most of its points but did not agree with the suggestion that responsibility for the Survey should be transferred. *The Times* of 28 March 1942 gave the report a warm welcome: 'The development of a national social survey machine was one of the most interesting wartime social innovations . . . an active and practical research body the justification of which is pragmatic . . . it would appear necessary to bring to the notice of potential users the facility for investigation which the Survey provided'. *The Times* also thought that 'some at least' of the Survey reports should be published. 'Research on this scale is something new in sociology. It is concrete evidence of the advance of democracy . . . a new and quantitative bridge between the central Government departments and the people of the country. It looks as though the wartime Social Survey has come to stay'. Sympathetic accounts of the report also appeared in *The Economist* and *Nature*.

Such enthusiasm, although pleasant to the ears of the small group of researchers who were struggling to create an effective organisation, seemed a little premature. By the summer of 1942, the staff comprised two senior researchers and four junior researchers aided by interviewers, 24 coders and Hollerith machine staff, and a small management group. The staff, with one exception, were not civil servants: they were employed by the Survey, which received a monthly sum of money to finance its studies. I was the exception: a civil servant, a member of the MOI's Home Intelligence Division and responsible to its head, Dr Stephen Taylor. Dr Taylor, who later became a Minister, was an enthusiastic advocate of the Survey. Indeed, without his continuing support it is unlikely that the Survey would have survived to receive the Select Committee's endorsement. He was the main contact between the Survey and other departments during the first few years and took a close interest in the organisation of the work. In February 1942 he drew up *Regulations for the Organization of Individual Surveys* which proposed a systematic procedure for handling Survey work. But more important were the regular reports he made on the Survey's progress, which provided the basis for decisions on finance and staffing. In his September 1942 report he described the work which had been done over the first year, and commented 'I think the quality of the Survey's work can best be judged by an examination of its recent reports. These reports are not easy to read but I am increasingly satisfied with them; and so, as far as I can judge, are the user Ministries'.

By 1943 the Survey had an increasing and ever more varied array of customers with whom continuing relationships had been established, and had effectively developed the use of its original authorised budget and staff. In that year, 17 separate surveys were undertaken, in many cases with samples of more than 2,000 people. The fixed team of interviewers, sometimes called the regional interviewers, were proving very useful for short, quick studies of household problems of special interest to the Board of Trade and the Ministry of Food. The mobile team worked on surveys where more intensive methods seemed necessary or where the subject matter seemed more than usually sensitive. The Building Research Station of the Department of Scientific and Industrial Research (DSIR), and later the Ministry of Works and the Scottish Office, were becoming interested in the social dimensions of topics on which their scientific staff were working, and found in the Survey very willing collaborators. The Ministry of Health was trying to cope with many new problems of what would today be called health education and needed to know much more about the attitudes and habits of the relevant sections of the population. The Ministry of Labour was moving towards the mobilisation of women. The Survey staff were interested in showing how the sample survey method could be adapted to many different problems and were convinced that they had something new and important to contribute in many fields. And they were beginning in a small way to spread the gospel.

Sampling was a matter of some concern. In some circumstances, where suitable registers were available, random (probability) sampling was used. Chapman's Scottish Housing Survey in 1943 was an example. But sometimes the timing of the survey and the urgency with which information was needed meant that the regional interviewers were asked to use their accumulating information about their fixed locations to produce samples which were controlled within known limits – such as proportions in particular industries, in addition to sex and age quotas – but which were some distance from random. The limitations of such samples were acknowledged, and in the summer of 1943 I used an invitation to talk about the Survey to the British Psychological Society to discuss population sampling. The merits of random sampling and the limitations of quota sampling or any method which permits individual interviewers to determine the selection of respondents were underlined. The audience, however, were not very impressed. They were more interested in the nature of the material collected in surveys than in detailed discussion of how surveyed individuals were selected. The suggestion that psychologists should also study whole populations rather than confine themselves to special groups, like students, was also not welcomed. The paper, however, was also sent to the Survey's advisers, and was quite well received by them. Another paper, analysing the contribution of survey methods to administrative problems, was also given that year.[2]

These public forays and the steadily developing work programme raised the spirits of the small staff. They felt that their work was becoming acceptable and that the Survey's continuing contribution to government needs was more assured. They began to turn their attention to developing methods and tackling more ambitious projects. But all was not to be plain sailing. About the middle of 1943 the government, in the period preceding vital turning points in the progress of the war, put pressure on departments to reduce their civilian staff. The Survey, as part of this exercise, was asked to reduce its field staff. This meant that some Survey customers had to be told that work on their behalf would have to be curtailed. This particularly affected the mobile interviewers who were used on the random samples, and some of the customers most affected protested vigorously.

Control of the Survey's expenditure was very tight. Each individual survey needed MOI authorisation, which was only given after Treasury had given its authorisation. This might involve a reference back by the Treasury to the originating customer department. The public expenditures involved were relatively small, and it could be no encouragement to possible customers to know that a request for Survey work might involve them in argument with the Treasury. Authorisation was also needed for an annual budget and staff complement, and the proposed budget had to be supported by evidence of actual surveys requested. Many surveys in those early days were requested at very short notice and it was impossible to predict more than a few months ahead what topics would be under investigation. Some ingenuity was necessary to deal with such difficulties. But few surveys were, in fact, frustrated by the circumstances under which the Survey worked. This may be because the MOI had the main responsibility for negotiating the Survey's annual budget and authorisation for individual surveys. But there was also at that time a great willingness on the part of Survey staff to demonstrate their ability to undertake surveys on new topics, and that brought in new customers.

Dr Stephen Taylor and Dr Percy Stocks, the chief medical statistician in the General Register Office (GRO), at some time toward the middle of 1943 had discussed the assertions of some medical practitioners that there had been an increase in the numbers of people seeking medical attention. The Ministry of Health had no data which would permit any check. Stocks thought it unlikely that there had been an increase, and that many changes had taken place since the start of the war that may have led to increasing attendance at doctors' surgeries without any real accompanying increase in the amount of illness. He thought that there was 'no way of establishing this except through your organization'. The Chief Medical Officer of the Ministry of Health asked him to discuss possible arrangements with WTSS, and it was decided to run a pilot study in order to test the method and to establish the response that might be expected from a random sample. The pilot survey was carried out on three separate random samples during the winter of 1943–4 and the results published in the ministry's bulletins in the early summer of 1944. Dr Stocks and his colleagues found the results useful, and the Survey began to develop the organisation necessary to do the survey on a continuous basis. The sample needed would take up a third of all the interviewer resources available. An extra, part-time field force was proposed, and Stocks formally put the proposal to the Chief Medical Officer: 'Of the usefulness of such a continuous survey for measuring the progress of health in general I never felt any doubts and I am now satisfied as to its practicability'. With the full backing of the Ministry of Health and Treasury authorisation the survey of sickness and medical consultation went ahead.

The survey was critically important to the development of WTSS. It was not the first continuing study, but it had obvious relevance to the discussions going on at the time about the possibilities of a more comprehensive health service. It also marked the first major change in the field organisation which had been used from the beginning of the Survey's activities. The use of part-time interviewers suggested the possibility of great elasticity and economy, provided suitable recruits could be selected, trained and supervised. The experience gained on the Survey of Sickness was to prove important later on.

Perhaps for the Social Survey the new continuing survey was also important because it associated the unit with the public discussion of proposals for change in many social and economic spheres, which marked the turning point of the war. Sir William Beveridge in 1942 had presented his report on a social insurance scheme which assumed a national health service and a high level of employment. On 17 July 1943 the Minister of Health announced a royal commission to enquire 'into questions of the trends in the population'. On the same day, Professor Carr-Saunders, one of the Survey's scientific advisers, wrote to *The Times* 'we have no information whatever concerning the number of families with one, two, three or some other number of children ... and this information would be as useful in relation to housing as to demographic problems'. The Medical Planning Commission set up by the British Medical Association (BMA) issued in 1942 a draft interim report with some far-reaching suggestions for the improvement of medical services. This and many other proposals for change in the health services were discussed in the white paper, *A National Health Service*[3] published in 1944. In 1943 a white paper on *Educational Reconstruction*[4] heralded the 1944 Education Act. In May 1944 another white paper, *Employment Policy*,[5] discussed the government's intention to 'accept as one of their primary aims and responsibilities the maintenance of a high and stable level of employment'. The British Association had set up a committee to discuss scientific research on human institutions, and in August 1943 the proposals of this group were published. They were concerned with the promotion of social science and argued its contribution to the general welfare. They also discussed the relationship of research and the collecting and publishing activities of government. They thought that the need for development in the social sciences called for 'the constitution of a British Council for the Social Sciences'.

Another aspect of the changing needs of administration was examined in a pamphlet published in 1945 by the Institution of Professional Civil Servants (IPCS), *Post-war Organization of Statistics in Government Departments*. The pamphlet noted the range of data which the white paper on employment policy had specified as necessary, and urged the need for continuous series of statistics – 'research should be made into the statistical aspects of social questions and the results published'. And the pamphlet records *The Economist* of 11 December 1943, on the existing wartime statistical apparatus: 'It must not be broken up, it must rather serve as a starting point for the statistical service that is wanted'.

It seems clear that the climate of opinion was favourable to the kind of activity with which the WTSS was associated. But, although it agreed with the 1942 Select Committee that public acceptance would be more likely if the Survey mainly worked for other departments, the MOI still thought that the less public attention it attracted, no matter what its work, the better it would be for all concerned. Towards the end of 1943 the RSS invited the Survey to present a paper about its work. Kathleen Box and Geoffrey Thomas prepared a paper which described very simply and directly what the Survey did. The President of the RSS courteously advised the Director-General of the MOI and invited participation in the discussion. He responded in a friendly way, but added 'I do hope that it is not intended to publish this paper in any journal of the Society. It is not our policy to give any publicity to the work of this organization which conducts a series of rather delicate enquiries related to the work of other Government Departments'. This reply surprised the RSS, some of whose members were customers of the Survey and very aware of its activities. Later in 1944 other research officers had some initial difficulty in getting permission to describe their work in professional journals, but eventually accounts were published.

At the end of 1944 I reported to the Scientific Advisory Committee on the work done so far. My report noted that by that date just over 100 separate enquiries had been done, with samples varying from 500 to 5,000, of which 28% had been concerned with Board of Trade interests in consumer needs and shortages; 25% with food and nutrition for the ministries of food and health; and 18% related to various publicity and information activities, including the Ministry of Health's educational campaigns. The remaining proportion was distributed over a wide array of topics. I also noted that the tendency during the three years was for samples to get smaller, but for topics to be examined more intensively. Consequently, each study was likely to require more headquarters work of coding, analysis and reporting. At the end of 1944 the total permanent staff complement was 101, of which roughly half were fieldworkers and half technical, clerical and research staff. The decision to recruit an additional part-time field staff was noted, and the necessary accompanying task of recruitment and training. The report acknowledged the need 'to develop more system-atically than we have done the devising of experimental situations which would enable us to confirm the verbal information which we get' from interviews, which were still the main research method. The growing internal specialisation in coding, tabulation and sampling was noted, and the attempt to develop some kind of specialisation in subject matter. 'The outstanding feature of the Survey's staff at the present moment is that most of them are people who have developed their present skills in large scale social surveys by a process of self education and learning from their experience at the Wartime Social Survey'. The tone of this report was not defensive. It was quite a bold statement of what had been done. It looked forward, and concluded 'If technical developments are to take place it would seem desirable to reach decisions about the Survey's future activities so that the Survey staff can make their own decisions as to where their future field of work will be'. This was to be a rather lengthy process.

Towards the end of 1944 Dr Stephen Taylor had told WTSS staff that 'the Minister of Information has decided to discontinue Home Intelligence weekly reports and to disband the Ministry's Intelligence machinery at the end of December 1944. The work of the Wartime Social Survey is not affected by this decision'. It seems clear that the earlier decision that the Survey should mainly work for other departments meant that their interests would be affected if the Minister had included the Survey. Dr Taylor continued to be the Survey's channel for staffing and financial discussions with the MOI and in February 1945 remarked that reports were taking longer to complete than in earlier years. This was one of the effects of more detailed planning and more careful reporting, which reflected more careful attention to matters of design and analysis, but also implied that unless the Survey's staff was to grow, fewer topics could be studied. Because of this, Dr Taylor had suggested that some of the requested surveys, which were nearer in scope and subject matter to market research work, should be contracted out to commercial organisations. Up to a third of the budget for 1944–5 was so allocated.

The authorisation of part-time interviewers for the Survey of Sickness and their necessary supervision, together with the proposed contracting out and the supervision required for that, implied that some kind of reorganisation of Survey headquarters staff would be needed. It seemed that this was going to be a period of pressure and change – and none of it could wait on any decision on the Survey's future. So the work went on and reorganisation was considered as if there was some kind of assured future. It was becoming clear inside the organisation that movement towards greater internal specialisation would improve the technical level of the work. But such a move would only become profitable if the total turnover reached an adequate level. Increasing the scope and volume of the Survey's work would therefore permit better work. But this possibility cut across other pressures in the government to constrain the activities of the temporary organisations set up to meet wartime needs. At such a time, proposals for reorganising, let alone expanding such bodies, were bound to raise difficulties with the Treasury. In my proposals for the 1945–6 budget I suggested that more use be made of part-time interviewers for other types of survey as well as the Survey of Sickness and urged that the supervisors who recruited and directed the work of part-timers should themselves become fulltime staff. Some of the money allocated in the previous year for contracting out some surveys could be used to cover the extra cost, leaving the residue for contracting out or for other uses of the part-timers. It was still the intention to keep the fulltime interviewers for those surveys where their experience and training were needed. Extra technical staff, coders and tabulating staff would be needed for the extra fieldwork proposed. To permit further specialisation in such areas as sampling and statistics some extra research staff would be needed, and the Survey could make good use of a librarian. Overall, these changes would take the headquarters staff total from 58 to 79. As expected, Treasury's response was to ask for much more detailed information about each extra post and to query the proposed salary levels, particularly of the supervisors.

After the argument had been launched but before it was settled, Dr Taylor left the MOI and prepared to contest a seat at the forthcoming general election. It was decided shortly afterwards that the Survey should stop all interviewing during the July 1945 election campaign to avoid any risk of confusion with canvassing. The Social Survey became the responsibility of a civil servant,

Bernard Sendall, who had worked at the highest levels in the MOI and who had become the controller of the home divisions. In July 1945 he argued that an attempt should be made at a 'general settlement of the Survey's future. 'I do not see any reason why we should await a general decision about the future of the Ministry of Information before tackling this problem. The Survey has never been an integral part of the Ministry . . . there are various possible homes for it and the sooner one is selected the better for all concerned'. The senior staff of the Ministry agreed, and I was asked to produce a memorandum setting out my own ideas, which would be the basis for discussion.

Others, too, felt that decisions were needed. On 25 July a *Times* leader asserted 'No single duty imposed on the new Government is more urgent or important than the collection and dissemination of the facts on which public policy must be based . . . Policy in the future must rest more than ever on the widest and freest interchange of information between the Government and the community'. The article referred to the 'fragmentary public knowledge of the valuable work of the Wartime Social Survey' and to many reconstruction issues which had recently come under parliamentary and public debate.

> In every instance the argument has been conducted without the indispensable minimum of up to date factual knowledge . . . Early Government pronouncements are also needed on the future use of the Wartime Social Survey and similar agencies for the hundred and one daily tasks of investigation which should precede every important development in the social services and social policy.

I produced my memorandum in August 1945. It described the scope and variety of the Survey's activities and its organisation, stating that the staff had grown with the work and that in the absence of any body of work in the universities dealing with appropriate methods, the Survey had developed its own. Over 300,000 interviews had been made covering 120 separate enquiries since June 1941. 'No Department which asked for the Survey's services at any time had ceased to request further information. . . . Under more settled conditions where administrators had learned the value of social research and tried to anticipate their problems more clearly social research could play an increasingly valuable role.' Possible future subject areas were suggested, based on developments in policy and government action which were already occurring, including 'the consumer expenditure and budget studies which would be needed for economic surveillance, health surveys, housing design research, attempts to measure the degree of success achieved by the social services, possible work for Royal Commissions'.

The memorandum did not ask for any major staff changes or increased budget, but emphasised that 'the Survey can attract the best people only by offering conditions of work comparable with other Government research bodies and by permitting the publication of research reports when appropriate'. It concluded by proposing that a government social field research organisation should be continued as an interdepartmental service, which wouldn't impinge on any university research but would make available for government departments 'social research techniques which could help in their work'.

After the election the new controller agreed that 'the word Wartime be dropped'. He then prepared a discussion paper based on the memorandum which slowly circulated through the higher levels of the MOI. Some of the Survey research staff began to look elsewhere for more assured employment. Requests for new surveys continued to flow in. The Ministry's paper[6] differed in some respects from the memorandum, but said clearly 'there is need for a continuance of enquiries by the Social Survey on behalf of government departments; the Social Survey might continue to be linked with the Ministry of Information or its successor, though alternatives are mentioned'. The trend of the argument in the ministry paper, however, was rather against the alternatives and for continued association with the MOI.

Responses from the Treasury were mixed. It eventually agreed that the field organisation should be strengthened but could not agree to the appointment of a senior person to supervise the technical sections. But proper coordination of the various technical sections was critical, especially in dealing with the backlog of reporting which had developed. The Treasury had granted some extra research posts to help with this, but in November 1945 they were withdrawn and Treasury wrote 'we are now looking for *further* reductions in WTSS staff'. The problem for the Survey was that more intensive exploitation of survey data required more technical work; the more serious the problem under investigation the more care needed for analysis and reporting. Pressure could not be put on staff to work harder. Extra temporary staff did not solve the problem. And, given the discussions about the Survey's future, it did not seem wise to decline the more serious projects – which quickly renewed the problems of analysis and reporting.

Treasury also refuted a proposal that Survey research staff should be graded equally with the researchers among their customers at the Ministry of Works and other government research units. 'To a great extent', said the Treasury 'the value of the Social Survey lies in its flexibility and in the fact that it can obtain information on a great variety of general subjects from a wide field. This seems markedly in contrast with the work of scientific staff proper'.[7] The implication was that a narrow focus on limited subject matter, and not the method of working, was the hallmark of the scientist. This illustrates a continuing problem for the Survey in staffing discussions. While the Treasury accepted the Survey's contribution, it had difficulty in discerning the essence of its approach and working method.

On 17 December 1945 Clement Attlee, Prime Minister of the new government, announced the dissolution of the MOI and in the following March described to parliament the new organisation for official information services. A Central Office of Information was to provide publicity services which all departments would normally be required to use. But no decision about the Survey was included in the statement. It had proved more difficult to reach agreement on its location and organisation than on the other functions of the COI. Parliamentary questions to the Prime Minister and letters to Treasury ministers made some kind of decision a matter of urgency.[8] The Treasury told COI officials concerned that it accepted the MOI paper, and on 14 February 1946 the MOI put to the Treasury draft terms of reference which described possible Survey functions and recommended the continued existence of an advisory committee, the availability of the Survey to all departments and 'on suitable terms and conditions' to other bodies, and publication of reports 'subject to the consent of the body for whom the work was done'.[9]

Discussion then moved to one of the new official committees set up to oversee the Government Information Services.[10] The Chairman made it clear that 'there was general agreement by the Departments which had used the Wartime Social Survey that some service of this sort should continue since it had a permanent part to play in efficient Government administration'. There had been some criticisms of its work and a feeling that it should be brought under closer control. The MOI officials present argued that the Survey's reports 'had reached a generally high standard of accuracy and objectivity' and some of the criticisms were 'probably caused to a large extent by user Departments leaving the "briefing" of the Survey to their public relations staffs rather than to the technical divisions concerned'.

The committee agreed that the Survey should be transferred to the new COI but that this decision should be open to later review. It recommended that some contracting out should be allowed but it was essential that this work should be coordinated. The committee also considered the extent to which Survey services should be made available to organisations other than government departments. 'It was felt that surveys should continue to be undertaken, when appropriate, for bodies such as the Medical Research Council and that there might be occasions when it would be in the public interest for such facilities to be extended to non-governmental bodies.' The committee discussed the activities of the Scientific Advisory Committee and thought that, while it had been helpful in the early days, it had met very infrequently and should now be dissolved. The staff of the Survey should be absorbed into the civil service. The committee agreed to report to ministers accordingly.

A few days later the controller was informed that the Treasury had just told the MRC that they would be charged for the whole cost of any study which they had asked the Survey to carry out.[11] Moreover, following an inspection by Treasury Hollerith machine experts, and their conclusion that all the junior technical grades should be standardised at a low level, the Treasury had now laid down salary scales which were leading to an exodus of staff at this level.

In May 1946, Political and Economic Planning (PEP) produced a broadsheet titled *The Social Use of Sample Surveys*.[12] It began with the assertion:

> One of the age long complaints of mankind has been that the measures of government however well intentioned simply do not fit the habits of common life . . . it has become absolutely vital that the state should have an accurate knowledge of the ways of thought and action and of the environment of the people for whom laws or services are intended . . . the social survey is an instrument still in the early stages of development by which this vital information can be obtained.

The broadsheet referred to the 1942 Select Committee report and then went on to discuss the Survey's work against the general background of government sample survey work for all the main departmental users. The discussion ranged over the customary methods and criticisms of survey research and concluded 'the facts set out should be enough to prove beyond question that the social survey is an essential tool in social policy, and indeed in government policy... there are the strongest arguments in favour of the maintenance of the Social Survey unit as part of the governmental machine'.

In some sectors of public life, then, the climate was favourable to the permanent incorporation of a wartime creation into peacetime government. But when Herbert Morrison, Minister responsible for the COI, put the matter before Cabinet, there was little agreement.[13] The fact that departments were spending considerable sums on surveys done by commercial market research firms seemed to some good reason for all government survey research to be so done. Others could not see why the kind of information produced by the Survey was necessary for administrative purposes. But contrary views were also expressed. No doubt some ministers were concerned about a possible loss of control over their own information work. It seemed that there was no very clear understanding of the Survey's actual and potential contribution. Morrison was asked to consider the matter further and bring it back to Cabinet later. There were further discussions among officials and some private exchanges between ministers. It seemed that some ministers were not fully informed on what the Survey had done for their departments. A government pledged to far-reaching reforms and sure that such reforms were long overdue would necessarily have some members who could not easily accept the suggestion that their administration might need yet more information about the condition of the people – even less so, studies of opinion made by a non-political organisation.

In July 1946 Morrison went back to the Cabinet and firmly put the case again.[14] The Survey was to continue under the COI,

> the precise arrangements to be subject to review at the end of two years... The work was to be carried out for Government Departments as an allied service and for other bodies on a repayment basis. [This left obscure the position of the MRC which was not a department, but a grant-aided body.] The aim should be to entrust all new surveys to the Social Survey except in quite exceptional circumstances and ultimately to transfer all Government survey work to it. But for the time being Departments which had continuous long-standing commercial surveys should be free to continue these arrangements.

On 8 July 1946 the Cabinet accepted these proposals.[15]

I was accordingly asked to make my proposals for a staff complement and budget for a permanent organisation. My response was ambitious and attempted a detailed description of the apparatus needed for carrying out a continuing programme of work with at least two surveys in the field at any time. One of these would be the continuous Survey of Sickness, and the other might come from any part of the government's total span of interests that could be helped by survey research. My proposals were the first attempt to describe and argue the case for the various specialist functions needed for the kinds of research of which the Survey had experience, and which might be anticipated from its contact with what was going on in government. It was done by a discussion of the techniques and academic disciplines relevant to the work and how these translated into the numbers and kind of staff needed for a programme of the current size. For once, I assumed that there was no longer a need to justify the existence of the Survey; the need now was to build the organisation. The emphasis of my response was on developing the specialist sections – sampling, coding and analysis, and on a major change in fieldwork organisation. I proposed to transfer completely to part-time local fieldwork and redevelop an appropriate field supervisor function.

Some of the proposals had been presented piecemeal before but had not gained acceptance. Over the previous year, as a result of decisions to award relatively low salaries, there were in post 16 coders, tabulators and computing staff against a complement of 25. Five research officers and two senior research officers had left. No doubt part of this turnover was natural to a period of change following the end of the war, and as women were released from various wartime compulsion orders and demobilisation proceeded, some very promising young researchers began to make their way to the Survey. But the position in the technical sections was very unhappy. Since the fulltime interviewers were to be given up, the extra posts needed to strengthen the technical sections could partly be found from within the existing total numbers, but extra research staff were also needed, especially if some time was to be spent on methodological research. The total cost of the proposed new complement was about 16% more than the cost of the existing staff. Much of the extra cost arose from requests for upgrading posts and for the suggested work on improving methods. Everything was discussed amicably within the COI, and eventually the proposals were put to the Treasury in October 1946. The subsequent exchanges were still going on in the following June. During this time the changeover to part-time interviewing staff was agreed. Some extra research posts were conceded, but no change in their gradings and no changes at all in the technical sections on which the heaviest emphasis had been put. In May 1947 it was pointed out that unless something was done about technical staff it would be necessary to stop fieldwork in the following month to allow technical staff to catch up with the mounting backlog.

While these prolonged negotiations were proceeding, the new members of staff began to make contributions to Survey procedures and methods which were to shape design and operation in the future. They came, some of them, from operational and scientific research units, and were used to devising studies aimed at specific problems from the design of jet engines to the analysis of aircraft accidents and aerial photographs of bomb drops. Among the recruits was Percy Gray, whose work on sampling methods, assisted by Tom Corlett, eventually achieved international recognition. Leslie Wilkins' studies on prediction methods opened up a new approach in criminology, and Jack Fothergill took over the work of machine tabulation and showed how it could be applied to nutritional studies, the factor analysis of opinion data and much else. Geoffrey Thomas and Kathleen Box, who had joined in the first four months, had by this time become experienced veterans, and had soon been joined by Gertrude Wagner and Bob Willcock, also from Mass Observation. They all rapidly adapted to a statistically oriented organisation and made their own individual contributions to many different aspects of the work. Muriel Harris, who had been trained in the teaching of deaf children, began to systematise interviewer training and briefing after a spell in fieldwork; and another distinctive individual contribution came from an anthropologist, Bertram Hutchinson, who introduced new techniques in town and country planning surveys. Dennis Lambeth started work on coding techniques which was substantially developed by Amelia Harris before both of them moved over to research; and a major contribution was made by Bill Kemsley and David Ginsberg in working out and testing methods used for consumer expenditure work, especially the methods of household budget surveys.

Their innovations were made against a background of economic crisis and great advances in social legislation. The period leading up to and immediately after the 1949 devaluation was a time of intermittent political stress accompanied by very tight policies on public expenditure and staffing. Learning had to be done on the run. Methodological work was done while substantive studies proceeded. There was no set house style. Individual research officers were allowed – indeed encouraged – to question, and to create the most suitable approaches to their own work. But since internal specialisation was a condition for all, there had to be, and was, a high level of cooperation and mutual criticism.

Inevitably the delays in reaching agreement with the Treasury led to the proposal that its Organisation and Methods Division should be allowed to examine the structure and staff and advise on what might be done. This was the first of many such investigations carried out where deadlock had been reached in straight discussion. This group talked freely with Survey staff at all levels and were given evidence of what was being attempted. As has just been noted, this was a time when Survey methods were being reshaped and many experimental approaches were being used. The new researchers had come from work where they were used to a questioning approach to what they tackled, and it was not surprising that the O&M people came to believe that firmer conclusions could be reached about an appropriate structure and rates of working than anyone in the Survey felt was realistic. At a time when an attempt was being made to develop specialist skills, it did not seem right to combine responsibility for sampling or coding, for example, with other responsibilities, or to attempt to set rates of output for fieldwork or computing. But there was agreement in some matters and very slowly, aided by the sympathetic and persistent support of the COI senior staff, some useful changes were made.

The work, of course, went on. Geoffrey Thomas continued his studies of the circumstances and attitudes of particular sections of the labour force and, in particular, carried out for the MRC a study of miners certified with pneumokoniosis. Kathleen Box and, later, Bob Willcock developed a series of surveys examining public opinion for a group of officials running an economic information campaign. Leslie Wilkins used the Survey of Sickness to collect information which helped him to predict the demand for National Health Service (NHS) hearing aids. The Survey of Sickness also produced data for the regular reports of the Registrar General. Percy Gray did some of the early house design surveys and produced as a by-product a report on the British Household, which built on Kathleen Box's earlier study. Many of these surveys were published with the agreement of the customer departments, and published reports began to carry the names of their authors on the cover – unusual for civil servants.

At the Treasury a different official had taken over responsibility for dealing with the Survey, and the unresolved staffing matters had to be explained again. During the summer of 1948 there were two further complications. One of the usual biennial economic crises had blown up, which meant a halt to any increase in staff, especially in the information services. At this time also the Central Statistical Office (CSO) began to press for a start on the programme of consumer expenditure surveys which government economists and statisticians saw as part of the economic intelligence necessary to fulfil the promise of the Employment Policy paper. To accommodate the consumer expenditure work during a staff freeze would have been difficult: to tackle it while some staffing proposals were already a year or so overdue seemed beyond the bounds of possibility. But the situation was a stimulus to further change, and some of the current programmes were cut, which helped the existing staff pressures and gave the consumer expenditure work, rightly, some priority. The Survey of Sickness, too, continued with a larger sample to meet the request of the Registrar General's department, and there was still space for some new ad hoc surveys. So despite the pressures, the general scope of the Survey's work programme was maintained, although some prospective customers had to be told that they could not be accommodated.

Towards the middle of 1949, a year after the standstill, the COI returned to Treasury with the case for four principal level posts to be responsible for four main groups of work.

> On the basis of the last three years of experience of the Division's problems or difficulties we are seeking to give it a structure strong and flexible enough to enable the demands upon its services to be met ... Survey work has developed very considerably since we became responsible and is today on a much sounder foundation ... it has developed definite lines of enquiry which enable us now to make out defined areas in which there is a continuing demand.

The four groups were health and work for the Registrar General, consumer expenditure, manpower and social problems, and government information campaigns. It was also proposed that the four posts should carry responsibility for overseeing a particular technical function. In arguing the case for these changes, I emphasised the way Survey staff had developed with the work they had done. Senior posts could all now be filled with experienced researchers who had entered the Survey at a low level and had been given responsibility and the opportunity to contribute to a developing and changing organisation. The four principal posts were granted, enabling me to delegate some of my too wide span of direct responsibility.

The manpower standstill at the end of 1948 had also started off other trains of thought. No doubt the Survey staff numbers had appeared somewhat anomalous for a parent organisation whose main purpose was government publicity and whose staff were under such pressure. It was felt at the highest levels that the Survey's location within the COI was unsuitable when 'three-quarters of its work has nothing to do with the Information services'. One of the implications of this was that the COI senior staff had no special qualifications for supervising, assisting and improving the technical aspects of the Survey's work. Further, it seemed wrong for the Survey to be part of a department which had been attacked for reasons which had nothing to do with the Survey. But, as in 1944, nobody could think of an appropriate alternative. I had emphasised the importance of independence and objectivity in all the Survey's work, and thought the ideal location would be in association 'with those responsible for considering over the long term social and economic issues for which survey data was needed'. In the meantime, as long as the COI would have the Survey, there it had to say.

The decision on the four principal posts in August 1949 released a vein of optimism. Spirits were further raised by a request in September from the Lord President's Office. This noted the White Paper on Scientific Research and Development published in 1949 and said that the 'Advisory Council on Scientific Policy had recently decided to issue a new and somewhat fuller memorandum on Government Scientific Organization . . . Social Science should not be overlooked'. A note about the Survey's scientific organisation and responsibility should be included, and I was asked to provide this.

A new Home Controller, T Fife Clark, had by this time joined the COI from the Ministry of Health, where he had had working contact with the Survey. His appointment coincided with a new memorandum from me, repeating the case for consolidating the Survey's work into a fairly settled programme, in which the Survey of Sickness, the consumer expenditure work and information related activities were all given agreed parts of the budget. A more settled programme would bring some stability to the work and enable methodological developments to proceed. It also seemed that both the Survey of Sickness and the consumer expenditure work could be used as bases for meeting other government research needs.

The COI had accepted this case and indeed had urged it on the Treasury. The changing economic situation, however, led to uncertainty in the policies of departments, reflected in changes in their expressed need for survey research. After the Ministry of Food had been absent as a customer for some time it began to ask for work at short notice. The Board of Trade, also at short notice, asked for a series of surveys. In both cases the demand was related to questions about the end of rationing. The Ministry of Housing, which at the end of 1948 had quite firmly ruled against survey work on housing, in the following spring asked for work to be done very quickly on housing waiting lists. All this made it difficult to stick to any agreed priority for a work programme which could ensure that resources were available for topics of most importance to the government as a whole.

My memorandum tried to find some way through this difficulty. It pointed out that:

> It is clearly not possible to organize efficient fieldwork at very short notice apart altogether from the difficulty of replacing work to which we had already committed ourselves . . . it would seem that the best way of ensuring that the wisest use is made of Survey resources is to keep the Survey in touch with administrative developments and

growing social problems continuously ... I therefore make the suggestion that an Advisory Committee be formed of civil servants whose day to day duties will ensure that they are in touch with the kind of administrative problems which are likely to need survey assistance.

And a number of departments were suggested. This proposal was given a favourable reception, but it was to be many years before any machinery was set up to coordinate demand for the Survey's resources.

Since the Survey had become part of the COI in 1946, all the staff, including myself, had been 'temporary' civil servants. The establishment of staff into the Information Class, which began at the end of 1949, marked the formal integration of Survey staff into the civil service. It also meant that a renewed effort would be needed to secure appropriate grades for the technical staff, who became part of the Information Class and remained so for over 30 years. This was not altogether attractive to some potential recruits. Researchers who were seeking a career in the professional groups developed in the post-war civil service – psychologists, statisticians and so on – would not believe that time spent in the Survey would be very helpful.

In the years immediately after the 1946 Cabinet decision there were many surveys, mainly supervised by Geoffrey Thomas, done to help recruitment to industries which were central to immediate economic problems, such as coal-mining and textiles. Some of the long term problems of employment policy were also explored, such as the continuing movement of women into the labour force, and labour mobility. The latter topic was examined in a survey designed also to provide data for an LSE study of social mobility. The LSE part was done on a repayment basis. Gray's work on aspects of house design continued; Hutchinson did town-planning work in Scotland and London; the consumer expenditure programme was developed by Kemsley and Ginsburg, and Wilkins developed further his prediction methods, producing a very accurate prediction of the likely demand for war medals. He also carried out an ambitious study of adolescents for a group of departments variously interested in recruitment to the services and employment. Nutrition surveys were done of social groups, and techniques were developed for studying exhibitions as one of the media used by the government information services.

Alongside these studies of particular topics there came a flow of technical papers steadily establishing foundations for the Survey's future work. The change in the field force from fulltimers to part-timers had directed attention sharply to problems of recruitment and training. It was clear that a continuing central function would be essential and that it would have to focus on the kind of subject-matter involved in Survey studies, using what was known already. Beyond this it would be necessary to move experimentally. A psychologist, Glyn Evans, joined the Survey with a remit to tackle these problems and he was soon working with Muriel Harris. They devised test procedures, and examined fieldwork and the layout of questionnaires.[16] Other researchers contributed to this examination of the interviewing process.[17] The failure of the Gallup Poll to choose the winning candidate in the 1948 United States presidential election stimulated a lively discussion within the Survey, and members of staff contributed to an international debate in the journals. Papers were written on various government publicity activities and their effects.

One of the notable achievements in the development of the Survey's methods was the work on sample design. Most surveys done before 1946 used some version of random sampling, but about one in four used a combination of random and quota sampling. The proportion with any non-probability element dropped from 26% in 1946 to 3% in 1948. From 1949 onwards, random sampling was used on all but a few occasional surveys. The methods developed were described in a paper given by Percy Gray and Tom Corlett to the RSS in February 1950.[18] It gave a brief theoretical discussion of multi-stage and stratified random sampling, to provide the basis for a description of the sample designs appropriate to different costs, conditions of fieldwork and the level of sampling error acceptable for particular studies. It noted the possible stratifications and the method used for selecting areas (first stage units) in which interviews would be done with a probability equal to the size of their populations. It described the available registers, from the National Register, used in many early surveys, to rating records and the Electoral Register, and their possibilities for different kinds of population. The paper also made the first attempt to examine the effect of non-response. It concluded 'our experience of survey work suggests that sampling errors, being readily calculable, are the least serious errors. Human errors on the part of the interviewer or memory errors on the part of the informant are less easily detectable and measured'.

The paper was read to a crowded meeting of the RSS and was very well received. It had obviously filled a need. Dr Frank Yates, an eminent statistician, remarked that the paper presented for the first time the formulae giving the sampling error of two-stage random sampling with probability proportionate to size; it also introduced practical methods for sampling on the basis of probability proportionate to size. The paper's description of the methods developed, and the use of available registers, had clearly made random sampling a more accessible method for serious researchers. At the end of 1950 a Survey methodological paper took the discussion of the Electoral Register further. This was an important contribution as the register is published and available to all; in later years it was heavily used by the Survey.

By 1950 the headquarters staff complement had risen to 90, of which 14 were occupied in field recruitment, training and control, and 38 in research design and reporting. There were rather fewer staff actually in post, but the technical sections had clearly demarcated functions and the unit was working as an integrated whole. This does not mean that procedures had solidified. Since new topics were being tackled all the time, procedures had to be developed or modified accordingly. This was very evident in the consumer expenditure work, the results of which were closely scrutinised by government statisticians. The slim pamphlet *General Notes for Interviewers on Consumer Expenditure Surveys* (1949) was progressively enlarged to include the results of the experimental household budget studies in Kemsley's *Some Technical Problems in Planning Budget Surveys* (1951). Muriel Harris's *Handbook for Interviewers* appeared first in 1948. A second edition was prepared in 1950 and this, too, eventually gave way to a much more detailed handbook. In 1950, following the departure of Glyn Evans, Bob Willcock took over the work on interviewers and interviewing.

These technical developments could not always be simply implemented. Often, experimental work needed financial authorisation, and this had to be argued through. Gray and Corlett had hit on the use of the 'J index' as a stratifying device which could make fieldwork cheaper by permitting closer clustering by economic status. The J Index was simply the proportion of the electorate in any area who were jurors (for whom there was a property qualification).[19] To make the idea work it was necessary to classify all areas accordingly, which would require some time and money. The purpose was not in question. £400 was required, and possible savings in field costs would be about £2,000–3,000 each year. The reaction of one official whose approval was necessary was 'Whilst I am not able to dispute this case on statistical grounds, some of which are out of my depth, I am not convinced of its validity'. Others were 'doubtful'.

Eventually the matter was resolved, as were the problems of finding junior and clerical staff. There was always a shortfall of the numbers agreed after arduous negotiations, and when strenuous efforts were needed to fill the empty posts, the direct instruction of the senior establishments officer was 'There is an excessive number of clerical officer vacancies in Social Survey and we must make a special effort to fill some of them'. Decisions were being made about which body would carry out the proposed 1953 Household Budget Survey, and it was important for the Survey to show that it could cope with the heavy paperwork involved. The Ministry of Food had also decided to transfer the National Food Survey to the Social Survey in 1953: this, too, would depend upon assurances that the clerical work entailed could be handled. Both these decisions turned out to be critical for the Survey and it seems clear that their importance was appreciated by the COI officials concerned.

In 1951, the position looked fairly healthy. The Survey's annual budget had grown since it became a permanent part of government, from £63,000 to £133,000, and the headquarters' staff had increased by about 50%. A growing number of customer departments were becoming accustomed to using the Survey, and despite the perennial staffing problems there was within the Survey a conviction that progress was being made and that there was widening public recognition of what we were doing. *Nature* had published a long and positive article on the Survey. I had been asked by the British Association to give a paper in a symposium on operational research in war and peace,[20] and the Statistical Commission of the United Nations' Economic and Social Council had asked for an account of the Survey's work. In 1950 moves were made to set up a new British Sociological Association (BSA) in place of the Institute of Sociology, which had ceased to function. I was elected to the provisional executive committee which had the task of 'establishing the new association and of initiating relevant activities', and in 1952 I was asked to join the BSA sub-committee appointed to study and report on the training, recruitment and employment of sociologists.

There seemed to be good ground for optimism. However, there were national economic problems, and the outbreak of the Korean War emphasised them. On three occasions before 1951, as a result of economic downturns a halt had been called to increases in staff: after that date, more serious effects were felt. Restrictions on staff and budget had begun to affect all sections of the government information services, including the Survey's work for them, but they did not have dramatic effects because the work used only around a quarter of the Survey's budget.

After the 1951 election, the new administration led by Winston Churchill reduced the Survey's Vote for 1952–3 to £112,000 from the 1951–2 figure of £133,600. The staff was reduced from a complement of 100, with 90 actually in post, to 81. It is interesting to compare this decision with comments made at the time. The Financial Secretary to the Treasury, replying to a detailed and well-informed statement by an opposition member, Elaine Burton, about the work of the Survey, said:

> In the first place the Social Survey is somewhat anomalously placed in the COI ... it would certainly be administratively possible to place it elsewhere ... I entirely agree that in the examples which she quoted and indeed in others she did not quote it has proved fully worthwhile and undoubtedly resulted even in the stricter narrow financial sense in substantial gains to the State. It is therefore being continued. We agree that some surveys should continue ... and we propose to concentrate the resources of the Survey on those of more direct and obvious values ... I can assure the Hon. lady that there is not the slightest intention of abandoning those surveys which are worthwhile and particularly those of the kind to which she referred.

Among the surveys to which Miss Burton had referred was the Survey of Sickness. After the new administration took office, the Treasury had addressed enquiries to the Ministry of Health about its use of this survey. The ministry had replied noting the purposes which the survey could serve, but following this pressure the Minister of Health decided to stop the survey, and informed the Treasury accordingly. The Survey was then asked how many people were employed on the Survey of Sickness, which led to further staff cuts from 81 to something under 65. By October 1952 the staff in post had fallen below 60, from an agreed complement of just over 100. Severe adjustments were necessary. The amount of fieldwork possible in 1952–3 was drastically cut from the previous year's level; a major change was made in the field organisation, and responsibility shifted to a headquarters group aided by some mobile staff. There were cuts in the technical sections and in the research staff. But the organisation held together and prepared to move into a new and different phase.

Notes

[1] *Second Report of Select Committee on National Expenditure* HMSO, 1942.
[2] Louis Moss, 'Social Research at the Service of the Administrator', *Public Administration*, October–December 1943.
[3] Cmnd 6502, HMSO, 1944.
[4] Cmnd 6458, HMSO, 1943.
[5] Cmnd 6527, HMSO, 1944.
[6] INF 1/273, Part II.
[7] INF 1/278, December 1945.

[8] INF 1/281, 5, 14 and 15 February 1946.
[9] INF 1/281, 14 February 1946.
[10] CAB 134/306 1 March 1946.
[11] INF 1/281 5 March 1946.
[12] *Planning*, No 250, 24 May 1946.
[13] CAB 128/5, April 1946.
[14] CAB 129/11, July 1946.
[15] CAB 129/6, 8 July 1946.
[16] Social Survey Methodological Papers M Series, M16a, 16b, 23, 30, 32, 33, 34, 47.
[17] *ibid*, M 28, 29, 35, 36, 43.
[18] P G Gray and T Corlett, 'Sampling for the Social Survey', *Journal of the Royal Statistical Society*, series A, Vol CXIII, part II, 1950.
[19] P G Gray, T Corlett and P Jones, 'The Proportion of Jurors as an Index of the Economic Status of a District', COI, 1951.
[20] 'Advancement of Science', February 1948.

3   1952–7: Climbing back

THE SURVEY HAD SURVIVED, but it had been damaged. Perhaps most important, the staff at all levels had been given a sharp warning that establishment as part of the civil service was no guarantee of a research career. The cuts in staff and financial provision meant that many former customers were also warned that they might have to look elsewhere for the kind of information that the Survey had provided. If the experience gained by the staff in the preceding years may be regarded as a form of accumulated intellectual capital then that, too, was threatened. Over the next few years much of that capital was lost, as some of the second generation, those who had joined since 1945 and had developed with their work, began to look elsewhere. Between 1952 and 1957 five middle-level staff, all of whom might be regarded as potential leaders, had moved. In time they became: deputy director of the Home Office Research Unit and professor of criminology; head of research for a political party; managing director of a leading market research firm; head of research for a major food distribution firm, and director of a government-funded social medicine research unit. At the Survey they had been responsible for sampling, tabulation and coding as well as taking increasing responsibility for research projects.

And yet the government's public pronouncements and policy interests in the 1950s did not obviously imply a lack of interest in social research. Two of the outstanding ministers of the period were R A Butler and Harold Macmillan. Macmillan had electrified the 1951 Conservative Party conference with an appeal for a vastly expanded housing programme. Butler had built up the strength of his party's research organisation and was later, as Home Secretary, to set up one of the first specialist research units in any government department. *The Times* obituary of him noted, of the people he drew into the Conservative Party research organisation, 'They gave post war conservatism an up to date but distinctive image – making plain its commitment to full employment and the Welfare State while presenting a recognizable alternative to socialism by reclaiming a prominent role for individual initiative and private enterprise in the mixed and managed economy'.

Macmillan, too, had published *The Middle Way*, in which he argued for a 'mixed system' including 'industries and services which have reached a stage of development when their conduct requires to be governed by much wider social considerations than the profit-making incentive alone'. This confirmed the acceptance of the much wider government responsibility which had become general in the war and postwar years. Towards the end of the 1950s he gave powerful support to the development of the government statistical services and, eventually, he was to initiate the Robbins enquiry into higher education.

While there were others, too, in the 1951 Cabinet who strenuously defended the changes in education and other social services,[1] there was also growing concern at the continuing increase in expenditure on the NHS. This concern may have led to the pressure to stop the Survey of Sickness. As the survey developed, it would have shown the nature of the demand for health services and to what extent it was met. The abortive study of general practice, which began as part of the last few months of the Survey of Sickness, showed how the survey might be used. In the decision about the Survey's future this point was never overtly made, but the Public Accounts Committee had drawn attention to the increasing cost of the NHS,[2] and in 1953 the government set up the Guillebaud Committee 'to review the present and prospective costs of the NHS ... to advise how in view of the burdens on the Exchequer a rising charge can be avoided'. Whatever the public ideological position of leading members of the government, to judge from past experience it was going to be the day to day decisions of those responsible for authorising and staffing the Survey that would determine its future. Throughout its existence, its ability to respond to opportunities and to use whatever resources were available had been what counted, and so it was to be again. The Survey had to maintain its reputation as a skilled organisation, to show that its potential contribution was relevant, and to keep up the spirits of the staff. The first objective would be attained only by maintaining the technical level of the Survey's output and showing continued willingness to innovate methods and tackle new problems. This would also help with the other two objectives.

Survey staff made various suggestions on new fields of work, but most of these proposals made no immediate impression. Large parts of the civil service were cutting back, and proposals from a section of the government which it was clearly intended to reduce could not have seemed very wise politically. But they helped to keep the Survey visible, and also helped maintain a sense of involvement, while demonstrating that it would be more fruitful to respond to proposals which the political requirements of departments themselves inspired. There was clearly going to be a change in the Treasury's willingness to authorise surveys and it quickly became evident that proposed surveys which would previously have been authorised wouldn't survive. To some extent this was inevitable: as the political environment changed, so would the content of the Survey's work programme. The financial picture was markedly affected by the reductions. Redundancy arrangements for Survey staff whose posts were abolished had to be painfully negotiated. Stock had to be taken of the likely field of work. Decisions had already been made which gave a short breathing space. The National Food Survey, which had been done for some years by a commercial research organisation, was due to move to the Survey in 1953. The Survey had already shown that it could do the work for rather less money. It had also been decided that the Survey would do a substantial part of a large household expenditure survey in 1953–4 (the forerunner of the Family Expenditure Survey), designed to provide up-to-date weights for the Retail Price Index. So despite the fall in the number of new surveys, there was some foundation for a 1953–4 fieldwork programme. Both surveys demanded much detailed and technical office work.

There were also some interesting new customers. The 1946 Cabinet decision had allowed the Survey to work for non-departmental customers if they repaid the costs. The Oxford Institute of Statistics had obtained a grant from the Nuffield Foundation to study personal savings along lines pioneered in the USA. They asked for the Survey's help and offered to pay; the Treasury was interested in the topic and authorised the three annual surveys involved. The London Transport Executive was interested in studies of travelling habits in its region. The Road Fund provided finance for some of the road safety studies which had been urged by a select committee. The Ministry of National Insurance, defending itself from suggestions that social security provision was leading to growing early retirement, asked for the Survey's help with the design and analysis of a major study of reasons for retirement. The work of a Nuffield Hospital Design unit had suggested a radically different organisation of ward nursing: the Ministry of Health asked the Survey to set up an experimental study to test the recommended changes. The growing interest of the Home Office in criminological research prompted by the Howard League and a parliamentary select committee led to a Survey study of Borstal records which examined factors associated with recidivism. The Ministry of Agriculture, aware of the small enterprises excluded from the regular agriculture census, asked if the Survey could devise a method for estimating the number of pigs and poultry produced by small-scale food producers.

This was a remarkable assembly of new projects. None of them concerned subjects which the Survey had touched previously and the methods developed to explore them were equally varied. The Nursing Survey designed by Bob Willcock involved time sampling and observation at short intervals of what nurses were doing under the traditional system and, later, the new system. Geoffrey Thomas developed a recording system for the Travel Survey, and Wilkins devised the new analyses of existing records on which the Borstal survey was based. The Pigs and Poultry Survey involved locating small producers, not only in rural but also suburban areas. It was done by Gray's and Corlett's unprecedented use of postal methods, and the demonstration that postal enquiry could be made to work well on some topics turned out to be very important for subsequent Survey studies.

As well as these technical inventions, the methodological interest in the basic techniques continued: papers on other aspects of sampling by Gray and his team,[3] and more work on interviewers and interviewing by Willcock and Muriel Harris.[4] This work was proving to be of interest to others. In December 1953 the Association of Incorporated Statisticians organised a weekend school on modern sampling methods. The Survey was asked to contribute and produced five out of the eight papers given at the meeting. They included accounts of sampling methods and interviewing techniques and problems, and a paper by Amelia

Harris that was one of the first accounts of coding given anywhere.[5] The final paper, by Fothergill and Wilkins, examined analysis and interpretation.[6] It concluded with a comment that epitomised the spirit of that group of Survey staff. 'An attitude of mind is perhaps more valuable than any tools of analysis which might be used. Scepticism and an intuitive appreciation of the meaning of numbers, plus an ability to collaborate with other workers in the research unit are what are mainly required of the statistician engaged on sample surveys'. Some years later, these papers were reproduced in *Readings in Market Research*, published by the British Market Research Bureau. In 1952 I was elected as Chairman of the Market Research Society. So the Survey's troubles had not made it introspective or defeatist.

The work of the years after 1952 included a declining number of studies related to the information services. In his statement to the House in 1952 the Financial Secretary had, by his public reference to the 'anomalous' situation of the Survey in the COI, raised again the question of location. And in May 1952, responding to a parliamentary question, he said 'On average over the last few years surveys undertaken to assist information activities have been 17% of the work of the Social Survey and surveys for other administrative purposes 83%. The proportions in the 1952–3 Vote provision are five and 95% respectively'. A year later, replying to another question in the House, he said of the 1953–4 Vote 'none is for information work; the whole is for other work'.

It was, no doubt, this fact which led to another enquiry by the Treasury at the end of 1952. This had two main objectives: to estimate the 'probable level of demand for the Social Survey over the next few years' and 'the proper location of the Social Survey within the Government machine'. The first problem was approached by considering the Survey's actual work since 1946. This had been rising until 1952, when political decisions, described earlier, reduced activities and staff. If the political will remained the same, the future level of demand could be expected to continue at that reduced level. Departments had in fact been warned by that decision, and advised by the Survey, to expect only what the reduced Vote could provide. Nevertheless, the enquiry was scrupulous. An analysis by type of survey showed that changes in, say, the balance of ad hoc and continuing surveys would affect the size and make-up of staff. It also showed that the main existing customers would continue to ask for the Survey's services. A limitation of this approach to estimating future demand is that it cannot take into account new developments, either of demand, as departments are confronted with new problems, or of technical innovation, enabling the Survey to take on completely new types of work.

Because the Survey's methods were statistical, the Treasury argued that the Survey was 'an extension of the Government's statistical services'. This turned out to be a good prediction in the long run, but in 1952, despite the make-up of the 1953–4 programme, it inevitably failed to provide for the full variety of work to which the Survey contributed. A possible connection with the DSIR, which had been a customer since early days, was considered, but although it was agreed that there were some 'affinities' the statistical nature of the Survey's work was thought to distinguish it from the 'general run of the work of the DSIR'.

This view obviously underrated the use of statistical methods in most scientific analysis, the growing interest of the DSIR research stations in the economic and social aspects of their work, and the major question, affecting all the DSIR's work, of the importance of these factors in gaining acceptance and use of its research output. In addition, the report accepted the 'common service' aspect of the DSIR's work, which was shared by the Survey. It is not clear whether all the senior officials of the DSIR would have welcomed a decision to locate the Survey with them. There were, of course, powerful units within the department which, at a time of financial stringency, felt they should give priority to their own work. But a senior official, Alexander King, in March 1953, gave an enthusiastic account to the British Sociological Association of the DSIR's interest in the use of social science for its purposes.

The report suggested that 'on the whole the CSO seemed the most suitable home'. This conclusion doomed the report. The CSO was part of Cabinet Office and it was never likely that it would agree to absorb a unit whose prime purpose was public contact with individuals on behalf of other departments. Since the DSIR had been ruled out, and location in any one major user department was thought to be inimical to the common service basis, the outcome of the report could only be the maintenance of the status quo. For the Survey this seemed a pity. Although the COI officials had been consistently helpful and had loyally implemented the 1946 Cabinet decision, everybody concerned agreed with the Financial Secretary that the situation was anomalous – and clearly destined to remain so. This meant that any ministerial coldness about the COI would continue to make life difficult for Survey, regardless of the minimal relationship between what the Survey was actually doing and the main purpose of the COI. To argue within the COI against a continuing connection while relying on its good offices for day to day support was clearly difficult, if not invidious, but it was necessary to do so.

Between 1952 and 1957 the total headquarters staff stayed at the reduced level while the cash level of the Vote slowly increased in response to civil service wage increases. Given the cost of the continuing National Food Survey it would have been difficult to take on the array of new types of survey and their heavy demands on office staff if it had not been for one positive outcome of the 1952 cuts. It had been agreed with Treasury at the time of the cuts that the Survey would be allowed at times of special pressure to use part-time staff at headquarters. The coincidence of the 1953–4 Expenditure Survey and the National Food Survey was accepted as such a time, and field staff began to work at headquarters. This helpful procedure continued for some time, and the numbers of fieldworkers so employed increased, enabling the Survey to fulfil its commitments and to take on some of the new, more demanding, work described earlier. Without this the Survey would have stagnated. But the practice raised a problem. The civil service unions, at a time of staff cuts, were naturally suspicious of the use of fieldworkers for work which in other circumstances would have been done by clerical or executive officers. However, the COI was not at all sure that the Survey was less vulnerable, and had noted that requests for Treasury Survey authorisation were still being refused. They therefore accepted the case for continuing to use part-timers, but it was understood that the whole situation would be kept under review. With the aid of this innovation and other exercises in adaptability, the Survey managed to survive the most difficult years in its history.

By 1954–5, the situation, though still unstable and precarious, had enough promise to encourage a positive statement from me about future arrangements. In March 1954 I made a strong case[7] for continuing to use part-time interviewers to eke out headquarters staff. The proposed work programme was somewhat larger than the previous year and since it included only one continuing survey (the 1953–4 Household Expenditure Survey ran for only one year) it would have a larger proportion of ad hoc surveys. Very little provision could be made for actual staff increases, so the use of part-timers was the only way this expansion of work could be carried out. The possibility of using them for technical work such as coding, and drawing samples, meant that we could offer them more security – an important point. Our rates of pay for fieldworkers were lower than those in commercial market research, which made the Survey uncompetitive. The COI officials found the case 'sound and persuasive', and the Treasury was willing to accept it. It was also agreed that some lower level clerical posts could be provided.

Discussion of the work programme and proposed Vote for 1954–5 proceeded as in previous years, but had some unusual features. Departments had been asked in the previous autumn to indicate what work they would call for in the next financial year. The responses gave the basis for a proposed programme which was discussed inside the COI: the agreed programme would then, normally, have been discussed with Treasury. This time there was an extra stage. At the suggestion of the Treasury, customer departments attended a meeting at which they were invited to comment on the proposals. That is, officials of particular departments of differing professional backgrounds and status were asked to say what they saw as the merits and demerits of research proposals designed to meet the needs of other departments. They found the situation awkward. Civil servants are normally expected to speak for their own departments in the light of their knowledge of the policy background, unlike at professional meetings, where mutual criticism of and comment on research methods is expected. Those present, though they freely commented on the objects and methods of the individual studies, felt that they had insufficient knowledge of projects other than those sponsored by their own departments to grade them in any agreed order of priority. It was also felt, despite the severe examination of individual projects, that there was no substantial project on the list which could be regarded as unnecessary: if some of the larger requests were reduced in scope they would still serve a purpose, but the loss of value would be disproportionately high in relation to any savings.

This response could hardly have been expected, and the Treasury proceeded the next day to suggest cuts in all the departments' requests. This suggestion was negotiated between the Survey and the Treasury. As a result, the proportion of agency services (those done against repayment) rose from around 22% to just over 26%. The total Vote rose from £89,000 in 1953–4 to £107,200 in 1954–5, and although pay increases devalued the rise, in money terms the Survey's Vote moved steadily upward from then on.

Table 1 Items in suggested 1954–55 programme

Sponsor	Allied Service Description of project
Ministry of Food	The National Food Survey
Central Statistical Office	Consumer Expenditure enquiries needed for purposes of the annual White Paper on National Income and Expenditure
Ministry of Labour	The coding of the Ministry of Labour enquiry is, as expected, running some months behind field work and provision (£5,000) is needed to complete the job. Apart from this the department have asked for provision (£3,000) for one enquiry for administrative purposes.
Board of Trade	The Board of Trade prepares and publishes monthly indices of retail trade. These are based on returns made to the Board by traders and are one of the most important indications of the level of home economic activity available. The returns are voluntary and from time to time steps have to be taken to renovate and replenish the lists of retailers giving the information month by month to the Board of Trade. This work of renovation has now fallen much behindhand, to some extent because we were unable to give the Board of Trade an adequate allocation last year. It is proposed that the Social Survey now recruit new panels of retailers willing to volunteer the information required. There is also some provision for a further British Industries Fair study.
DSIR	This provision is for several different interests in DSIR including the Building Research Station, Headquarters Division concerned with Human Factor in Industry and the communication of scientific and technical information, the Food Research Station and the Fire Research Station.
Home Office	Studies of the working of the Approved School system and the results of applying the Survey's Borstal enquiry findings; analyses of court records of crimes of violence and some small scale work for the Chief Scientific Advisers division related to Civil Defence.
Ministry of Health	Some dietary enquiry work on special groups and a specimen study of the labour economies which a reorganization of nurses' duties would make possible. This latter results from preliminary enquiries which suggested that certain forms of reorganization would make it possible to defeat the continuing shortage of nurses by the more efficient use of the existing numbers. It would be the job of the Social Survey to collect detailed records of the time spent on different duties before and after such reorganization in a small number of hospitals which agreed to take part in the experiment.

Sponsor	Allied Service Description of project
Ministry of Agriculture	Studies of the small scale production of pigs, poultry and horticultural products designed to replace information formerly accruing from the administration of rationing schemes (now discontinued) and needed to estimate Exchequer liability on guaranteed price schemes, farm incomes and costs for purposes of the Annual Price Review and to provide the basis for government agricultural and food import policy.
Scottish Office	The Scottish Home Department is interested in the welfare of the Herring fishing industry. It is proposed to analyse the records of the National Food Survey to see what information can be obtained about the consumption of Kippers and the factors associated. Some small scale enquiries are suggested related to problems of the Scottish Education Department.
General Register Office	A comparison of the illness records obtained from general practitioners and those produced by the Survey of Sickness techniques in order to show the value of future work on Survey of Sickness lines.
COI	The normal provision for interviewing training plus a provision (£500) for the analysis of the National Film Library records which is being made continuously for Films Division.
	Repayments
Oxford Institute of Statistics	A study of the distribution of personal savings and all forms of liquid assets, using techniques adopted in previous studies so as to show the effects of changes in recent years.
Ministry of National Insurance	Further work in the large scale enquiry now being made into the effects of retirement pensions on willingness to continue work beyond the statutory retirement age.
London Transport Executive	An extension of the work now authorised for Road Research Laboratory designed to produce information useful for the organization and development planning of the passenger transport services in the London area.
PEP	Employment experience of graduates with special reference to the employment of Arts graduates in industry. This is the Waterfield project which Treasury last year were willing to include in our programme.* It is now financed out of Conditional Aid and will be carried out jointly by Waterfield and PEP (*SS1018 8 11 1952).
Howard League	A study of the records and home circumstances of young prisoners designed to show the effects of prison sentence. This is the long term project which Treasury have agreed in principle (SS216/1) and for which we have to make an annual provision.

Table 1 continued

Sponsor	Allied Service Description of project
Ministry of Transport	An enquiry related to Road Safety with special reference to the new Highway Code.
Scottish Council	An enquiry into some of the factors which relate to the efficiency of small firms in Scotland. This would be part of a larger scheme to be undertaken in Scotland and financed out of Conditional Aid.

So the beginning of 1954 was an important point in the Survey's fortunes. With hindsight, it seems evident that the situation had stabilised. Repayment work was making a considerable contribution, and most of the Survey's old customers and some new ones wanted to use the services of the unit if resources permitted. In the years since 1952 the research staff had shown great flexibility and willingness to tackle new, different subjects, and a transition had been made to a different fieldwork organisation which helped ameliorate the staff reductions at headquarters.

In 1955 there was another general election. This time there were no traumatic results for the Survey. In 1957 Harold Macmillan became Prime Minister, and a rather different atmosphere in government became evident. This did not mean that pressures on the Survey from its various controlling authorities ceased – rather, the opposite. It was almost as if the realisation that the Survey had survived stimulated the feeling that all its operations should be looked at critically. The inspections that followed were done by COI administrative staff and Treasury staff inspectors. Because of the reduced staff and an uneven flow of work, there were peaks and troughs in the internal pressures. When work was urgently needed all possible resources were employed, so the result of an inspection might well depend on when exactly it was made. If this fluid staffing – a working reality – was measured against normal civil service gradings, it was inevitable that there would be a problem. The various inspections generally led to conclusions that some posts, particularly at clerical and machine-operator level, were overgraded. The invariable response to this was that lower grades failed to recruit any staff. The expanded use of part-timers drew renewed attention: it was pointed out that this was 'a little irregular and if the Social Survey was on an even keel there might be a case for tightening up'. The Treasury inspector, however, noted that without part-timers there would have to be a fairly substantial rise in the numbers of clerical and ancillary staff, and the system had the obvious advantage of enabling staff to be adjusted to fluctuating workloads. So the COI and Treasury felt able to live with this fact of life. In the middle of 1955, after some intensive research on commercial market research interviewers' pay, a case was put to Treasury for increased pay for interviewers when employed in the field, and this was agreed.

The former Home Controller, T Fife Clark, had by this time returned from his post outside the COI and was now Director General. At the end of 1955 he asked for a further inspection – the third general review in three years. It was made by a middle-level number of the administrative staff, whose main duties were staffing matters of the COI's information work. His report, early in 1956, was imaginative but, to Survey staff, somewhat unworldly. He found that the 'work of the Division is subject to severe peaks', which affected the amount and quality of work.

> At the present time it is not easy to plan a detailed programme of work very far ahead. Often there is uncertainty as to whether a survey in the work programme will in fact be undertaken. In 1955–6 there were 36 surveys in the programme but in the course of the year twelve of these were deleted and twelve others substituted. Sometimes the purpose and scope of a survey can be changed significantly in the course of initial discussions with the result that the pattern of fieldwork, coding, tabulating and computing differs considerably from what had been originally planned ... we would like a strenuous effort to be made to change the conditions.

This was hardly news to anybody and it was unlikely that anything the Survey could do would change the circumstances under which customer departments decided that they needed survey research. Many years later, it was found that even support from the centre of government didn't much help to change the way in which surveys were requested.

The report found that the allocation of surveys to different levels of staff was not very systematic. Senior staff in control of technical sections were allocated quite difficult surveys to carry out while still controlling their sections, and some of the most senior research officers were supervising the continuing surveys and some of the expenditure surveys. Developing an acceptable method of bringing new people forward and training them was certainly a problem. Given the small number of research officers (eight at all levels) to cover the whole range of Survey work, the 16 controllers of technical sections provided the only available source of people knowledgeable about the Survey's methods. My practice was to regard them as a pool of talent and to look for research opportunities for them. It was untidy to work this way, and there was a problem of controlling their sections while they were running research projects, but the method had produced some excellent researchers, and showed the whole technical staff that there were possibilities for some of them to move into research. The report argued that 'there is a temptation for the Director by this means to take on more work than the Division is equipped to do'. This was a matter of judgment. To me it seemed that the fewer rigid lines between different parts of the Survey the better. And freedom to move between technical and research sections was, however untidy, very productive – it was the Survey's development of such technical functions as sampling, fieldwork and coding that helped to build its reputation.

Some of the suggestions for improving internal control of the work seemed positive and helpful, and were promptly implemented. Among the changes were improvements in the centralised training and supervision of fieldworkers, and to help with this Muriel Harris produced a new edition of the *Interviewers' Handbook*. It was certainly the case that there were more customers than the small staff could efficiently handle, but to refuse surveys that offered some kind of challenge seemed impossible – to the existing staff, this was the Survey's central purpose. The difficulty of matching staff to demand was especially frustrating to those who were trying to keep up a reasonable standard of work in the technical sections, and during 1955 and 1956, as noted earlier, three of the most promising middle-level staff left.

During this time discussions were going on in committee about further work related to the Retail Price Index. Following the big 1953–4 household expenditure survey in which the Survey had participated, the Ministry of Labour's Advisory Committee recommended a small-scale continuing household budget survey. The statisticians who had been considering what statistics would be needed for employment policy had noted that the Survey's expenditure survey work had been suspended during the 1953–4 survey, and agreed that to understand expenditure trends, it was necessary to be able to relate expenditure to family circumstances and income. They therefore supported the Advisory Committee's proposal. The proposed survey would give up-to-date information on changes in expenditure, the relative incidence of direct and indirect taxation, and income received in cash and kind from social services in different classes of household.

Who should do the work? Early in 1955 the Treasury announced that it should be done by the Survey. The Ministry of Labour objected and the COI Controller, briefed by Survey staff, responded at some length. The argument revolved around such issues as the response rate and cost of doing the work through Survey staff or through the ministry, which proposed to use local office staff for fieldwork and pay overtime rates where necessary. The experience of the research officer at the Survey who had specialised in expenditure work was, of course, very relevant, and his efforts contributed heavily to the discussion. This was one officer whose work the COI inspector had thought was overgraded. In the middle of 1955 the Treasury summoned everybody concerned to a meeting, listened to all views and told the ministry in September that it saw no reason to depart from the allied service provision within the COI. The ministry did not accept this, and went higher up the ladder – to no avail. At the end of 1955 it finally accepted the decision. The Family Expenditure Survey (FES) started as a Survey project in January 1957, designed by Bill Kemsley, and has continued ever since.

The Treasury decision left some questions unresolved, such as who would tabulate and analyse the survey results. One of the Survey staff who had left had been in charge of its tabulating and computing section, so clearly it would be folly for the Survey to take this on. Later, in 1956, the Ministry of Labour agreed to tabulate the results and also to publish an annual report. There were also the questions of the sample size and, quite important, whether the Survey could increase its staff to cope with this major addition to its programme. The FES started without a decision on that point. But the decision to let the Survey do the work was critical, and the work was entirely appropriate for it. The field costs were a relatively high proportion of the total cost and, apart from the coding operation involved, the burden on headquarters staff was limited. It proved to be a Survey of central and continuing importance, and has become a source of information used by many parts of the government.

The Survey's position had also been strengthened by the Treasury's decision to upgrade my post, as Director, to the equivalent of the Assistant Secretary level. The COI had first suggested this in 1951, and in 1955 raised it again, stressing the range of the Survey's activity, the development of its technical levels, its general standing as a research organisation and its future prospects. This time the Treasury agreed, implicitly recognising the justice of the case and, presumably, the Survey's continuing contribution to government. But there was to be no quick solution to the resources problem. The FES made heavy use of fieldworker time and a recruiting drive was launched. At the end of 1956 the Survey raised the question of allocating part of the Vote to a fund for pilot studies, to be done at an early stage of the development of individual surveys, and enabling decisions on design to be made much earlier. This was not agreed.

These management problems did not stop the work on new kinds of survey, but made it more difficult. In 1955 Gray carried out an operational research type study of the use of the Medresco hearing aid – one of the first empirical surveys of the way parts of the NHS were working. Fothergill examined the actual contribution made to nutrition levels of young children by welfare food supplements. Willcock began a series of road safety surveys evaluating the effects of propaganda and ground-level control. He used sampling methods to study the movement of vehicles and pedestrians in selected streets which he compared with the intentions of experimental schemes. In 1956 Geoffrey Thomas carried out a survey of industrial establishments which aimed to measure promotion prospects in different industries and different sized firms to compare with the more general theories of industrial motivation then being discussed. The earlier work on postal surveys suggested a method for an ambitious study made in 1957 – the first for a royal commission – for the Royal Commission on the Remuneration of Doctors and Dentists. Kemsley used professional registers to collect, by post, details of the earnings of a large number of different professions. The information provided a framework within which the commission could assess proposals for doctors and dentists. For the Central Advisory Committee for Education concerned with further education, the Survey studied young people who had left school in 1954 and 1955 to discover what had happened to them – to compare those who had taken some form of further education with those who had not, and to try to establish what conditions favoured participation. A sampling scheme was devised which worked through the different strata (local authorities, schools, children) in a way which was to be used frequently in future educational surveys, and parents and children were interviewed. In the same year, 1957, a very different study was made, based on many groups of farmers. It tried to establish, for the National Agricultural Advisory Service (NAAS), how farmers acquired new technical information, what part NAAS officers played, and what might be more profitable procedures for them to use. Perhaps most interesting of all was the survey designed at the request of the Ministry of Housing towards the end of 1957. This asked for an evaluation of the effects of the Rent Act – a highly contentious piece of legislation – and marked the entry of the Survey into housing statistics. The survey was designed to show a before and after effect. The second stage and the consequent report came two years later.

By the middle of 1957 the FES was fully launched and it seemed that the time was right to attempt to get the organisation on a more permanent footing. I produced a paper which stressed the importance of the technical facets of the Survey's work and linked them to staffing.

> For many years now Social Survey staffing has depended in the main on the COI manpower ceilings . . . I am convinced that this is the time to insist on Social Survey staffing being considered as part of the Government statistical and research apparatus rather than as part of the Government Information and Publicity apparatus . . . The basis for an Allied Service Social Survey unit is that it provides a convenient means of bringing together the technical specialists needed for a field research organization and spreading the overhead costs which are thus built up over a large output. Economies result from this arrangement and only in this way can the expense of a high technical level of work be justified. Since the field is growing new technical questions arise continually. Improvement and change in methods are necessary if the confidence of Departments is to be maintained.

I went on to say that continuing staff shortages prevented this, and hampered internal training and the essential experimental work. The paper formally presented the sequence of technical activities involved in the survey procedure which had gradually been adopted by the Survey and illustrated their relevance and importance by descriptions of recent and current studies. It pointed out that the disappearance of so many middle-level staff had made the staffing arrangements somewhat lopsided. 'There now exists no real promotion ladder for technical or research staff inside the Survey.' Part-timers had helped to meet the problems caused by staff limitations, but now that the programme was expanding again so many part-timers would be needed that all the manpower restrictions would be breached, and 'unless they worked practically full time they were not a real substitute for HQ staff . . . We can sum up the situation by saying that the Social Survey is falling behind its responsibilities as a research organization . . . we are not doing our work as quickly as we should'. Steps should be taken to publicise the service so that likely demand could be predicted as far in advance as possible, and this would enable a basic minimum figure to be agreed as the foundation for the annual Vote.

It seems contradictory to stress staff limitations and then suggest that measures be taken to expand and stabilise the work programme. The Survey was already having to turn away customers and it was clearly felt that the time had come to move out of the situation where the use of part-timers was hiding a real staff shortage. But if they were to be replaced by a fulltime headquarters staff, it would be necessary to take on enough work to keep them occupied – only then could the organisation continue to be economic. I was, in fact, advocating a permanent arrangement and was seeking a way to match resources with demand. I suggested a Vote of around £110,000: a 'staff adapted to such a figure would enable the Survey to cover programmes varying from £100,000 to £125,000 a year with the use of temporary staff for peak loads only'. These proposals were fairly modest. They would provide for a staff of 80 at headquarters, compared to over 100 in 1952, and their cost was somewhat less at 1957 prices. The paper was put to COI in the middle of 1957. It was discussed informally with Treasury and at the end of the year there followed another inspection. The outcome was not known until the following year.

Notes

[1] See the account of 1953 Cabinet papers given by Peter Hennessy and Peter Walker in *The Times,* January 1984.
[2] *Fourth Report Committee of Public Accounts,* Session 1950–51, HMSO, July 1951.
[3] Social Survey Methodological Papers M Series, M60, 63, 64.
[4] *ibid,* M48, 54, 56, 69.
[5] *ibid,* M67.
[6] *ibid,* M68.
[7] COI AD 1/14 April 1954.

4   1958–67: On a rising tide

THIS WAS A PERIOD of vigorous activity and growth in which many possibilities opened up, though not all doors were open to the Survey. The level of real resources in staff and money did not begin to change until 1960–61. But, despite the staff losses of previous years, the Survey now seemed assured of a continuing role. It had accumulated a number of steady customers and developed a lively internal scientific activity around the extension and development of methods designed to meet new purposes. As techniques developed, so did ideas about the most efficient organisation and the appropriate staff structure. The tasks in this period were to adapt methods to the needs of Survey customers, to gain acceptance for the developing ideas on organisation and staffing, and then to accumulate the necessary staff.

Between 1958 and 1967 real resources (the annual Vote deflated by changes in staff costs) increased by about four times and headquarters staff by three times. Very little of this occurred to start with, though this was the time when the Survey was learning how to achieve and maintain a satisfactory performance on the continuing Family Expenditure Survey. This meant, above all, recruiting, training and managing an adequate field force. The rate at which new ad hoc surveys could be mounted was somewhat reduced: the range of topics covered, if anything, increased. As a result of the increased pressure I informed the COI Home Controller that until the staffing situation changed it would be necessary to 'ask some of our possible customers to do without our help and some proposed surveys must be put off until later in the year'. Some order of priority was essential, and would have to have a strong political element – some surveys seemed more important for public policy than others. There was no formal apparatus for making such decisions: in its absence the COI Controller, with no policy authority, would have to decide. Thus the question of location was, inevitably, raised again. This situation made it urgent to proceed with the proposed staff increases: otherwise, despite the increasing interest in its work and capabilities, the survey would have to accept a permanently limited role. It was this growing interest which made it difficult for the COI to do nothing about it, although experience had shown that staff changes did not come easily.

The response to my restructuring proposals came in the report, in January 1958, of the ensuing staff inspection. The reaction to this report, both of Survey staff and the COI's Director of Establishments, was amazement. The report proposed that the internal technical specialisation developed over the years should be so modified as to be almost liquidated. Many research and technical posts, it said, should be downgraded; some technical sections – coding and sampling – which had little in common should be merged, and field service (carrying the brunt of the FES work as well as the full range of ad hoc surveys) should also provide all the clerical aid needed by research staff, who would have to organise their own supervision of all technical work done for them. The only point of agreement with my proposals was that the time had come to cease relying on part-timers for headquarters work. If this report had been accepted, the Survey would have been forced back to a situation rather like that of its earliest years. It would have become impossible to meet the needs of most of its current customers. The report was shown to all the Survey's senior staff. Their comments, and mine, were sent to the Treasury staff inspector, who was invited to come back to the Survey to discuss them. By this time he was no longer a staff inspector: he was engaged on other duties and would not be able to discuss the response 'for some time'. In the following years all the staff inspection judgments which had so amazed the recipients were reversed, but meanwhile it was for the Survey to find some way of accommodating the increased programme or, if this was not possible, to reject it. But discussion of staff improvements would, of course, be related to the scale of Survey activities, and to work to a stationary programme would suffocate the growing demand and lead to a stagnating organisation. So somehow the programme was carried out. This would not have been possible without the missionary attitude of the existing staff who took on the added responsibilities. In 1958 a new administrative officer, Sam Witzenfeld, was appointed – the third in four years – and in the years ahead he was to make a major contribution to the work. Extra staff came a year or so later, and posts were upgraded to reflect the increased responsibilities. The need for strong technical sections specialising in particular functions had been finally accepted.

The general climate of opinion at the beginning of this period seemed favourable. With the Macmillan government there grew a pervasive public sentiment that things were going well, epitomised in the Prime Minister's statement that people had 'never had it so good'. The economic statistics seemed at first to support the government's determined optimism, but the Chancellor's attempt at a balanced budget in 1957 was rejected, and a new Chancellor budgeted for a deficit, eased hire purchase regulations and lowered interest rates. The boom that followed was capped by a general election in 1959 which produced the third consecutive Conservative Party victory. However, the economy did not perform as expected and in 1961 more urgent action was initiated. The government made an attempt to enter the Common Market, and set up the National Economic Development Council and the National Incomes Commission. A credit squeeze and a wage freeze for civil servants followed. So the initial optimism was followed by events which were much less favourable to expansion. This was part of the background for discussions on staff increases, and helps to explain the extended timetables involved.

Within the government apparatus other moves were taking place, leading to the work of the Plowden Committee and major developments in the procedures for tracking, recording and deciding public expenditure. The Plowden Report[1] emphasised the importance of surveying expenditures and changes in prospect, the measurement of expenditures against resources, and of one kind of expenditure against another. The existing system was for individual departments to deal with their problems in isolation, but the public interest, said Plowden, required a more collective approach – more interdepartmental working. The report's interest for the Survey was in the repeated emphasis on the need for greater use of 'quantitative methods in dealing with public expenditure problems ... We believe there should be active consideration of the wider application of quantitative techniques both to policy and to management ... We favour a more systematic attempt to bring together the work done by different Departments in similar fields'. All this seemed very relevant to the methods and output of the Survey. The responsibility for developing the appropriate personnel and management services was thought by the committee to be with the Treasury; of course, since the Survey provided a common service, Treasury ministers from the beginning had been responsible to parliament for estimates and for answering any questions on Survey staffing, efficiency and methods.

It seems clear from the Plowden Report that experience of the expanding expenditure on the NHS and especially the heavy capital outlay on hospitals had made a marked impression. In January 1962 the Minister of Health, Enoch Powell, announced a ten year hospital plan[2] and at the same time invited local authorities to draw up ten year development plans for their health and welfare services. Much of the data on which the plan rested came from hospital inpatient statistics collected from the regions by the Ministry of Health and produced in collaboration with the General Register Office from 1958 onwards. In May 1962 the Minister examined these statistics and, to an audience of hospital administrators, pointed out the difficulties in drawing firm conclusions from them. 'Until we are satisfied that we have eliminated the inaccuracies which at present abound we must not use as pretended statistics what is no more than conglomerated fiction ... Statistics are a tool of management and a basis for planning. To get them right and to want to get them right are signs of a service which is alert and self-critical, which wants to identify with certainty the things which need doing.'[3] Clearly, those responsible for the NHS and the accompanying local services had been alerted to the need for better quantitative data. This gave a strong impetus both to the development of official statistics and also to the rapidly growing research programme which the ministry began to promote.

During this period there was no organised discussion with the Survey of any special contribution it might make deriving from its experience, methods and staff. It is not clear why this was the case. The Medresco surveys and nutritional surveys described earlier had been done directly. Surveys of the elderly and their need for and use of services had mainly been done on repayment terms for non-government bodies, but with the active support and endorsement of the Ministry. When a concrete need existed the Survey might be called in, but this clearly depended on departments' awareness of the Survey's research potential and past contributions. The continuing FES produced data which was more directly relevant to the work of the economic departments, and it wasn't until much later, when social security interests were merged with those of the Ministry of Health, that the new department's economists began to use FES data. It seems evident that a continuing survey, modified in the light of experience and adapted to administrative needs, could have produced a flow of information which would have provided a factual framework for many of the small-scale studies which eventually began to emerge from the academic network financed by the Ministry and the new department. During the same period, the Ministry of Housing was encouraged to launch a stream of Survey studies which provided just such a framework for describing the housing situation. The 1960 Housing Survey was the first major step in this work. It was followed by a study designed to help the Milner–Holland enquiry into London Housing (especially in the rented sector), and by other national surveys and a succession of regional studies. In 1963 the Ministry of Housing inaugurated a fully fledged statistics division under a professional statistician.

Between 1958 and 1963, apart from the housing surveys, a wide range of ad hoc studies and another major continuing survey, the International Passenger Survey (IPS), were organised. For the Home Office, Bob Willcock did studies of public experience of drunkenness, of the home circumstances of young offenders and of the impact of deterrents to crime. In 1960 Roma Morton-Williams, using samples of police and public, studied police public relations for a royal commission. In 1961 Selma Monsky examined many aspects of the staffing of children's homes, at that time a Home Office responsibility. These surveys were all of special populations and most of them involved several different groups and their interactions. Concern for improving labour efficiency led to the Amelia Harris study of labour mobility in 1962, and work by others on the employment histories of people who had obtained Higher National Certificates in various fields of technology, and the contribution of farm institutes to the technical development of farmworkers.

In 1961–2, Percy Gray collected detailed information about the use of motor cars for the Ministry of Transport, using diaries and interviews to record day to day travel patterns, mileage and the purposes of journeys. A feature of the 1958–63 period was a succession of studies for the Post Office, designed to explore their customers' needs and to open up consideration of some longer-term issues, reflected in trends in the use of the telephone and postal services. One of the Prime Minister's initiatives led to the Committee on Higher Education (Robbins Committee) which began a major research programme to explore the size and composition of the present and potential take-up of tertiary education. This occupied a major part of the Survey's research in 1962, in studies run by Bill Kemsley and Roma Morton-Williams. Two rather unusual studies were also done at this time. They were both concerned with an environmental nuisance which was forcing itself on public attention – noise. Aubrey McKennell, working with the Building Research Station, designed a survey of the impact of noise from road traffic in London. The study design incorporated physical measurements of noise and interviews with the people affected. He built on this experience in the second survey, which investigated the nuisance caused by aircraft around London Airport.

Perhaps one of the most striking developments was the extension of postal methods, traditionally low rated as a research method. Gray and Corlett had shown earlier how postal enquiry could be used to contact a scattered population and in 1960 they successfully dispensed with interviews altogether for another pigs and poultry study. In 1961 Christopher Scott brought all the Survey's experience on postal studies together with the work of others in a paper given to the RSS.[4] Interviews were still the main method of the Survey, but a research design often incorporated interviews and records, or interviews preceded by a postal component. Knowledge of the interviewing process and of the most effective use of interviewers remained central, and was reflected in a series of methodological studies of interviewer variability.[5]

But the major innovation of the period was the International Passenger Survey which began in 1961, and marked a sharp break from most previous Survey work. It was designed to provide information about emigration/immigration and expenditures by tourists and travellers, and has made a continuing and growing contribution to population assessment at a time of much public discussion about immigration. The survey is on a very large scale. Some hundreds of thousands of people are sampled and interviewed very briefly as they move through ports and airports. Geoffrey Thomas originated the design and negotiated the complex arrangements needed to sample and contact travellers and to ensure that as little interference as possible was caused to passenger movements. Airport control, Customs and shipping lines were only some of the bodies whose cooperation was essential. Thomas was also responsible for organising a completely separate team of interviewers able and willing to work the unusual hours required, and he supervised the survey for over 16 years. This survey, which uses very short interview schedules on a very large sample, is at almost the opposite end of the spectrum from the FES and many of the ad hoc studies, which use very detailed interviews on relatively small samples.

It seems clear from this brief description of studies done between 1958 and 1963 that the Survey staff were able to mount a very wide range of studies and to innovate relevant techniques. What was done in the studies noted, and in housing and transport, was in marked contrast to the absence of the Survey from the studies of the NHS promoted by the department during this time, despite the emphasis of senior officials and ministers on the need to develop the numerical assessment of NHS work.

Before 1958, social research using survey methods as a mainstream academic concern had not made notable progress: research in universities was still sporadic and uncoordinated. The pre-war mode of unrelated individual contributions still dominated and this meant that many problems of which there was growing uncomfortable public awareness were not scrutinised by the tools available to social science. Without support from foreign foundations there would have been even less work on public issues. In 1957 the DSIR had set up a Human Sciences Committee whose backing led to the award of some research grants and fellowships, mainly related to the study of human factors in productivity. In 1960 this was still a very minor part of DSIR interests: 23 grants out of 525 in that year and two research fellowships out of 75 were for human sciences.[6] In 1961 the British Academy produced a report on research in the humanities and social sciences, which asserted that such research had 'relatively declined during recent decades'.[7] This was the outcome of a major expansion of the physical sciences at a time when financial resources for the human sciences had not grown, and the report argued that there should be 'some authority which could allot funds, as does the DSIR, for special requirements'. At about the same time the DSIR Research Council reviewed its support for research in the human sciences, and agreed that it needed to be increased. A flow of industrially oriented projects resulted, marking an important landmark for the growth of empirical industrial research in Britain.

By 1963, social science had forced itself onto the public agenda. One of the last acts of the Home Government in 1963 was to set up the Committee on Social Studies, called the Heyworth Committee after its chairman. The committee's remit was to 'review research at present being done in the field of social studies in Government Departments, universities and other institutions and to advise whether changes are needed in the arrangements for supporting and coordinating this research'. In the following January, the Minister for Science, Lord Hailsham, spoke to the British National Conference on Social Welfare on the social sciences. He said he had become

> increasingly preoccupied with what seem to me three of the central problems of the twentieth century – the preservation of what is essentially good and permanent in civilization in an age of change, the necessity to make perpetual adjustments and radical innovations in social and political machinery in order to take account of changes in technical processes, and above all the need for political expertise and social awareness in attaining these ends . . . To some extent the key to those questions lies in the social sciences or studies, and it was for this reason that why my colleagues and I initiated a full scale enquiry into their range and adequacy now proceeding under Lord Heyworth . . . Science is after all nothing more than systematic thought applied to systematic observation and measurement. Judged by these standards social studies require to be science based . . . Moral and political judgments are indissolubly part of them, but to be effective these need to be informed by practical scientific techniques, not the bogus stuff which can creep in so easily but the real thing, measuring, predicting, testing and correcting.

The Minister went on to develop the theme of technical change and its social consequences. 'Obviously we need to study anew our means of living together . . . our communities are, in the last analysis, mechanisms for the collective sustaining and enjoyment of a man's life as a social being; and it is probably time that we put into that task an amount of deliberate and informed social thinking and planning at least as great as the thinking and planning that goes into an aircraft cabin or a man-carrying rocket'. It was a characteristically ebullient speech, delivered at a time when it was clear that a general election was only a few months ahead and when the opposition party had begun to talk of modernisation and the application of science to national problems. But it gives, perhaps, some insight into contemporary ministerial thinking. The Macmillan impetus had petered out; the Plowden Report had crystallised thinking about economic and financial 'forward looks' and suggested the appropriate mechanisms; the ten year plans in health and social services had begun to focus attention on a more highly organised management in these areas, and in every sector the need was expressed for a more quantitative approach. Demand for survey work within the government was clearly growing, and the Heyworth Committee was to prove of key importance, both for official support of social research and in the affairs of the Survey. The committee and its eventual report (in 1965) provided a marked stimulus to departmental activity. The committee asked all departments to respond to two questionnaires, sent out in July 1963 and April 1964, which asked about their use and financing of social research. An interdepartmental committee of civil servants, set up to exchange information on Heyworth, circulated all the responses to all the departments so, for the first time, departments became fully aware of research sponsored by other departments, and of other departments' views on the government organisation of social research.

Among these circulated papers was the Survey's response to Heyworth, which took into account discussions I had had with some of the major departments about the potential of the Survey and the use of survey research for many purposes, official and academic, in the USA. Its main points were:

– The programming system was not efficient. It did not produce a list of projects which necessarily rated the highest priority for the use of Survey resources and it might be advantageous if the Survey concentrated its efforts on a more limited range of subject matter, maybe in the form of longer-term programmes each related to the interests of several departments.

– The use of the Survey in future would depend on whether departments acted on the conclusions of the Plowden Report and made more effort to apply quantitative methods to their planning and evaluation.

– Government use of survey research was haphazard and unplanned. Departments were not well informed about the social research which was being financed by government. This must mean that total expenditures were not yielding maximum benefit. Regular meetings of departments financing research would encourage exchanges of experience on the most and least profitable exercises, and highlight the most important subjects of common interest. This would also provide some order of priorities for the Survey.

– Government research programmes, which were now developing fast, were not distinguishing clearly between academic interests and the operational interests of the departments that were financing them.

– The staffing of the Survey was not improving in line with the growing programmes and expenditure. The inappropriateness of the Information Class and the conditions of service were not facilitating recruitment, especially of middle-level staff.

– A strengthened Survey could be of assistance to all users of government financed research and could help to mobilise and supervise resources outside its own staff.

In 1964 there was a change of government and a great deal of enthusiasm for a programme of modernising the government and the country. In many ways this was a continuation of the Macmillan era, which had been a period of growth for the Survey. The new government, however, had first to deal with the results of a very expansive financial programme in the last year of the preceding government and a balance of payments crisis. This did not make for relaxed discussion about civil service salary problems. But the most immediate effect on the Survey was the break-up of the DSIR and the distribution of its parts to different departments. This disrupted the good relations which the Survey had had with the DSIR from very early days, and added to the Survey's work-programme difficulties.

In the interval before the Heyworth Committee reported, the Survey's Vote continued to increase and the desultory discussion with Treasury about organisational matters continued. The Vote for 1965–6 had been agreed at £710,000 – an increase of 40% on the previous year. In March 1965 three assistant director posts were agreed and a total of 28 new posts. In October 1966, after the report, a fourth assistant director post was agreed: the four posts were filled by Thomas, Gray, Kemsley and Willcock. In November 1967, the management structure was rounded off by the award of principal posts for the heads of the technical sections and the appointment of Geoffrey Thomas as Deputy Director. These senior posts recognised that with the expansion of the work programme a large management element had entered into the work. In April 1967 the research staff in post numbered 72 and the total staff was 158 – more than twice the size of the Survey in 1961, when the expansion began. Real resources had increased by more than three times in this period. A substantial part of this was needed for the continuing surveys, which made heavy demands on operational money, and for contracted-out work such as the National Food Survey and, later, the National Travel Survey.

The Heyworth Committee reported in June 1965. For academic researchers its main recommendation was that a social science research council should be set up to finance social enquiries and to provide for postgraduate awards and fellowships. For the Survey, some of its recommendations followed the suggestions in my submission, but others were quite unexpected – and there was one major disappointment. This was the committee's rejection of the proposal that government should set up an organisation which would review the experience of all major government users of survey research, coordinate their efforts and make their experience widely known throughout government. The committee may have felt that the proposed research council would carry out this function: the years that followed proved it wrong.

The committee noted the Survey 'has given valuable service to Government by means of ad hoc surveys', but it thought 'the arrangements for using the Survey reveal weaknesses which must be corrected if it is to make a full contribution to the work of Government'. The Survey, it thought, was

> being inefficiently used because: (a) its purposes are not properly understood by all departments and it is sometimes asked to carry out work which ought to be done by departments themselves or commercially; (b) there has been no means by which demands can be coordinated and so the Survey cannot plan a coherent programme and cooperation between departments in any one enquiry is fortuitous; (c) the Social Survey has no easy means of keeping in touch with those aspects of departments'

policy which lead to demands upon it. Its skill and experience are not brought in early enough to contribute to decisions about which problems it can best tackle; (d) the contribution which the Survey could make to the development of survey techniques, the training of research workers and the accumulation of a coherent body of knowledge as a background to Government administration is lost as a result of its being regarded purely as a service organization.

If these criticisms were to be met, interdepartmental machinery would be required 'through which the demands of departments could be rationalized'. The committee recommended that 'the Social Survey be transferred to the Treasury and that there should be created an Interdepartmental Committee under Treasury chairmanship composed of the main user departments and of the Social Science Research Council to advise on the programme of the Social Survey'.

Some of this was in line with what the Survey had been saying for a long time, but it was not easy to see how the actual recommendations would lead to any improvement. Since its inception the work of the Survey had, in fact, been under Treasury supervision, as were all the central services. Not only did the Treasury authorise the annual programme of work and Vote: it also considered all the individual surveys as they were submitted for authorisation, and had therefore been in a position to query priority or to suggest possible combinations of interest. The Survey, in its evidence to the committee, had itself urged the creation of an interdepartmental committee to review the government's experience of financing social research done inside and outside government, and to make regular appraisals of how to ensure its needs were met. To consider the work of the Survey in isolation from research done elsewhere at government expense would not improve matters. The committee itself had agreed that since departmental research programmes were 'becoming more ambitious, the total demand on resources for research and the allocation of resources will need to be scrutinized centrally'. But on such a scrutinising committee Heyworth was noncommittal: it 'might be unwieldy . . . it will grow if it is needed'.

The recommendation that Treasury should take direct responsibility was unexpected, and seemed all the more curious in view of the other listed supposed shortcomings of the system. Since the Plowden Report, responsibility for spreading awareness of techniques that might improve managerial efficiency and, particularly, the spread of methods that would help to develop quantitative appraisals, had been with the Treasury. But nobody was inclined to oppose any proposal that appeared to solve the problem of a more appropriate location for the Survey than within the government's information service.

In August 1965 the recommendation that Treasury should take over was officially accepted and in November the decision was announced in the House of Lords. At about the same time the Minister of Education moved a motion in the House of Commons to approve the order setting up the social science research council. At the end of October the Treasury began to take steps to implement the recommendations that concerned the Survey. The government background to these developments was not encouraging. The climate for research was very favourable – 'modernisation' implied some scrutiny of old arrangements and consideration of new ones. However, the cycle of 'stop-go' economic policy which had been inherited from previous governments continued, and there were periodic balance of payments difficulties. The stops included freezing government salary changes. They reached a climax in 1967 when the government felt it had to enter into negotiations with the International Monetary Fund (IMF). This was just about the time when discussions about the new arrangements for the Survey were finalised.

During these prolonged discussions about the Survey's future, the regular procession of surveys continued. The internal pressures were simply accepted as a continuing challenge – part of the working environment, eased from time to time by staff increases and a de facto creation of a better structure. In 1963 and 1964 some major studies were mounted. The Allen Committee, appointed to examine the impact of rates, reflected the growing concern about the financing of local government. Information collected in the course of the FES showed how people at different income levels were affected. In 1964 another large housing survey was done, followed by a study of housing in Scotland and a series of regional housing surveys. Also in 1964, the National Travel Survey inaugurated a series of surveys designed to record passenger movements, which could be related to regular traffic censuses. In 1964 and 1965 studies of smoking habits and attitudes towards smoking were made, arising out of the official recognition of the association between smoking and lung cancer. In 1964 a major survey on primary schools was made for the Central Advisory Committee for Education, and thereafter for some years surveys were requested on some aspect of education. In 1966 there was a survey designed to help evolve proposals for raising the school leaving age, followed by a survey to help clarify thinking on changes in sixth form curricula.

In 1963 and 1965 more nutrition surveys were done using the methods developed earlier. In 1965 and 1967 work was done for the Maude Committee on Management in Local Government and the later Royal Commission of Local Government. During this period work was also done on other strata of the public services: the Fulton Committee on the Civil Service needed descriptive information on the social background of civil servants, which was provided by a postal survey (1967), and the staffing of the fire service and the police was reviewed in the same year. In 1963 a survey was designed to help with recruitment to the army and in 1964 there was a survey to examine the way the jury system was working. In 1965 and 1967, welfare services that mainly helped the elderly were studied, and in 1966 there was a further survey in the series for the Home Office on the penal system.

In 1965, 1966 and 1967 a series of surveys was made for statistical divisions of departments. One of these, on women's employment, studied the growing participation of women in the labour force (1965). There was a Post Enumeration Survey to check the efficiency and quality of the Census in 1966, followed by a study of family intentions, designed to improve population forecasting. This survey had been thought too delicate a subject for a government instrument to tackle; in fact, it led to no difficulty at all and a respectable response rate. In 1966 the Royal Commission on Industrial Relations asked for a study of many groups of people involved in trade union activities. The growing use of the FES for social security purposes led, at the end of 1967, to a decision to double the sample.

This work, between 1963 and 1967, was the usual mixture of surveys making factual examination of existing situations and studies of opinion and attitude, often both within the same survey. Many of the surveys noted embraced more than one population. Thus the education surveys covered teachers, parents and pupils, whose responses could be related; the Milner Holland Survey of London Housing included landlords and tenants; the Maude Committee survey studied councillors and electors, and the survey of police and the public studied both. The opinion and attitude surveys used scaling methods and factor analysis of different populations.[8] The use of postal methods was developed further – the Maude Committee survey in particular used a large postal survey to collect descriptive information about 3,000 councillors, of whom 600 were later interviewed,[9] and some information was obtained on about 96% of the councillors sampled.

The internal committee set up in January 1966 to coordinate response to Heyworth became known as the Committee on Social Science Research (CSSR). Its formal terms of reference were rather close to those proposed by the Survey to Heyworth and to the Treasury in 1963. It was chaired by the Treasury and met for the first time in April 1966. In parallel, a Programme Committee, also chaired by the Treasury, was set up in March with the narrower aim of discussing the Survey's proposed annual programmes and advising the Treasury accordingly on the annual Vote. There was no clear division of function between these two committees. And if the intention had been to integrate the Survey into the expanding government social research activity, it would have been more logical to arrange for the CSSR to act as its parent body rather than the Programme Committee – a more restricted committee, which even excluded some of the Survey's customers. This was probably due to confusion or ignorance rather than intention. The Registrar General, for example, was not invited to join it because it was thought that his office had 'never commissioned work from the Social Survey', though in 1966 the Survey carried out a major Post Enumeration Survey to check on the quality of the Census, for which the Registrar General was responsible. This was not a promising beginning for a body which was supposed to help develop a more 'coordinated' programme of work and to advise on priorities.

In 1963–6 the Survey's Vote had grown from £418,000 to £710,000, an increase of about 70%. Data collected by the CSSR showed that departmental expenditure on research, excluding the Survey's Vote, had grown at twice this rate in the same period. The expenditure of the Department of Education and Science had increased from £53,000 to £316,000, and that of the Ministry of Social Security from £64,000 to £172,000. After these two came the Home Office. A large part of the Ministry of Social Security expenditure had been on the time of its own local staff, but for most departments the greater part of this expenditure was on contracts and grants to outside research organisations. The dispersal of the DSIR had increased the in-house capacity of some departments, and the Survey's expansion in these years was not exceptional. It was part of a more general movement in the government's use of social research.

The development of the large continuing surveys was making a major contribution to social statistics. It was therefore inevitable that when in January 1966 the Estimates Committee turned its attention to government statistical services it asked many searching questions about the work of the Survey and the possibilities of developing the scope of the FES even further.[10] Professor Claus Moser, examined on his views about manpower statistics, emphasised the role of large-scale sample surveys. Professor Balogh thought the Survey should do more opinion and attitude research on economic matters. The Registrar General, after describing the costs and uses of the Population Census, argued that 'there is really no competition between censuses and sample surveys' and explained the different contributions which both types of enquiry made. He went on to say:

> Even now there is call for close working relationships between the two organizations [Social Survey and GRO]. It seems almost certain that the sampling aspects of census work will grow. There is much sampling expertise in the Social Survey and we shall try to make as much use of this as possible. The need to test census procedures and to measure the quality of census results is now recognized. All this means that the staff of the two organizations should and do consult frequently. The important thing is that people in both organizations should know each other and be able to exchange ideas and learn from each other's experience.

The chairman of the Estimates Committee asked the Registrar General if it would be appropriate for the GRO to be represented on the Programme Committee, to which he replied 'I would certainly welcome an invitation'. The Estimates Committee thought that 'development of social statistics in the next decade comparable to that which has taken place in economic statistics in the last is to be looked for. It is their view that development should be coordinated at every stage and that the CSO should play an integral part in achieving it'.

While these parliamentary deliberations were taking place, and thus in practice helping to define the Survey's role, the work of the internal committees proceeded. The CSSR had quite extensive terms of reference, and if it had indeed undertaken an active and critical review of the government's use of social research, it would have provided the necessary framework for examining the Survey's past contribution and helping to decide how its programme should be shaped in the future. But while departments did provide the CSSR with information about their research expenditures and staffing, as described earlier, this excluded work done by the Survey because it did not involve payment. Since the Survey was the largest in-house research unit this meant that the CSSR's tabulated figures were deficient. However, they were circulated, but the CSSR did not attempt any analysis of its data collection. And the committee does not appear to have discussed the use made of the Survey by its members. No reference was made to the discussions of the Estimates Committee. The CSSR met only four times in its three years' existence from April 1966 to May 1969 – a period of substantial expansion of departments' research activities, when many of the problems of expansion and control must have been common problems. There is no published account of the committee's deliberations and no indication of what guidance, if any, the Treasury was given.

Towards the end of the committee's existence there were developments in the ministerial responsibilities for the social services, and discussion about whether the committee should narrow its interests from the social sciences to the social services. For departments which would not be too happy about a scrutinising committee which might impinge on their areas of sovereignty, this notion would have had some appeal. In 1969, noting that the committee had done very little 'coordinating', the Treasury informed it that its future membership would be limited, and responsibility for a much limited role as an exchange centre for information and contact with the SSRC would be transferred to the Office of the Secretary for the Social Services.

The Survey's Programme Committee was a more active body.[11] It was the first time that most of the Survey's customers had ever been assembled, though with notable exceptions such as the Board of Trade and the GRO. The committee met four times in 1966, and various papers were prepared for it, including several submitted by the Survey. The first of these, titled the *Social Survey's Role and Programme,* noted the recent growth of the Survey and the large part played by the continuing surveys and by contracting out due to staffing problems. It went on to analyse the advantages and disadvantages of a central research unit: a large output permitted specialisation inside the unit but meant that output was very heterogenous; there was technical sophistication and the chance to combine the needs of different customers, but there were limitations on the cumulation of subject knowledge; its resources and technical experience were available to any part of the government, but programmes were somewhat unpredictable. The paper went on to say that producing mass statistics was probably not the most useful way to use the Survey's resources and experience, and it might be better to concentrate those resources on longer-term interests of departments. This would require discussions with departments about their developing research interests, and better contact between them and the survey. But deciding which part of total government research should be done by the Survey and which by other agents would require a body like the CSSR to review all government work.

Most of the participants accepted this analysis, but the Chairman, in summing up, made no reference to CSSR. Rather, he asked departments to say what survey research they had sponsored and to guess their future needs, distinguishing work done by the Survey, work supervised but contracted out, and work wholly contracted out (see Table 2). This information was discussed at the second meeting three months later.

The numbers in Table 2 relate to projects of unequal scope – thus the FES counts as one project, as does the very large International Passenger Survey. But they show that for the departments participating the Survey was, at that time, the dominant resource. To some extent this could be misleading. The definition of survey research would have been interpreted as research of the sort done by the Survey. A study carried out by an academic researcher, which employed some form of sample survey but was reported with an emphasis on theoretical interpretation, might well be excluded. Indeed, scrutiny of actual projects

Table 2 Review of sponsored surveys

	Social Survey done or managed	Social Survey not involved	Total
1962–4	15	2	17
1964–5	10	7	17
1965–6	15	9	24
	40	18*	58

* 3 with Survey advice but no other involvement.

sponsored by departments in these three years shows that many which are excluded from the table are not very different from some that are included.

Departments' forecasts of their future needs were not very firm, but using the information about past use, trends and future needs, the Survey produced another paper for the third meeting of the Programme Committee in July 1966. This paper, *Future of the Social Survey*, emphasised the constraints of staff limitations but forecast a total output of around £850,000 for 1967–8, and of £1,000,000 three to four years ahead. (In fact, the 1967–8 Vote was £850,000 and that for 1969–70 £1,061,000.) The forecasts assumed that the proposed extension of the FES would go ahead, but there would have to be periodic reviews of actual work programmes in the light of the committee's decisions on their desirable scope.

The paper suggested some criteria for deciding the make-up of the programme from year to year: the Survey should continue to work on a variety of topics and to employ a mixture of social scientists, but it would be economical and technically efficient to concentrate resources on some selected subject areas; the Survey should only be used for large statistical surveys where departments' statistical divisions could not provide necessary resources, and there should be no more mass statistical surveys like the International Passenger Survey; a continuing effort should be made in discussion with departments to concentrate resources on continuing and longer-term research needs.

The Chairman, summing up, said there seemed to be 'general agreement with the broad tenor of the Director's recommendations'. The discussion showed, he said, that while some kind of central reference point for government survey work was desirable, complete centralisation should be avoided because of departments' existing commitments and relationships with university researchers. This was completely compatible with the suggestion of an extended advisory role for the Survey, and in any event manpower limitations would not permit the Survey to contemplate doing more than a part of sponsored survey work. It would essentially be a cooperative enterprise, in which each side would provide what it was best equipped to, so that the Survey's direct and indirect contribution to government survey research could be much advanced without undermining departments' ultimate responsibility for obtaining whatever survey material was needed for policy.

Between April and July 1966 the Survey and the Treasury attempted, once again, to reach agreement on an appropriate class and salary structure for the Survey's staff. The COI was still formally responsible for the Survey, but since it was clear that other arrangements would soon be made, the Survey made most of the running. The discussions followed changes made earlier, when the fast-growing work programme supplied the main impulse. These changes resulted in a framework first proposed many years earlier in which a senior research component, with responsibility for managing sizeable sections of the annual programme, was strongly supported by clearly defined technical functions. About a quarter of total expenditure went on research and technical staff who comprised about half the total staff. This proportion did not vary a great deal over many years, and reflected the practice of seeking staff changes as the Vote and commitments to carry out specific projects increased. The structure in 1966 was not well balanced. There were too few at the middle levels to ensure adequate supervision, technical development and the reserves needed to cope with new demands; there were too few at the middle and higher levels to offer reasonable promotion prospects. Many left after initial training and participation in a few projects, and Survey experience was used to the advantage of other organisations inside and outside the civil service.

The contribution of the Survey's fieldworkers, too, was not overlooked: as surveys became more intensive, their work became more onerous, and the selection of suitable people became more important. In March 1965 a scheme based on a detailed analysis of the interviewers' work, compared to the work of and conditions offered by market research firms, was put up for consideration. It proposed a graduated scale in which trainees, trained interviewers, interviewers with a minimum experience of ten surveys, and a group who were completely mobile and used for auxiliary training purposes as well as the most demanding surveys, were paid on an increasing scale. This was eventually accepted.

From the Survey's point of view, it was important to recruit and maintain a research staff from different social sciences. If they were to have reasonable promotion prospects they would have to be able to move to professional posts elsewhere in the civil service, which could best be done if they were members of the established classes for social scientists – economists, statisticians, psychologists and so on. It was important, too, for all members of the staff, not only research staff, to see a promotion ladder open to all and related to the different functions carried out. Members of the technical staff had made valuable contributions to the work and many had moved into the research section at all periods in the Survey's history. A common scale and promotion ladder seemed critical. Pay scales for psychologists, scientific officers, statistical officers and research officers were higher than those available for Survey staff. Promotion prospects, too, were better. Survey staff's experience was worth more to them outside the Survey than in it.

All this presented difficulties for the Treasury. Different classes were subject to criteria established over time and agreed with the relevant unions. Any special arrangements for one organisation would be viewed as precedents to be followed in many other areas, which would embroil the Treasury in continuing debate. Much better from its point of view would be the adoption of some existing class and its criteria. Its choice of a convenient grouping, which had been often discussed previously, was the Research Officer Class. This class had been devised to provide an umbrella for a very broad collection of individuals for whom no other class seemed relevant. Most of its members were not doing social research and many of them had no experience of survey research. Applying the criteria used for the Research Officer Class to the Survey would have eliminated most of the technical sections and split the staff into two groups with very different career prospects. It would also have meant that existing members of that class elsewhere in the civil service would have been eligible for promotion to the Survey regardless of their lack of Survey experience. Graduates recruited to the Survey, on the other hand, might be moved after gaining some years' experience – just when they were becoming useful – to other departments with a complement of research officers. And people recruited to the Survey specifically for the few social scientists' posts (psychologists, statisticians, economists) would certainly be expected to move on promotion elsewhere in the service. It seemed to the Survey that these proposals would not only offer little improvement – they might even make the situation worse. All the arguments on both sides were taken back to the Programme Committee with the intimation that there had been a failure to agree. It is remarkable that for a whole generation everybody agreed that the Information Class was not suitable for the Survey, but no one could produce a satisfactory alternative. The committee reiterated its view that something had to be done to help with the Survey's staffing problems.

At the next meeting, in September 1966, the Ministry of Labour produced its proposals for extending the FES and later adding a second parallel interview survey. In all this would call for samples four times as large as the pre-1967 survey. The same meeting also received a paper prepared by the committee's Secretary, a Treasury principal, suggesting a completely different method of budgeting – that is, preparing the Vote and financing the work. This was unexpected, and proposed a change from a system which had worked since 1941. I prepared a counter-proposal and both papers were debated at the next meeting, in January 1967.

The Survey's Vote was compiled on the allied service principle: that is, the principle that the Survey provided, on request, a common service to any part of the government apparatus, and that the costs for this service were met from a sum clearly identified in estimates presented to Parliament. The assumption was that some activities are best evaluated by Parliament, and that the work involved is best done by a specialist body handling a greater part of the government's requirements, either by providing the service through its own staff or by contracting for the services of organisations outside government.

The Treasury argued that the system gave no clear indication of what government expenditure should be. The Vote simply reflected the total demand for customer departments as amended or agreed with Treasury at estimates time, and Treasury had no yardstick for reaching its decision. If departments had to pay for the services of the Survey, it was argued, then the sum of what they were prepared to pay each year would give much better guidance. It was assumed in the paper that since research formed such a small part of departmental activities, the sums involved would be such small proportions of departmental votes that they would have little difficulty in financing them. There was no acknowledgement of the fast-growing totals of research grants which departments were giving to academic researchers (apparently without the help of any 'yardstick' for the Treasury); nor was it noted that, given this large and growing academic resource, if departments came to the Survey, this would be because of a calculated judgment that the Survey could meet particular needs more satisfactorily. This was especially true since every survey project had to be related to a policy requirement and defended if necessary by the minister of the customer department. By ignoring this, the Treasury paper curiously avoided the political component involved in every Survey study.

The Survey response noted that the Treasury's proposals assumed that the repayment principle would, in a way not described, enable departments to place a market value on a piece of research. Experience showed, however, that the value of a particular piece of research changed with the changing pressures on policy. A request for a survey would necessarily be based on a judgment at any one time that attempts to respond to these pressures could be aided by a particular survey study, designed jointly by administrators and researchers, which could be defended politically if necessary. And it was to meet such needs that the Survey, its techniques and working methods had been developed. The more it could be ensured that long-term needs were met by a particular piece of research, the more certain it would be that the costs involved could be justified. This was one of the requirements for developing the Survey's programme that the committee had discussed and agreed. Similarly, it was desirable that particular projects covered as many departments' needs as possible. Because the FES did this, it had been recognised as successful. It would, however, be difficult, if not impossible, to allocate the costs to the growing number of Survey users.

But apart from these arguments of principle, perhaps most important, the Survey argued, was the practical difficulty the change would involve. The Survey's Vote was compiled on the basis of discussions with departments before the beginning of the financial year and before precise costing could be done, by means of pilot studies or analogies with previous work. At that early stage, cost could be only roughly assigned. So apart from studies carried over from one year to the next, much of the Survey's programme was tentative. Some of the studies mooted earlier would not be done, some not discussed at all in the early days would, as the financial year evolved, assume greater political importance; and there were always royal commissions or departmental committees deciding without much notice that they needed new information. The existing system could cope with the balancing act required to deal with these eventualities. But some kind of Vote was necessary to provide for headquarters staff and the costs of fieldwork if, as projects crystallised, it was needed. The Survey's central Vote provided a pool from which necessary resources could be made available. If all possible customers had to provide on their own Votes for such eventualities, clearly a much larger total sum, much of which would not be spent, would be needed, and would be dispersed among many Votes. The Treasury then, far from having a better yardstick, would have difficulty finding out what the total demand was. Finally, said the Survey, the committee had agreed on the Survey's future role and programming. This assumed that a qualified and experienced staff specialising in providing survey research shaped to meet government needs would be available. A central Vote would provide the basis for it: without such a Vote it was problematical.

The committee discussed the two papers and agreed that the Treasury should be asked to redraft the paragraphs dealing with budgeting. The Chairman said the report should say that the matter would be looked at again, but departments still had strong doubts about how it would work in practice and whether it would provide any improvement on the existing system. The same meeting noted that the Vote for the next financial year had been compiled in the usual way and that the Treasury had agreed the sum of £850,000 for 1967–8. This compared with £710,000 for the year in which the Heyworth Committee reported.

During the year in which the Programme Committee was discussing and agreeing on the future role and programming of the Survey, there had been no discussion of the Survey's future relationship with the Treasury, which was supposed to be responsible for it. Early in January 1967 I was told that it was proposed 'to appoint an administrative head' of the Survey when it formally separated from the COI, and that an Under Secretary would be appointed to this post. The appointment was to take effect on 27 February. This was something of a surprise to the members of the Programme Committee, who had been studiously analysing the Survey's future role for the last year and to whom these proposals had not been mentioned. The new administrative head, T R Kingdom, formerly of the Assistance Board, had no experience of the Survey's work, and had not seen a Survey report before he arrived. And this was at a time of major change for the Survey.

On 17 February a Treasury Minister announced in the House of Commons that arrangements for reconstituting the Survey were complete, and that 'the Social Survey will become a separate Department as from 1 April 1967. Revised Estimates will be presented to the House in due course'. The new administrative head was to be called Controller, and I was to continue as Director and chief professional officer. The new department would be known as the Government Social Survey Department and would continue to be responsible to Treasury ministers. Urgent discussions took place to get agreement on the administrative arrangements for the new department, which would be very small by Whitehall standards: administration would, therefore, bulk large. As the new Controller noted to the Treasury, 'the housekeeping overheads are bound to look disproportionately high'. A net increase of eight staff was requested, taking the total administrative staff to 23. The total Survey staff in post in April 1967 was 150.

The constitution of the new department seemed to settle the old question of a more appropriate location for the Survey than in the government information service, though the issue had neither been discussed with customer departments nor argued in any statements made about the new arrangements. The Heyworth Committee had certainly recommended that the Treasury should take responsibility but had scarcely demonstrated that this would necessarily be an improvement; and as subsequent events showed, the decision took little account of changes in the government apparatus which were in the making before the announcement of the new department. However, its creation certainly signalled official recognition of the continuing contribution of survey methods to government, and must therefore be noted as one of the more important landmarks in the Survey's history.

Notes

[1] *Control of Public Expenditure*, HMSO, July 1961.
[2] *A Hospital Plan for England and Wales*, HMSO, 1962.
[3] Minister of Health in an address to the Institute of Hospital Administrators, 4 May 1962.
[4] 'Research on Mail Surveys', *Journal of the Royal Statistical Society* Vol 124, 1961, and Methodological Papers M80, 100, 104 and 121, also discuss the use of postal methods.
[5] Methodological Papers M82, 94, 112, and 121 are examples.
[6] *DSIR Report of Research Council for 1960*, HMSO, May 1961.
[7] *Research in the Humanities and Social Sciences*, Oxford University Press, 1961.
[8] See Methodological Papers 114, 119, 124, 125, 126, 127, 128, 129.
[9] *ibid*, M121.
[10] Fourth Report from the Estimates Committee, Session 1966–67, Government Statistical Services, HMSO, 1967.
[11] Most of the material for this account comes from COI files SS 41, 41/1, 41/2 and 41/3.

5   1967–70: A government social survey department

THE LATER MONTHS OF 1967 and the following years were dominated for the government by the decisions flowing from negotiations with the IMF. The National Plan was abandoned, there were cuts in government spending, the credit squeeze was tightened. The first French veto on British entry into the European Economic Community followed. In November 1967 there came devaluation and, in 1968, a new Chancellor of the Exchequer with a further credit squeeze and more taxation. These measures were followed by an improvement in the balance of payments, but a deterioration in industrial relations as trade unionists sought to regain the position eroded by the decisions of previous years. In 1970 another election led to a change of government from Labour to Conservative, with Edward Heath as Prime Minister.

Alongside these disturbing economic events there was a procession of social and administrative changes. It is not clear how the nature and direction of these changes were shaped by the economic background. Perhaps economic turbulence had by this time become expected, making business as usual, or perhaps more activity in other spheres of government, all the more important if the appearance of a government in control of events was to be sustained. Thus the appointment of Professor Moser, a social statistician, to head the Central Statistical Office, was seen as one aspect of the declared intention to modernise the apparatus of government. Another was the appointment of a committee to review the civil service, under the chairmanship of Lord Fulton. Speaking to a press conference in June 1968, Lord Fulton said 'we accepted that our enquiry was widely regarded as part of a general reappraisal of the country's institutions; education as a whole had already been under the scrutiny of a series of committees from Robbins to Plowden; and other parallel enquiries – on eg Trade Unions and Local Government – were contemporary with our own'.

In November 1967, eight months after the new department began, the Treasury finally issued a circular which formally notified departments of the future role of the Survey and set out 'the relationship between the Survey and user Departments that has been proposed by the Social Survey Programme Committee and accepted by the Treasury'. The accompanying *Note by the Treasury* followed, along the lines agreed in the discussions of the Programme

Committee. It is reproduced as Appendix B. The circular seems to have had little practical effect, and it is unlikely that any department changed its research policy as a result of it.

Inside the departments research budgets grew, particularly where, as in the Ministry of Health, a rapidly expanding network of academic units was created on the supposed model of the Medical Research Council. The head of the civil service, Sir William Armstrong, speaking at a conference of the Social Science Research Council (SSRC) in 1969 noted 'the very marked increase in the interest of Government in social science research . . . the total amount of money over the years 1965–6 to 1968–9 spent by government departments on social science research increased from £1 million to about £1.7 million . . . almost the whole of that growth was in research commissioned by departments to be undertaken by research outside the government service'. He noted also the growing use of commissioned research by royal commissions and committees of enquiry, and went on to emphasise changes in the internal organisation of government departments 'made with a view to organising research more systematically and bringing it into closer contact with policy . . . most departments have had a statistical unit for some time but the connection between the work of those units and policy making has often in the past been rather sketchy'.[1]

In the social departments, the organisation of fully-fledged statistical units headed by professional statisticians had, in fact, been quite recent and changes in the orientation of government-sponsored research were seen a few years later as urgently necessary. Sir William's comments, then, may have been a little optimistic and it is notable that his talk at no point mentioned the Survey, which had been involved in many of the developments he noted and which only a year or so previously had been constituted as a separate department. It may be, too, that the abrasive language used in parts of the Fulton Report about the alleged limitations of managerial competence in the civil service made it appear helpful to stress a positive development – a more sympathetic attitude towards social research. Earlier in 1969, Sir William had said in a BBC interview, 'As I see the way our system has developed, the Civil Service is the connection between politics and reality, between politics and facts. We do a good job if we provide politicians of either party with the most accurate mirror and interpretation of ongoing reality with which we have to deal . . . (this isn't) in fact a neutral position; the position is the efficient and humane management of the affairs of this country from a basis of reality'.[2] These sentiments express well the function that the staff of the Survey perceived themselves to be carrying out.

These sentiments were one aspect of the general movement towards raising the competence and responsiveness of government, which was finding expression in many different ways, of which the Fulton Report was one example. Another was the *New Presentation of Public Expenditure* put by the Treasury to the Select Committee on Procedure in April 1969. This followed the logic of the Plowden Report and proposed an annual statement by government of what it saw as the prospect for public expenditure for a number of years ahead. The idea was to try to ensure a better based public discussion.

Economists in government had clearly taken the lead among other professional civil servants concerned with social science topics, and had begun to reach some conclusions about research that was relevant and useful for government policy. In a paper given to a conference jointly organised by the Civil Service Department and the Public Administration Committee in April 1969,[3] Maurice Wright described these conclusions. 'Research paid for by Government must be justified on the grounds that it would improve decisions and policies. Some attempt must be made to evaluate the likely pay-off of the research on these terms before it is begun. Research done internally by departments themselves was likely to be more effective than work commissioned outside. An additional advantage of internal research is that experience and expertise is built up and retained within the department'. Wright suggested that the new Civil Service Department should develop a research unit to promote administrative research. 'Ideally it would have a permanent nucleus of people to lead and coordinate research studies throughout the Service and would include sociologists, psychologists, economists and statisticians'. Much of this was in line with Survey experience and, indeed, had been among proposals for improving the programming and internal structure of the Survey.

The 1966 Estimates Committee had drawn attention to the need to bring official social statistics up to the levels established in post-war economic statistics, and the appointment of a social statistician to head the CSO was seen as a sign that further change was expected in this field. In April 1968, a parliamentary question had elicited from the Prime Minister an indication that other developments had been in prospect for some time.[4] Mr Edward duCann had asked about a study of government statistical services commissioned by the Prime Minister in April 1966. This had not been published, but was taken together with proposals made by Professor Moser as the basis for changes within the CSO which strengthened its coordinating role in government statistics. These changes were described in more detail in *Statistical News* by Professor Moser in May 1968.

Among the developments promised were a more integrated system of official statistics; an improvement in the usefulness of statistics to government and other interests – business, trade unions, economists and other social scientists, and strengthened contributions to methodological advances in statistical work and 'our relations with the academic and research world'. The choice between a centralised statistical system and one in which individual departments had their own statistical units was described, as was the decision to maintain the existing decentralised system, largely because it ensured stronger links with senior policymakers. This in turn required a more powerful means for coordinating the whole statistical system, and changes designed to achieve this were set out. 'The CSO will take responsibility for the Government's overall statistical programme and the priorities within it . . . and will move towards a comprehensively phased programme of current statistical work up to five years or more ahead'. The work of a proposed Business Statistics Office, to centralise much economics statistics collecting, was described, and the article referred to

the possibility of similar developments in the collection of data from households and individuals. For example a study has begun of the costs and uses of continuous household surveys on the model of the Current Population and Labour Force Surveys (in the USA and other European countries) . . . we are also looking at organizational aspects of social statistics including arrangements for censuses and surveys.

The implications of the CSO Director's statement were twofold: first, organisational aspects were under review, and second, some kind of continuous household survey was being considered. The total programme was very ambitious, and the statement about organisational aspects a little premature. In the following month the Prime Minister, asked about the possibility of transferring responsibility for the Survey from the Treasury, said that existing arrangements had only been working for over a year and 'it would be premature to consider a change now before the developments in the Government statistical services' he had referred to in his reply to the question of 2 April. The public signals were a little mixed, but it seemed that further changes for the Survey were not ruled out. The manner of Professor Moser's announcement also indicated that he felt authorised to make decisions about the Survey's activities and organisation. This seemed to ignore the existence of the Programme Committee, which had presented its report on the future programming of the Survey at the beginning of 1967. Since the Treasury had accepted the report as providing the guidelines for the future, the CSO statement also raised questions about the Treasury's responsibility for the Survey. But there was indeed some substance behind it. Speaking much later, at a conference of the International Statistics Institute, the Prime Minister praised the efforts of government statisticians to put into effect the recommendations of the Estimates Committee. 'I am able to give you first hand assurance that in this work the Director of the CSO has the complete support of the Government . . . and authoritative backing by the creation in this country of a standing Ministerial Committee chaired by the Minister of State at the Board of Trade.'[6] The CSO and its Director, then, had assumed a much larger role in the affairs of the Survey, and there was ministerial support for its interventions.

The conclusions of government economists on internal research as the most profitable organisation of government-sponsored research were not universally followed. Sponsored educational research, for example, was done largely outside government. On the other hand, the departments which had inherited relatively large research units from the break up of the DSIR, naturally met a substantial part of their research needs through such in-house units. The Home Office developed its research through a mixture. Its own unit, perhaps because of special problems of confidentiality, dealt directly with a wide variety of problems but the tradition of financing academic units was also maintained. The Ministry of Health's policy was rather different. It, and later the DHSS, had practically created an external network, based on an implicit model of the best way of getting a department's research needs met. The model is closely related to that of the Medical Research Council and it seems that a substantial part of the work done originated in the interests of researchers. There was also an assumption that in-house research units were not capable of establishing 'credentials of quality and independence in research'.[7] This assumption contrasts with the practice of at least some parts of the Ministry of Health in asking the Survey to undertake some of the most substantial descriptive and analytical accounts of various aspects of the health and social services done in those years.

Over the period 1967–70 many Survey studies were done for the ministry, almost all of which were organised, as was most of the Survey's ad hoc work, by direct negotiation between the Survey and the relevant administrative division. One such study, a National Dental Survey (1968), was notable for its unprecedented collaboration between academic dental schools and Survey staff in surveying a major area of concern to the NHS. During the same period, a comparably major study was made of the incidence of physical handicap and related medical and local services (1968–9). This, for many years, supplied the only data available of the numbers of people with different kinds of physical disability and the public help they were getting. Other Survey studies during this period, sponsored by different divisions of the department, were concerned with prescription charges (1968), smoking habits (1969), complaints about treatment in hospitals, family planning (1970), and the home help service (1967). None of this Survey work has ever been criticised for failing to achieve the necessary 'credentials of quality and independence in research'.

These health studies were only part of the Survey's work during this phase. Following on the earlier work done for the Royal Commission on Trade Unions, a series of surveys for the Department of Employment dealt with aspects of youth employment, the effects of the Redundancy Payments Act (1969), the possible scope of dismissal tribunals (1969), attitudes towards work in the new towns, and other employment-related topics. A major study of housing in London (1967) and in West Yorkshire (1969) continued the series of housing surveys which had begun 10 years previously. Opinion surveys were done on shopping hours, liquor licensing, attitudes of deceased persons' relatives to coroners' enquiries, and reactions to possible changes in British Standard Time. Continuing the earlier surveys on aspects of education, work was done on sixth form curricula, teacher wastage and the careers of arts students. In 1970 a major study was done on public opinion about devolution. Some of this work was done for committees or commissions set up to study specific topics, but departments also turned to the Survey as part of the normal government machinery. Accompanying the stream of survey reports were papers examining, describing and making public the methodology involved. Kemsley described in some detail how the FES was carried out, and how a simplified version of the FES income questions could be used in other surveys.[8] Bynner and McKennell[9] examined the methods used in work on attitudes towards smoking and aircraft noise.[10] More analytical work was done on interviewing, and Jean Atkinson, who had taken over from Muriel Harris some years earlier, distilled the experience of many different surveys in *A Handbook for Interviewers*. This was published and rapidly became widely used outside the Survey.

The idea of a possible new continuing survey – a major challenge – came from Professor Moser's reference, noted earlier, to the need for a household survey modelled on the American Current Population Survey and the European

Labour Force Surveys. Normal Survey procedure was to define, in close collaboration with a commissioning department, the policy purposes which a proposed study was to serve and only then to elaborate a detailed design. So the purpose served by these foreign surveys was examined in some detail. Discussions then took place on what British government purposes could be served by a continuing survey. It became clear that some of the objectives of the foreign surveys were already being met in other ways – at that time registration for employment provided data as an acceptable alternative to the large US household survey, whose primary purpose was the measurement of employment – and other objectives were not felt to be relevant. On the other hand, there were government needs which could be met in a continuing survey of households, and a study could be designed to meet several such needs within one continuing multi-purpose survey. This would be very different in scope and design from what was originally suggested by the Director of the CSO. It would cover several subject areas (housing, health and education were only some) but would not displace the need for the detailed ad hoc surveys which departments requested. One household interview would provide basic information about several topics, but could not be expected to provide the usual detailed enquiry on any one particular subject of special policy interest. It was necessary to get this point clearly established, and the CSO accepted this important condition. The survey was listed as a separate pilot study in the proposed programme for 1969–70, which was considered by the Programme Committee in December 1968. The starting date for the main survey, if the pilot was successful, was tentative, and would depend on resources. Further staff would be needed, and general civil service manpower limits were being strictly enforced.

The decision to begin work on a multi-purpose survey as an addition to the Survey's existing programme was not easy to make. The staffing problems which already existed would not be eased by an additional continuing commitment, especially as from 1967 onwards the FES sample was doubled. On the other hand, by the end of 1967 the main staffing structure had been agreed in principle. It was now a question of filling posts within the manpower ceiling rather than arguing about the ceiling itself. It was also clear that some kind of multi-purpose survey was central to thinking in the CSO about the future shape of government social statistics and, given the ministerial support for Professor Moser, this fact had to be given weight. The Survey's preliminary soundings had shown that there was wide support for such an additional source of continuing social data and, provided the technical design of the survey could be developed in accordance with the Survey's existing procedures on sampling, interview design and interviewer standards, there seemed a fair chance that a successful study could be started.

So a commitment was made, resources for a major pilot study were assembled, and the work went ahead. In this case I had to assume the senior management responsibility for the survey, but the development work was done by an enthusiastic group headed by Bob Barnes and Mary Durant. Parallel discussions took place in many of the statistical groups in the departments who were involved. These discussions were especially necessary, since some rather unrealistic ideas on possible sample size and possible questions had to be examined in the light of likely resources and general Survey experience. The decision to go ahead with preliminary work on the survey opened the door to a continuing technical debate with the CSO and the department statisticians who would be the customers for the results. By the end of 1969 the survey had been approved in principle and the major pilot survey went ahead in February 1970. The main survey was launched in the following October, and the later history of the survey, which came to be called the General Household Survey (GHS) is described subsequently. It has become one of the most widely used sources of social data both in and out of government, and since 1971 an annual report on it has been prepared by the Survey.

It is clear from the continuing record of work done over this phase of the Survey's history that its new departmental status, with the changes in responsibility involved, did not greatly affect its work. Some of the studies initiated in this period are among the most important contributions made. From 1966–7 to 1970–71 the annual Vote grew from £761,250 to £1,220,000; between April 1967 and September 1970 the numbers actually in post grew from 158 to 204. Of course, from its early days the Survey had been a self-generating unit. While it had always been necessary to work through some controlling department, the technical organisation of the resources made available had been a matter for internal decision. The Treasury's assumption of responsibility did not result in any changes in programming or technical organisation. It had always been necessary to explain and justify proposed organisational changes, and the discussions about staffing matters continued with the same people. Given its accumulated experience of survey work, it was unlikely that the Survey would be pressed into decisions about methods of working or the internal distribution of functions and resources which did not seem reasonable. The situation, however, could not have been easy for the new Controller, since the organisation for which he was now responsible was very different from the Assistance Board and the Ministry of National Insurance from which he came. They were large, regulation-bound departments which had done very little of the kind of research he found going on in the Survey.

Staffing problems were more worrying. The decision to double the size of the FES sample and, later, to add the GHS implied a major increase in field staff. This would take some time and delay the date from which the new information would begin to flow. Professor Moser felt that he must do what he could to alleviate the situation. This led to a request in the summer of 1967 to produce a formal statement about staffing difficulties, and the Controller thus found himself quickly involved in one of the most difficult areas of Survey administration. He was briefed on the structural problems and lack of promotion prospects for technical staff, and then jointly with the Treasury prepared a document on the staffing situation. In September 1967, out of a total complement of 177, there were 134 actually in post – a shortfall of nearly a quarter. A large part of this shortfall was in clerical officers, but among the research and senior technical staff 10 posts out of 89 were vacant – a deficiency in the key research posts that affected all the activities of the organisation. It must be recognised that in 1968 there was a comparable proportion of unfilled posts throughout the main civil service statistical grades – it was not only the Survey which suffered from these deficiencies. But for the Survey, there was a special need to get an urgent review of the interviewers' pay scale.

It is not possible to say exactly what factors influenced the decisions made on Survey staffing in the later months of 1967. It may have been evidence of the continuing growth of demand, or the political backing of the CSO's Director, or even a gradual acceptance of the logic of the argument for changes in the Survey – but some change there was. In November 1967, as mentioned earlier, a Deputy Director, Geoffrey Thomas, was appointed; a week later the top posts in the four technical sections (sampling, field, coding, computing and tabulating) were upgraded, and some additional posts were awarded elsewhere. But there was still no agreement on appropriate salary scales, so it was still not possible to offer salaries that equalled those available to other professional classes. One possible consequence of this was the poor response to advertisements. The only way to fill the new posts was by internal promotion, which was satisfactory to those concerned but did not help to increase the numbers of experienced people at the middle levels. By October 1968, out of a complement of seven principal Survey officers, only three were in post.

The hints about the possible restructuring of the mechanisms for producing social statistics did arouse some concern among the senior staff of the Survey – especially the suggestion that some of the senior posts might be filled by recruits from other professional classes without survey experience. There was a strong wish, arising logically from the Survey's history, for one class throughout the organisation and freedom of movement between technical and research sections. And it was feared that the incorporation of, say, statisticians might lead to divisions within the Survey. It was because of this feeling that staffing proposals had always argued for grading and salary scales parallel with those of statisticians and psychologists, but not for posts for people formally graded as such. During 1967–8 it was suggested by Treasury that some Survey posts should be allocated for a limited number of other professionals but, as with the proposal to put Survey staff in the Research Officer Class, this was so hedged about with qualifying and limiting conditions as to be impractical. This, in the event, was rather fortunate: such an intrusion would not have helped with the management of scarce research resources. The publication of the Fulton Report in June 1968 with the suggestion that all classes in the civil service might be abolished and replaced by different grading procedures seemed to change the terms in which previous discussions about the appropriate class for Survey staff had taken place.

This continuing concern with classes and grades was kept active by the failure to recruit enough suitably experienced people to fill the posts available. Part of the explanation for this is probably to be found in the growing funds made available by government for academic research, coupled with academic notions of what research is and should be. The fact that a continuing study like the Family Expenditure Survey was being used ever more widely would not necessarily lead graduates to want to work on the detailed operations involved in collecting the data. There was more professional glory to be sought in intellectual leadership for political and administrative change. This too was the period of student upheavals within universities and the flourishing of a concomitant culture of revolt against aspects of the status quo. Such an atmosphere was hardly likely to facilitate recruitment to an organisation which emphasised a rather sober approach to the investigation of social issues. For those who were attracted to the possibilities of work in research there was also the flourishing market research industry, where movement, excitement and promotion promised rather more than could be expected from a small part of a large apparatus – especially if this was part of the much maligned bureaucracy.

In the following year there was the problem of finding finance for work on the GHS. The original proposal had not been costed and until technical details had been tested and agreed it was difficult to put a figure on it. Treasury was naturally unwilling to authorise expenditure on a project which still lacked the formal sponsorship of any one department. So although the programme for 1968–9 included provision for pilot work on the survey, there were difficulties in deciding what should be done about provision in later years. Some kind of forecast of this was necessary for the 'forward look' at expenditure now becoming mandatory. It was eventually decided that the CSO should be the formal sponsor.

The Controller and I had the indispensable assistance of Sam Witzenfeld in arriving at and keeping within staff and budget ceilings during these years of uncertainty, change and continuing pressure to limit public expenditure. These were also years in which the Survey's scope and willingness to innovate was not frustrated by the staff limitations – a credit to the contribution of all the technical sections to the development of research designs and their successful operation as well as the work of research staff, to whom credit was most usually given.

Despite the time spent in these years on organisational discussion, there had, in fact, been very little change in programming arrangements and no movement on a system for allocating priorities. At the annual meetings to decide the recommended Votes for 1968–9 and 1969–70 the Programme Committee had been given the usual round-up of departmental replies to the Survey's call for proposed projects to be done or at least started in the next financial year. These had been very roughly costed but not yet authorised. To these was added the estimated cost of continuing surveys, training requirements and the cost of completing projects already authorised and started. The programme submitted to the committee for 1968–9 is shown in Table 3. The large proportion needed for continuing surveys stands out. It was because of these figures, which imply a substantial failure of the programme to meet needs, that the Programme Committee had emphasised its view that the Survey should not take on any more continuing mass-statistics exercises.

The actual out-turn in 1968–9 was £890,000, which was very close to the estimate. The Programme Committee made no suggestion about the order of

Table 3 Proposed Programme and costs 1968–9

	Total GSS costs £	Operational £	Staff and admin £
I *Continuous requirements*			
Training/Methodological			
Family Expenditure Survey			
National Food Survey			
International Passenger Survey			
Consumer Durables			
Housing Data			
National Travel (1966)	448,700	320,000	128,700
II *Carry-in and already authorised*			
Nutrition			
Dental Health			
Home Help Service			
Aircraft Noise			
London Housing			
Measurement of Long Distance Travel			
Safety in the Home			
Coroners			
Drug Taking			
Police and Fire Services (Management)			
Police and Fire Services (Recruitment)			
Penal System			
Weather Centres			
Sixth Form Functions			
Parental Attitudes of Secondary Schoolchildren			
Family Intentions			
Post Enumeration Study			
Youth Employment			
Local Government (Scotland)	226,100	132,300	93,800
III *New and ad hoc projects*			
Suggested discounted allocation for new ad hoc projects (Estimated undiscounted total £517,000)	225,200	120,700	104,500
	900,000	573,000	327,000

Note: No specific provision has been made for enquiries possibly required at short notice for royal commissions, departmental and inter-departmental committees, etc.

priority of the new ad hoc surveys: the Chairman simply said that the Director would have to work this out as best he could in the light of staff resources and the actual progress made with continuing projects.

The total requested for all work in the 1969–70 programme was £1,003,000.

New ad hoc surveys within this total came to £286,000 – an increase over the previous year but still less than half of the preliminary estimated costs of all new ad hoc projects suggested by departments. Given such figures it is not difficult to understand why some departments felt that, at least as an insurance policy, some other possible research resources should be developed.

In 1968–9 just under 40% of total expenditure was on staff. Over 60% of the total Vote was spent on operational costs – field costs, payments to keepers of FES budgets and contractors. In the latter category came the costs of contracting out fieldwork and coding on the National Food Survey, coding work on the IPS and some ad hoc surveys. About 35% of all operational expenditure – 22% of total expenditure – was on contractors for a mixed supply of services. Between 1962 and 1969, staff costs, field costs and contractual payments ranged as shown in Table 4.

Table 4 Social Survey costs 1962–3 to 1968–9: percentage of total

	Staff and administrative	Field costs	Contractual payments	Other
	%	%	%	%
1962–3	35	46	14	5
63–4	36	47	13	4
64–5	33	44	20	3
65–6	34	33	30	3
66–7	37	33	25	5
67–8	33	34	29	4
68–9	38	34	22	6

Between the same dates the proportion of operational expenditure spent on continuous and ad hoc surveys ranged as follows:

Table 5 Continuous and ad hoc surveys: percentage of operational expenditure

	Continuous	Ad hoc
	%	%
1962–3	68	31
63–4	61	38
64–5	70	28
65–6	69	30
66–7	65	35
67–8	56	43
68–9	59	39

Small proportions (not included) went on training and methodological work. A major part of the continuous expenditure was on the IPS: the important part played by the continuing surveys is clear. In later years this proportion declined a little, to the benefit of ad hoc surveys. This resulted from a deliberate decision to make as much provision as possible for ad hoc work, to maintain the scope of the Survey.

The Government Social Survey Department had begun its life in April 1967. Less than a year later, discussion of an alternative arrangement began. In his May 1968 article in *Statistical News* the Director of the CSO, Professor Moser, said 'we are looking at organizational aspects of social statistics including arrangements for censuses and surveys'. Apparently what was in mind was to combine the Survey with the General Register Office and thus to produce for social statistics a parallel to the Business Statistics Office, with its responsibility for collecting economic statistics. It seems that, some months previously, he had been authorised to develop these notions and in February 1968 a study group had been set up to consider relevant proposals. Neither the Survey nor its Programme Committee, which was supposed to represent its customers, had been consulted on these developments, although it seemed clear from Professor Moser's earlier intervention on staff shortages that in some circles it was thought that the work of the Survey and the CSO should be more closely integrated. However, most of the discussion about Survey staffing had been bilateral, between the Treasury and Survey, and agreement on the main structure, if not its grading, had been reached before the study group was set up. A further complication was the sentiment inside the Survey against integration with the statistical apparatus of government. In March 1968 the Chairman of staff side of the Survey Whitley Council had told the Controller of his objections to incorporating statisticians. 'If in fact statisticians and staff in the existing grades worked side by side the latter would resent the presence of people with a higher salary maximum than the Principal Social Survey Officer and a generally higher status in the Civil Service'.

The fact that arrangements for the Survey were under discussion again so soon may indicate that the decision to set it up as a separate body was not well considered. However, it had arisen out of the Heyworth recommendation made in 1965 and was probably accepted in principle some time before that. By 1966 it was becoming clear that greater stress would henceforward be put on the development of social statistics, and that the Survey was regarded as a necessary contributor. So the work of the Programme Committee, its report early in 1967 and the issue of the Treasury circular in November 1967 were events which moved separately but in parallel with the changes in government statistics which were taking place or under discussion. It seems strange, however, that the two developments should not have been brought together until 1968. The Heyworth Committee was apparently asked to consider the future of the Survey in 1963. Until 1967 it was not clear what arrangements would govern it, and in 1968 these arrangements were once more in the melting pot. These uncertainties may not have prevented the flow of work and the political contribution made to government, but they could not have helped to attract suitable staff or to persuade those who were recruited that they had a settled future.

The study group was set up at a time of considerable optimism about the contribution of statistics to government. The emphasis of its proposal was on the rather idealistic target of setting up an all-embracing data system. As in the proposal for the GHS, the exact government purposes which would be served were not clear, but it was apparently thought that since censuses and surveys were alternative methods, bringing them more closely together would enhance the contribution of each, and, theoretically, improve decisions about which method would be preferable for particular purposes. This view underestimated the historical development of the two separate organisations and the way their work programmes actually developed in response to need. The techniques of census and surveys were distinct and the staffs concerned were, rightly, specialised. This was particularly true of field staff: Survey interviewers did a very different job. This had not prevented the Survey from helping with the preparation and evaluation of the Census by designing appropriate sample surveys. It had not been necessary to merge the two bodies to achieve that or in order to design surveys which produced material relevant to the GRO's demographic research. And in the Registrar General's other field of interest – medical statistics – it was a quarter of a century since the Survey of Sickness had been devised by the War Time Social Survey at the request of the GRO's chief medical statistician.

On the other hand, there was an interest in ensuring that sample survey data emerging from studies designed to meet the needs of Survey customers was consistent with and helped to amplify data produced by the Census, and collaborative effort would be needed for that. There were, however, interdepartmental statistics committees which existed for such purposes and there were limits to what would be expected here. Most surveys covered a very small part of the population. The data they produced could be used in some cases to help elaborate on Census findings, for example, on education, housing or employment, but the two sources could not be linked in some kind of universal database. It might be that a combined organisation in which both bodies made their separate contribution would appear more attractive to potential recruits because of the very broad subject-matter it would cover. This could only be shown after the event, and when further resources and perhaps decisions on a competitive grade and salary structure had emerged. It was quite clear that in the immediate future resources for both organisations would be strained. So the main weight of the proposal had to be on the future and what might be done as new tasks and new resources emerged. It could not be for the staff of the two organisations to decide on the future programme: a population census would be taken and the FES would continue because they met expressed needs, and the future programme would reflect the interest of government. A Survey contribution to an extended function of the proposed new office had already emerged in the shape of the GHS, which was being designed around the expressed interests of a group of departments and was accordingly turning out rather different from the initial proposal.

No formal statement was made about the discussion on the merger proposal, but Survey staff, through their union, IPCS, became aware that discussions were going on and made representations to the Controller. They were told nothing, since what was involved was a change, if a small one, in the machinery of government, which was normally treated as confidential. The idea of merging the Survey with the GRO, which had many statisticians and whose subject emphasis was on population studies, suggested to the staff that the scope of the Survey would be narrowed, that the statisticians would have disproportionate weight in the new organisation and that Survey staff would be split between different grades. There was, too, a fear that even as statisticians were thought to be compilers of statistics which others, especially economists, interpreted, so the Survey might come to be regarded as producers of data for the statisticians in the new department to use. All these worries were made known to those discussing the proposal, but since the new office would be considered part of the statistical service, it is not clear how much weight would be given to a worry that statisticians might have too much say in what was done.

There were similar worries about the top management of the proposed office. The head of the GRO had over the years not been a professional statistician and at the time of the discussions was a former senior administrator from the Ministry of Health. But there were plans for a deputy director of the new office who would be a professional statistician and to whom the various divisional heads would be responsible. The implication was that the professional and technical aspects of Survey work would indeed come under the continuing supervision of a statistician, and also that the head of the office, if a non-professional, would always have professional statistical advice available on all future developments. So for the Survey many of the old fears and doubts resurfaced. When the decision was made and announced it seemed that some attention had been paid to these worries.

In his speech to the International Statistical Institute on 10 September 1969, the Prime Minister, after referring to various improvements made to government economic statistics, said:

> We consider that the development of social statistics is no less important than that of industrial statistics. Parallel to the Business Statistics Office we now envisage an arrangement under which the collection and processing of certain data on the social side is centralised with a combination of censuses of population, social surveys and vital registration and statistics in one organisation ... In the collection and publication of these statistics we need to look more at the social condition of individuals, households and families, the inter-dependency of social groups and the extent to which social problems are inter-related ... we are of course fortunate in already having a very important regular source of information about households in this country through the Family Expenditure Survey which for many years now has provided information about the expenditure and other characteristics of households at various income levels. And very shortly we will be piloting a second household survey which will provide for regular study of other crucial factors.

This statement certainly made the decision public but the Controller had been given no advance notice. On 18 December the Prime Minister,[11] responding to a parliamentary question, announced:

> As a further stage in improving the Government's Statistical Services the General Register Office and the Government Social Survey Department are to be merged into a new Office of Population Censuses and Surveys. The new office will be closely linked with the CSO and the Director of the CSO and the head of the new office will

together under the general direction of ministers guide the direction and planning of its survey, censuses and statistical work . . . day to day ministerial responsibility will be exercised by the Secretary of State for Social Services. Social surveys will continue to be undertaken by the new Office for other government departments and the new arrangements do not affect the responsibility of individual ministers for matters of Departmental policy arising on such surveys.

It was decided that the new office would start on 11 May 1970, and the CSO began to draw up proposals for its organisation. It was not clear from these just how much autonomy the Survey would have, but the proposals were not obviously related to the actual working processes needed in designing and developing surveys. If the last sentence of the Prime Minister's statement was to have real meaning, some account would have to be taken of these realities.

As with most decisions about the work, staffing and organisation of the Survey, this critical decision had taken some time and left many unanswered questions. The delay and uncertainties had taken their usual toll. Several middle-level research staff had left and there were still real staffing problems. It was clear that the Survey had been moved into the government's statistical orbit without any decision on the grading of staff who would henceforward find themselves working alongside statisticians. For some of them this presented no real change: the big continuing surveys and many of the others had been developed with departmental statisticians. Other researchers, however, had long been accustomed to working directly with administrators or the staff of public committees and commissions and their sentiments were different. The views of the Survey's senior staff were expressed in a note signed by all of them which was sent to the head of the new office. This is reproduced in Appendix C. It shows that the staff in general took a positive view of the possibilities opening up but were very concerned that established survey procedures should be allowed to continue.

The decision to set up the Office of Population Censuses and Surveys (OPCS) did, however, appear to settle finally the question of an appropriate location for the Survey. The GRO, with its long-established responsibility for reporting on many aspects of the 'condition of the people', was a logical partner for the Survey. Certainly the Survey's capabilities would much extend the reach of the OPCS and its record over many years had demonstrated that its methods were publicly acceptable. Indeed, the addition of the techniques it had developed to the GRO's established procedures would help the new office to make an enhanced contribution to the needs of government in circumstances which were very different from those in which Chadwick advocated the GRO's inauguration. The purpose, however, was still the same – to describe the social situation in such a way that responsible government could decide how best to act.

For me too there was a major decision. I had been Director for 30 years, and now that the Survey had been found a satisfactory location in government, I felt it was time for change. I informed the head and deputy of the OPCS that I no longer wished to be Director of the Survey, but wanted to go on working in the organisation. There was an experienced deputy director ready to step into my shoes and a major staffing problem to be solved if the General Household Survey was to start. I could contribute by taking responsibility for a large share in the research work and above all by helping to make the GHS a reality. My proposal was agreed and a new Director, Geoffrey Thomas, was formally appointed on 28 May 1970.

Notes

[1] *SSRC Newsletter,* 7 December 1969.
[2] *The Listener,* 30 January 1969.
[3] *PAC Bulletin,* May 1969.
[4] *Hansard,* Col 75/76, 2 April 1968.
[5] *Hansard,* 18 June 1968.
[6] *Statistical News,* 7 November 1969.
[7] Cohen, *Portfolios for Health,* Nuffield Provincial Hospitals Trust, 1971.
[8] Methodological Papers M144, M146, M14.
[9] *ibid,* M149, M152, M153, M154.
[10] *ibid,* M143, M136, M140.
[11] *Hansard,* 18 December 1969.

6 1971–81: The research expansion and after

THE GENERAL ECONOMIC AND POLITICAL turbulence noted earlier continued during this period and was even more marked. Indeed, halfway through the period there occurred a sharp break with the public policies of the past generation as Britain was compelled to call on the IMF for assistance. But throughout this time attempts at structural and constitutional reform continued despite the economic uncertainties. The Heath government carried further the policies of amalgamating departments as part of the search for greater administrative efficiency, inaugurated a Central Policy Review Staff (CPRS), reformed local government, pursued the attempt to join the Common Market and tried to achieve some acceptable degree of political devolution.[1]

In an effort to improve administrative machinery, it also brought in groups of businessmen and promoted management methods which owed something to recent American developments. The CPRS was one element in this effort. Its function was 'to enable the Government as a whole to take better policy decisions by assisting them to work out the implications of their basic strategy in terms of policies in specific areas, to establish the relative priorities to be given to the different sectors of their programmes and to ensure that the underlying courses of action are fully analysed and considered'.[2] But there had, over the years, also been some development of ideas within the administration. A former permanent secretary, Sir Richard Clarke, discussed these contributions in public lectures organised under the auspices of the new Civil Service College.[3] He considered the emergence of the 'giant' departments which 'reflects the thought that it is more efficient to operate with ten large departments than with over 20 smaller ones'. He showed how following the Plowden Report, which had led to Public Expenditure Surveys (PESC) there had emerged the idea of the Programme Analysis Review (PAR) 'providing for submission by departments of statements of objectives and statements of priorities for central consideration before the process of allocation begins ... Departments will have to organize themselves to produce their PARs as well as their PESCs'. What was being proposed was a more rational system of reviewing government activities which took full account of political necessities but attempted to provide a basis for more orderly and better-informed decisions. It seemed a logical sequel to the changes which had followed the Plowden reforms, and it is notable that the lectures reflected growing calls within the government apparatus for improved decision making.

The new spirit of purposeful enquiry is well illustrated in a speech made at the annual conference of the National Foundation for Educational Research by Margaret Thatcher, then Education Secretary, on 1 December 1970.

> The increasing pressure of educational needs on available resources meant that the Department could not continue indefinitely to spend large sums on educational research just because it was a good or wise thing to do ... By the late 1960s it was becoming clear that a policy of general support for educational research on a basis of patronage could not be relied on to produce results of practical value to the Department ... There was a growing need for facts and objective views which only research could produce to illuminate emerging problems ... In these circumstances there was clearly only one direction that the Department's research policy could sensibly take. It had to move from patronage to a basis of 'commission'. This meant the active initiation of work by the Department on problems of its own choosing ... It meant focussing of issues which offered a real possibility of yielding usable conclusions ... Officials must think hard about the problems that are likely to face them, to expose these problems to people whose background and approach will – if they do their job properly – lead to awkward questions. It requires them to take cognisance of the results as an integral part of the resources available to them in their daily work.

This view of government-financed research was echoed in the recommendation of the head of the CPRS, Lord Rothschild, that all such research should be on a customer-contractor basis, that departments should decide what research was relevant to their policy purposes and then find researchers to do it. For nearly 30 years the Survey had worked precisely in this way, and it seemed that research, especially on the social aspects of public organisation, was to have a more positive role. In the 1970s many kinds of social research saw unprecedented expansion. In their study of the development of social research in Britain Cherns and Perry noted the increase in the number of students in the social sciences and pointed out that 'the expansion in the teaching of social sciences led, almost unnoticed, to a major growth in potential research capacity. British universities have enjoyed a staffing ratio far more favourable than most countries. The stability of the ratio in public policy and the principle that the university teacher's contract includes an obligation to conduct research means that where increase in staff accompanies increase in students, research capacity is enlarged'.[4]

So during the early 1970s there was a growth in available research capacity, and it seemed that if government money was available to finance research there would be people and organisations ready to use it. From this time onwards for some years, much larger funds for academic research became available. In the DHSS and the Department of the Environment small in-house research units were created which used some of these extra resources, and with this general increase in government-funded research the resources available to the Survey also grew.

The economic background to this surge in social research activity provided a marked contrast. During the Heath government's first years, there were cuts in government expenditure and in taxes together with a credit squeeze and high interest-rates. Some of the policies of these early years were later reversed but the long-term background was not encouraging. Unemployment had been at historically low levels. By autumn 1972 it had risen noticeably and regional differences were becoming marked. Cairncross, a former chief government economist, has noted that 'while full employment retreated from one decade to the next inflation gathered strength. Between 1964 and 1972 the rate of inflation accelerated to 5.4% and over the next three years to 15.8%'.[5] In the years before 1971 'when the Government's weakness vis a vis the trade unions had been plainly demonstrated by its retreat on the policy announced in 'In Place of Strife' [government proposals for trade union reform] the increase in hourly earnings accelerated. In 1970 and 1971 the rise in weekly rates exceeded 12% and in 1972 it reached 16%. Then came a dramatic crisis in world commodity prices and in the price of oil in 1973 and with it a sharp increase in prices in Britain. Wage rates accelerated once more to a 26% increase in 1974 and again in 1975. Import prices doubled in the two years 1972–4'.

Together with these staggering price changes there were also changes in the labour market as married women moved, in increasing numbers, into employment. 'Most of the addition to the working population were women workers. Estimates of working population put the increase in women between 1965 and 1975 at one million and the decrease in men at 700,000'.

In 1974 following a national miners' strike there were two general elections leading to Labour governments and a relaxation of attempts to control wages – awards in some industries reached 30%. A National Enterprise Board was set up and massive support offered to some industries including British Leyland. None of this dampened inflation or the deterioration in the balance of payments. In 1976 the government applied to the IMF for help and there followed major cuts in public expenditure, a growth in unemployment and a check to inflation. However, outside the public sector, wage increases continued and gradually the inflationary climb was renewed. 1976 marks a major break with the expansionist aspects of the early years of this period.

In 1979 there came another change of government, to the Conservatives under Margaret Thatcher. Many previous policies were reversed including those of previous Conservative governments. The government cut taxes and public spending and in particular pressed for a reduction in the size of the civil service. The statistical services were sharply affected and to many observers it seemed that the Survey had been singled out for particularly harsh attention. These events are discussed later in more detail. The early years of the new government were made more difficult by an international economic downturn. Unemployment increased steadily, though eventually inflation began to decline. A MORI opinion poll showed that between February 1979 and December 1981, while the proportion naming inflation as 'the most important issue facing Britain today' has declined from 38% to 12%, the proportion naming unemployment had risen from 10% to 65%.

This, then, was the economic background to the expanding research programmes in government departments. There seems little relationship between the economic crises of the period and these programmes, which seem rather to reflect social commitments embalmed earlier in the political process. Subject matter, research methods and research organisation varied with departments. They probably varied even more between research organisations with which departments negotiated. The criteria of research methods employed by the departments varied widely. In some, attempts were made to adhere to the strict letter of the Rothschild doctrine. This was more easily done where researchers were members of an in-house research unit, although even here all was not plain sailing.

The development of department-financed social research in recent years shows some common elements and some variation between departments. In common was the public stance up to 1979 at least, following Rothschild, that research is financed and defended by departments in order to inform policy. Also common was the interest in social research as a means to obtain an assessment or illumination of the social component in the topic researched. Without some form of organised investigation it was assumed that policy could not be adequately assessed, defended politically or developed. Departments' interest is in the help that research can give with burdens of administration. The interests of researchers may thus sometimes be quite close to administrative needs, but sometimes pointed in quite different directions. The variation between departments was in the research resources used and in the degree to which people outside departments helped to shape research programmes and decide how resources should be allocated.

Where, as a result of decisions made in earlier times, specialised units such as the Road Research Laboratory or Home Office Research Unit have become continuing parts of departments, these units have become the natural focus of purposeful departmental research and an essential element in the departments' commissioning of non-governmental researchers. In these cases the main decisions on research programme content seem to be made in the department. In the absence of long-established units it seems that departments have put their main research emphasis on academic or independent researchers, as in the Department of Education and Science and the DHSS. Here, a large part of programme content is much more likely to be influenced or even shaped by non-departmental interests. Although most departments have set up some kind of apparatus for assembling departmental research interest – the research requirements committees of the Department of Environment or the research liaison committees of the DHSS – there are marked differences in the extent to which non-departmental people help to shape the programme. In the DHSS a continuing effort has been made to involve outside people in developing a research programme. The Buller committee, set up to advise the DHSS on research to match policy needs, suggested that by 1982 perhaps half of the social research programmes financed by the DHSS originated in researcher interest. It may be that traditions of independent medical research influenced this situation, or perhaps the absence of any internal continuing tradition of direct research sponsorship. It seems clear that while accepting financial support, some researchers have not happily accepted an obligation to direct their energies to topics that the department regarded as priorities, so although the department finances many research units, there is a constant complaint that research resources are difficult to find.

These developments have formed part of the background against which the Survey carried its contribution to government into a further decade. There was no Rothschild shock for the Survey. It had always designed its studies in cooperation with departmental personnel to meet expressed departmental needs. But the growth of research committees in departments did not help with the problems of developing logical work programmes which employed Survey resources on priority problems. This was not because all or most departmental research programmes concerned topics or required methods of which the Survey had no experience. Part 2 shows what the Survey contributed to a wide range of government interests and much of this is not very different from some of the work sponsored under new research programmes. In earlier periods, however, the Survey's work programme had grown in direct response to the needs of particular sections of departments: now, the situation was much more complicated. As research programmes grew, departmental relationships with academics and independent researchers multiplied and so did departmental commitments to these researchers. The clearest example of this is the system of 'rolling contracts' developed by the DHSS. In earlier days, too, the growing statistical divisions often had responsibility for the 'research' interests of departments. In the 1970s, research became a separate interest and the research apparatus more autonomous. The new Director of the CSO, Sir John Boreham, urged government statisticians to concern themselves very closely with policy needs. In his presidential address to the Royal Statistical Society in November 1979 he said 'Our skill is as much in drawing inferences from uncertain data as from collecting them and we would be abrogating what I regard as the central part of our responsibilities if we left this task to others whether they be politicians, administrators or economists. The aim is to aid government management, decision and policy making'.[6]

Since the founding of OPCS the Survey had been formally part of the Government Statistical Service and the statistical divisions in the departments were one of the channels through which departmental requests for survey research came forward. There seemed to be no such direct route for requests from the new research empires and indeed it was not always clear just what the relationship between statistics and research was in any department. However, individual divisions, such as those concerned with family planning or the dental service or nutrition in the DHSS, could and did come directly to the Survey as customers. But their doing so might depend upon knowledge of a past contribution by the Survey and this procedure did not ensure that a new topic for which Survey resources and methods might be relevant would come forward. The connection with statistics sometimes did not help. Administrators, not themselves statistically aware, might have a view of what statistics were or could be used for which was somewhat distant from that of the CSO Director. There was also a certain vagueness about what research was and how it was done – an attitude not clarified by some of the theories of human behaviour in social situations or the relationships between government and governed or the deficiencies of 'positivism' as an approach to research that were academically respectable at the time. So it cannot be said that the 1970s was a period in which the actual contribution of the Survey to government became easier to see.

In the period 1971–81 the record shows that as well as the continuing surveys, which contributed to increased demand, a large and varied range of ad hoc work was done. Some of the major social preoccupations of the time are reflected in work done on housing, mobility and the effects of increasing road traffic. Several National Travel Surveys (1972–5) brought the mobility picture up to date, and it was given more detail by a 1975 study of pedestrian movements. In 1972 a major study was mounted to measure some of the effects of traffic noise. A national picture of the housing situation was produced annually by the GHS, which updated information produced by the decennial Census. More detailed examination of some aspects of housing circumstances was made in ad hoc studies. In 1973–5 surveys were carried out to monitor the effects of housing legislation on availability, cost and condition of unfurnished rented accommodation. In 1976, attitudes of tenants, landlords and owner-occupiers to letting were studied to assist in a review of the Rent Acts, and in 1978 more work was done on the privately rented sector. In 1978 and 1979 households sharing accommodation or in which there were 'concealed families' were studied to find out if this was from choice or lack of other available housing and, separately, if unmarried persons sharing accommodation would prefer alternatives. In 1977 a study of vacant properties was done to establish the reasons for and the duration of the vacancies.

In 1973 and 1979 the adequacy of existing methods of advertising and filling vacancies in the construction industry was studied and an attempt was made at examining the mobility of manual workers in the industry. Throughout this period studies were made for the Department of Employment. In 1972 more work was done on industrial relations and in 1977 earlier work on reasons for retirement was updated. In 1973 and 1975 employment services were studied and in 1978 and 1980 there were studies of training activities which had become the responsibility of the Manpower Services Commission and were developed to meet growing unemployment among young people. In 1972 an attempt was made to identify influences on girls' career patterns and the factors that might limit their ambitions or prospects, and in 1980 a major study of women in employment updated earlier work. During the period the GHS kept a running check on movements in the labour force, recruitment, reasons for absence and job satisfaction. But for many aspects of labour-force movements the survey was not on a large enough scale to give the detail required when unemployment began to grow. In 1973 the Survey did the fieldwork on part of the much larger EEC biennial Labour Force Survey. Several studies were made in connection with possible changes in industrial legislation. In 1976 opinions at many levels in industry were examined on possible developments in industrial democracy. In 1977 the effects of and attitudes towards protective legislation limiting women's shiftwork were studied.

The Survey contributed a fair amount to the work of the DHSS during 1971–81. GHS, in the section devoted to health, revived the continuing record of illness and medical attention which had not been available for 20 years. From 1971 onward survey research in the field not only maintained this record but also offered an available vehicle for related health topics. So when in 1971 a committee of enquiry was investigating complaints against the hospital service a sample of people who had recently been in hospital could be quickly provided. Every second year a series of questions about smoking habits was put to the whole GHS sample which, over the years, recorded the marked changes that were taking place. When American studies and the publicity they achieved seemed to indicate that aspirin could help people troubled with heart complaints it became important to observe repercussions in this country because it was also believed that aspirin was associated with stomach bleeding. Some baseline was needed to measure the impact of the publicity and, at short notice, the GHS was used to create one.

In earlier times the Survey had studied recruitment to nursing, and in 1971 the Briggs Committee was once again concerned with the training and recruitment of nurses. It was also felt that many trained nurses had given up nursing on marriage but might, under suitable circumstances, come back to it. The Survey traced and interviewed women who had noted their nursing training in the course of the 1971 Census. Some years later the Survey studied the work of community nurses. In 1976 studies were made for a committee of enquiry into the training and disposition of mental health nurses. In 1977 when a royal commission was examining the NHS a study was mounted of people's experience of hospitals and their attitudes towards this experience. About the same time, for the DHSS, a survey was designed to examine access to primary health care at the general practitioner level. The Survey also cooperated towards the end of the period in studies of people who were not registered with GPs and of the work of junior hospital doctors. These more detailed studies of the health service and some of its personnel supplemented the results of the continuing record of illness and medical attention provided by the GHS.

In 1974, 1976, 1978 and 1981 surveys were made of drinking and smoking habits, which updated work done many years earlier. In 1972 and 1978 further work on dental health was done which examined changes in dental hygiene since earlier studies. In 1978 a new study of family planning services examined the changes that had occurred since they became a public responsibility. More specialised surveys were made of the effectiveness of the Department of Employment's vocational assessment facilities for disabled and other disadvantaged people (1974), the services devoted to the use of hearing aids (1972) and the use of the existing range of NHS wheelchairs together with consumers' views on how these services operated (1974).

None of this work arose from DHSS discussions with its own research network, although of course published Survey reports helped to shape the climate in which those discussions took place. Perhaps the only Survey study done to meet a need expressed in a Research Liaison Committee research strategy programme was one on the needs of the elderly, designed to investigate the social circumstances of the elderly, particularly the very old, living in the community (1976).

The GHS provided a stream of information on educational levels and training, all of which could be related to occupation and incomes. But apart from this the education department was not a major user of the Survey during this period. It did ask for a survey to estimate the take-up rate for free school meals and the reasons for non take-up. It also asked for studies, based on the FES, of the expenditures of graduates and undergraduates which could be used to help with decisions on student grants, and it was interested in the girls' career patterns study mentioned earlier.

Given the impact of inflation during this phase it was inevitable that the Retail Price Index and everything connected with it would become central to much official preoccupation. This made it all the more necessary to resist the continuing pressure to increase the scope of the FES and thereby risk its acceptability and response rate. But nevertheless the FES was used ever more widely for purposes additional to its main function. The income data it provided had become much more detailed and now pressure grew to widen the income section of the GHS in order to supplement FES data. Eventually during this period the income sections of both surveys were made comparable and more useful for such work as that of the Royal Commission on the Distribution of Income and Wealth. In 1977 it asked for special studies to assist its examination of the 'economic, social and other factors which give rise to low incomes', although feasibility studies for a survey into wealth distribution showed that this was a subject that could not be handled by social survey enquiry.

The FES of course continued as a main source for official economic studies and there were other surveys at this time also concerned with income and financial circumstances or decisions. In 1973 an annual survey for the EEC of consumer buying intentions began. Its purpose was to assist economic appraisal. In 1975 the Layfield investigation of the rating system led to surveys examining the impact of local rates, the effects of changes in rates and public understanding of the rating system. In 1973 the GHS had provided a sample which was used to establish the proportion of households eligible for and taking up rent rebates or allowances. The housing surveys of rented properties mentioned above had, of course, paid attention to rent levels, as had the surveys of the elderly and reasons for retirement. Late in this phase the Social Security part of the DHSS began to sponsor surveys of low income families. In 1980 at the request of the Treasury the Survey assisted a major academic study of taxation, incentives and labour supply. Interest in incomes, income disposal and its consequences had clearly become a major aspect of Survey activities.

Before the merger the Survey had cooperated with the GRO on enquiries into the efficiency of the Census of Population and on collecting information which might improve population projections. This interest was given an extra political impetus when the 1971 Census showed that estimates in some important regional centres had overestimated population size and had resulted in a misallocation of rate-support funds. There was thus continuing interest in population studies which might help in this connection, and an additional impetus to this work was given by the report of the Population Panel and the 1977 Demographic Review. In 1972 there was a follow-up survey of women who had taken part in the first Family Intentions Survey, and in 1976 a major study of family formation. Post-enumeration surveys were made of the 1971 and 1981 censuses and in response to some public discussion a survey was made in 1971 of public attitudes to the Census. In the lead-up to a possible 1976 Census and the eventual 1981 Census, questions were pretested and a great deal of work was done on testing ethnic questions. Throughout the period the GHS produced data at the national level which could be taken with Census results to give a continuing stream of demographic data and descriptive accounts of changes in households, families and family intentions.

As well as this work responding to problems posed by a wide array of departments, there were also studies during the period, resembling work done in earlier years, which were related to matters of law or the activities of public institutions. Reconsideration of some aspects of social security organisation brought the Survey into studies designed to help with changes in local office management by examining the experience and opinions of claimants; a committee reviewing the work of crown courts wanted to know how well individuals understood the procedures followed and how this affected their choice of options open to them at different stages; the incidence and effects of legal and other representation before industrial tribunals was studied, and the working of family property law in Scotland raised some issues on which survey research threw some light.

The outstanding development of the period was the General Household Survey which contributed to many different subject areas and also facilitated work on several ad hoc surveys. During this time, at least until the 1979 general election, the position of the Survey as part of the continuing apparatus of government seemed to strengthen and become more assured. Survey research became part of the accustomed armoury of official investigation and enquiry. It also became clear that no procedures had developed to relate the Survey's work programme systematically to all the other work going on in government – what the Survey was asked to do reflected very different arrangements in different departments. The Survey responded when asked to help and on the whole its responses were regarded as satisfactory by its customers, though in many cases they would have welcomed quicker responses than the Survey's staffing position allowed. And when a major study was underway, such as the access to primary care work which was of interest to the Royal Commission on the National Health Service as well as the DHSS, it did not help that two out of the three research officers concerned went on maternity leave just at the time when the collected material became available for reporting. The staff ceiling of research officers in post had never allowed for any reserves to cope with such situations.

It may be that a more settled programme, or at least one which could have been planned over a longer timespan, would have helped, but this seemed impossible given the variations in demand from year to year. For example, work for the Home Office was very limited: the earlier work with the police on public drunken behaviour was not followed up by other studies, and the work on the penal system was followed by only one other study in the same area and period.

The major surveys on hospitals and community nurses came along many years after concern about the organisation and costs of the NHS had grown into a major public issue. This was characteristic of many surveys done during this time. They employed methods which had long been available but were not called into use until rather late in the day. The interest displayed in the early 1970s at senior government levels 'to ensure that the underlying courses of action are fully analysed and considered' (Edward Heath, 1970), and the emphasis given by Sir Richard Clarke to the importance of regular and systematic analysis of government programmes and how well they were achieving their stated objectives had somehow not led to a more systematic employment of the Survey.

The experience of the GHS is of special interest in this connection. Its eventual design was very different from the original CSO proposal, which was to produce a British copy of some of the large labour force surveys of other countries. At the time there was no evident demand for such a survey, but a continuing survey of some of the main social statistics topics was of interest to many departments. 1971 was the first full year of the survey and by 1981 it had become recognised as one of the most widely used sources for both government and academic research. Accounts have been published regularly of the many official purposes for which the continuing stream of GHS data is thought relevant; each year's design has to be approved by customer departments and each year an account of its varied uses has to be given. But until the initiative was taken to construct the survey and make it available, the latent demand did not surface. It seems that regular review of government objectives based on direct examination of what is being achieved does not come easily. After the 1979 change of government the Programme Analysis Reviews, which Clarke had seen as the necessary method for reviewing work done before Budget allocations were made, were stopped. They had been regarded as confidential appraisals of particular areas of policy, so the methods used were not open to discussion.

It is a matter for speculation if the cultivation of academic research networks by the Home Office, the education department and the DHSS made it less likely that the Survey would develop more settled work programmes in these subject areas. In contrast is the regular use of the Survey for studying varying aspects of the housing situation and the increasing interest in income and expenditure data. Given the procedures for authorising the Survey's work and the need from very early years for clear commitment from its customer departments, it was unlikely that the various arrangements made for implementing the Rothschild recommendations would affect the Survey's work. They did not. A conscious and persistent attempt to integrate the Survey with other research resources, in-house or academic, to develop departmental research programmes aimed at making the best use of resources would have been much more important – but this did not happen.

The reorganisation into OPCS interrupted for a while the flow of technical papers that had always accompanied the studies. But the GHS was developed with a critical eye to the validity of the data produced and annual reports reproduced the results of experimental variations of questions, analysed response in some detail and calculated sampling errors for the complex sampling design used for the survey. (These are different from the so-called 'sampling errors' frequently and misleadingly quoted for public opinion surveys.)

The highly successful exploitation of the postal survey method was examined in the light of doubts about the comprehensiveness of the population registers used for sampling, and attention was turned to the use of postcodes as an alternative. It was shown that they were usable and could be computerised, which would greatly facilitate the drawing and listing of samples. Later, they became the preferred frame for selecting samples of the general population and for all the continuing household surveys. They gradually replaced the Electoral Register for many purposes, previous work having shown its limitations for sampling some sections of the population.

A methodology bulletin appeared twice a year from 1977. It regularly reported pilot work done on substantive surveys, reviewed particular problem areas and summarised relevant work on methodology done by other survey organisations. During 1979 it contained papers on interviewer coding of occupation and industry; procedures for dealing with multi-household addresses; current issues in field methodology; conditional inference; partial-order scalogram analysis; family budget survey experiments; household concepts particularly in multi-occupied dwellings; statistical estimation for small areas; rating and valuation lists as a sampling frame and other topics.

The Survey's Vote during this phase multiplied by about four times. But most of this simply reflected the inflationary effect of changes in civil service rates of pay which, during this period, increased by more than three times. There were corresponding major increases in interviewers' hourly rates which led to substantial changes in the cash costs of surveys based on large amounts of fieldwork. The continuing surveys were sharply affected. It must also be noted that with the inauguration of OPCS various administrative functions such as finance and establishments work moved to central management, which means that there is a discontinuity in staff numbers and costs between the earlier phases and 1971–81. A further discontinuity occurred in the middle of the period when Survey computing staff became part of the OPCS Computer Division. The figures in Table 6, which take account of changes in pay rates, provide the best indication of the movement of real resources within the period.

The change between 1970–71 and 1971–2 reflects the changing administration's handling of the combination of two separate Votes for the two combined departments. In 1975–6 there is a marked increase which reflects provision for major housing and mobility (travel surveys) work and substantial increases in interviewers' pay. After 1975–6 there is only marginal change in real resources. However, within the total there were changes in the disposition of resources mainly reflecting the inauguration of the General Household Survey in 1970 and its first full twelve months in 1971. There was also a substantial use of resources for the pilot and feasibility study of the proposed one per cent continuing survey, described in more detail later in this chapter, and for work on Labour Force Surveys for the EEC.

Table 6 Resources 1970–71 to 1981–2

	Deflated Vote* £	Vote £
1970–71	326,203	1,220,000
1971–72	269,118	1,098,000
1975–76	333,333	2,380,000
1976–77	324,082	2,382,000
1980–81	329,995	4,428,000
1981–82	341,547	4,990,000

*Deflated by change in civil service payscales as measured by an index of relevant payscales based on the year 1941 when the Survey began operations.

Staffing changed over the period as shown in Table 7.

Table 7 Staffing 1971–81

	Total complement	HQ staff in post	Research staff in post	Assistant research staff in post	Others in post
September 1971	196	177	111	55	66
April 1973	202	198½	124	65	74½
September 1975	242	210½	120	53	90½
September 1976	239	218½	132	64	86½
April 1977	239	209½	117	47	92½
April 1978	220	202½	111	45	91
September 1980	217	203	50	7	153
September 1981	194½	182½	46	2	134½

Staff numbers actually employed reached a peak in 1976, but the Survey's computing staff then moved to the OPCS Computer Division. Taking that into account, the total staff engaged full time on survey research reached a peak in 1978–9. The other major change in the table reflects the reclassification, described later, of most of the technical staff overlapping junior research staff. These people were in 1979 transferred mainly from assistant research officer grades to posts in the administrative classes. The effect is illustrated in the two righthand columns of the table. A higher proportion of all staff were until 1974 in the assistant research officer grade. They reflected a continuing recruitment drive and, notionally, could all move up the research hierarchy as they gained experience. After they were regraded they were rather more likely to seek their fortunes elsewhere. The need for a continuing recruitment effort is shown by a comparison of the two lefthand columns: throughout the period there were vacancies, greatest in 1976 and 1977.

It had been argued that one of the positive outcomes of the merger with the

GRO would be a much enhanced computer capacity, but delays in producing 1971 Census tabulations were clearly a major source of embarrassment, and computer difficulties during the early 1970s provided some of the main problems in completing Survey projects. The first two years' work on the GHS were handled successfully by a contractor and the reports concerned were widely circulated and welcomed. A decision was then made, on the advice of the CSO, to bring the computing in-house and develop the use of new British computer programmes. This turned out to be a mistake. It caused a delay of some years before the analysis of the GHS could be brought up to date. Other Survey work, on ad hoc surveys, was handled by a small team using commercial machines. In 1974 a formal decision was made to set up a Computer Division in OPCS to handle all OPCS analysis including Survey projects. All Survey computing staff were transferred to this new division in 1976, as noted earlier, a move that caused some disquiet. It broke with the tradition the Survey had established of arranging teamwork on all surveys in which all technical stages of the work could be integrated in an agreed project programme. It seemed to Survey staff that the move would disrupt the cooperative approach in which all the different phases of a survey made their agreed contribution, and they protested strongly. The Survey Director spelled out at some length the procedures developed by the Survey, and criticised in some detail the proposals for shifting responsibility to Computer Division. As a result, assurances were given that there would be no 'root and branch change in the methods followed by the Survey computing unit ... the unit attached to Survey will continue to be manned by Social Survey Officers and recruited as they are now ... present staff will not be moved elsewhere in Computer Division except by agreement with the head of the Survey ... there will not be any change in the close working relationship between Survey computer unit and the research and specialist branches of the Survey'. On 1 November 1974 the Computer Division assumed responsibility for Survey's computing, but the misgivings continued. A 1977 internal report, describing a further reorganisation of Computer Division, indicated that the Survey's insistence on close working relationships between all those concerned with the different technical functions was not misplaced. It noted that

> 'experience during the first two years showed that responsibility for a particular job was too diffused for effective control and that communication between customer and people working on his job was unsatisfactory. From January 1977, as a result, the Division was reorganized to create topic-orientated branches handling population and medical statistics work. The branch handling Survey work had always been topic orientated so no change was needed in that case. The creation and staffing of Computer Division in 1974 caused some dislocation. We now feel that the initial organization of the Division was not well suited to continuous interactive working between CD and customer divisions'.

Another immediate concern of the senior managers of the new office related to a very old and much debated problem – the appropriate civil service class for Survey staff. The time was favourable to a relaxation of the former tight divisions. Speaking to the Institute of Personnel Management in October 1971, Sir William Armstrong, head of the home civil service[7] described the process of merging many of the previous classes based on methods of entry and educational qualifications to make it easier for non-graduates to compete on equal terms with graduates. The divisions between administrative, executive and clerical classes were abolished in January 1971 and all the staff absorbed into a single administration group with a single promotion ladder, while maintaining recruitment to different rungs of this ladder. A similar grouping was proposed for the scientific classes and works group. The objective was the same as for the administration group: 'to make arrangements which allow for staff movements and promotions without regard to former class divisions ... Posts must not be regarded as the exclusive preserve of particular groups unless some specific qualification is a genuinely essential feature of the job'. There was also to be an extension of 'opportunity' posts – 'jobs in which the work is expected to benefit from their successive occupancy by people with different backgrounds and skills ... we hope this will enable individuals to broaden their experience by coming into contact with those of other disciplines'.

To those inside the Survey who had argued fruitlessly for many years that its work needed a mixture of research staff drawn from many social science disciplines, this must have sounded right, even if some decades too late, but it was still not clear whether the new doctrine would be applied in practice to Survey staff. The issue was raised early in 1972 because a decision had been made to create an occupational group of Information Officers and to apply to it all the new formulae described in Sir William's paper. The Survey staff were formally members of the Information Class but were recognised as a distinctive group, and clearly were not appropriate members of the new Information Class. At that time there were 107 Survey Officers in post. The disciplinary background of those with university degrees was as follows:

Economics	11
Accounts and business administration	4
English	4
Languages	5
Physical Sciences	5
Mathematics	9
Sociology	12
Anthropology	4
Statistics	4
Other social sciences	12

The classification and grading problem had existed since the establishment of the Survey in 1946 and had defied all efforts at resolution. The Survey was now part of a department where all the senior management and most of the professional staff were in the Statistician Class. The majority of the Survey's professional staff did not have the appropriate qualifications for that class and most of them would not have welcomed an offer of membership even if it had been possible. For a mixture of reasons which are unclear, the authorities had at this time also decided not to keep the Research Officer Class in its current form. It was accepted that in many departments research officers were employed on work which could not realistically be described as research. This, of course, was the classification which Treasury had for many years pressed on the Survey as the logical answer to all its classification problems: if the Research Officer Class was to change and the Statistician Class seemed not possible or desirable, what were the alternatives?

A possibility was the merged administration group, but the experience and qualifications of Survey staff did not match those on which the new group was based. But a further proposal was being aired – the formation of a government social science group. Most of the Survey staff had the relevant qualifications and experience, and were certainly doing research; this seemed to be a solution. The CSO was consulted and took a rather different view, that the most desirable outcome would be to integrate the Survey staff into statistical grades wherever possible and to dispose of the rest in the administration group. But OPCS managers were firmly in favour of a social science group. It would give a professional identity and would provide reasonable career outlets. Given the doctrine of 'opportunity posts' members of other classes, such as statisticians, could take up some of the Survey positions from time to time, and presumably members of a social science group could sometimes do work which otherwise would be done by statisticians. One of the complications of this discussion was the existence of recognised groups of economists, statisticians and psychologists which had achieved formal status and did not want to be submerged in a new class – particularly one which would include less prestigious social science disciplines than their own. It was urged that, alternatively, potential members of a social science group should be given the opportunity, if they had the qualifications, to join these existing classes. In the usual civil service manner these ideas were being discussed during 1972 by responsible officials to reach agreement on their presentation to the trade unions: formal discussions began in July 1973.

In November 1975 they were brought to a halt as a result of national economic difficulties leading, among other measures, to a national incomes policy applied stringently to the civil service. The unions were told that 'further discussion of the present proposals cannot be pursued during the current phase of national incomes policy since the proposals would involve an increase in the pay scale maximum of individuals regraded to a higher grade in the new structure and discussion thereof cannot avoid kindling pay expectations'. This seems a rather thin excuse for terminating discussions that had gone on for nearly 30 years and had acknowledged the existing arrangements as 'nonsensical'. In a letter to the IPCS the Civil Service Department said 'it is clear that your comments upon the proposals and department's own views thereon force us in any case towards a more fundamental reappraisal. Accordingly we are exploring possible alternative avenues which lie within the limits of current income policy'. Whatever followed from these explorations did not affect the Survey. In 1976 they culminated in the Civil Service Department's acceptance of the status quo.

But some change did occur. In 1978 a decision was made to offer membership of the administration group to any Survey staff who volunteered for it. Promotion from here might involve movement to any section of the civil service, and would also mean that recruitment for administration group posts within the Survey might also draw on other departments. The argument for this change was that within the Survey grades there were blocks of technical specialist work not essentially different from that performed elsewhere by members of the administration group. The impetus came more probably from the attempt to set up a social science group. In the event the professional staff of the Survey decided to remain where they were, but many of the technical staff accepted the regrading offer, and the long-maintained unity of Survey staff was dissolved. In 1987 the long-established link with the Information Officer Class was finally broken, when Survey staff were regraded into a new Social Survey Officer Class.

The new location of the Survey had, by design, incorporated it into the expanding government statistical network. This led to participation in the array of committees which formed the framework within which statistical matters were discussed. The continuing surveys were seen as important contributors and the senior officers of OPCS were bound to consider this part of survey work as more relevant and important for their main interests than the ad hoc surveys which might originate from other sections of government. At the same time, they were attempting to develop a new government department and to integrate the different parts of two separate organisations into a working whole. They were bound to emphasise this aspect of organisational change and perhaps to underestimate aspects of Survey organisation developed during many years of concentration on building integrated survey procedures.

The difficulties arising out of unsatisfactory population estimates in 1971 were bound to direct attention to attempts to improve this side of OPCS work. A continuing One Per Cent Survey was proposed, partly because it was believed that it would help to provide smaller area statistics. This was unlikely for anything smaller than regions or sub-regions. But the proposal was given further impetus by the Labour Force Survey carried out by OPCS for the EEC. That the work on the One Per Cent Survey went as far as it did is only explicable in the context of the discussion, in the statistical committees, of a 'package' of statistical instruments, where it was envisaged that something smaller than the Census but bigger than most surveys was needed to implement the 1920 Census Act which laid on the Registrar General the duty to measure the 'number and condition of the population'. This judgment was based on an appraisal of existing social statistics and their limitations, particularly when viewed against the flood of social legislation which was characteristic of the epoch and the encouragement to monitor its effects, promoted by new ideas on management information.

The Survey's demographic work originated before the merger, as did its studies designed to improve the Census: both continued afterwards. But the political uncertainties of the first part of the 1970s, culminating in the last-minute decision to stop a proposed 1976 Census towards which much of this work was aimed, was not a very encouraging start to the development of an improved package of social statistics. Similarly, attempts to develop ideas about extending the utility of the Electoral Register came to nothing. The work on the proposed One Per Cent Survey used resources which might have been used more fruitfully elsewhere, perhaps on ad hoc surveys which were abandoned or done elsewhere. There were other diversions of resources which limited what could be done on ad hoc studies: for example, on the insistence of one of the statistical committees, methodological work on the FES was increased and staff were diverted for this purpose. This truncated work on a study of young people moving into employment being done for the same department. Another research officer, studying the employment of coloured teenagers, was moved onto developing possible Census questions on ethnic origins. Later on, one of the assistant directors was appointed Head of Census Division. All these alternative employments of Survey staff could obviously be justified in their own right: the Survey's problem was in its failure to recruit acceptable research staff as replacements. It has been argued when the merger was under discussion that a larger organisation, carrying out a wider programme designed to improve social statistics, would help recruitment. Experience showed that this had not happened. The growth of research staff in client departments had opened up other work avenues. Not only were possible staff now working elsewhere; it was also possible that research staff in departments felt they lost control over surveys at the stage when operational responsibility passed to the Survey, with its wider experience and expertise. This, if true, was not very encouraging for those Survey staff who normally expected to work with departments developing their own small research units.

Whatever the combined effect of these developments, it seems clear that despite the expressed statements in the 1967 Treasury circular (appendix B), the contribution from ad hoc surveys was somewhat less after the merger than before it. The senior staff of the OPCS had all been drawn from various branches of the statistical service, and while they did their best to help the Survey carry on with mixed programmes of continuous and ad hoc surveys it was inevitable that they would give extra weight to the main statistical output for which they were responsible.

The creators of OPCS might well have felt that they had laid foundations for some permanent solutions to the Survey's problems of location and organisation, and its relationship to the rest of government. In fact, during this period, tendencies slowly crystallising over the years emerged more sharply, and within the Survey different strands of opinion on the most appropriate work organisation were expressed. This was probably inevitable. There had been a long period of indecision about the location and organisation of the Survey beginning in the years before the Heyworth Report (1963–5). The new Social Survey Department (1967) came under question within a year or so of its creation. There were further delays after that in setting up OPCS. The feeling was that no group of people within the government had been subject to such indecision. Most important, the decision to join the Survey, which had grown as a general research facility available to all parts of the government, to the rapidly growing statistical service, did raise questions about the future scope of services to other parts of the government at a time when departments were expanding their social research interests and looking for usable resources.

The situation was not made easier by frequent changes of Survey Director –

five between 1970, when I resigned as Director, and 1984. Two of the changes were due to the incumbent reaching retirement age, and for five years the post was occupied by a chief statistician (and former Survey customer) from outside the Survey.

Directors of Social Survey

1941–70   Louis Moss
1970–77   Geoffrey Thomas
1977–82   Frank Whitehead
1983   Roma Morton-Williams
1984   Bob Barnes

It was inevitable that the first change of Director would lead to a change of management style. In the early days there had necessarily been a great deal of spontaneity and organisational elasticity. The main effect had been a response to opportunity to demonstrate what survey methods could do and a gaining of resources and staff on the basis of these demonstrations, and it had always seemed important to maintain the unity of the staff – research officers and specialists. Now the Survey had grown, and with the development of the four continuing surveys its work programme year by year had begun to take on a more settled structure. The ad hoc surveys within that structure were always sufficiently numerous to justify a large part of the annual Vote, but their origin and subject matter were, as always, unpredictable. So the new Director, Geoffrey Thomas, following his own judgment produced at the end of 1972 a paper which discussed several alternative schemes of organisation. Among them, some ideas stand out. There was a proposal that one of the four assistant director posts be used to coordinate the specialist sections and take responsibility for progressing their work, providing a more formal link with research staff. There was an emphasis on managerial responsibilities which would be shared by all the assistant directors and, of course, the Director. And there was some emphasis on the need for firmer control of ad hoc projects at a lower level.

The paper provoked a great deal of discussion. The 'coordinator' proposal would give added strength to a most important feature of the Survey's organisation but for some people it threatened to separate off the specialist sections and could perhaps be divisive. The IPCS welcomed the proposals generally, but said that it would prefer something rather 'more radical'. Some of the research staff, too, were a little apprehensive about changes which they anticipated might involve them in heavier workloads. The new internal organisation inaugurated on 3 September 1973 reflected most of the Director's proposals. There followed a period of active discussion about staff training, very much influenced by the suggestion, discussed earlier, that a new social science group should be formed. If this was to be based on graduate recruitment then a large part of the specialist staff would be assigned to the administration group, and for them a different approach to training would be necessary. A member of the research staff eventually produced more radical proposals, among which was the idea of project groups. The suggestion was that for each new survey a group representing research and specialists should be brought together, and disbanded when the Survey was completed. It was not clear how functions such as training, which might involve participation in several consecutive projects, would be carried out, nor how the responsibility of the directors or the coordinator would fit such a loose scheme. But the origins of the proposal lay in a certain dissatisfaction with the existing organisation and the way it influenced promotion prospects. The thrust of the argument was for a much more fluid structure and of enhanced possibilities for movement of individuals.

In 1975 Geoffrey Thomas produced new proposals which tended in the opposite direction. He suggested that there should be a division between the continuing and the ad hoc surveys, that each group should become the responsibility of a senior director and that the Director of the Survey should be upgraded accordingly. This proposal followed on the retirement of two of the three assistant directors, Percy Gray and Bill Kemsley. Thomas had earlier noted, in an internal paper, 'the Division's resources have increased very considerably since 1970 – 35% more operational money spent in real terms, 33% more staff since 1970. This increase has largely been absorbed by an increase in the number of continuous and repeated surveys. It is likely that continuous and repeated surveys will remain a growth area while the demand for ad hoc work will remain fairly constant'. In fact the increase in resources was about 19% in real terms and much of this was absorbed by the GHS. He went on to examine some of the organisational problems of the Survey and noted the effect of retirement on the pool of experience available. 'Experience of the last two years has shown that the division of ad hoc work between Groups has led to a relatively inefficient use of manpower. This suggests that all ad hoc work should be under one command. The logical consequence of that is to put the continuous and repeated surveys under a separate head'.

It was assumed that there was a common basis to the organisation of all the continuous surveys: in fact, they were rather different. There was, for example, nothing in common between the organisation of the IPS and the FES – indeed, the IPS had its own separate field staff. The GHS staff produced an annual report based on the material collected at the request of many departments. The Survey had never produced an analytical report on the FES: this was done by the main customer, the Department of Employment. Fieldwork and coding on the National Food Survey had been contracted out to a commercial research firm for many years. Moreover, it was also suggested (elsewhere) that to this grouping of continuous surveys would be added responsibility for the proposed One Per Cent continuous survey – a major undertaking in itself – and other possible continuing work. There was already great variety of purpose and method in the continuing surveys; if new surveys were started this would be increased, and continuing surveys would then take up something approaching 90% of the Survey's operational funds. There was even less identity of purpose and method between the ad hoc surveys. Survey staff, already upset by the separation of the computer section, were likely to fear the further divisions of staff and resources which would follow this proposed separation, and it is likely that internal turbulence was increased by this proposal.

In 1977 on Thomas's retirement the third Director, Frank Whitehead, was appointed. He came from the DHSS but was well acquainted with the Survey as a former customer. He rapidly absorbed the very mixed collection of proposals for change and responded within a few months in an emollient and positive manner. His response had been discussed with all senior Survey staff, and he was therefore able to say to OPCS management, whose views had also been taken into account, 'I think you can take it that this is now a broad consensus'. His proposals setttled most of the discussion. He judged that

> by corporate management it is possible to ensure that research resources are allocated efficiently ... given the range of projects at least three different Directors are necessary to lessen the load on the head of SSD ... professional work needs re-examination with a view to seeing how much could be done with the help of other classes ... given a more homogenous staff we believe it would be possible to ensure greater flexibility of movement within SSD to ensure that the majority of officers have experience in all relevant aspects of survey design ... to set up project teams does not seem to make the most efficient use of resources and has the major difficulty of making it more difficult for management to ensure reasonable accountability and productivity and to keep costs within bounds.

Whitehead accepted criticisms of recruitment, training and career development and noted that it was 'difficult to plan careers effectively and at the same time react intelligently to changes in the programme of work'. One of the elements of Thomas's proposals had been a methodology section to specialise on techniques improvement. The new Director accepted this: 'We think it important for there to be a separate methodological unit to pursue certain studies free from the distraction of other duties and this is now in existence'. A year or so later this unit became the basis for a further regrouping as the effects of reclassification began to impinge. A Methods Design and Analysis Group was formed to work with all groups responsible for particular projects and give consultancy advice on techniques, design and resources to any part of the government that approached the Survey for this kind of help. Eventually responsibility for sampling was brought within the orbit of the same group.

This period turned out to be fruitful, though was no doubt very distracting at the time. It might be viewed as a time of transition to a more coherent organisation and management, and as usual, none of the arguments and decisions affected the work itself. Given the eventual outcome and the way the views expressed so vigorously by the Survey staff were absorbed and reflected in the new arrangements, the events of this time seemed to have followed in a Survey tradition, whereby the Survey from time to time remade itself in the light of experience, new needs and changing resources. And events were to show that the changes made in 1977 were timely. During 1978 a general election was expected but did not happen. In 1979 there was an election and a change of government to the Conservatives under Margaret Thatcher, which brought a very different philosophy about the scope and organisation of the public sector. The Survey once again found itself under attack, perhaps more seriously than at any time since 1951. Clear ideas about effective organisation were to prove important for survival.

The making of major changes in government may often be discerned some time ahead – at least, with hindsight, such changes appear to have an inevitability. The pressures on the Survey following the election were the continuation of a process that had begun some years previously. In 1976, after the negotiations with the IMF, the expansions in research and statistics of the preceding decade were halted, and a general process of financial stringency was applied throughout government. Much greater changes took place or were considered subsequently. For example, the issue of repayment for services given by one part of the government to another was reviewed in 1978. The conclusion was 'there is a presumption against repayment unless a good case can be made out. Cases should be considered on their merits'. The new government interpreted the election results as a mandate for change in many areas and in particular for drastic changes in the civil service. On 22 May in answer to a parliamentary question, the Minister for the Civil Service said 'The Government is committed to making economies in Civil Service manpower. As a first step the Civil Service pay component of the 1979–80 cash limits will be reduced by three per cent'. Since inflation was at a high level and wages everywhere were increasing, this decision meant an immediate halt to recruitment and a rundown of staff as retirement and other natural losses made their effect felt.

As part of OPCS the Survey shared in any decisions applied to the statistical service. It was therefore involved in the next stage of the 'economies' – consideration of possible savings of 10–20% on staff levels. Following discussion on the changes that would be necessary for such savings the government, on 6 December 1979, announced cuts in civil service manpower. OPCS was to lose 275 posts and a budget reduction of £1.3 million was to be achieved by 1984. Twenty-four posts were to be taken from the Survey and there would be consequent cuts in expenditure on staff and fieldwork, most of which were to be achieved by 1981–2. An overall reduction of about 11% was envisaged and it was argued that the proposed reduction might reduce the usefulness of the major continuing surveys to customer departments, but would not jeopardise their most important aims.

In order to achieve the 11% overall reduction a rather larger reduction would be needed in staff and finance earmarked for ad hoc surveys. The savings proposed in the continuing surveys were not at first based on detailed examination – that came later. These surveys were mainly used by sections of the statistical service, but there were no continuing customers for the ad hoc surveys. There were many former customers, but their views on the surveys' value were not systematically sought as were those of the customers for the statistical surveys. This ad hoc part of the work of the Survey had done much to build its good reputation. It was part of the government's social research effort carried out in many different forms, and was seen by departments as such. It would have been logical, and perhaps more effective, to have considered the ad hoc surveys in a review of government social research, and not solely as part and parcel of the statistical services whose scope and methods were rather different. Since the review which did take place was directed by the head of the Government Statistical Service, a separate appraisal of the ad hoc surveys would have required an early initiative from the service that was not forthcoming. OPCS had been created on the initiative of a previous head of the CSO. At that time, a pledge had been given that the inclusion of the Survey in the statistical service would not diminish the work on ad hoc surveys designed to meet specific policy needs.

The reductions announced were only the beginning. In January 1980, Sir Derek Rayner, a retail store senior executive who had played some part in the work of the team of businessmen brought into the Heath government in 1970, was asked to oversee the review of the Government Statistical Service which had already begun. Speaking at a meeting of the Royal Statistical Society some months later Sir John Boreham, head of the CSO, welcomed the review.[8] He said 'the underlying policy behind the review was to look for reductions in the Statistical Service as part of the Government's general aim to cut the size of the Civil Service as a whole'. It seems from this statement that while the review was presented as an attempt to improve efficiency and achieve greater value for money, the conclusion had been, in part at least, agreed before the review was carried out. The Rayner method was to encourage civil servants to review themselves: to select members of the service to be reviewed and encourage them to look critically at the work being done, making recommendations for changes that might increase value for money. Under an elected government this raises questions about the judgment of value, the pricing of the benefits to be set alongside the cost, and it is not easy to see how in a political system the value of a policy is arrived at. What, for example, is the value of an acceptable Retail Price Index or a reliable system for calculating national income?

The team of two people appointed to review OPCS did not, perhaps for these reasons, reach many firm conclusions, preferring to transfer responsibility to a central review group directly responsible to Rayner. On the ad hoc surveys their comment was:

> The Social Survey Division machine is a highly technically competent organization without many parallels outside. The Division does not compete with the private sector ... those companies are not necessarily capable or competent of undertaking the type of policy orientated enquiry demanding the very high degree of technical excellence and comprehensive analytical reports which SSD carries out ... it seems probable that the surveys which are done should be considered value for money but the Central Review team may wish to consider whether any survey can be identified which should not have been done and whether this could be foreseen at the time the original decision was taken.[9]

The central review team thus had remitted to them the main task of somehow extracting from the Survey the savings in manpower and money which, according to Boreham, were 'the underlying policy of the review'. Their report and recommendations were adopted as the second part of Rayner's *Report to the Prime Minister* in December 1980. The title is important: it notes a feature of the review which is critical for the approach adopted. Boreham and Rayner were both acting under the aegis of the Cabinet Office, at one remove from the Prime Minister. They were, in fact, both attempting to implement a political decision already taken at the highest level of government.

Under such circumstances it was difficult, if not impossible, for others to raise considerations which in different circumstances might have been stressed more forcibly. For example, the appropriate size of a multi-purpose survey like the Family Expenditure Survey or the General Household Survey was normally decided by professional judgment and, given the continuous pressure on Survey resources, was unlikely to be much more than the minimum acceptable level for its stated purposes. Confronted with a government-backed recommendation that something less than this should be done, normal professional judgment is difficult unless equally strong political weight can be brought into play. No cuts were in fact made in the FES. On the other hand, the CSO was the sponsor of the GHS, and it accepted a cut in the sample size. It is interesting to note that when this survey was originally discussed, the CSO were hoping for a sample seven times as big. During the eleven years of its existence one of the repeated comments on it by customers was that the sample was too small. So when the review team suggested a cut it could hardly have been on professional grounds.

The Rayner review team's recommendations fell into four parts. The first, and perhaps most important, was that 'the Division should continue to act as a central coordinating body for government survey research and provide a technical and managerial advisory service as required by departments. Departments should consult it about surveys before undertaking or contracting out work within its competence'.

All the other recommendations made it more difficult for the Survey to act accordingly. It is not quite clear what the review team had in mind on this point, which was taken as an official position on the Survey, repeated in the House of Commons and used in part answer to a large body of critical comment. It is almost as if the review team, having suggested a radical dismemberment of the Survey, felt that it had to reassure its critics that everything remained unaltered. While the other recommendations were pressed hard, very little support was given to implementing this acknowledgment of a continuing function in government for a central survey research unit.

Secondly, the review team proposed reductions in the scale of the continuing surveys and gave a backhanded endorsement to the GHS. 'In principle there is sense and economy in the idea of a continuing multi-purpose survey . . . it is true that to axe the survey would be likely to create an outcry that the government does not want to know about the well-being of its citizens.' The team acknowledged that the GHS was designed to meet the needs of a large number of departments for information about the economic and other circumstances of households: 'OPCS has a long list of departmental uses to which the survey data has been put'. They went on, nevertheless, to recommend a cut in the size of the survey. A reduction in sample size would, of course, reduce the number of separate social groups covered in adequate numbers, so this recommendation would make the GHS less useful and less value for money. This error of judgment was compounded by the review team's wish elsewhere to see the reduced GHS used more often to replace ad hoc surveys.

Another recommendation was that proposals should be worked out for three alternative cuts in the size of the International Passenger Survey, of which the most drastic would cut the cost by over 80% and yield a sample size too small to serve much of the survey's purpose. Eventually a much smaller cut was agreed. A proposal from which major savings were anticipated was the merging of the National Food Survey and the Family Expenditure Survey. At this time there were substantial differences in the response to the two surveys and it was felt that, given the political importance of the Retail Price Index and the part the FES played in this, it would be wrong to raise doubts about the reliability of the FES. Although substantial effort was put into trials of a combined survey, the merger did not go ahead.

The review team was perhaps most trenchant on the ad hoc surveys. 'It is doubtful if government has so large a requirement for its own operation as the OPCS capacity indicates.' The source of the doubt is not identified. The review was concerned with the future work of the Survey, and the surveys which might be requested in the future had not yet emerged, so it is not easy to understand how such a speculation might be warranted. The review team made no attempt to accept the challenge from the OPCS to consider 'whether any survey can be identified which should not have been done'.

The fourth part recommended that since the review team did 'not believe that the Allied Service arrangement brings sufficient sharpness to departments' decisions about the need for, form and cost of surveys . . . the aim should be to contract out all the ad hoc social surveys where private costs are less than those of OPCS. We also recommend surveys conducted by Social Survey should be on repayment terms'. Departments would have to pay for such work out of existing departmental budgets. This meant that other departmental research commitments, such as sponsoring academic research, would have to be cut if departments wished to use their existing funds on work done by the Survey. It therefore meant a cut in the total funds available for social research.

This recommendation followed a peculiar logic. It assumed that if departments had to repay, they would be more efficient purchasers of research services. The demand for ad hoc surveys, however, was not continuous. Many departments were only occasional customers and were not, therefore, experienced buyers. As described earlier, even where scientific advisory groups had developed, departments had still not managed to harness all the research resources they required. The commercial providers which the review team expected to solve this problem were mainly engaged in quite different kinds of work from government surveys, and their staffs were deployed accordingly. Government work taken from the Survey and divided up between them would provide only very limited extra work for any one organisation and it was unlikely that they would change their usual arrangements to meet it. The market in such circumstances would not resemble any 19th century model. Presumably the review team had made its first recommendation because it thought that departmental customers needed advice on the technical aspects of their social research requirements. No attempt is made to clarify the problems which would result for the Survey in carrying out this function for departments free to operate in a non-existent market – problems exacerbated later, when it was expected to compete vigorously with the commercial providers. It also seemed to be assumed that departments asked for surveys in a somewhat lighthearted manner – a judgment that could only have been made in ignorance of the very earnest discussions inside departments before decisions are made to begin a survey. The procedures, frequently involving ministerial consultation, have been described in earlier chapters. They meant that any department requesting Survey help had to accept public responsibility for the cost and for all interviews with members of the public. This had been the situation for more than 40 years before the review team began its work, and there was available information on how the allied service principle worked in practice over many years. There was even a period, described earlier, when regular meetings of all the Survey's customers took place under the chairmanship of the Treasury in order to review experience year by year and consider an appropriate budget, to be settled by direct negotiation with the responsible Treasury officials. So the available evidence contradicted the team's judgments on this issue and perhaps undermined the recommendations that followed.

It is, however, interesting that the team did not propose repayment for the continuing surveys. By their nature these surveys are stable in design and it is easy to estimate and predict their costs, whereas the ad hoc surveys range over the whole field of government, deal with a very mixed collection of topics, employ very different designs and are not predictable. Many sections of government are only occasional customers and do not have research budgets to use in the way suggested by the review team, which is why the allied service system proved helpful and effective in meeting their needs for survey research.

The review team assumed that its recommendations for contracting out and repayment would inevitably lead to a decline in demand for the services of the Survey. The reductions in staff following earlier decisions would have led anyway to a reduction in output, but the review team went on to recommend further reductions, on the assumption that their recommended cuts in the continuing surveys and changes in financing the Survey's work would prove possible. They calculated staff at 235 in 1980, of whom almost 100 worked on the continuing surveys, leaving 135 for ad hoc work. 'If all but a handful [of ad hoc surveys] were contracted out or stopped we estimate savings of up to 100 staff.' Such savings would have left 35 staff for ad hoc work and for the coordinating and the central consultancy function that had been emphasised. The review team were suggesting a cut in staff of something over 40%.

However, the review had made recommendations, not decisions. It was now for departments to consider and decide what procedures would safeguard their Ministers' interests and assure their policy needs. The savings proposed by the review were described as 'potential', and various groupings of civil servants were set up to examine the possibilities. Where it was felt that the recommendations could be accepted they were, and decisions were made about their application. But some cases were not so clear. The review team had expected large savings from its proposed merger of the FES and the National Food Survey. The Department of Employment, however, were unable to accept any cuts in the FES sample and believed that the merger would diminish the acceptability of the Retail Price Index, which was too important politically to threaten in this way. Of the three options proposed for the IPS, the smallest cut was accepted and applied during 1982–3. The cut proposed in the size of the GHS was applied from the beginning of 1982.

During this period there were occasional newspaper stories about changes in other government social research arrangements. One, on 27 November 1980 in *New Society*, described substantial changes in the Home Office Research Unit, the oldest departmental social research unit, founded in a very different era of Conservative government. In April 1981 a White Paper was published,[10] which simply repeated the Rayner Report and paid little obvious attention to the issues raised by departments. There was one exception to this. Whereas the review team had assumed that price could be used as the sole criterion to ensure value for money, the White Paper was a little more circumspect. It said 'Arrangements for commissioning ad hoc surveys will be reviewed to make greater use of the private sector when this can do the work as effectively and at lower cost than the public service'.

The White Paper was followed up very quickly by the head of the CSO who, in May 1981, commissioned a member of the Civil Service College staff, J R Merchant, to 'review the arrangements' for the various functions it was expected the Survey would carry out. This was the third successive review of the Survey's situation in three years. It was expected to find ways of dealing with all the problems the interdepartmental discussions had thrown up, and in particular with arrangements for the ad hoc surveys. The Merchant review was made during a period of quite active professional discussion of the Rayner proposals, and in particular of its intended effects on the Survey.

In June 1981 a special meeting of the Royal Statistical Society was called to enable Fellows to express their views about the cuts in the Government Statistical Service. Over 200 members attended, an unusually large number, many of whom were government statisticians. The meeting was very lively and some of the speakers were loudly applauded. It was clear that the professional conscience of many of those present had been aroused by the Rayner review and its reception by the government and some of its officials. Sir John Boreham opened the discussion, remarking that his 'post bag was not overflowing' and to judge from this the OPCS and its Social Survey Division were the main subjects of interest. He made it clear that the purpose of the review was to look for reductions in the statistical service as part of the government's general aim to cut the size of the civil service, and he outlined the main recommendations. He particularly welcomed the statement by the Prime Minister assigning increased responsibility for the CSO and claimed that the review was consistent with remarks made by the previous head of the CSO, Sir Claus Moser, in his presidential address to the Society.

Sir Claus, who was present, said he believed the government might regret the cuts proposed. He hoped that the government would regret the cut in social statistics. He was shocked that the White Paper and the departments had not identified the losses of information. He thought it was misguided to propose cuts in quality checks and verification: 'We should rethink the switch from government surveys to the private sector'. Another speaker at the meeting commented that the review was 'a cost benefit exercise without adequate study of the benefits'. A proper review, it was said, would have looked at the economic, social and political consequences of reshaping the government statistical services. Government needed to be accountable to Parliament and the people, and the provision of statistical data was one means of assessing the impact of government policies. Several speakers pointed to the lack of argument and support within the reports for some of the recommendations. There was no clear statement of the implications of many of the cuts. The *Statistical News* summary of the meeting says 'In conclusion the general mood of those who contributed to the meeting was that although a review was to be welcomed this particular Review was poorly conducted and too narrow in its objectives'. The President of the RSS followed up this meeting with a letter to the Prime Minister describing the feelings expressed at it.

On 2 July a Manchester MP raised in the House of Commons the question of the effect of the Rayner Review on the Survey and repeated at length some of the points quoted above.[11] In reply, the DHSS minister noted the Rayner recommendations and commented that a further review of the commissioning of ad hoc surveys was being made and that 'Ministers will not take final decisions' until this report was available. He added 'many think that value for money will be best achieved by preserving a strong ad hoc survey capability in the Social Survey Division and that it is a possible outcome'. He repeated the assertions made frequently over the previous few months that the Survey would continue to act as a central coordinating body for government survey research and that departments should consult it before commissioning surveys. 'This emphasises the high regard that is held for the technical competence of the Social Survey Division. It is significant therefore that Sir Derek Rayner's report accepts that all the present functions of the SSD should remain intact but that the size should be questioned'.

On 15 July the Chairman of the Social Science Research Council wrote to Sir John Boreham expressing anxiety that the desire to achieve economies should not inflict lasting damage on the quality of government statistical work. Its high reputation, he said, had been the product of the high calibre of professional statistical expertise which the service had set out to recruit.

> One area where this has come to be particularly crucial is survey research. The Social Survey has set a standard which the rest of the survey profession has felt obliged to emulate. The pressures of the market place are such that a general deterioration would quickly set in were this topmost standard to be removed. It will be difficult for the staff to maintain their expertise and research creativeness if they are no longer to be involved in the planning and carrying out of the ad hoc surveys themselves. Apart from this threat of a general deterioration of standards the proposals seem bound to end the effective existence of the Division as a centre of social science research making contributions that have a significance far beyond the strict confines of government.

It may be that these remarks, and the fact that their substance is repeated in all the responses made to the substantial official correspondence on the topic, show that an impression had been made on the government: it seems clear that at that stage some questions were still open. The Merchant Report, commissioned by Sir John Boreham, might still be of some importance in the final decisions.

In September 1981 Mr Merchant presented his report.[12] In many respects, despite his terms of reference, the tone of his discussion was rather different from the self-assured voice of the Rayner review team. He emphasised that sample surveys were 'an essential part of the formulation and implementation of many policies. They cannot be regarded as optional and this study is not concerned with whether the Government should have access to ad hoc survey information, but how it should have that access . . . I also conclude that social surveys are not necessarily like market research and that a good social survey manager has an unusual mixture of knowledge and ability'. This attitude conflicts with the standpoint of the Rayner review where the opposite assumption is made – that any market research organisation which tenders successfully on the basis of cost comparisons can do all that is required. Merchant said that 'the complexity of social surveys contrasts with market research surveys. The latter are often considerably simpler in their objectives, their questionnaire design, their sampling method and their report. Proven ability in market surveys is therefore no guarantee of good social survey work'. In further diagreement with the review team he outlined the reasons why surveys are in many cases necessarily complex and why specialised knowledge and experience is needed if the desirable quality is to be achieved. 'The foundations of this quality are the thorough immersion of the Social Survey officer in the client's problem, the long and careful gestation of the sample and questionnaire design, the use of probability samples, the high standard of the field force and coding section and the sequence of training and quality control built into the system.'

Unlike the review team, Merchant did not assume that throwing open the departmental demand for surveys to the private sector would lead automatically to the disappearance of demand for the Survey's services. He accepted the principle of repayment but recommended that 'the repayment mechanism itself be allowed to determine the size of the SS Division'. To this end he proposed that the Survey should compete with market research tenderers for government surveys and because of the need for equal competition, steps would have to be taken to ensure its ability to make decisions about details of its own expenditure in the same way as private sector companies. 'The Survey should be freed from normal civil service control on some expenditures and, presumably, on staffing.' His acceptance of repayment thus leads a long way in the direction of the Survey becoming independent of the civil service and of the OPCS. Merchant made no attempt to reconcile this conclusion with the frequently stated intention to retain a specialised government survey organisation – a central coordinating body which would advise departments on how their needs might be met. Nor did he reconcile it with his previous comments on the differences between government surveys and the general run of commercial market-research. The report highlighted the difficulties of proposing a straight competitive repayment mechanism within the controlled conditions of a government organisation. It cannot be said that it provided a satisfactory and workable answer for many of the problems created by the review. Above all, it failed to solve the main problem of maintaining a government apparatus with service-wide responsibilities for which experience and training were necessary, while accepting major cuts in the permitted work programmes on which the experience and training must be based. At no point did Merchant or the Rayner review ask what was the minimum work programme needed to provide the staff necessary for this purpose.

Merchant did, however, comment on the review team's staffing proposals. He noted the assumption of 'potential savings' leading to a marked reduction in staff, and commented 'it seems likely that this was something of a rough estimate but I have been unable to reach any firm conclusions about the likely reduction in demand. I do feel in practice however that because of the importance of survey research to many Departments and their high regard for SSD abilities the decline might not be quite so dramatic as has been suggested'. His way out of this difficulty was to suggest allowing the repayment mechanism to establish demand and to assume that there could be a long enough transition period in which 'resources will have to be reduced carefully'. It is interesting that despite their belief in the benefits of market mechanisms, neither the review team nor Merchant were ready to contemplate the Survey competing successfully and retaining enough customers to maintain its staff at existing levels. This had been ruled out by the need to cut staff, and much of the tortured argument in both reports is due to this.

Some of the reactions to the Merchant Report must have been unexpected. Both the Rayner review team and Merchant had made confident assessments of the differences between most market research and most Survey research. The review team attempted to diminish the importance of the difference by its bold statement that the Survey and the rest of OPCS were 'too research minded, too perfectionist', that the Survey too often provided a 'Rolls Royce' product rather than the 'budget' reports which were more suited. Merchant went out of his way to emphasise that the differences related essentially to government requirements. Among those given the Merchant Report for their comments was the Association of Market Survey Organisations (AMSO), which describes itself as 'the trade association of 28 leading private sector survey organisations whose work in the UK amounts for approximately two-thirds of the commercially available market'. In a letter to Sir John Boreham in January 1982 it said:

> we should like to point out that such surveys are often of great importance to public and private sectors of British industry and not only government ... We totally disagree with the Merchant statement that the work of the Survey researchers is not closely paralleled by the majority of commercial survey work. The statement is untrue, there is no supporting evidence and reflects an ignorance of commercial survey organisations ... There is no doubt in our mind that there must always be a role for SS Division in respect of consultation with their clients ... In our dealings with senior staff at OPCS we have developed great respect for their research knowledge, attention to detail and the importance they set on maintaining high standards. It is on this executive role we feel SS Division should be concentrated.

The letter raises the suspicion that perhaps neither the Rayner review team nor Merchant correctly understood the work of market research firms. There were, possibly, other aspects of work important for government needs that were not fully investigated – for example, the experience of departments that commissioned studies from market research firms. The AMSO proposal was that the Survey should take responsibility for all the design stages and allow the private sector to do the fieldwork. This proposal was also echoed in some of Merchant's suggestions. It assumes that the recruitment and training of field staff for commercial research purposes is adequate to cope with designs specified by the Survey, and contradicts earlier comments made by Merchant on the importance of the Survey's interviewing staff and the fact that experience of the conduct and reception of field interviews is quite an important part of the skill applied to interview design. But the AMSO reaction does emphasise the weight given by all survey practitioners to the experience needed in the design stages of surveys, which implies the need for the Survey to have a large enough programme to provide the experience required to act as a central government source of advice and coordination.

The contradiction between the review team's assertions and the Merchant discussion is interesting, and shows that the recommendations of the former were very far from self-evident. The political decision to reduce staff and the change to repayment, however, made it difficult for Merchant to provide a workable proposal, and only time could show the actual outcome of departmental need for survey work in a period where such constraints were imposed. These were, of course, years of uncertainty and worry about the future of the organisation, reflected in the loss of some research staff. To this was added the effects of the increased movement of specialist staff following reclassification into the administration group. The balance of work shifted towards the continuing surveys, which by 1984 accounted for about 70% of the Survey's work. Nevertheless, throughout the period following the first announcement of staff cuts in 1979, Survey staff continued to respond to the requests of departments for a flow of ad hoc studies related to continuing policy interests.

Surveys for the DHSS in 1981–2 examined further the use of tobacco and alcohol and, particularly, smoking among secondary school children. Another study explored possible explanations of the high incidence of alcohol-related problems in some regional health authorities. In 1981 a post-enumeration study evaluated the quality of the population Census and, for the Home Office, the different methods used to compile the Electoral Register were examined. This latter work was part of a series of studies which resulted in limiting the use of the register for sampling purposes.

Following changes in the provision of school meals there was a nutrition survey of schoolchildren designed to provide a seven-day record of all food and drink consumed. In Scotland, the health department asked in 1982 for a survey to examine the use of family-planning services, the incidence of and demand for sterilisation, and the trend in unwanted pregnancies. For the Home Office Prison Department a survey of prison staff was done in 1982 to provide information about staff opinions on working conditions and the ways in which they could be improved. Some help was also given to the Home Office Research Unit on a study of the workloads of crown courts and magistrates' courts. An enquiry in 1983 into hardship among unemployed people, with special reference to financial aid received, was carried out for the DHSS. A major survey of disabled people was designed in 1985 to update and extend the work done 15 years previously and, in particular, to cover mental disability and disability among children. The Survey was asked by the Department of Transport to carry out the National Travel Survey in 1985–6 after the two previous surveys had been contracted out. Many of these studies carried forward earlier work and were thus able to draw on accumulated experience, but new ground was covered too.

The dominance of the political factor in the fortunes of the Survey is well illustrated by the contrast between the early and later years of its history; between growing recognition and integration in the government apparatus and the later, very pointed, attack. The Survey shared these difficulties with many other publicly funded bodies. Within government there was a change of emphasis from the developing systematic appraisal and evaluation of public programmes to decision-making using a language which blended management information and economic rhetoric. The Survey survived all the enquiries into its operations and weathered the changes. By 1984 it had organised, for the Department of Employment, a major continuing survey of the labour force, underlying still further the shift of the Survey's energies towards continuing statistical studies.

Notes

[1] *The Reorganisation of Central Government* Cmnd 4506, HMSO, 1970.
[2] Prime Minister in answer to a parliamentary question 29 October 1970.
[3] Sir Richard Clarke, *New Trends in Government,* HMSO, 1971.
[4] Cherns and Perry, 'The Development and Structure of Social Science Research in Britain', in Crawford and Perry (eds), *Demands for Social Knowledge,* Sage, 1976.
[5] Sir Alec Cairncross in R Flond and D McClosky (eds), *The Economic History of Britain,* Cambridge University Press, 1981.
[6] Sir John Boreham, *Journal of the Royal Statistical Society,* Section 'A', 143, Part 1, 1980.
[7] Sir William Armstrong, Personnel Management in the Civil Service, HMSO, 1971.
[8] *Statistical News,* HMSO, August 1981.
[9] *Initial Study of OPCS,* OPCS, August 1980.
[10] *Government Statistical Services,* Cmnd 8236, HMSO, 1981.
[11] *Hansard,* Cols. 1127–1136, 2 July 1981.
[12] J. R. Merchant, *The Commissioning of Ad Hoc Surveys,* Civil Service College, 1981.

PART TWO

The Survey's contribution to government

A PUBLICLY FINANCED RESEARCH UNIT must at all times be prepared to give an acceptable answer to the question 'what does it do?', and the answer must appear relevant and useful to the purposes of government. Between 1941 and 1981 the government changed 11 times, often changing overt political philosophy at the same time. In that period many hundreds of surveys were done and major continuing studies were mounted and developed to become part of the political and intellectual scene. Every one of those surveys was done only because one or other department formally asked for it and the Treasury approved the expenditure. Because governments change in response to changing political pressures, the history of the Survey as a government research organisation can be seen in the changing focus of its work, the changes in weight given to particular topics in response to the changing voice of government. The most useful framework for a description of what the Survey does must then be subject matter, the topics with which individual surveys were concerned. In what follows, an attempt has been made to show how interests changed and how the procrustean survey method was adapted to these changes of interest. The scope and variation is great, and it is probable that the Survey has contributed to the review of more different topics than any other comparable organisation.

The description of surveys and when they were done emphasises the contribution made to the assessment of particular problems. The continuing surveys provide measurements of selected indicators of social or economic situations. As they accumulate over time they may reveal trends which help to indicate the emergence of a continuing problem, such as the continuing increase in one-parent families or the numbers of elderly people living alone, or they may reveal progress in a sector which was worrying and where action has been taken, such as the decline in cigarette smoking or the reduction in the rate of inflation. The ad hoc surveys, when repeated, like the family planning or dental health surveys, serve the same purpose, but in very much more detail so as to indicate possible lines of further action. But no survey ever provides more than part of the picture that government needs. Intra-departmental debate, political pressures, external professional opinion and budgetary constraints all play their part in shaping the eventual judgment about appropriate policy and public action. It would not be possible to disentangle this mixture for more than a few of the many surveys described. What came out of the studies is shown by quotations from the reports, selected to show the main findings bearing on the problem to which the survey was related. These assessments by the researchers of the time, written for the people who asked for and would use the results, give the flavour of the work done and also show just what it was that the Survey contributed to the governments it served.

7. Housing design, housing statistics, planning, noise, mobility

THE BALANCE OF THE SURVEY'S WORK in the area now covered by the Department of the Environment has changed over time. Although work on aspects of housing or human settlement has continued over the whole period of this history, there are marked differences in the subject matter of the surveys done in different periods.

Until 1957, very little work was done on housing statistics, but from then on surveys for this purpose were wanted almost every year. In early years, on the other hand, surveys were organised to build up knowledge of many physical aspects of houses and their occupants' attitudes to features of design. Another early series of surveys studied the broader aspects of environment relevant to town and country planning. The object of these two groups of surveys was to help improve the design of new post-war housing and the planning of new settlements. Very little was done in the last 20 years on either group: the change in emphasis accompanied administrative or political decisions about particular kinds of research activity. Throughout the whole period there were clearly times when particular subjects were more acceptable, or perhaps more obviously necessary, because government responsibilities had widened.

Housing design

The Building Research Station (BRS) of the DSIR first asked for surveys to help develop its work. In 1942, surveys were made of interior lighting and heating. The first of these interviewed households selected by random numbers in streets indicated by electricity authorities. It examined artificial lighting in all main rooms and used light meters to measure the intensity of light in certain working locations. This material was related to housewives' opinions. In 1943 a similar study was made of noise in dwellings and its effects. In 1947 the Chief Scientific Advisor's office asked for a study of domestic water heating. An Electoral Register sample was used to describe cold water supply and water heating appliances used for bathing and clothes washing. As was usual with these surveys, opinions were requested on the degree of satisfaction with these appliances in relation to region, income group and presence of children. In 1950 the early study of sound in dwellings was taken further, and in 1952 there was a study of space heating.

Table 8 The main heating appliance of the main living room. Post war Local Authority sample – Lighting and Space Heating (1942)

	Proportion using appliance			Proportion satisfied with heating		
	North	South	North and South	North	South	North and South
	%	%	%			
Central heating	–	4	2	..	..	..
Solid fuel						
Ordinary open fire	24	28	25	88%	88%	88%
Improved open fire	39	48	43	90%	89%	89%
Range or cooker	32	9	22	85%	78%	84%
Stove	1	1	1	..	..	..
Independent boiler	2	6	4	..	80%	82%
Others	2	4	3	..	..	..
	100	100	100			
All households	1,066	777	1,843	87%	86%	87%

.. Base numbers too small.

These were population surveys. A study more closely related to usual laboratory procedures was made in 1952, the *Sound in Flats Survey*. Three selected blocks with differently constructed party walls were chosen where BRS facilities for sound measurement could be employed. Residents were asked about different kinds of noise – airborne or structure borne – which they could hear and which annoyed them. This study, interestingly, showed that physical measures of noise did not necessarily correlate directly with what people heard or how much annoyance it caused. Some years later a possible explanation was developed in another survey for BRS; much of the BRS work on noise in dwellings was summarised in 1954 by Parkin and Stacey.[1] In 1952 and 1955 further studies were made for the BRS of water heating, and this time information about expenditure was also collected from the authorities concerned. This was part of a programme to determine requirements for low-cost housing by assessing user experience and ability to pay; the samples were selected accordingly.

A rather different survey was requested in 1960. The BRS decided that it needed to know more about the market for the publications that recorded its work and recommendations. Using Ministry of Works registers of building firms, the Survey constructed stratified samples of managing directors and contract managers in a range of local authority areas. It was possible to show whether or not firms doing different kinds of building work used techniques of varying newness and what they thought about them. This information was used to classify the firms' progressiveness, and this classification was then used to illuminate other data collected about awareness of available techniques, the media available to spread knowledge and who within the firms made the decision to try new methods.

By the end of the 1950s much new housing, private and public, had been built and attention had turned to other features of design. In 1959 and 1960 work was done on the special housing needs of older people, children's play spaces on estates and the problem of access arrangements in high blocks of flats. This last study focused on several alternative types of arrangement, distinguishing enclosed access and open air access. Since the object was to assess the views of users, the study concentrated on tenants who had occupied their dwellings for a year or more and who had experience of particular types of access scheme. This meant that blocks had to be selected accordingly, so the sample populations were highly selective. They were not comparable to the Survey's population studies but were nearer to those used for experimental studies.

From this time on, such design studies were less likely to appear in Survey work programmes. In April 1965 the DSIR was dissolved and the BRS was transferred to the Ministry of Technology; this was, no doubt, part of the 'modernisation' policy of the period. Two years later the BRS returned to an enlarged Ministry of Public Buildings and Works which in 1970, under a different administration, became part of the Department of the Environment. At this time, in this field as in other sections of government, much greater emphasis began to be placed on involving academic researchers, and there was an impression that the government was less interested in direct policy-related studies.

Planning

In 1943 the Department of Health for Scotland, through its Scottish Housing Advisory Committee which was considering post-war development, asked the Survey to mount a study to help the committee's deliberations on new settlements in Scotland. For the *Location of Dwellings in Scottish New Towns Survey* a random sample of selected wards in an array of towns was chosen, but limited to houses rated at less than £30 per annum – 'houses in which it was to be expected that the families of the working class were likely to be found'. The survey examined the dwellings and many features of daily living, reasons for choosing the house, opinions on moving and preferred locations. An interesting feature of this survey was the attempt to assess convenience of location in relation to measured distance from various frequently used facilities like shopping areas, schools and so on.

This survey was followed by a series related to planning exercises in different parts of the country. In 1944 the Ministry of Town and Country Planning asked the Survey to produce, by sample enquiry, a great deal of descriptive information for the use of planners who were being financed by the Ministry as an experiment to produce a plan for Middlesbrough. In 1947 the same department asked the Survey to study a London borough, Willesden, focusing on the possible interest in and potential for movement to a new town. The survey, *Willesden and the New Towns*, described geographical and social characteristics and opinion on existing facilities, housing and the use of social amenities, together with interest in moving out of the area and the limiting conditions that might affect movement. A feature of the survey was the attention given to the effects of movement out of the area on the age structure of the remaining population. The 1943 Scottish study was followed by a similar study in Glasgow which also examined the possibility of movement to new towns.

Table 9 Scottish miners: 'What occupation would you like for your son?' Scottish Mining Communities (1945)

	No.	%
Anything but mining		47
Anything but mining, plus a trade		7
Anything but mining, plus a profession		1
Mining		3
Trades, eg bricklayer, carpenter		17
Professions, eg teacher, draughtsman		5
Let child choose		10
Undecided, not thought about it yet		7
Others		2
No answer		1
Sample of all boys still at school	635	100

In 1945 the Department of Health for Scotland, faced with a problem which combined industrial and planning aspects, brought in the Survey again. The coalmines in Lanarkshire were becoming exhausted, but new pits were being developed further east in Fife and other areas. Exploiting the new areas would only be possible if miners were willing to move. Under what circumstances could this happen? For the *Scottish Mining Communities Survey*, expanding and declining areas were selected, both in predominantly mining and mixed population areas. The Survey studied mobility patterns and the experience of other occupations of miners and members of their families, as well as attitudes to mining of miners and their wives. The latter were also asked what they thought of mining as an occupation for their sons. These facts were related to willingness to migrate. It was shown that the worse the housing situation, the more willing people were to move, but mining was regarded very unfavourably and a move to mining in a new area even more so. But when the possibility of different occupations in new areas was posed, willingness to move increased substantially, though much less so among older men, and the views of miners were different from those of their wives. Even when a very positive view of mining in new areas – 'new highly-mechanised pits' – was presented, substantial opposition remained. A feature of this survey was a questionnaire put to schoolboys expected to leave school in the near future which used the method of paired comparisons to assess opinion on a range of occupations, including mining. The results were no more encouraging than those from their parents. In 1948 the Survey examined rural depopulation in Scotland for the Department of Health.

These studies were all concerned with planning questions, and covered most kinds of living in areas and many different aspects of living. They combined different methods of data collection – interviewing, physical measurement, questionnaires – with the immense possibilities offered by population sampling techniques applied to many different populations. Together with the BRS work and the noise studies, they offered the possibility of a many-sided attack on the emerging problems of urban life. But this possibility was never realised: a different view was taken of research location and operation. After 1964 an enlarged Ministry of Housing and Local Government took over some of the research responsibilities, and in 1966 a decision was made that research related to planning and urban settlement would be undertaken by a new body, the Centre for Environmental Studies, jointly financed by the ministry and an American foundation. The Survey did not take part in the discussion, but it was clear that it would not be asked directly to do any more work in that field.

Housing statistics

Most of the surveys mentioned so far inevitably produced, as by-products, descriptions of the demographic and social characteristics of the households involved. This, with the possibilities of representative population sampling, meant that much information of interest to people other than the immediate sponsor emerged from surveys, data which would have been difficult or expensive to collect themselves. In 1945, a survey covering a stratified random sample of over 11,000 households drawn from rating lists yielded information which it was thought would be sufficiently useful to record in a separate report, *Population and Housing*. It gave nationally representative information about household composition, income groups by household size and some regional analyses, and as there had been no Census since 1931, it began to fill a gap. A similar report, *The British Household*, was produced in 1947.

These reports had not been requested by the authorities responsible for housing, and were mainly used by others. In fact, between the end of the war and 1957, only one survey concerned with housing in England and Wales had been requested. Waiting lists for public housing were maintained by local authorities. They provided one means of assessing the unsatisfied demand for housing at a time when it was thought necessary, because of shortages of men and materials, to give priority to other national needs and limit the number of houses built each year. It was thought, however, that some people would register with more than one authority, so a simple addition of all waiting lists would provide inflated figures. The Ministry of Health and Housing asked in 1949 for a survey to give the true picture: it showed not a great deal of duplication, so the large waiting-list total did not overestimate demand. Since there was no Census until 1951, it is difficult to understand why the Survey was not used to supplement in detail the very limited available information about many aspects of the housing situation.

After the 1951 election the constraints on housing were removed, and year after year the numbers of new houses, both private and public, increased. It was no doubt the feeling, which could not be verified by the limited supply of housing information, that a major change in the housing situation had occurred, which led the government into producing a proposal to begin the decontrol of rents, which had been controlled since the closing years of the first world war. Such a measure was very sensitive politically, so it was surprising that while the Bill was being debated the Ministry of Housing asked the Survey to design a study which would evaluate its effects. This was to be combined with the collection of information needed to update the Retail Price Index. Ministers understood that the survey could not be kept confidential, and their approval of it envisaged the possibility of publication.

The sample was to relate to all domestic rateable units in England and Wales except those owned by local authorities, which were not affected by the Rent Act. Since control limits varied, the sample would need to discriminate between London and elsewhere. The first sampling proposals made by the ministry did not meet the requirements. The Survey provided a much more detailed proposal involving variable sampling fractions so as to increase the numbers around the control limits: this was shown by subsequent results to be more appropriate. Since the intention was to evaluate the effect of the Act, a 'before and after' study was needed, which meant that the first stage had to be prepared in great haste so that it could describe the situation before the Act came into force. After some 20 months all the rating units for which full information was collected on the first round were revisited.

It had been thought that one possible result of rent decontrol would be that as rents rose, some households occupying more space than they wanted to afford would move, and their places would be taken by those needing more space and willing to pay more. The survey showed that there had, in fact, been a slight increase after the Act in rateable units that might be considered under-occupied. The 1956 White Paper,[2] which opened the discussion of the Bill, suggested that the immediate effect of the increases proposed would be to decontrol 750,000 accommodation units. The survey showed that the actual number decontrolled was 367–391,000, and the survey report points out 'It is clear that insufficient data were available to make reliable estimates at the time of the preparation of the White Paper'. The survey showed in some detail what had happened to the accommodation units which were decontrolled, and the survey results also made it possible to estimate how many new tenancies every year would be affected by another provision of the Act, by which new tenancies were automatically decontrolled. But most of the discussion of the Rent Act was about its possible effect on the actual level of rents, and in the period after it came into force a very wide range of 'guesstimates' were made. One of the main conclusions drawn from the survey report (published in full as a White Paper in 1960)[3] was that the information available to the Ministry of Housing was very limited. It seems that the Survey's contribution to the assessment of the Rent Act persuaded the ministry of the potentialities of survey research, since thereafter surveys on some aspects of housing have appeared in the Survey's programme almost every year.

Table 10 1957 and 1959 net rents paid for unfurnished non-service tenants (1959)

		Average 1957 rent			Average 1959 rent			Increase per cent
		£	s.	d.	£	s.	d.	
Metropolitan London								
Below control limit	Occupier unchanged	0	14	0	1	2	4	60
	New occupier	0	12	1	1	9	7	145
Above control limit	Occupier unchanged	1	12	5	2	9	2	52
	New occupier	1	16	3	3	13	2	102
Rest of England and Wales								
Below control limit	Occupier unchanged	0	9	4	0	13	1	40
	New occupier	0	12	9	1	0	2	58
Above control limit	Occupier unchanged	1	5	5	1	13	11	33
	New occupier	1	10	0	2	12	3	74

The 1960 *Housing Survey* was the first major housing survey covering the whole national stock of dwellings. It was designed to show the extent of under-occupation and overcrowding, the pattern of tenure and the distribution of amenities. When in 1962 the Ministry reviewed its available information for policy decisions, this survey featured very largely, as a possible contribution to be renewed every few years. The survey report showed that half of the rateable units in England and Wales were erected before 1919, and most of these belonged to the private rented sector. The great majority of local authority housing was, of course, built in the inter-war and post-war periods. The survey estimated the fitness and future life of the housing stock on the basis of three questions put to the local authorities about the rateable units in the sample. The local authorities were first asked to classify each rateable unit according to its fitness or unfitness. The second question asked them to estimate the expected life of the unit on the assumption that no repairs or improvements, other than ordinary maintenance, were carried out. The third asked whether the unit was likely to be pulled down due to town planning, redevelopment or any other scheme during the next five or five to 15 years. The estimate of 622,000 unfit

Table 11 Estimated number of dwelling rateable units, and the accommodation units therein, according to their fitness for habitation and approximate length of life in their present condition and the likelihood of their being pulled down within the next 15 years. Housing Survey (1960)

	Greater London			Other conurbations			Non-conurbation			England and Wales
	Rateable units	%	Accommodation units therein	Rateable units	%	Accommodation units therein	Rateable units	%	Accommodation units therein	Accommodation units therein
	Estimates, thousands		Estimates, thousands	Estimates, thousands		Estimates, thousands	Estimates, thousands		Estimates, thousands	Estimates, thousands
Fitness for habitation and approximate life, in present condition, of rateable unit:										
Unfit	47	2.0	57	243	8.9	254	303	3.5	311	622
Fit and with a life of										
under 5 years	31	1.3	38	30	1.1	30	142	1.6	142	210
5 but under 15 years	143	6.2	181	292	10.7	326	607	7.0	615	1,122
15 but under 30 years	519	22.3	712	446	16.3	484	1,708	19.6	1,760	2,956
30 years or over	1,588	68.2	1,837	1,722	63.0	1,755	5,964	68.3	6,135	9,727
Totals	2,328	100.0	2,825	2,733	100.0	2,849	8,724	100.0	8,963	14,637
Rateable units which are likely to be pulled down (for any reason) in the next:										
5 years	55	2.4	73	146	5.3	146	243	2.8	267	486
5–15 years	79	3.4	103	265	9.7	276	271	3.1	275	654
Those likely to remain after 5 years, according to present programme:	2,194	94.2	2,649	2,322	85.0	2,427	8,210	94.1	8,421	13,497
Totals	2,328	100.0	2,825	2,733	100.0	2,849	8,724	100.0	8,963	14,637

This Table includes unoccupied rateable and accommodation units. It also includes 30 rateable units in Greater London, and 33 outside, whose length of life was not estimated. These rateable units have been distributed, in proportion to the frequencies obtaining in the samples of which they form part, among the rest.

accommodation units which resulted from these questions showed reasonable agreement with the ministry's estimate of 600,000 in February 1961. Only small proportions of these unfit units were considered by the local authorities to be capable of repair at reasonable cost: one seventh in Greater London, none in the other conurbations, and about one in 15 in the non-conurbation areas.

In the period following the Rent Act a great deal of public attention focused on the use, maintenance and management of rented accommodation and the relations between occupiers of rented accommodation and private landlords. The problem was not only that of 'Rachmanism', and the terms of reference of the Milner Holland Committee, appointed in 1963 to consider the situation, were far wider. What was required was a review of rented housing conditions in London as a whole. The introduction to the committee's report commented that no official study of London's private landlords had been attempted before; 'it is on this aspect of rented housing that so much guesswork has been lavished and to us it was a matter of surprise that so little is known about it'. In reference to the information collected by the committee the report says 'The most important single survey, for our purpose, was in fact that undertaken for the Ministry by the Social Survey ... the *Housing Situation* in 1960'. This underlines the importance of designing any public survey with attention to those technical

Table 12 Overcrowding and under-occupation by type of letting. Privately rented accommodation in London (1961)

Privately renting households

	Controlled tenancy (unfurnished)			Not controlled				
				Unfurnished			Furnished	
	Singly occupied house	Singly occupied purpose built flat	Part of house or flat	Singly occupied house	Singly occupied purpose built flat	Part of house or flat	Mainly parts of houses	All types
Number of bedrooms* available to household	%	%	%	%	%	%	%	%
1	2	37	52	7	36	57	90	46
2	31	53	39	30	43	31	7	32
3 or more	67	10	9	63	21	12	3	22
	100	100	100	100	100	100	100	100
Bedrooms available compared with a standard	%	%	%	%	%	%	%	%
Two or more less than standard	2	3	5	2	3	6	4	4
One less than the standard	7	9	13	9	16	22	25	15
Equal to the standard	26	61	63	42	62	57	67	55
One more	38	27	17	26	15	14	3	19
Two or more in excess	27	—	2	21	4	1	1	7
	100	100	100	100	100	100	100	100

Table 12 (contd)

	Controlled tenancy (unfurnished)			Not controlled				
				Unfurnished			Furnished	
	Singly occupied house	Singly occupied purpose built flat	Part of house or flat	Singly occupied house	Singly occupied purpose built flat	Part of house or flat	Mainly parts of houses	All types
Number of habitable rooms* available to household	%	%	%	%	%	%	%	%
1	—	8	3	—	3	4	57	12
2	—	8	18	—	17	26	23	16
3	—	33	50	4	22	42	13	27
4	30	44	22	28	37	17	4	23
5	47	6	6	31	13	5	2	14
6 or more	23	1	1	37	8	6	1	8
	100	100	100	100	100	100	100	100
Average number of rooms per household	4.94	3.38	3.13	5.05	3.70	3.15	1.75	3.40
Persons in relation to habitable rooms								
Persons per room	%	%	%	%	%	%	%	%
Over 2	—	1	1	—	1	3	8	2
Over 1½ up to 2	—	3	3	—	3	7	18	6
Over 1 up to 1½	5	6	9	7	6	16	8	9
Number of persons equals rooms	8	20	19	14	25	21	49	23
Rooms per person								
Over 1 up to 1½	17	26	28	27	27	28	9	23
Over 1½ up to 2	28	26	18	26	25	16	6	19
Over 2	42	18	22	26	13	9	2	18
	100	100	100	100	100	100	100	100
Average number of persons per room	0.55	0.69	0.74	0.62	0.72	0.88	1.14	0.74
Proportion of overcrowded households according to part of the 1957 Housing Act	—	1%	3%	—	1%	4%	2%	2%
Sample	172	77	237	57	106	214	174	1,043†

*Only rooms available for sole use are counted. Unusable and any sublet rooms are excluded. A kitchen counts as a habitable room only if meals are eaten in it.
†Includes six cases which could not be assigned by type of letting.

details that ensure a survey's utility, not only for immediate purposes, but also as information available for subsequent public use. The survey designed for the committee, *Privately Rented Accommodation in London*, collected data from tenants and landlords and was able to use both the Rent Act survey and the 1960 housing survey to indicate change in the size and composition of the private rented sector. It examined the amenities of controlled and uncontrolled property, rents paid in relation to valuation levels and different types of accommodation and, in particular, it discussed the effect of the Rent Act between 1957 and 1963.

These three surveys initiated a continuing stream of studies. In 1964 the data collected in 1960 were updated and some new issues examined. The 1964 government reviewed the housing situation in the context of the shortlived National Plan in a White Paper, *Housing Programme 1965–1970*.[5] Once again it was noted 'reliable and up to date information is required – knowledge about population and household changes; about housing stock, its tenure, equipment and condition and the incidence of overcrowding . . . the Government's decision to carry out a sample census of Population and Housing in 1966 will materially improve national and local information . . . to supplement the census regular surveys will be carried out on a scale sufficient to provide at least for the most important items indicators of current trends. A series of sample surveys in depth will be undertaken into the housing conditions in the main conurbations'. In 1965 a housing survey was carried out in Scotland and a series of regional surveys followed. Much of the information collected in these studies helped with the *National Dwelling and Housing Survey* in 1977. The Survey lent its experience and technical expertise to the Department of the Environment for the design and operation of this immense survey designed to replace the cancelled Census of 1976. The survey was far beyond the capacity of the Social Survey and was carried out by a consortium of agencies working directly to the department. Much of the subject-matter of all these studies, has since 1971, been surveyed regularly in the multi-purpose General Household Survey, which thus provides a continuing series on the topics covered.

The 1965 White Paper emphasised the continuing decline of the privately rented sector. It drew attention to the way public housing had, since a peak in 1954, steadily declined and thus had failed to replace the disappearing private sector; it concluded 'the only remedy is an increase in public sector building'. Nevertheless, it also emphasised the importance of private rented housing, and the continuing public interest in this sector was marked by another review of the Rent Act, announced in 1975. In connection with this the Department of the Environment asked the Survey to survey the opinions of private landlords, private tenants and owner occupiers on letting. The *Attitudes to Letting Survey* in 1976 sampled households in a selection of wards where private renters outnumbered owner-occupying households. The intention was to concentrate fieldwork on areas where renters could be most economically located, and a consequence of this method was that no national picture could be drawn. The survey looked at different kinds of landlords – companies, housing associations, resident, non-resident – and the distribution of all rented property between them, as well as how the characteristics of rented property varied with type. The attitudes of tenants and landlords to letting were investigated, as were their opinions on how laws and regulations affected landlords' actions and willingness to let.

Table 13 Lettings by type of landlord by density of occupation. Attitudes to letting (1976)

Densely rented areas of England and Wales 1976

	Type of landlord making the letting						
Density of occupation	Resident individual	Non-resident individual	Company	Charity/ housing association	Non-charitable trust/executors	Public body etc	All types†
	%	%	%	%	%	%	%
Persons per room							
Less than ½	26	35	37	30	47	29	33
½ or more but less than 1	35	37	43	45	42	58	43
1	31	24	16	16	9	10	19
More than 1 but not more than 1½	4	2	2	9	2	3	3
More than 1½	2	2	2	—	—	—	2
	100	100	100	100	100	100	100
Information not obtained	2	—	1	—	—	—	7
	%	%	%	%	%	%	%
Bedrooms available compared with standard							
2 or more above standard	1	14	9	3	16	13	10
1 above standard	6	20	30	19	43	40	24
Equal to standard	74	56	55	70	37	41	56
1 below standard	19	9	5	7	4	5	9
2 or more below standard	—	1	1	1	—	1	1
	100	100	100	100	100	100	100
Information not obtained	4	5	5	—	4	2	30
Lettings for which tenant interview obtained	88	321	218	141	55	69	1,068†

In 1978, the scale of the 1977 *National Dwelling and Housing Survey* provided a sampling frame for a direct follow-up survey of the rented sector which unlike the attitudes survey provided, economically, nationally representative data. The report on this study was a combined effort of the Department of the Environment and the Survey. The 1977 survey also provided the basis for a group of follow-up studies on particular topics. Large-scale surveys (of up to $\frac{1}{2}$% of the population) give opportunities for economical studies of particular sections of the population. A large-scale labour force survey was being planned for spring 1977 and provided a convenient sampling frame for a rather special study. There had been growing concern about the apparent number of vacant dwellings in the country and the loss of housing implied. But estimates of the total number were difficult and information about ownership and other characteristics was scarce. *Empty Housing in England* looked at different methods used for making such estimates in much more detail than had been attempted elsewhere. The survey investigated ownership, regional distribution, the previous history of the properties, their condition and why they were vacant.

Noise

The rather ambitious survey of noise annoyance in central London, in 1961, was based on noise measurements made in 257 randomly selected locations in an area 35–40 miles around Charing Cross. Around these locations clusters of houses were chosen, and were supplemented by an additional random selection of households in the same areas. The inhabitants were asked about the amenities and disadvantages of their area, desires to move, other indications of low satisfaction and sources of annoyance. Detailed questions were then asked about noise from various sources and its ranking as a source of annoyance. The survey showed that traffic noise was more likely to be heard than other noise and was more likely to bother people than any other source of annoyance. The responses to questions and the physical measurements were assessed against a scale of personal susceptibility which helped to bring out the effect of personal differences on the responses. In this way further light was shed on the 1952 *Sound in Flats Survey* findings.

Noise was becoming an issue of some importance. Not only was road traffic and the concomitant nuisance growing; so was air traffic, and some highly successful pressure-groups were springing up. The government responded by setting up the Wilson Committee which in 1962 asked the Survey to study noise around London Airport. It was first necessary to obtain physical measurements of aircraft noise in the area of the survey and to assess the numbers of aircraft heard at any one point. These measurements and assessments were made by the Ministry of Aviation and were used extensively in analysing the other data collected during the survey. The measurements made it possible to demarcate areas in which noise from aircraft was at different levels – noise level strata. The sample drawn from the survey was designed to ensure that there was an adequate number of interviews in each stratum to enable comparisons to be made between the different noise levels.

Interviews were carried out in which informants were asked first about their general reactions to the neighbourhood, then what they considered to be its advantages or disadvantages. They were then asked to rate noise from all sources, followed by detailed questions about noise from aircraft and the inconvenience, if any, it gave them. The interview was designed so that the results of different questions could be combined. Where the answers formed consistent patterns it was possible to construct 'attitude scales' which could be used to measure, for example, degrees of annoyance. By this means it was possible to relate annoyance to the physical measurement of noise. The main conclusions were that first, there was a considerable correlation between the complaints that had been made in the past and the degree of annoyance revealed by the survey. The survey showed that the complainants were fairly representative of the people highly annoyed by aircraft noise. The main difference between the complainants and those who were equally annoyed but had not complained was that the complainants tended to come from those sections of the community who were likely to be more articulate.

Secondly, the survey provided a scale by which it was possible to measure the

Table 14 Distribution over noise levels of the total population and the 'annoyed' section of the population. Airport Noise Survey (1962)

PNdb stratum	Percentages			Absolute numbers	
	% of total population in stratum a	% of stratum annoyed* b	% of total population annoyed* c	No of people annoyed* d	No of people in stratum e
103+	3	68	2	28,000	42,000
100–102	6	51	3	42,000	84,000
97–99	7	48	3	42,000	98,000
94–96	13	36	5	70,000	182,000
91–93	27	24	6	84,000	378,000
88–90	22	23	5	70,000	308,000
85–87	11	16	2	28,000	154,000
Up to 85	11	10	1	14,000	154,000
Annoyed*			27	378,000	
Remainder			73	1,022,000	
Total	100		100	1,400,000	1,400,000

*For these data the 'annoyed' refers to those having a score on the annoyance scale of 3.5 or above. The population is that within a ten-mile radius of London Airport: 1,400,000 adults. Entries in column (c) are derived from those in columns (a) and (b) eg 68% of 3% gives 2% (rounded). The numbers in column (e) corresponds to the percentages in column (a) and those in column (d) to column (c).

degree of annoyance caused by aircraft noise. The area around Heathrow could be divided into inner zones containing comparatively few people, most of whom were intensely annoyed, and outer zones containing a large number of people of whom progressively smaller proportions were intensely annoyed. There were, in fact, people intensely annoyed by the noise at all levels of exposure covered in the survey: 10 per cent of the adult population in the outer zone were very annoyed. In contrast, about 25 per cent of the adult population of all zones were unconcerned by the noise whatever its level. The Wilson Committee agreed that the survey provided a basis for establishing a combined number and noise rating (NNR) defining the total noise exposure that caused annoyance. The relationships demonstrated between the annoyance scales and actual physical measurements led to a decision that a definite line could be drawn around part of the area, within which the annoyance and disturbance caused by aircraft noise could be regarded as so unreasonable that some kind of compensation should be made. The committee recommended in 1963 that the government should give grants to soundproof rooms in private dwellings in some areas around Heathrow, and eventually the Minister for Aviation announced 'we have decided to accept the principle ... grants amounting to 50% of the cost of soundproofing will be available'.[6]

Some years later an attempt was made to study noise pollution nationally, but this was less successful, mainly because of the difficulties of arranging acceptable sound measurements nationwide and because it proved difficult to focus the study on particular policy problems at a time of much change in departmental responsibilities. Nevertheless, it seemed from the general experience of noise studies that at least one feature of the environment could be examined to help judgments on appropriate policies. The government set up the Noise Advisory Council in 1970 to 'review progress in the prevention and abatement of noise'. By 1973 noise regulation had extended to the effects of new road building, and here again a physical measure became the deciding factor. In 1980 the Noise Advisory Council recommended an extension of government responsibility and noted that 'to gain some indication of the size of the problem various social survey reports and estimates of the number of people exposed to high levels of noise were examined',[7] and calculations were made of the numbers who would be affected by these recommendations, and their possible cost.

Mobility

The growing nuisance of traffic noise had drawn early attention, but was by no means the main problem presented by rapidly growing road traffic. Much more important in terms of inconvenience and public expenditure was the need to plan the use of roadways and to judge where capacity could be increased, either by traffic management schemes or road building. These problems became central to all consideration of urban development: this was most obvious in London, and in the early 1950s the London County Council was involved in a large-scale study organised by American traffic consultants.

Back in 1943 the Survey, as part of the attention to living problems highlighted by the war, had studied difficulties in getting to work. Some 10 years later, in the 1954 *London Travel Survey*, it began to develop the techniques necessary to describe population movements over large areas. The survey was organised jointly with the Building Research Station and the London Passenger Transport Board and was the first in a series of regular studies – National Travel Surveys – which was later taken over by the Ministry of Transport and then the Department of the Environment. Before the first of these national surveys was launched the Survey had paid considerable attention to the fastest growing traffic element, private motoring, in a series of quarterly surveys over the period 1961–4. The samples were based on private households and detailed information was collected for all cars and all license holders. For all household cars, the interviewer placed a mileage book for recording the driving done in the car on seven consecutive days following the day of the first interview, and noting the mileometer readings. A sub-sample of recorded days was chosen on which to collect, by interview, more details of journeys made and passengers carried. The data produced was related to information about cars and their drivers, the timing and purpose of journeys and the mileage involved. A useful by-product of these surveys, and of the very careful attention given to design and recording procedures, was that the mileage and other driving experience data for different kinds of drivers gave baselines for calculating true exposures to the risk of road accidents.

The surveys also helped to define the motoring contribution to attempts to cover all means of transport for all purposes in the National Travel Surveys carried out in 1963–4, 1965–6, 1972–3 and 1975–6.[8] The 1972–3 survey was carried out completely by the Survey, but after the development stages the others were handled elsewhere. The purpose of these surveys was ambitious. They tried, with some success, to describe all journeys made for all purposes by all modes of transport – private, public, cycle or pedestrian, using a combination of record and interview. Anything less comprehensive would not have shown the choices made between alternatives, which decided the overall pattern of movements and which gave traffic engineers, planners and economists an adequate base for decisions on major public expenditures. But although the information helped to describe the current situation, it is not clear what other studies would have been needed to predict future traffic problems.

Perhaps even more ambitious was a survey which since 1961 has grown into a major Survey undertaking – the *International Passenger Survey*. Tourism has in the last two decades become a major item in the UK balance of payments as more citizens travel abroad on business and holidays and more visitors spend money in this country. In 1961 the Tourism Committee of the EEC recommended the sample survey method for collecting tourism statistics. A relaxation of exchange control made estimating UK residents' expenditure abroad difficult, and the large credits earned from visitors impossible to calculate. At the same time it was becoming clear that the growing political importance of emigration and immigration data needed a more adequate base than was provided by the methods then available. It seemed that both migration and expenditure data could be

Table 15 International migration: occupation, 1971 to 1980. International Passenger Survey

United Kingdom thousands

Year	All persons	Professional and managerial	Manual and clerical	Students	Housewives	Others	Children	Employees as a percentage of all persons
Immigrants								
1971	199.7	43.4	55.4	32.4	24.2	11.0	33.3	49.5
1972	221.9	50.0	55.9	35.2	22.6	14.7	43.4	47.7
1973	195.7	47.1	56.8	29.0	16.9	11.5	34.5	53.1
1974	183.8	48.0	45.8	31.0	16.1	6.8	36.1	51.0
1975	197.2	48.7	50.3	28.2	23.2	13.2	33.5	50.2
1976	191.3	52.2	41.1	29.3	25.7	8.6	34.4	48.8
1977	162.6	43.2	37.3	25.6	20.4	6.1	29.9	49.5
1978	187.0	45.6	32.5	35.5	23.9	9.4	40.1	41.8
1979	194.8	52.8	34.7	34.8	26.7	8.1	37.7	44.9
1980	173.7	44.5	32.4	29.5	24.3	6.9	36.1	44.3
Emigrants								
1971	240.0	51.0	87.2	11.0	30.6	9.5	50.7	57.6
1972	233.2	49.1	83.7	15.3	24.7	13.5	46.8	57.0
1973	245.8	51.1	87.0	11.7	30.9	13.1	52.0	56.2
1974	269.0	62.1	96.9	13.2	30.9	9.0	56.9	59.1
1975	238.3	60.4	73.5	4.7	27.3	17.1	55.3	56.2
1976	210.4	70.3	55.9	9.5	22.2	11.0	41.4	60.0
1977	208.7	65.8	61.8	17.6	24.4	6.7	32.3	61.2
1978	192.4	55.5	56.1	23.7	20.4	6.4	30.4	58.0
1979	188.6	57.9	51.8	26.2	17.2	4.9	30.7	58.1
1980	229.1	64.8	62.3	29.2	24.3	6.0	42.4	55.5
Balance								
1971	−40.4	−7.6	−31.8	+21.4	−6.4	+1.4	−17.4	
1972	−11.4	+0.9	−27.9	+19.9	−2.1	+1.2	−3.4	
1973	−50.1	−4.0	−30.2	+17.2	−14.0	−1.6	−17.5	
1974	−85.3	−14.1	−51.1	+17.8	−14.8	−2.2	−20.7	
1975	−41.2	−11.7	−23.2	+23.5	−4.1	−3.9	−21.8	
1976	−19.1	−18.1	−14.8	+19.7	+3.5	−2.4	−7.0	
1977	−46.1	−22.7	−24.5	+8.0	−4.0	−0.6	−2.4	
1978	−5.5	−9.9	−23.5	+11.8	+3.4	+3.0	+9.7	
1979	+6.2	−5.0	−17.1	+8.6	+9.5	+3.2	+7.0	
1980	−55.4	−20.3	−29.9	+0.2	—	+0.9	−6.3	

125

provided by the same survey, provided the difficult sampling problems of surveying a moving population transported by various means could be solved. The survey was sponsored by the Board of Trade and the Population Statistics Division of the GRO. Later, the Department of Trade and Industry and the CSO became the regular users of the expenditure data and the OPCS (which by then embraced the GRO and the Survey) the principal user of migration data. In the first year a stratified random sample of international air routes was made. Gradually, coverage was extended to all the principal sea and air routes and eventually 200–250,000 interviews were being done each year. The deployment of interviewers was and is a major task, so much so that initially a separate branch of the Survey was developed for this one large study. Interviewing at ports is related to the expected volume of passengers, interviewing costs and sampling variance: the number of shifts at each port throughout the year is determined accordingly. Passengers arriving or departing are counted, and every 1 in Nth passenger is interviewed, where N is fixed for each port and ranges from 1:1 to 1:50. A very short interview is critical: one of the main conditions of the work at very busy sea and airports is that it does not impede the free movement of passengers. The overall response rate, despite very difficult interviewing conditions, has remained at well over 80% for many years.

Notes

[1]'Recent Research on Sound Insulation in Houses and Flats', *RIBA Journal*, July 1954.
[2]HMSO, 1956.
[3]*Rent Act 1957: Report of an Inquiry*, Cmnd 1246, HMSO, 1960.
[4]Milner Holland Committee 1963 *Privately Rented Accommodation in London*.
[5]*Housing Programme 1965–1970*, Cmnd 2838, HMSO, 1965.
[6]*Hansard*, Col. 413/4, 10 March 1965.
[7]*Noise Advisory Council: A Study of Government Noise Insulation Policies*, HMSO, 1980.
[8]P R Smethurst, 'The National Travel Surveys', *Town Planning Review*, April 1967.

8  Health and social services

THE SURVEY'S CONTRIBUTION to the development of health services began very early and has continued over the greater part of its history. Over several generations there has been concern with nutrition, with measures designed to prevent illness, with the recruitment and deployment of nursing staff and doctors, and with the organisation of help for various forms of physical incapacity. In the war years these problems became more acute, but the national will to mobilise all available resources for war purposes was also reflected in many fields of civil administration, and in a determination on the part of the health authorities to use any available resources and methods to ensure the welfare of the home front. This resulted in a very positive attitude towards the major problems of health service administration, to which the Survey staff were able to respond.

After the war, discussion of plans for a National Health Service seemed to many a natural development of wartime determination to do what was necessary to provide a full range of health services for all. There is no doubt that the collaboration on wartime interests between the Survey and the Ministry of Health played a substantial part in the decision to maintain the Survey as a continuing part of government in 1946. Even after the major setback following the change of government in 1951, the responsible departments still sponsored an array of surveys, sometimes developing work which had been started earlier and sometimes opening up topics which had not previously been tackled. The main wartime contributions were in two areas: nutrition and health education. The ministries of health and food had a major joint interest in observing and maintaining scientifically acceptable levels of nutrition in the whole population.

Nutrition

The Ministry of Food's main concern was with distribution, but since supplies depended greatly on shipping it had also to ensure that the best use was made of what was available. This led to a flow of publicity encouraging people to 'eat more potatoes' or mixed-grain wheatmeal bread, or other commodities that were in stock. It also meant continuing concern with the public reception of messages related to distribution or to any difficulties. The Survey report on wartime food problems in 1941 examined some buying habits, queuing, milk and egg consumption and reactions to Ministry of Food advertising. Wheatmeal bread had been bought by less than a quarter of all households, and the regions where more people had tried it had the largest proportions giving it up. About one third were unable to identify it, the proportions ranging from one quarter in the higher social category to half in the lower social groups. The report investigated the effect of publicity and attitudes towards this attempt to change food habits. Marked differences were shown in regional and social group consumption of milk and eggs, and the report attempts to show if various priority schemes were guaranteeing consumption by the groups for which they were intended. Some 20% of households had queued during the seven days before the interview, ranging from about 37% in Scotland to 8% in the eastern region, but many objected to queuing and did not do so, while minorities of those who queued did so four or more times in the week covered. In order of frequency, fish, cakes and confectionery, meat, biscuits and groceries were the commodities for which people queued. A clear majority of housewives preferred 'the wireless' as a means of communicating information about food – 60%, compared with 36% choosing newspapers. While only very small proportions had experienced most of the other methods used to explain and help, 75% remembered seeing the *Food Facts* notices the ministry inserted regularly in newspapers.

A very different survey for the Ministry of Food, *A Typical Day's Meals* (1942), concentrated on particular groups in the working population and sought information about the food items they had consumed in the previous day and where they had eaten them; whether packed meals were taken to work, and attitudes towards canteens, British restaurants and cafés. The analysis by occupation showed some major differences, but perhaps the most interesting feature of the report was the attempt to classify types of meal in terms of supposed nutritional adequacy, and to examine by this means the intakes of different occupation groups. This study was seen as a preliminary effort in a field which required much more precise measurement, but it does give an interesting description of a basic activity under very difficult circumstances.

During 1942 and 1943 the Ministry of Health undertook a vitamin feeding experiment with elementary schoolchildren in some English towns, in order to test the effect of a daily intake of multivitamin capsules. It was necessary to get a measure of the nutritional value of the children's ordinary weekly diets: quantitative methods were required, and following experimental work by Dr Bransby of the Ministry of Health, homely measures were proposed. Tablespoons, teaspoons or cups were used for vegetables, breakfast cereals, jam, sugar and milk, and portion sizes of meat, cheese, potatoes and puddings were compared with actual-size photographs. Fat used as spread was weighed or estimated by interviewers and all food supplements and sweets were recorded. School meal helpings were obtained from schools, and Survey interviewers visited homes at least every other day. The quantities obtained in this way were translated into nutrients. It was realised that these homely measures would certainly not be as accurate as weighing, but experimental work gave an indication of the possible extent of over- and underestimation. On the whole the method led to some

Table 16 Milk consumption (1942)

Regional distribution	Scotland	S Wales	N Midlands	NW	N & NE	Midlands	SE & London	South	SW	East	Total
						Percent					
Less than 2 pints	35.3	18.3	12.2	15.6	27.0	8.1	22.4	13.0	9.2	11.5	19.0
2–3½ pints	49.5	69.0	60.1	59.0	58.1	75.2	62.4	61.1	65.9	5.8	61.2
3½–5 pints	10.3	8.9	16.9	17.2	10.2	12.4	11.4	16.7	13.4	16.7	13.1
More than 5 pints	4.9	3.8	10.8	8.2	4.1	4.3	3.8	9.2	11.5	13.8	6.7
Sample	*329*	*180*	*213*	*424*	*443*	*259*	*518*	*162*	*216*	*174*	
						Percent					
3½ or more pints per head	15.2	12.7	27.7	25.4	14.9	16.7	15.2	25.9	24.9	30.5	19.8

Distribution in special groups	A	B	C	D	Total
			Percent		
Less than 2 pints	14.2	9.6	16.9	27.7	19.0
2–3 pints per head	52.5 (±7.4)	63.1 (±4.2)	63.4 (±0.9)	58.7 (±1.1)	61.2
3½–5 pints per head	19.1 (±5.8)	15.7 (±1.0)	13.4	10.4	13.1
More than 5 pints per head	14.2 (±5.1)	11.3 (±0.6)	6.3	3.2	6.7
Sample	*183*	*573*	*1,087*	*1,061*	

Table 17 Consumption of eggs (1942)

	Scotland	S Wales	N Midlands	NW	N & NE	Midlands	SE & London	South	SW	East	Total
						Percent					
Median	0.86	1.83	0.84	0.80	0.83	0.96	0.84	1.75	0.75	0.97	0.80
Upper quartile	0.43	0.61	0.42	0.40	0.42	0.48	0.42	0.38	0.39	0.49	0.43
Lower quartile	2.87	3.89	3.71	2.48	2.2	3.05	2.13	1.77	1.80	2.96	2.46
Sample	*313*	*182*	*220*	*424*	*454*	*276*	*457*	*164*	*217*	*184*	*289*

overestimation but gave usable results that could be analysed in some detail, and made a contribution to the developing work at the Ministry of Health. It was realised early on that cooked foods would lose some of their nutrients during preparation: an attempt was made to estimate such losses by getting housewives to describe how they prepared vegetables, what proportions were thrown away, how they were cooked and what was done with the cooking liquids. The Dunn Nutritional Laboratory of the Medical Research Council then reproduced these methods in the laboratory and calculated nutrient losses.

Table 18 Average intake for one week of nutrients expressed as a proportion of League of Nations standard, analysed by food expenditure group. Typical days meals (1943)

	Food expenditure group (Calcium, Vit A and Vit C not weighted according to age)		
	Expenditure per head, per week		
	Less than 11/-	11/- less than 15/-	15/- less than 25/-
	%	%	%
Calories	95	105	117
Protein (A+V)	103	111	123
Calcium	56	64	65
Iron	95	109	116
Vit A and Carotene (inc Cod Liver Oil)	92	132	126
Vit B1	126	134	150
Vit C	113	149	152
Total sample	*43*	*124*	*103*

From 1942 onwards the Ministry of Food carried out, through a commercial agency, a food expenditure survey using a household budget method. Later, this survey became a Survey responsibility. In addition to recording expenditure the study, later called the *National Food Survey*, also weighed foodstuffs which were translated into nutrients. In 1957 fieldwork and coding on the NFS was contracted out, to free resources for the new continuous Family Expenditure Survey. These investigations brought nutrition studies into people's homes, and by devising methods which could be applied to selected large groups they produced data on which judgments could be made of many facets of nutrition affecting the population. The demand for such studies from the two ministries reflected the urgent pressures of keeping a population fed adequately, and also the extension of scientific nutritional work to ensure that national decisions about available foodstuffs could be given a rational foundation. They led to a public concern for adequate nutrition which continued after the war. In 1947 a

Table 19 Average intake for one week of nutrients expressed as a proportion of League of Nations standard, analysed by age of child. Typical days meals (1943)

	Age of child								
	5 yrs old	6 yrs old	7 yrs old	8 yrs old	9 yrs old	10 yrs old	11 yrs old	12 yrs old	13 yrs old
	%	%	%	%	%	%	%	%	%
Calories	140	139	119	114	109	102	99	95	91
Proteins	147	148	127	125	115	111	105	99	93
Calcium	61	67	56	64	63	58	62	63	65
Iron	125	122	110	109	100	100	107	100	94
Vit A and Carotene*	112	135	103	132	115	110	119	128	126
Vit B1	167	164	158	143	141	135	133	126	119
Vit C	117	127	117	137	140	137	154	157	160
Sample	23	45	39	59	68	40	40	82	26

* Cod Liver Oil included.

study of housewives' nutrition, using a food weighing method, was made in four areas. Because of doubts about older people's diets in 1950, a study was done in collaboration with the Department of Social and Industrial Medicine of the University of Sheffield, which had also arranged medical examinations for the whole sample. The level of physical fitness could therefore be related to food intake.

Perhaps the most detailed analysis of nutritional data by then was the study of young children's diets (1951), which was based on samples drawn from children's ration records. It had two main purposes. The first was to measure the intake and source of the main nutrients of five age-groups up to five years of age. This was compared with intakes recommended by the BMA in 1950. The data from this survey was compared also with pre-war nutritional work, and the conclusion drawn was that 'on the whole it appeared that the nutritional level found in the present enquiry for a representative sample of children was as good as the pre-war nutritional level of middle-class children'. The second purpose was more narrowly focused, and is stated in the first sentence of the introduction: 'The need for the survey arose from the Treasury's desire to reduce dollar expenditure on orange juice'. Various supplements (described as welfare foods) had been made available for children and pregnant women, including orange juice, as a source of ascorbic acid (vitamin C). The problem was to decide what contribution this supplementary orange juice made to ascorbic acid levels. The first part of the study provided detailed information about the sources of measured nutrients, and within these data the intake of Ministry of Food orange juice could be separated and related to various categorisations of the population.

Thus it seemed 'the proportion of children taking MOF orange juice increased from 13% in the £5 a week group to 60% in the over £10 a week group'.

Welfare foods survived that inspection and in 1955, following a transfer of distribution to local authorities and an apparent decline in take-up, another study was launched. The *Take-up of Welfare Foods Survey* found that the proportion taking up some welfare food during the three months prior to interview was almost identical to that found in 1951. 40–50% of under fives were not taking the ministry's orange juice and higher proportions were not taking cod liver oil. About 40% of expectant mothers had neither orange juice nor vitamin tablets during the week prior to interview. But there was little evidence that any change in habits was due to the change in distribution arrangements. The report examines the effect on breastfeeding and the use of National Dried Milk of the post-war growth in use of proprietary brands of baby foods. There had been an apparent decline in breastfeeding from 1953 onwards and an increase in the use of proprietary dried milks. This survey followed a period of sharp contraction in the work of the Survey following the 1951 change of government. Despite this, the 1955 survey showed that some continuity had been preserved and this made it possible to note change in habits since the first survey. The work on diets of pre-school children and expectant mothers was renewed in 1967 when rationing and other constraints on supplies had gone and a general raising of living standards had taken place. It is interesting to link with the early work two later studies on infant feeding.

The early arrangements for observing and advising on nutrition had given way to a more formal Committee on Medical Aspects of Food Policy located in the DHSS. In 1974, following a review of infant feeding and the effects of current practices on the wellbeing of infants, the committee concluded that human milk was the best food for babies and therefore recommended that mothers should be encouraged to breastfeed their babies, preferably for four to six months. The Ministry adopted this recommendation as official policy. It appeared that there had been a decline in breastfeeding at least until the early 1970s, by when it seemed that the majority of mothers made no attempt to breastfeed. But there was a lack of up to date information on the topic and the department asked for a survey which would provide a base from which to monitor the success of the policy. The survey *Infant Feeding* in 1975, with follow-up surveys in 1976, showed that about 51% of babies had been breastfed initially. This was higher than might have been expected from other work, mainly small local studies. Analysis showed that first births, education beyond 18, husbands in non-manual occupations and residence in London or the south east were all associated independently with a higher incidence of breastfeeding. The report shows how estimates of breastfeeding standardised for these factors could be calculated, and this method showed that, taking other factors into account, single mothers were much less likely to breastfeed.

This first survey was followed five years later by another more limited one. A feasibility study showed that in terms of response rate and the quality of data collected a postal method would be suitable, except for attitude questions, which were therefore excluded. The 1980 postal sample produced results which compared well on all main variables with the 1975 survey. There had been a significant increase in breastfeeding, from 51%–67%, and the change was greater with second or later babies. Although similar differences according to social group, education and region were still found, the prevalence of breastfeeding was greater at all ages up to nine months. This survey showed how determined action by professional officials could, in a relatively short period, lead to significant changes in widespread social habits. It also demonstrated the importance of associated attitudes and thus of health education.

Health education

The wartime nutrition campaigns were science-based despite their utilitarian objectives. Some of the early surveys were equally focused on very immediate problems. In 1942 the Ministry of Health, concerned with what was thought to be the growing problem of venereal disease, decided to break the taboo on public discussion of the problem. A broadcast by the Chief Medical Officer was followed by parliamentary debates, a national conference and subsequently by a substantial press and poster publicity campaign. It was important for the ministries of health and information to know the public reaction to this activity and whether its objectives had been attained. A first survey soon after the advertisements appeared showed that 86% of a sample aged between 14 and 50 claimed to have noticed them, and 92% were in full agreement with the publicity given to the subject. This public support encouraged the Ministry of Health to increase the scale of publicity, and a more detailed survey, the *Campaign Against Venereal Diseases*, was organised to assess effectiveness. The sample for this study was aged 16 to 60, and respondents were selected by occupation group at places of work in all regions. Housewives were interviewed in their homes. Only about 1% of contacts resulted in a refusal to respond but, given the topic, it seemed important to get a good record of response, and interviewers were asked to note their impressions of respondents' attitudes to being interviewed. Although all interviewers were women there was little difference between the attitudes of men and women. The survey showed that the publicity had indeed been widely noticed – more so than that of other campaigns at about the same time, and proportions around 90% agreed with the actions of the Ministry of Health. The effectiveness of the advertisements was tested by questions about their contents. Respondents were asked if they knew the names of the diseases, how they were spread, what were the symptoms and what might be their results. Analysing this data, the conclusion was drawn that the majority who claimed knowledge did have reasonable knowledge. Only small proportions claiming knowledge showed by subsequent answers that their knowledge was limited, and this was balanced by a small proportion initially denying knowledge (perhaps through shyness) who showed later that they had a certain amount of accurate information. This study showed that, provided a political lead was given, the Survey could tackle a sensitive topic in a manner which did not embarrass a commissioning department and which opened the way for wider communication with the population.

Another problem that could only be solved by enlisting wide attention and prompt action was the need for immunisation of children against diphtheria, and a series of surveys was conducted in 1942, 1945 and 1951 to try to find out why the proportion of children immunised had not risen to the level necessary to keep the disease under control, and had indeed threatened to fall much lower. It was shown very early that while a majority of mothers, despite the publicity campaigns, could not say what caused diphtheria or what were its dangers, two thirds could say how it could be prevented. This was almost equally true in 1942 among 'higher' and 'lower' social groups, in different regions of the country and in areas with good or bad immunisation records. At the time of the early enquiry, about 17% of immunisation had been done by the doctor for payment, and here there was a sharp social gradient. All three studies examined the use of clinics and publicity issued through schools as well as the general media. The 1945 study noted, as had the earlier one, that 'a considerable amount of ignorance as to the cause of diphtheria had not prevented mothers from having their children immunised'. The series of surveys, in effect, monitored progress and documented change in public consciousness as well as the part played by schools, doctors and clinics over the period. They showed that some kinds of publicity directing attention to action produced positive results where accompanied by other appropriate administrative measures.

Smoking and alcohol

In another area which later became one of major concern, policy and associated action developed more slowly. A cautious statement on the association between cigarette smoking and lung cancer was made by the Ministry of Health in February 1954. There was a rather more definite reply to parliamentary questions in May 1956,[1] but the Minister at that time resisted the suggestion that an information campaign 'as widespread as the campaign against diphtheria and in favour of immunization' would be appropriate 'in the present state of knowledge'. Between that time and the mid 1960s the public stance on tobacco smoking relied mainly on individual actions, influenced increasingly by a growing adverse public sentiment. Survey work on this topic began in 1964 after a government decision to sponsor major publicity campaigns designed to influence attitudes. The series of surveys of adults, adolescents and schoolboys carried out for the Ministry of Health examined behaviour and opinion in great detail, and attempted to construct a coherent set of propositions about why smoking began, the conflicting attitudes of smokers, why some people gave up and so on, all shaped to provide some kind of rational basis for the public education campaign. The survey report, *Adult and Adolescent Smoking* (1964) began, as do most Survey studies of attempts at public persuasion, by examining the pattern of behaviour, and in particular the initiation and growth of the smoking habit among different groups. The report noted a powerful trend towards early experiments with smoking on the part of successive generations of females which was examined as part of the general relationship between initiation and becoming a regular smoker. The effect of social factors was examined and the attitudes of respondents' parents were shown to 'have an important bearing on smoking behaviour'; even more important was the actual behaviour of the parents.

The report argued that if people could say when they smoked this would give useful clues as to why they smoked. It developed a typology of smokers on this basis and suggested that different strategies for deterring different kinds of smokers would be more efficient than any generalised appeals. The behaviour and habits of the groups distinguished by this typology were tested against all the other data, factual and attitude, collected during the survey and helped to indicate the 'most profitable target groups for antismoking persuasion'. Possible appeals were tested against the data, and the report warned against some as likely to produce a 'boomerang' reaction because there was too much of a gap between the argument of the persuader and the standpoint of the recipient.

The work on adolescents and adults was followed by a study in 1967 of schoolboys aged between 11 and 15. Schools in the sample in which previous health education campaigns had been conducted seemed to have had little success in reducing smoking despite the high level of awareness of lung cancer and its association with cigarette smoking. Children who smoked had strong defences against giving up – 'rationalizations for continued smoking gathered strength as smoking experience increased'. The report, *The Young Smoker*, showed that smoking experience was associated with poor academic achievement. Those who fell behind others in their work tended to be the first to take up smoking. Smokers were attracted much more than non-smokers to the social life of older teenagers and such differences could emerge at relatively low levels of smoking. Some main motivations for smoking were identified and were shown to become more powerful as the boys grew older and among those attending secondary-modern and comprehensive schools rather than grammar schools. Among relevant factors were parents' permissiveness in allowing smoking in their own homes, but the main attraction of smoking for these schoolboy smokers was 'the toughness that it represents'.

Subsequent surveys studied smoking among health professionals as the most obvious images of the message about the connection of smoking and ill health. In 1981 another major study of current attitudes and behaviour was carried out. Meanwhile, the inauguration of the General Household Survey in 1971 facilitated monitoring of the more basic facts about smoking behaviour.

Comparable surveys on alcohol and its effects began much later, in 1969. In 1968, however, the Home Office, concerned by the substantial increase in offences of drunkenness, asked the Survey to investigate the social factors behind these trends. Discussions took place with chief constables and led to a decision to conduct an investigation among the police themselves as firsthand observers. The resulting study is described later (p 227).

The first study of general alcohol consumption was designed and carried out in collaboration with an academic researcher at Strathclyde University. In 1972

Table 20 Cigarette smoking by sex: 1972 to 1982. General Household Survey (1982)

Persons aged 16 and over (Great Britain)

	1972	1974	1976	1978	1980	1982
	Percentages					
Men						
Current smokers						
Light (under 20 per day)	28	25	22	22	21	20
Heavy (20 or more per day)	24	26	24	23	21	18
Total current smokers	52	51	46	45	42	38
Ex-regular smokers	23	23	27	27	28	30
Never or only occasionally smoked	25	25	27	29	30	32
Base = 100 per cent	10,351	9,852	10,888	10,480	10,454	9,199
Women						
Current smokers						
Light (under 20 per day)	30	28	24	23	23	22
Heavy (20 or more per day)	11	13	14	13	13	11
Total current smokers	41	41	38	37	37	33
Ex-regular smokers	10	11	12	14	14	16
Never or only occasionally smoked	49	49	50	49	49	51
Base = 100 per cent	12,143	11,480	12,554	12,156	12,100	10,641

the first more usual population study was done in Scotland. This was followed by a survey in England and Wales six years later, and in 1981, using an experimental design, an attempt was made to see why some regional health authorities had a much higher incidence of alcohol-related problems than others. The main thrust of this study was to show if regional differences could be explained by the different types of neighbourhood regions contain. The concomitant differences in social pattern and behaviour might, it was thought, help to indicate the most suitable kinds of publicity aimed at restraining alcohol consumption.

Family planning

In his 1968 report the Chief Medical Officer of the DHSS emphasised the importance of family planning to family wellbeing: 'about 200,000 unwanted pregnancies are thought to occur each year ... There is need for a systematic health education campaign involving mass media to educate people in the benefits of planned parenthood'. These statements encapsulated the major changes that had taken place in official outlook over previous decades. Having originally accepted the idea of family planning for health reasons only, and empowering local authorities to provide accordingly, the Ministry of Health, as a result of growing voluntary action and propaganda, changed its stance. The activities of the Family Planning Association (FPA) were of continuing importance from 1936 onwards, as were the rather positive recommendations of the Royal Commission on Population in 1949. Even so, when the NHS was created there was no mention of family planning. It was given respectability in 1956 when a Minister of Health visited the FPA premises for the first time. In 1960 the FPA saw half a million patients, and at about this time the pill was introduced in Britain. Previous taboos began to disappear quickly. The 1967 Abortion Bill increased the level of public discussion and pressure on local authorities to give more urgent attention to a memorandum from the ministry drawing their notice to the importance of family planning and encouraging them to cooperate actively with the FPA. At that time local authorities were only authorised to provide services for married women who had medical reasons for avoiding further pregnancies. A Private Member's Bill in 1967 widened the powers of local authorities and brought them under the cover of the NHS. It also led to a request to local authorities to report on action taken.

In June 1968 the FPA published an account of what local authorities had done to implement the 1967 Act. Three quarters of them had set up only restricted services or taken no action. About 15% had set up a full service. The FPA did its best to help local authorities by negotiating agency services with them. In 1971 the DHSS negotiated an agency scheme between the FPA and the hospitals, and for the FPA to provide a domiciliary scheme for local authorities. The central importance of the FPA in actual service provision seems clear, as is the policy of the ministry in sponsoring its activities. By 1974 the FPA had increased to around 1,000 clinics, and in fact prepared the ground for the incorporation of all family-planning services in the reorganised NHS in 1974. By this time developing policy had survived many changes of minister.

The two relevant studies made by the Survey in 1970 and 1975 must be viewed against this background. Of the first survey the Minister said in March 1970 that it would 'cover all aspects of the service including publicity . . . to find out whether the facilities now available meet the requirements of the people who use them and also ways in which they might be improved . . . to enquire of those who do not use the existing services to find out whether other sorts of provision are needed or whether there is no expressed demand for services amongst these people'. The survey would serve as a basis for future guidance to local health authorities on ways in which the family-planning service should be developed. By the time the survey *Family Planning Services* was ready to begin, another minister in another administration was in office, but he too authorised the survey. To some extent the design of the survey drew on the experience of the *Family Intentions Survey* which is discussed on page 213 and which included questions about contraceptive practices. Married women aged 16 to 40 and single women aged 16 to 35 were interviewed. It was found that 24% of married women were currently using the services and 43% had never used them. About one third of those who had never used them and a quarter of past users considered it unnecessary to do so. Forty-four percent of women who had never used contraceptives said they knew of no readily available source of contraceptive knowledge, 36% knew of no clinic and 24% knew of 'nowhere' as a source of information. Clinics were considered less accessible than GPs. The report examined in some detail stated difficulties in reaching various services. Over 40% of past working-class users of the service thought that clinics were expensive, but cost does not seem to have been a deterrent to the majority of never users since most of them did not know the cost of clinic charges, and 68% did not know what their GP would charge.

Experience and opinions on current services were examined. On the whole, current users were more likely to hold favourable views of the service than past or never users, and the reports of those who had used each source of advice showed that clinics, in comparison with GPs, were less accessible, more costly and less attractive in that they provided less privacy and were more embarrassing to use. The 1970 report said 'It seems fairly clear that inadequacies in the service deterred some women from seeking advice and drove away others once they had done so and on the whole clinics had more disadvantages than GPs . . . however 38% of the never users did not expect sympathetic advice from their doctors'. The report considered what would have to be done to attract more people to clinics. The use and acceptability of different contraceptive methods was considered. About one third of the women at risk were using either the least reliable method (withdrawal and safe period) or none. About one third were using the pill or intra-uterine devices. Use of the pill was increasing, and it was the most commonly used method by those married after 1965. Past planning failures were examined. It seemed that only 61% of last pregnancies were planned and the report considers 'high risk' groups in this context.

Six per cent of single women were current users and 10% had used contraceptive services at some time. Only 32% of never users who were at risk knew of a convenient source of advice; 42% said they knew of a clinic but only a little over a half of these knew its exact whereabouts. Like married women more of them considered clinics more difficult to use than GPs, but over half of the never users at risk who expected difficulty said the trouble was locating a clinic. The report said 'at the present time ignorance or uncertainty take precedence over and colour most other aspects of acceptability' and discusses the consequent effects. Changes in contraceptive practice as age increased, and attitudes towards different methods and future family intentions were also examined.

This first survey was made before the services were integrated with the NHS and therefore reflected the period when, through the FPA, there had been a gradual increase in available services but fairly widespread gaps in availability. By 1975 contraceptive services had become available from the NHS free of charge, and the DHSS accordingly felt the need to get some measure of the new situation. In asking for a second survey the department noted the full cost of a comprehensive, free family-planning service and said that this expenditure 'justifies further enquiry along the lines of the 1970 study . . . which has proved invaluable in the creation of a family-planning service within the reorganised NHS and in providing advice to the new health authorities on its development'. The request noted some of the possible changes in attitude and sexual behaviour and in particular noted 'the difficulty of planning to meet the needs for contraception of young women between 16–20'.

The new survey was planned accordingly and the analysis of the resulting material was discussed in some detail with departmental officials. Apart from extending the age range covered the sampling method was the same, and the same method of cohort analysis was used to show how behaviour had changed within and between generations. The report showed a considerable increase in the proportion of women using the services and that use had become more persistent. In between 1970 and 1975 the use of the service had grown in every cohort and social class; it was suggested that the initial upsurge in use of the services occurred at about the time the pill was introduced and that it had increased at a constant rate ever since. Since free services were only introduced in 1974 and 1975 it was not possible to show if this had accelerated the rate of increase in use. 'The experience of women using the service was similar in both surveys; each outlet, GPs and clinics, were more or less as easy or difficult, pleasant or discomforting to use in both years'. However the services were catering for many more women in 1975. There had been changes in the contraceptive method used: 'The increase in service use was accompanied by a corresponding growth in the use of the principal service specific method – the Pill and, to a lesser extent, the IUD. Use of the less effective methods had declined but so also had use of the relatively effective condom. Whilst about one quarter of single women (16–35) used contraception in 1970 the proportion rose to 45% in 1975'. The proportion using the pill had grown from 9% to 36%.

Sterilisation was of growing importance and by 1975, 13% of women under 41 or their husbands had been sterilised, compared to 6% in 1970. The report argues that comparison of all and planned pregnancy rates indicates that the fall in third and fourth pregnancies which had led to the fall in fertility especially in the 1970s was 'largely but not entirely brought about by improved contraceptive practice rather than by a change in intentions'. The reduction in later unplanned pregnancies was especially marked among the wives of manual workers and therefore tended to reduce the historic differences in fertility between the social classes. 'The main area in which some improvement in services was needed had to do with women's feeling of embarrassment in using them – although only a minority reported such feelings.' A quarter of the women who had not used the service said they would prefer advice from a woman doctor. Most clinic doctors were women but the majority of GPs were men: more women GPs might, therefore, reduce one deterrent.

Hearing

Demand for the various NHS services in the early years proved to be much higher than was anticipated. There was in fact very little previous estimation of need, but one of the very few areas which was studied in advance related to the proposed Medresco hearing aid. The *Prevalence of Deafness (1948) Survey* was done for a Medical Research Council Committee which was trying to estimate the number of hearing aids likely to be required when the NHS came into being. No data based on physical examination of the whole population was available – lack of time and resources precluded this possibility so, as an alternative, a method developed by an official of the US Public Health Service which classified hearing loss in terms of the patient's social disability, assessed by questioning, was used. The classification was correlated with the results of pure tone audiometric measurements. A large sample was available from the continuing Survey of Sickness and quite simple questions following the American experience were used, all relating to the degree of social disability suffered and providing information for a seven-category classification of deafness, ranging from 'no disability' to complete deafness.

This produced an estimate of just under 5% of the population aged 16 and over and 26% of those aged 75 and over with some degree of disability, and about half as many again with one defective ear. These estimates were analysed by region, industry, age and sex, duration of ailment, whether there had been any medical consultation or any experience of hearing aids, income, and so on. Since under 40% of those with any degree of deafness had seen doctors, estimates based on past clinical experience would probably have been deficient. Less than 5% of the deaf were using hearing aids and this covered a range of 3% in the lowest income group to 12% in the highest. But not all deaf people had severe disability and demand for an NHS hearing aid would vary according to attitude and motivation. So in addition all respondents were asked if they were prepared to have a physical examination and what they felt about wearing aids. It appeared that about 45% of the deaf said that they would be interested in a free hearing aid, but many of these people had, of course, no experience of what would be involved in getting an aid, and when this demand was assessed against willingness to pay and whether or not there had been any medical consultation previously, only about half of them seemed firm potential customers, which would mean around one quarter of the deaf. The report suggested that the quality of the NHS aid might affect eventual demand and that these estimates should be reviewed when the aid becomes a reality.

After the NHS aid, Medresco, was introduced the Ministry of Health asked for a study of users' experience and of the service problems experienced. By 1950 47 distribution centres had been set up in selected hospitals, each of which served three diagnostic centres. Interviews were made with a sample of patients issued with an aid, drawn from the records of ten distribution centres, for the *Medresco Hearing Aid Survey*, which was followed by another survey in 1955. In 1972 the Social Survey helped DHSS with a further study. This hearing-aid work may be described as operational research, since its main concern was to help improve the design and working of a service for a particular group of the population.

The elderly

The elderly population, which is increasing as a proportion of the total population, is of special interest. Older people's need for social and medical assistance is greater than most of the rest of the population: there has been a great deal of voluntary activity devoted to their needs and an increasing commitment by officials to see that their needs are met. Although the Survey has made many surveys which, like the Medresco study noted above, were specially relevant to the elderly, a substantial part of this work was financed by non-official bodies on a repayment basis, with the positive support of the appropriate government department. The National Corporation for the Care of Old People (NCCOP) was involved with many of these surveys.

In the *Reasons for Retirement Survey*, the Survey collaborated with the then Ministry of Pensions and National Insurance, whose staff interviewed a sample of people becoming eligible for retirement pension in four weeks in 1953. The Survey helped design the study and carried out some of the analysis but did not report. The study originated in questions about the proportions of people retiring and taking a pension at the minimum age possible and the part played by ill health or other reasons, such as an employer's compulsory retirement rules. Comparisons were made with the situation of those staying at work. A quarter of a century later the Survey returned to this topic, in the survey described on page 173.

The *Meals on Wheels Survey* carried out in 1958 began the development of an approach to the study of delivery of services which has had wide application. Under the 1948 National Assistance Act local authorities could contribute to voluntary organisations who were providing meals for old people, but could not provide such a service themselves. The NCCOP governors had become increasingly interested in the part played by such domiciliary services but found that very little factual information was available. In discussion with the Survey and with the agreement of the Ministry of Health a study was designed to show the scope and operation of the service, the contribution it made to needs, what kind of people received the service and whether there was an unsatisfied need. With the cooperation of the voluntary organisations a sample of current recipients was chosen, and a general population sample of males aged 65 and over and women aged 60 and over was also interviewed. The Survey's first contribution was to show what was actually happening: 40% of recipients got one meal a week and out of 720 recipients only 21 got a meal every day. The numbers wanting more meals were greater than those satisfied with what they were getting. Of the 453 schemes studied, 162 closed down for part of the year, some of them for 13 weeks in the year. The way recipients were selected was discussed with the organisers, and also how it was decided that meals were no longer needed. The circumstances of recipients were discussed with them – the location of family or friends, cooking facilities and mobility. Four per cent of the meals were free and 57% cost one shilling or more each. The report examines the production and delivery arrangements and the make up of the meals served. Organisers and recipients emphasised the value to recipients of the social contact involved. From information provided by the sample of non-recipients and from what recipients themselves said it was possible to estimate the numbers of potential recipients and the total number of meals required to meet their needs. It was clear that the service would be welcomed by many not receiving it. The production and delivery problems involved were examined.

From a study covering one service in the whole population, the Survey turned to a survey of the use in one authority of all services for the elderly. In 1961, at the request of the King Edward Hospital Fund, the *Lewisham Survey* sought to examine the use currently made by older people of available social services set up in one local authority area, and in particular to find out how well-informed older people were about existing services. It was done with the active cooperation of those responsible for running the services, who were interested in knowing what, if anything, could be done to achieve fuller utilisation.

As the local authority services developed during the 1960s it became clear that there were major differences in the scale of provision reflected in the 10-year plans of different authorities. The NCCOP governors doubted that these plans were based on either needs or what the authorities thought they could afford, and their doubts were shared by the Ministry of Health which, in an official circular, tried to stimulate more realistic reviews of services and plans. The NCCOP offered to finance studies which might help local authorities study their situation and, with the agreement of the ministry, negotiations with a range of local authorities in England, Wales and Scotland produced 13 areas in which authorities were willing to cooperate. The survey done in 1965 was not a national sample. Its purpose was to examine a range of locally provided services including housing, home helps and residential care, to ascertain through interviewing recipients and the officials concerned what criteria had been applied in selecting recipients, and then in each area to apply these criteria to a random sample of the population for whom the services were supposed to operate. In this way, actual local criteria were used to establish what need might be in each area, and a comparison of authorities would then show what proportion of need was satisfied by the varying criteria used by different authorities. This design was too complicated and time consuming to be applied nationally. The survey report, *Social Welfare for the Elderly*, describes how the design was applied and the purposes achieved, in a way that makes it possible for any local authority to make its own studies. Results could also be compared with the results of applying some professionally designed minimum standards or national norms.

Comparisons between the results of applying different criteria were also at the heart of another study, but here the emphasis was on international comparison. The survey, *Economic and Social Circumstances of Old People in Three Industrial Societies* (1962), compared situations in Denmark, the United States and the United Kingdom. It was financed by an official American grant and was not reported by the Survey which did, however, play a major role in developing the design, the interview, coding and analysis. The study was designed in such a way as to illuminate matters of special interest in each country, and also to produce closely comparable material in fields where the interest was in the way different systems affected the situations of elderly people. Such studies, if properly designed, can add extra dimension to the evaluation of policy in any one country. They stimulate consideration of alternatives and highlight the merits and deficiencies of alternatives as they have actually worked out for the populations to which they have been applied.

Without the financial support of non-official bodies it is unlikely that these

Table 21 Whether recipients have difficulty in doing certain things for themselves (Question 35) (elderly recipients by sex and age; chronic sick recipients in total). Home Help survey (1967)

			Elderly recipients								Non-elderly
				Sex				Age			Chronic sick
	Total elderly		Men	Women	65-69	70-74	75-79	80-84	85 & over	
All elderly and chronic sick recipients (base for percentages)	1112*		165	947	131	216	306	279	177	113
	No.	%	%	%	%	%	%	%	%	%
Going out of doors on own										
Totally unable to do	324	29.1	8.5	32.7	23.7	25.0	24.8	33.3	39.5	35.4
Has difficulty	346	31.1	21.8	32.7	31.3	25.5	35.0	32.3	29.4	40.7
Going up and down stairs on own										
Totally unable to do	255	22.9	9.7	25.2	19.8	17.1	21.2	24.4	33.3	31.9
Has difficulty	361	32.5	29.7	32.9	34.4	33.3	30.1	38.7	24.9	29.2
Getting about house on own										
Totally unable to do	37	3.3	—	3.9	3.1	3.7	3.3	2.2	5.1	9.7
Has difficulty	316	28.4	13.9	30.9	26.0	20.4	26.5	32.6	37.3	36.3
Getting in and out of bed on own										
Totally unable to do	26	2.3	—	2.7	1.5	2.3	2.3	1.4	4.5	8.8
Has difficulty	257	23.1	9.7	25.4	25.2	23.6	22.9	21.9	23.7	32.7
Washing self										
Totally unable to do	22	2.0	0.6	2.2	—	1.9	2.0	1.4	4.5	4.4
Has difficulty	209	18.8	7.9	20.7	29.0	15.3	15.7	19.0	20.9	29.2
Bathing										
Totally unable to do	348	31.3	12.7	34.5	29.8	27.8	29.1	34.4	36.2	30.1
Has difficulty	317	28.5	17.6	30.4	28.2	23.1	30.1	30.1	30.5	43.4
Dressing										
Totally unable to do	30	2.7	0.6	3.1	0.8	3.7	2.0	1.8	5.6	6.2
Has difficulty	245	22.0	12.1	23.8	30.5	13.9	21.9	24.0	23.2	31.9
Cutting own toenails										
Totally unable to do	357	32.1	14.5	35.2	29.0	27.3	31.0	31.9	42.9	40.7
Has difficulty	464	41.7	38.8	42.2	40.5	42.1	41.5	44.1	39.0	33.6
Has no difficulty with any	124	11.2	29.1	8.0	10.7	15.7	13.1	8.6	6.8	6.2

*Includes 3 elderly recipients whose ages were not given.

social welfare surveys would have been done. It was not until 1967 that the Ministry of Health asked for a survey in this subject area. This was the survey of the home help service, whose purpose was to describe the way the service was working and to see if there was any failure to meet needs. At the time of the survey about 90% of all recipients were elderly and nearly 70% were aged 75 years and over; some chronically sick people were also eligible. Unlike the meals service, at that time home helps were organised by local authorities. The survey report describes the organisation and then examines the circumstances of recipients; by comparison with a sample representative of all households, it brings out the special features of those then benefiting from the service.

The survey of the *The Elderly at Home* carried out for the DHSS in 1976 was more broadly based than the studies described earlier in this section. Its purpose was to describe the social circumstances of a representative sample of all people aged 65 and over living in private households. The report describes demographic, housing, income and health conditions. Physically, those aged over 65 to 74 were not much more severely disadvantaged than the next younger age-group. The next older group did show a moderate physical decline and a greater decline in social contacts. Thirty per cent of the elderly lived alone and 80% of those who lived alone were women; over 35% were women aged 75 or more at the time of the survey. Almost half the married couples had total combined net incomes of less than £1,500 a year. (At that time average earnings of full-time male workers were approximately £3,600.) About one sixth of elderly men and one twentieth of women were working at the time of the survey. Many had changed jobs on reaching retirement age. Nine out of ten were able to go out without assistance; this proportion reduced to less than half for those aged 85 or over, and 4.5% of all were permanently bedridden or housebound. The report describes contacts with welfare organisations, friends and relatives: 15% of all the elderly never visited friends or relatives. A majority did not go to any kind of social centre. Their interests, hobbies, and attitudes to life were also described.

This survey reflects the mounting interest in the growing elderly population but it took place many years after the demographic changes were known. It is equally difficult to understand why a lapse of 24 years occurred before another study of retirement was organised. *Older Workers and Retirement* was a study made in 1977 on behalf of and with active participation of DHSS and the Department of Employment. Since the 1953 survey there had been many changes in social security legislation which affected the incomes of retired persons. There had also been changes in the departments' professional personnel, such as economists with interests in econometric analysis, so departmental interests were shaped against a very different economic and social situation from that of 1953. The design of the survey had more far-reaching objectives, but some of the purposes were deliberately similar. While the earlier survey concentrated on those retired or about to retire, the new survey studied the process through which people moved on the way to retirement, so that people before retirement age – men aged from 55, women from 50 – and after it (to age 72) were included. The sample was not drawn from records but from a postal sift based on the Electoral Register, using a method previously developed by the Survey. The 1953 survey

Table 22 Type of household in which elderly people live (by age within sex of elderly persons). The Elderly at home (1976)

	Grand total	Men and women			Men				Women			
			Age			Age				Age		
		65–74	75–84	85 or over	All men	65–74	75–84	85 or over	All women	65–74	75–84	85 or over
All elderly persons WEIGHTED (unweighted figures)	3,869 (2,622)	2,571 (1,354)	1,089 (1,063)	209 (205)	1,540 (994)	1,101 (565)	384 (375)	55 (54)	2,329 (1,628)	1,470 (789)	705 (688)	154 (151)
	%	%	%	%	%	%	%	%	%	%	%	%
Type of household												
One elderly person alone	29.6	25.0	37.4	44.0	15.6	13.6	19.8	27.3	38.8	33.6	47.1	50.0
One elderly person with non-elderly spouse only	7.4	10.4	1.7	—	15.8	20.5	4.4	—	1.9	2.9	0.3	—
One elderly person with next generation only	6.7	4.3	10.6	17.2	2.9	2.0	4.2	10.9	9.3	6.0	14.0	19.5
One elderly person, non-elderly spouse + next generation	1.7	2.4	0.3	—	4.2	5.6	0.8	—	—	—	—	—
One elderly person with others	5.9	5.6	6.4	7.7	4.7	4.2	6.0	7.2	6.7	6.7	6.7	7.7
Elderly married couple only	36.7	40.2	33.1	11.5	46.0	43.5	55.5	30.9	30.4	37.8	20.9	4.5
Elderly siblings only	2.8	2.3	3.9	2.9	1.0	0.8	1.0	5.5	4.0	3.4	5.5	1.9
Elderly married couple with next generation only	4.1	5.1	2.3	1.4	5.1	5.5	4.2	3.6	3.4	4.7	1.3	0.6
Other combinations of two or more elderly persons with others	5.1	4.7	4.2	15.3	4.5	4.2	4.2	14.5	5.5	5.0	4.3	15.6
Total	100.0	100.0	100.0	100.0	100.0	100.0	100.0	100.0	100.0	100.0	100.0	100.0

Table 23 Personal mobility of elderly people (by sex and age). The Elderly at home (1976)

	Total	Sex		Age				
		Men	Women	65–69	70–74	75–79	80–84	85 & over
Elderly persons								
WEIGHTED	3,869	1,540	2,329	1,409	1,162	697	392	209
(unweighted figures)	(2,622)	(994)	(1,628)	(725)	(629)	(688)	(375)	(205)
	%	%	%	%	%	%	%	%
Mobility								
Bedfast permanently	0.3	0.1	0.4	—	—	0.4	1.0	1.9
Bedfast temporarily, usually housebound	0.2	0.1	0.3	—	—	0.6	0.8	1.0
Bedfast temporarily, usually goes out	0.3	—	0.4	0.1	0.3	0.3	0.3	0.5
Housebound permanently	4.0	3.3	4.4	1.1	2.5	4.9	9.7	17.7
Housebound temporarily, usually goes out	2.6	2.1	2.8	1.3	1.6	4.3	4.6	6.2
Usually goes out with assistance	7.6	3.2	10.5	3.2	6.6	9.6	12.5	26.8
Usually goes out	85.1	91.2	81.1	94.2	88.9	79.9	71.2	45.9
Total	100.0	100.0	100.0	100.0	100.0	100.0	100.0	100.0
Summary								
Bedfast permanently	0.3	0.1	0.4	—	—	0.4	1.0	1.9
Housebound permanently	4.2	3.4	4.7	1.1	2.5	5.5	10.5	18.7
Goes out	95.5	96.5	94.8	98.9	97.5	94.1	88.5	79.4

defined retirement as taking a pension, while the later survey defined it as stopping work whether or not a pension was involved.

The survey showed the gradual decline in proportions working before retirement and the very sharp drop thereafter: '29% of men aged 64 were already retired but at 65 three-quarters had stopped work'. The process was more gradual for women. The general sentiment favoured a more gradual process, but among those already retired opinion was more equally divided. For most the state retirement pension was clearly the key factor and gradual retirement 'was not in practice a reality for most men'. The report describes how people moved to retirement. Only a minority of retired men had moved through part-time work but women were much more likely to have done so. Practice and opinion on the state pension were discussed. Most part-time workers over pension age had claimed their state pension but many fulltime workers had not. Two-thirds of workers and the retired thought that men and women should get the pension at the same age, but this was reduced to less than half when the proviso was put that the pension age for women would need to be raised to pay for it.

The handicapped

Perhaps one of the most widely known of all Survey studies was the 1968 *Survey of the handicapped and impaired in Great Britain*. The survey had two immediate origins. The first was work done at Bedford College (University of London) in developing an array of devices for measuring physical disability. The Ministry of Health asked the Survey if they could be applied to a population sample in order to produce national estimates of the incidence of disability and of the social and economic problems it produced, what help was being received from local authorities and other agencies and whether more help was needed. The second interest in the survey came from the Department of Social Security which had for some time been under pressure from various groups (including the Disablement Income Group) to provide some assistance to disabled people. Some kind of attendance allowance for the disabled came under discussion. The department wanted to know if some measure could be made of how dependent disabled people were, their financial circumstances and the extra costs imposed by their disabilities. It was agreed to try to cover both interests: other departments, including the Ministry of Housing, then raised their interests.

Meanwhile, the Survey was testing the possibility of applying the Bedford College tests. The tests, broadly speaking, were related to movements necessary to the minimum activities of independent daily living – bathing, dressing, feeding, using the lavatory, getting into and out of bed. A version of these tests seemed possible but it was not clear how successfully they could be applied to

Table 24 Proportion of people with different degrees of handicap who are on the local authority register (general classes). Handicapped and Impaired in Great Britain (1968)

Degree of handicap			% registered		No. on which % based	
Very severe	1+2		13.9		101	
	3		18.7		551	
		(1–3)		17.9		652
Severe	4		9.0		410	
	5		11.7		1,010	
		(4–5)		10.9		1,420
Appreciable	6		6.7		2,457	
All handicapped		1–6		11.8		4,529
Minor/no	7		3.5		2,707	
	8a		1.8		2,935	
	8b		3.0		2,092	
All impaired			5.2		12,738*	

*Includes persons in categories 4 to 8 but who were not able to be classified further.

Table 25 Proportion of handicapped people with different degrees of handicap benefiting from various health and welfare services who are on the local authority register, compared with the non-registered handicapped. Handicapped and Impaired in Great Britain (1968)

Health and Welfare Service	Degree of handicap							
	Very severe 1–3		Severe 4–5		Appreciable 6		All handicapped 1–6	
	Reg. %	Not reg. %	Reg. %	Not reg. %	Reg. %	Not reg. %	Reg. %	Not reg. %
Home help	18	13	31	16	25	10	25	12
Meals on wheels	5	4	14	4	10	3	10	3
District or male nurse	48	39	19	13	10	7	23	13
Health visitor	19	10	13	6	13	4	14	5
Social worker	27	7	25	4	17	3	22	4
Occupational therapist	9	1	5	2	9	1	8	1
Physiotherapist	8	2	4	2	7	1	6	1
Chiropody	21	16	31	15	12	12	21	13
Visitor for the blind	2	2	—	1	—	2	*	2
Attends local authority centre for the physically handicapped	7	*	15	1	16	1	13	1
Attends centre for the mentally handicapped	—	—	—	—	—	—	—	—
Voluntary societies	2	1	1	*	2	1	2	1
In sheltered employment	3	1	3	*	4	1	3	1
Other service	2	2	3	1	1	1	2	1
None of these services	16	41	21	61	37	70	26	63
No. on which % based	117	535	155	1,265	164	2,293	436	4,093

*Less than 0.5%.

what would necessarily be a large sample distributed all over the country. The needs of the two main customer departments for information about social disability, dependence and financial burdens required detailed questions, which taken singly or in groups could provide a basis for classifying people into groups with varying degrees of dependence and disability. A rather lengthy interview would be needed, and coding and analysis would take some time.

A primary problem was to locate the disabled. There were registers maintained by local authorities but they did not seem comprehensive. It was decided to use the sift method, by which a large sample is sent a very simple questionnaire which can identify persons or events, and a follow-up interview is then done with those identified. To obtain reasonable numbers for interview it was necessary to send out 250,000 letters asking only if a disabled person lived at the address. Over 85% responded and, from these, samples were selected; eventually over 13,000 interviews were carried out. Various pressure groups began to make representations about the results and a flow of parliamentary questions followed, in no way halted by the minister's statement that 'the survey will be a formidable affair and tabulation and analysis will take some time'. In December 1969, a minister responding to further questions referred to 'this almost unique piece of work . . . we are grateful to the Social Survey for its efforts to contribute information about the severely handicapped in time for decisions about benefits for them'. This referred to preliminary results produced for the use of departments on the specific issue of the disablement benefit. The decision referred to estimates of the numbers of disabled falling into different degrees of severity. Without this information departments would not have been able to calculate the cost of the benefits at different possible levels. As public interest mounted and ministers prepared to respond it became tempting to use the existence of an incomplete study as part of a parliamentary defence and to become heavily committed to publication and use. None of this helps the operational progress of a study, and in this case everybody concerned showed understanding of the weight of work involved. By the time the report was published a great deal of public interest had built up.

The report showed that there were just over three million people over 16 years of age with some physical impairment. The proportion rose from about nine per thousand of the young to 221 and 378 per thousand for those aged 65–74 and 75 and over respectively. The proportions were different in the various regions of the country. Using data collected during the interview all respondents with some impairment, whatever the cause, could be classified into a number of categories indicating degrees of dependence. The numbers in the different categories in different age-groups were given. About 24,000 fell into the 'very severe' category – so severely handicapped as to need constant care and supervision every day and practically every night. A further 133,000 needed constant day care. Including those needing special care a total of just over 500,000 people, nearly three-quarters of them women, were very severely or severely handicapped and another 616,000 were appreciably handicapped, needing considerable support.

Over a quarter of the handicapped were women aged 75 and over. The proportions of those disabled to various degrees who were registered with local authorities were shown: those not registered but receiving other services, medical or social, must be added to get the total of those who had some official contact. But over half of the severely and two-thirds of the appreciably handicapped had no continuing local authority health or welfare service. The report described impaired housewives and those (nearly half a million) who could not do most of their household chores because of their disability. Mobility, leisure activities and attendance at clubs were described, as were employment and housing. While a third of impaired persons were retired and another third were housewives about one in five were working. The effect of handicap on employment was described in terms of employers, choice of job, journey to work and unemployment.

There was an unusual sequel to this work. As a result of legislation giving more powers to local authorities to help the disabled, it became necessary for them to become better informed about disabled in their areas. The authors of the Survey report prepared a guide to help local authorities carry out their own surveys – not necessarily on the same scale or in the same detail. The handbook was written with the more limited local resources in mind and, with the support of the DHSS, was sent to every local authority. Surveys with varying degrees of sophistication were done in 154 local authorities. Many of them had no social research sections at that time, so many of these studies were probably quite limited. Around half used social work staff as interviewers and over half used the authority's computer for analysis.

Nurses and nursing

The continuing growth of the NHS, somewhat unanticipated in its early years, together with its staff's changing attitude towards conditions of service, led to a flow of questions about the relationships of staff to the NHS. Later, when local health and welfare services began to grow they produced many similar staffing problems. These staffing issues were not separate from questions about the functioning of primary care and institutions. It cannot be said that the Survey made much of a contribution to these latter problems during the first half of its working life, but if the Survey of Sickness had not been so abruptly closed down in 1952 it could have made a substantial contribution.

The Survey did, however, investigate staffing problems in hospitals: from the war years onward surveys designed to help recruit and deploy hospital nurses were made at frequent intervals. In 1943 a campaign was launched to cope with a serious shortage of nurses, and to help design it, surveys of working women, schoolgirls and their mothers were carried out. The *Recruitment to Nursing Surveys* showed that attitudes towards nursing were generally favourable, and quite substantial proportions of women had at some stage considered a nursing career. But although it was clearly seen to be 'worthwhile and of service to the community', the prevalent ideas that possible recruits had about the conditions of service (long hours and lack of leisure) were obvious handicaps to recruitment. Most potential recruits were in fact uninformed about the changes in service which had followed the Rushcliffe Report. Many women had also to find jobs immediately on leaving school and the gap between then and the starting age for nursing (18) was not easy to bridge. A subsequent survey studied recent recruitment to nursing. This showed that student nurses were largely drawn from 'middle social and economic groups'. They had higher levels of education than others in the same age-groups and their fathers were largely in non-manual occupations. This contrasted with the finding of the first survey that people in the lower economic groups were less critical of nurses' working conditions. Analysis of the sample showed that voluntary hospitals relied more than municipal hospitals on recruiting middle-class girls. Fifty per cent of the recent recruits had had a longstanding wish to do nursing but many of them felt they did not have enough freedom or that they were 'treated like children', and long working hours and night duty were also the subject of complaint. They were somewhat critical of the publicity used for the recruitment campaign.

Other aspects of nursing were studied in subsequent surveys and an early study, *The Recruitment of Hospital Nursing Staff by Advertisement* (1949), attempted to assess the outcome and costs of advertising by hospitals. Hospitals on the Ministry of Health Management Committee lists were sampled and new entrants to these hospitals were sampled and interviewed. Twenty-six per cent of the staff of these hospitals were new entrants; 56% of new entrants had come from outside nursing services, mainly as pupil or student nurses, and 44% transferred within. Thirty-one per cent were unqualified nursing staff. Twenty-four per cent of them had joined in response to the advertisements – rather more men than women and rather more trained staff than student nurses. The average cost of advertising for those who had responded to advertising was a little over £12. This suggested that total expenditure on advertising by all hospitals was just over £100,000. Advertisements were only the second main influence on entering nursing – more important was knowing a nurse.

A very different type of survey was undertaken in 1954 and 1956. *Hospital Nursing Methods in a General Hospital* tested a proposed reorganisation of hospital nursing on an experimental scale. The Nuffield Provincial Hospitals Trust[2] had suggested that much of the discussion about the problems of recruiting and training nurses had not been based on information necessary to answer the question 'what is the proper task of a nurse?' They had therefore initiated a job analysis of the work of nurses. Their report made some serious criticisms and argued that 'a more rational use of available nurses is fundamental to the solution of present and future problems'. The Standing Nursing Advisory Committee of the Central Health Services Council considered the report and recommended that before changes in ward routine were made, experiments should be carried out in a number of hospital wards to test the efficacy of the changes proposed. In particular, the Nuffield group had suggested that there were many advantages to be derived from 'group assignment' as contrasted with 'work assignment'. (Under group assignment in a hospital ward groups or teams of nurses each undertake all the nursing care of a small group of patients, while under work assignment all the nurses in the ward perform specific tasks for all the patients.) Advantages were suggested both for patients and for training nurses, as well as in maintaining the interest of nurses in nursing duties. The NHS authorities asked the Survey to devise experiments with this end in view. The cooperation of four hospitals was obtained and appropriate studies were made in a medical and surgical ward in each of these hospitals. The studies involved 'before and after' observations in these eight wards.

A sampling system was devised by which observations were made of nurses' time sampled throughout the working day in the selected wards on a work assignment basis. During half-hourly periods throughout the day spot observations were taken every 15 seconds. Operationally this method avoided the need to record continuous narrative descriptions and to time the numerous activities of very brief duration which take place in hospital wards. All wards were studied by this method and a detailed account was obtained of all activities taking place in the ward, the nurses carrying them out, the time taken to carry them out and the condition of the patients concerned. After these preliminary observations, the wards concerned were reorganised on a group assignment basis and the new system put into operation. When the hospital felt that the new system had been working long enough to be established, a further week's observation using precisely the same techniques was made. Comparisons were thus possible of the whole range of work carried out within these hospital wards before and after the new method of nursing organisation. It was thus possible to show how the time devoted to different kinds of activities by different levels of nurse had changed. It was relevant to find out how nurses, patients and doctors felt about the new system and to consider their reactions together with the objective data obtained from the time-sampling studies. One of the methods by which this was done was to obtain details of complaints about their treatment in hospital from patients who had been in the wards during the two periods concerned. It was possible to show that the level of complaint dropped sharply under group assignment. The Nursing Advisory Committee accepted the findings of the survey and emphasised the advantages which might result provided suitable lay assistance was available for administrative work; the attitude of ward sisters would be important. They could not say whether group assignment would be a more costly system but thought it would provide more value for money.

Children's homes

Another problem area for institutional staff in the days before the major reorganisation of local authority social work was the staff wastage in children's homes. In 1961 the Children's Department of the Home Office asked the Survey if, acting in collaboration with local authorities all over the country, a study could be made to throw light on the situation and point to ways in which it could be improved. The study was designed with the active assistance of those in the Children's Department who were most concerned with this problem, especially the inspecting staff. Many children's officers throughout the country helped to shape the study. All local authorities were asked to give information about the number of children's homes they maintained and the staffing situation in them. This information by itself was of some value because it enabled a statistical appraisal to be made of staff turnover at different levels of employment, in different parts of the country and in different kinds of home. It also provided a basis, not otherwise available, for selecting a representative sample of all homes and of the people working in those homes as housemothers or assistants, for the study *Staffing of Local Authority Residential Homes for Children* (1961). These returns showed that in most homes vacancies were between 8% and 16% and the annual wastage rate was between 26% and 52% according to the type of home.

From the same local authorities the names of people who had left the service in the previous six months were obtained and from these lists a representative sample of those leaving the service was produced. Present and past members of staff were interviewed and asked about their previous experience and training, their attitude to different aspects of the work, how they felt about the practices of childcare on which the home was based, and what were the main attractions and disadvantages of the work. The hope was that by comparing the answers of those who had left and those who had stayed in the job, together with the information collected in interviews with the existing staff of the institutions, it would be possible to show the main factors on which action might be taken to reduce staff turnover or to make the work more attractive in the future. Thus both former and current staff were asked to rank various aspects of their jobs. Both agreed that long hours or not enough time off was the biggest problem. Leavers were asked whether there was anything which, if done, might have made them want to stay. It was possible, on the basis of assessments made by children's officers, to compare the answers of former staff members who had given different degrees of satisfaction while in the job. Using diaries completed by staff the report describes how working time was used. Taking into account the facts described and the opinions of staff at different levels the report suggested that turnover and wastage could be reduced by changes in recruitment methods, improving working hours and time off and taking steps to deal with the causes of problems in staff relations. There were, for example, differences between the perceptions of housemothers and assistants of how children were treated; and the trend towards smaller homes seemed likely to reduce wastage.

Doctors and dentists

Decisions about appropriate and acceptable salary scales in the public sector were perennial and in 1957 a Royal Commission on the Remuneration of Doctors and Dentists was given the task of comparing those of other professional groups of similar standing, and making recommendations on how future pay should be decided. To help the Commission the Survey organised a postal sample survey of professional earnings in ten different groups with comparable educational and professional standards. In all about 30,000 members of these professions cooperated. Later comparisons of salaries were made by a continuing review body using new data collected by the Department of Employment. But in 1981, in response to special problems concerning junior hospital doctors, the Social Survey, at the request of the review body, collaborated with the Office of Manpower Economics (OME) in devising a study of the hours of duty, hours of work and work activities of a representative sample of junior doctors and dentists in 16 health districts. This was based on a diary recording for seven days hours on duty and time spent on different work activities throughout each day. This work, including detailed checks on accuracy of diaries, was done by the Survey and reported by OME. The Survey showed the variations in contracted hours, hours on duty and hours worked while on duty by different grades of hospital doctor and different speciality groups. The review body said that 'in the light of the evidence from the OME survey we have concluded that existing levels of remuneration do not adequately reflect the amount of work and responsibility generally undertaken by hospital training grades ... we have therefore decided to recommend a higher percentage increase in basic scales of training grades'.

Mentally handicapped and community nursing

In 1972 the Briggs Committee returned to problems of recruiting and organising nursing work and the Survey arranged for a survey to help them. This committee had drawn particular attention to the nursing of the mentally handicapped and recommended that 'a new caring profession for the mentally handicapped should emerge gradually. In the meantime in the training of nurses in the field of mental handicap increased emphasis should be placed on the social aspects of care'. In 1975 The Jay Committee was appointed to examine the roles, training and career structure of nurses and residential care staff required for the care of mentally handicapped adults and children. The committee asked the Survey to study staff in hospitals and local authority hostels with special reference to how the emphasis on social aspects of the nursing work was related to residents' abilities, staff ratios and attitudes and staff training. Interviews were carried out in 1976 with 967 nurses in 56 hospitals for the mentally handicapped and 390 care staff in local authority hostels. The report, *OPCS Survey of Nurses and Residential Care Staff*,[3] volume 2 of the Jay Committee report, showed that half of the nursing and care staff worked part-time, but over 90% of nursing officers, ward sisters and trainee nurses worked fulltime. Almost two-thirds had no 'O' levels or equivalent, but about threequarters of the nurses in trained nursing grades were qualified in subnormality nursing. Twenty-seven per cent of all nurses were born outside the UK. Nursing staff had more experience of working with the mentally handicapped than hostel staff. Using assessments of residents' abilities and physical handicaps a classification was made of the units into four groups using cluster analysis. This put about a third of adult wards and almost all adult hostels into the high ability grade, a third in average ability and a fifth in low ability; 10% were described as non-ambulant (very low ability). Nurses working with lower-ability patients spent more time than those in other units on providing basic care. Staff working with higher-ability residents or in wards with relatively good staff ratios seemed to put more emphasis on helping their residents to do tasks like feeding, washing and dressing. Staff ratios on the whole were better in hostels than hospitals but this resulted partly from greater overtime and greater numbers of hostel residents attending an occupational centre during the day. Most but not all of the more senior ward and hostel staff had frequent discussions with staff from residents' occupation centres or with schoolteachers and had discussed the progress of at least one of their residents with a consultant within the last six months.

In general both nurses and hostel staff seemed to appreciate the value of developing the individual potential of mentally handicapped people. Their attitude towards whether to discourage or encourage sexual relationships among residents suggested this was an area they found difficult. About 40% of both groups of staff felt that more mentally handicapped residents or patients should be sterilised. The report examined the relationship between staffing ratios and the tasks carried out by staff and showed how nurses in wards with poor staff ratios had less time to spend on encouraging patients to help themselves. It also examined the various routines used to organise residents' daily lives and developed a scale indicating how many restrictive routines occurred. There were more restrictions in wards than in hostels but no differences were found on the restrictions scale between good and bad staff ratios in wards or hostels. During the week before the survey almost a fifth of residents had been visited by relatives, and voluntary workers had assisted in activities with residents in about half of the units. Staff were asked about the most important aims they had for their residents and the report examined how these views related to the ability level of the wards they worked in. The views of senior nursing staff seemed markedly different and the report suggested that senior staff might have over-optimistic views of what the ward nurses were trying to achieve. Lack of regular discussions with other professional staff and lack of influence over decisions on individual residents were related to dissatisfaction among nursing and hostel staff. Almost half of nursing or care assistants said they had not received any training or advice on how to deal with behaviour problems.

The home helps and meals on wheels surveys had also given attention to the staff problems involved in organising these services. These studies were concerned mainly with assistance given in the community. A later survey was concerned with the situation resulting from many changes which had taken place in the activities of nurses working in the community (1980). This report to the DHSS noted the 'increasing emphasis on providing health care in the community' arising out of such changes as early discharge from hospital, the trend away from home deliveries, the move of school health and family planning services into the NHS and the general move towards integrating community health services. It was important to cover all types of nurses and nursing auxiliaries, so as well as those employed in the primary care services – health visiting, district nursing and midwifery – it included school health, family planning, psychiatric, geriatric and other specialist nurses and nurses working with GPs. Those engaged on wholly administrative work were not included. Twenty-five health districts were chosen at random and a random half of all nurses working in them were selected from the lists of cooperating district nursing officers and, separately, from GPs in the districts. Nurses were interviewed and also asked to keep diaries for seven days recording their activities. Response in all groups was very high.

The report described the demographic characteristics, qualifications and training of the nurses, more than 80% of whom worked fulltime. Four-fifths of those who could be attached to general practice were: most nurses regarded themselves as part of a primary healthcare team and their contacts with other nurses as 'very good' or 'good'. These opinions were substantially less favourable for contacts with social services staff. Nurses gave their views on particular groups of clients who needed more care from nurses working in the community. Most chose the elderly living alone, but this was not necessarily the group with whom they would most like to spend more time. They were also asked to assess various aspects of client/patient care. Their judgments did not seem to be related to patterns of attachment and 'patch working' nor to the number of practices worked in. Substantial minorities thought they did too much travelling. Working time was analysed by using the diary data. District nurses, for example, spent 24% of their time travelling, 26% on non-clinical activities and 50% with patients. Health visitors, on the other hand, spent only 16% of their time travelling, 46% on non-clinical work and 38% with clients. The time spent with patients either in patients' homes or clinics was also analysed. The districts in the sample were classified by type[4] and an attempt was made to relate the variables used in the study (such as time spent on non-clinical duties or time spent travelling by district nurses) to the types of district.

Survey of Sickness

Most of the surveys related to services received were done after 1961, but the very early work – which was stopped – should be described because it shows what was started and what might have been done. In a 1947 paper Dr Percy Stocks, Chief Medical Statistician of the General Register Office, described recent developments in morbidity statistics.[5] 'In the past neither the Ministry of Health nor the General Register Office nor anyone else has been in a position to answer the simplest statistical question about the frequency of colds, accidents in the home, varicose veins, doctor's attendance and such like things.' He went on to discuss the initiation and contribution of the Survey of Sickness.

> The need for some index of the amount of illness, loss of ability for work and demands made on doctors in the civilian population became obvious in England about 1942 when alarmist rumours of deterioration in health began to circulate and were difficult to refute. It was alleged that nothing could be deduced from available notification and mortality data about total prevalence of illness. It was unsatisfactory that the Ministry of Health and the Government generally should have no reliable information about the total amount of illness and the effects it was producing and so in October 1943 we set on foot a new experiment to find out something about this and obtain a continuous record.

The method used in the early days was to sample the whole population. Each month a new sample was selected from national registration records and individuals were taken by interview through the whole range of incapacity and medical attention to obtain a record of what had happened to them in a limited period of time. The survey did not cover children under 16. The period covered at first was three months before the interview and 3,000 persons per month were interviewed. In 1949 the number was increased to 4,000 and the period covered decreased to two months before interview in order to reduce the proven effect of memory loss. The results were published in the Bulletin of the Ministry of

Health and the Registrar General's Quarterly Return, and by the beginning of the NHS in 1948 provided the prevalence and sickness rates by sex, age and income, and days per quarter of incapacity and medical consultation.

The inception of the NHS naturally drew attention to the amount of prevailing sickness and raised questions about whether the NHS had led to an increase in the numbers of people complaining about illness and the numbers of consultations with doctors. The Survey of Sickness was able to throw some light on these questions. An article in *The Lancet* (22 April 1950) by W P D Logan, the successor to Dr Stocks at the GRO, compared sickness prevalence, incapacity and consultations for the years before and after the NHS began. It showed that '5% more adults aged 16 and over had some illness and that the number of individual illnesses increased by 22% and the number of consultations with doctors increased by 13%. The increase was greater amongst women than men and greater among elderly than young adults. Since July 1948 the number of medical consultations amongst small income groups has greatly increased but among those with large incomes they have become less'.

Most of the reporting was done by the GRO but a full description of the methods used, noting the limitations, was given in a Survey report in 1946, *Survey of Sickness 1943–1945*. This had a foreword by the Chief Medical Officer of Health who said 'It is basic information of great value in adjusting our health services to the needs of the population'. Others were less welcoming. In his 1947 paper Dr Stocks had noted 'that misunderstandings do sometimes arise during fieldwork and I regret to say that some people, including doctors, who think any stick good enough to use against a Government Department do not hesitate to make political weapons out of such trifles'. Such political weapons eventually played an important role in the demise of the survey.

In January 1952 the Committee on General Practice was considering 'whether existing arrangements for engaging in general practice are such as to enable GPs to provide the best possible standards of service', and it had become clear to the committee that it had 'not obtained sufficient evidence from the "consumer" point of view'. The Ministry of Health asked the Survey to find out 'the extent to which patients were changing their doctors and the reasons for doing so; if people were going to doctors more than they used to and if their relationship with their doctors had been changed by the NHS; what the public felt about group practice; and to consider other current issues about the relationship of doctors and patients'. The Survey of Sickness provided an ideal vehicle for such a study. If several months' samples were used large numbers could be surveyed at little cost – three months would provide 12,000 people. One month's sample was in fact used. The report, *General Practice under the NHS*, showed the proportion using and not using the NHS at that date. About seven per cent were changing doctors in a year, mainly because of movement of patients or doctors: only a tenth of change resulted from dissatisfaction with the doctor or the treatment received. Seventy-six per cent of consultations resulted in a prescription and 100 consultations produced 115 prescriptions. The weekly rate of prescriptions per 100 persons was much higher for young women than young men but about the same for elderly men and women. It was much higher for those in low income groups than in higher, partly due to the proportion of old people in the low income group. The report describes the issue of certificates, referrals to hospital and the total attention required by a list of 3,500 patients during a year, and patients' opinions on attention received since the NHS started were also examined. A complete study would have needed three months' material, and would have permitted a path-breaking survey of how the NHS was viewed by its customers.

There had been a change of government in autumn 1951 and with it a change of attitude towards the NHS. The mounting costs provoked sharp criticism and a mass of allegations about the service's organisation which had little foundation. In 1953 the Guillebaud Committee was appointed 'to review the present prospective cost of the NHS ... to advise how in view of burdens on the Exchequer a rising charge can be avoided'. It was to be expected then that the Treasury would exert some pressure on the Ministry of Health and its new Minister questioned the existence of the Survey of Sickness. The administrators and professional staff concerned defended the survey and the outcome was in some doubt until a letter from a local GP arrived on the Minister's desk, protesting at the supposed breach of the doctor-patient relationship involved in the interviewing of patients. This settled the matter. The Survey of Sickness was stopped forthwith and the study of general practice fell with it. It was to be many years before the Survey was again permitted to study primary care and its recipients' attitudes. In the published Guillebaud Report there is a relevant comment: 'We are of the opinion that the knowledge at present available about the working of the NHS is inadequate and should be considerably extended and improved since it is only on this basis of such knowledge that the right decisions could be made for the future development of the service'. While some of the requisite information was to come from the flow of hospital statistics it also seemed that much could come from the application of survey methods. But not until 1971, when the General Household Survey began, was a continuing study of illness and consultation again part of the Survey's programme.

Dental health

Perhaps the most intensive study of a clearly defined section of the health service was the series of surveys on dental health for the DHSS. These were all done in close cooperation with dental schools and involved interviews of different population samples closely followed by dentists' examinations of the dental condition of respondents. By this means, physical condition could be related to a full range of descriptive data about the individuals concerned. The first study, *Adult Dental Health in 1968*, was done in collaboration with the London Hospital Medical College Dental School. It was the first time that such a national description had been attempted and it therefore ranks as a major addition to knowledge about the physical condition of the population. In 1973 a similar study was made of the dental condition a representative sample of schoolchildren aged five to 15. In this study a physical examination was done in schools and a home interview with mothers followed. In all about 13,000 children were examined and 3,000 mothers interviewed. In 1978 the adult study was repeated, this time in collaboration with the University of Birmingham's Department of Dental Health. The repetition provided measures of change over 10 years in dental condition and use of dental services.

The original survey had shown that 29% of all adults had no natural teeth. For each age-group in 1978 the situation was better: this was true in all regions but not to the same degree. In 1968, 45% of people in the north had lost all their teeth compared with 33% in 1978. The improvements were not equal in all age-groups and the degree of improvement was different for particular age-groups in particular regions. Women at both dates were more likely than men to have lost all their teeth, but both showed improvement in the 10 years. The greatest improvement among social classes was in lower-income groups with a reduction of 31% compared with 16% in the higher groups. Comparison of dentures worn seemed to provide evidence of a reduction in large-scale extraction, and this is supported by the increases shown in filled teeth among people who still retained some natural teeth. The proportion of filled teeth was compared with visits to the dentist. The actual physical condition of teeth (amount of decay) for both years is described. The interview information was used to investigate attendance at the dentist and attitudes.

Attitudes towards health services

The 1968 dental health survey marked a changing attitude towards involvement of the Survey in direct study of any part of the NHS. In 1971, the year the General Household Survey began, the Committee on Hospital Complaints Procedure, like the Committee on General Practice 20 years previously, saw the need to supplement its information with a more representative 'consumer' view, and in collaboration with an independent research organisation a survey was made of former patients and their views on certain aspects of hospital services. This was followed by a request from the Royal Commission on the National Health Service to study patients' experience of and attitudes towards NHS hospital services. One of the research secretaries of the commission has explained: 'most of the written evidence came from organizations within or concerned with the NHS. Two-thirds from organizations and a third individuals. Of individual submissions nearly half were from NHS workers or ex-workers. Evidence from members of the public was sparse and mainly anecdotal. This was one reason why surveys were carried out for the Commission'.[6] Two studies were thought relevant. One, *Patients' Attitudes to the Hospital Service*, was designed especially for the commission. The General Household Survey regularly asks questions about medical services received so it was possible conveniently to identify former patients, and personal interviews were carried out with them in 1977. The number of visits in a given period and illnesses treated were recorded. Over a quarter had been admitted within two weeks of being told they would have to go to hospital and nearly half were admitted within one month. Overall, one in five were distressed or inconvenienced by the wait for admission but among those who had to wait three months or more (about a third) the proportion rose to one in three.

Most made their own way to hospital and the demand for hospital transport seems to have been met even among the elderly. Asked about various amenities – TV, telephone, shop – most inpatients and outpatients said they had sufficient access. Washing and bathing facilities for most inpatients were satisfactory, but 15% were dissatisfied: overall complaints about washing and toilet facilities came from as many as one in five inpatients. Nearly half the patients complained of being woken too early. The proportions dissatisfied fell sharply after a 6.30 am waking time, but 27% said they were disturbed during the night and this was shown to depend on the size of the ward. Patients' attitudes to meals and to visiting times were examined as well as how they felt about the size and type of ward. Outpatients' experience of waiting and the appointments system were examined. The proportion feeling waiting time was unreasonable rose from 38% of those who waited 30 minutes to 60% of those who waited an hour or longer; when the wait was 30 minutes or more the proportion believing the appointments system is mainly for the benefit of the doctor rose to between half and two-thirds.

Privacy was mentioned spontaneously as a problem by only a few but the proportions rose when specific situations were mentioned: for example, 8% were 'bothered quite a lot' when being overheard or seen by other patients during their consultation, examination or treatment. About one in three inpatients felt they had not been given enough information about how they were progressing and nearly half of those who wanted more information felt they could not ask any of their doctors to tell them what they wanted to know. Substantial minorities had difficulty in understanding what the doctor was saying, some because 'doctors were foreign' and over half of these were worried or upset by this failure. The situation was similar for outpatients. Although it is official policy that outpatients' permission is asked if medical students are to be present one in four adult inpatients said that the doctor had discussed their condition or treatment as if they weren't there. Over half of these said they were annoyed or distressed, but 'The vast majority of patients found that all or most of staff (nursing, paramedical or non-medical) were considerate, or nice, or helpful'. No more than 5% were dissatisfied, and over two-thirds felt that nursing staff had done most to help them adapt to their hospital stay. The report describes other worries that patients had, what they felt about them and what they felt might help.

There are usually difficulties in summarising the degree of satisfaction or dissatisfaction about these different aspects of medical attention. The report took six aspects of the service which all inpatients would have experienced and found that 36% of all inpatients were satisfied with all six and a further 30% dissatisfied with only one. Of the latter, over half complained about being woken too early: if the time of waking could be shifted to 7 am the proportion satisfied with all six aspects would rise to around 54%. And if some improvement could be made in communications as well, two-thirds would have no complaints. A similar calculation made for outpatients showed that 46% were satisfied with all of the six items and 24% dissatisfied with only one. If outpatients were given more information about their progress the proportion satisfied with all six aspects would rise to 56%.

The other survey the commission was interested in, *Access to Primary Health Care*, had already been designed for the health departments of England, Wales, Scotland and Northern Ireland and was carried out in 1977. It followed the 1976 consultative document *Priorities for Health and Social Services in England*[7] which emphasised the importance of community healthcare in relieving pressure on hospital and residential services and recommended that priority should be given to the family doctor and other primary healthcare services. It was thought that changes in organisation leading to the primary healthcare team and the consequent attempt to provide integrated care and to develop health centres throughout the UK needed study. The survey was to examine access to treatment but not the treatment itself. Some of the descriptive information needed related to the GPs of individual respondents, who were all asked to give their GP's name. Every GP concerned was asked if he or she was willing to give the information on organisation needed for the survey, and just under 2% of the GPs whose names were available said they did not wish to give information. The information required was obtained for 95% of respondents who were registered with a GP. This survey was done 25 years after the study of general practice under the NHS was so summarily stopped. One of the results of that decision was to reduce the possibility of assessing change over time and after successive reorganisations of the health service.

The report began with a description of the kind of practice attended and showed that 42% of patients attended practices with an average list size of over 2,500 patients; 19% attended practices in health centres; a greater proportion of people in England attended practices in designated areas than in Scotland or Wales and 'there was virtually no difference in sex, age and social class of people using the different types of practice'. Grouping doctors in health centres might have been expected to increase the distance between homes and practices, but the distance was found to be only slightly greater for health centre practices than for others. But distance increased with the number of doctors in the practice. Ninety per cent of respondents said they found it easy or fairly easy to reach their doctors but this disguises some difficulty found among the elderly. Most people were content with surgery hours and the appointments system used, but 'between 10% and 15% of the sample as a whole were dissatisfied in any way with what was available at their doctor's practice'.

Most people found their doctors approachable ('easy to talk to, explained things fully') but this may depend on the patients as much as the doctors. Views on the surgery varied with age, the elderly being more likely to view surgeries as modern and welcoming, efficient. Health centre practices were more likely to be viewed by all as modern, spacious and clean. It appeared that the types of practice used and the way the practice was administered had 'remarkably little effect' on how often people consulted their doctors. There was no evidence that the more modern forms of practice organisation reduced the frequency of consultation, though distance from the surgery and large lists did have a small effect on the consultation rate. There was a 'remarkable degree of stability in people's attachment to their doctor's practices. The vast majority change practices only when they move or the practice ceases to operate'. The report described the frequency of home visits, for whom they were requested and variation by types of practice. The history of past attempts to contact doctors outside surgery hours is described and of past decisions to seek help from alternatives to the doctor such as pharmacists or hospital accident and emergency departments. 'It did not seem that the public frequently use' such sources of help. The report recorded the incidence of prescriptions and the location of pharmacists used. 'The great majority feel that they have reasonably easy access to a pharmacy.' Access and use of other primary services – ophthalmic, chiropody, dental – were examined with reference to location, use of private services and level of satisfaction. The report noted in conclusion the 'principal finding is that in general for most people the primary health care services are easily accessible . . . Evidence of difficulties or dissatisfaction was limited to a small minority . . . the newer forms of practice organization were generally no hindrance to accessibility'.

The royal commission recorded in 1979 some of the changes in research funding and responsibilities, and noted that 'Health Services Research has only been undertaken on any scale within the last decade . . . its development has been slow in comparison to clinical research . . . the present arrangements for funding and commissioning do not meet this requirement'. To meet the need the commission recommended the establishment of an Institute of Health Services Research with funding 'which would enable coherent research programmes to be developed'.[8] Any such development would need to utilise technical skill and professional competence not very different from that displayed by the Survey in surveys of the scope and type described in this chapter.

Notes

[1] *Hansard*, 7 May 1956.
[2] *The Work of Nurses in Hospital Wards*, Nuffield Provincial Hospitals Trust, 1953.
[3] Report of the Jay Committee on Mentally Handicapped and Community Care, HMSO, 1976.
[4] Webber and Craig, *Population Trends*, HMSO, 1976.
[5] P Stocks, 'Morbidity Statistics', *Public Health*, April 1947.
[6] Christine Farrel, *Policy and Politics*, Vol 8 No 2, 1980.
[7] *Priorities for Health and Social Services in England*, HMSO, 1967.
[8] Royal Commission on the National Health Service, Col 7615, 1979.

9 Jobs, productivity and industrial relations

LIKE THE WORK DESCRIBED SO FAR, surveys related to work and its rewards found an early place in the Survey's activities. The pressures and constraints of war paradoxically loosened previous patterns of working relationships; the composition and involvement of the labour force changed drastically. Faced with very difficult postwar circumstances where industries with a history of lasting depression became vital contributors to economic stability, attitudes towards the industrial mobilisation of working people were, necessarily, very different from those which prevailed before the war. This change is reflected in the efforts made to recruit workers to such industries and in a new-found willingness to reconsider the position and circumstances of particular groups of the population.

Early recruitment surveys

The government's attempt in the years following the war to increase cotton exports involved changes in working conditions in the industry coupled with a campaign to inform people about the country's economic difficulties and the part that cotton could play. The 1948 survey *Public Opinion in Lancashire Cotton Towns* was designed to help these efforts. It showed that the industry's past reputation did not help: nearly 70% believed that there had been objections to the industry. The report noted 'Cotton workers spoke of past bad conditions less frequently than the general population in the cotton towns but more frequently of "bullying and tyranny"'. Twice as many women, a majority of cotton workers, described lack of amenities. Only 20% voiced such objections about the current situation; comments on bullying had almost disappeared and low wages or bad conditions were mentioned much less. About a third of the general population sampled thought that the good times would last and another 10% thought that things would get even better. Against this positive view of 44% of the general population, over half would not venture any opinion or thought that there were bad times ahead. So there was a marked degree of pessimism about the future, rooted in the fear of foreign competition, though cotton workers were a little more optimistic than the general population.

Distinct from these general views were the opinions of the industry's workers on their own places of work: '80% thought conditions good or good on the whole'. Only very small proportions said that they disliked their jobs or wanted to change. By grouping responses to questions about the present and future of the industry a scale was produced (a 'satisfaction score') which was used to test 'the real willingness' of those outside the industry to enter it. But 'asked what improvements might induce more people to enter the industry a high proportion has no suggestions to make'. Only about a quarter of the general population and 38% of cotton workers knew about the possibilities of redeployment and of these about half were in favour of it. The great majority knew of the government's hopes for increased production as a contribution to exports and knew that the existing balance of trade was unfavourable, but a majority thought that cotton exports were already greater than before the war.

A year later, in order to measure the effect of the government's educational campaign the survey was repeated. Views on the past history of the industry, particularly among older people, had softened and fewer voiced objections to the industry than a year previously. However, pessimism about the industry had increased: 37% in 1949 thought there were bad times ahead for cotton because of foreign competition, compared with 17% in 1948. In 1948, 46% had thought that good or even better times lay ahead because of the world demand for cotton; in 1949 only 19% thought so. Between the two surveys an agreement had been signed with Japan to permit the importation of Japanese goods to the Commonwealth.

While the reputation of cotton and its future prosperity was mainly affected by fears of international competition, the situation in coalmining was rather different. The number of workers under 18 years old employed had halved between 1938 and 1945. Without a steady flow of recruits there could be no long-term hope according to the current view of increasing production, and in 1946 the Survey was asked to study the recruitment of boys to the mining industry. Samples of parents and boys in the six main coalfields were chosen from local food records, and the national registration schedules enabled a distinction to be made between mining and non-mining parents. The survey report noted that four out of every five miners came from mining families and this was also true of miners' wives. Hardly any boys from non-mining families were in mining. Any increase in the recruitment of boys would have to come from mining families. The great majority of boys or their parents were sure of the importance of mining compared with other industries, but a minority thought it was no longer important and the proportion rose to a quarter of all boys not employed in mining. Few parents had made plans for their boys still at school, but while most mining parents had considered mining as a possible occupation the majority had rejected it. Only one in five mining parents had decided in favour of mining and 6% of the boys wanted to become miners. This compared with 33% of the boys in mining families who were currently employed in mining. When boys from mining families went outside mining they were more likely to take up unskilled work than boys from non-mining families. The survey report records the advantages and disadvantages seen by respondents. Many more mining fathers (83%) saw disagreeable things about the industry than those who saw anything favourable (55%), and the discrepancy was even more marked among boys. The job was seen as unhealthy, dangerous, too hard and with poor prospects, and those who were not in favour of mining were more likely to judge that the miner had an inferior social status. Prospects for recruitment would depend on changing these views. While material incentives such as wages, job security and hours of work were rated by respondents as better in mining than in other industries, job interest, promotion prospects, and (among mining fathers who expressed an opinion) relations with management were thought to be worse. Nine out of ten mining fathers thought there had been improvements in the previous 20 years and it seemed that mechanisation might have a considerable effect on attitudes.

Nationalisation had just been approved by parliament at the time of the survey but there was not much knowledge of how this was going to operate. Three out of four mining fathers thought that it would lead to mining becoming a better job, expecting better conditions and organisation, 'fair play' and the chance to work for themselves or the country rather than for the owners. However, except among mining fathers these beliefs seemed to have little effect on attitudes to mining as a job.

The Survey studied mining recruitment again in 1946 in the survey *Men and Mining*, based on a general population sample. This was concerned with the general reputation of the industry as a factor in recruitment among the non-mining male population. The original intention was to make a parallel study of miners but the preface to the report noted that the 'National Coal Board was unable to agree to that enquiry being carried out'. When the men interviewed were asked whether people they knew talked much about miners and coal-mining only 51% said that people talked 'a lot' or a 'fair amount' about them, and among non-manual workers less than half did so. Asked what they thought was the main cause of the current coal shortage 27% said it was shortage of manpower and 11% said lack of up-to-date machinery. About a third of those who referred to manpower said that the shortage was due to bad conditions of work and the danger of the job. Two-thirds of the sample thought that nationalisation would make mining a better job, mainly because material conditions including pay and mechanisation would be improved and the strife of the past would be forgotten. These views were more frequently expressed in mining areas than elsewhere, and were supported by very favourable judgments on miners. Two-thirds thought they were good people 'doing a rotten job'. The report set such opinions about the industry and its workers against the actual past contacts of respondents: those who had not been down a pit or in a mining area gave a less favourable reaction than those who had. These views on the physical environment seemed to present formidable obstacles to recruitment – two-thirds of the sample thought working conditions were worse than in their own jobs.

Another aspect of the mining industry, which provided a rather different reflection of conditions and might have made its own contribution to recruitment difficulties, was studied in a survey *The Employment of Men With*

Pneumokoniosis carried out for a research unit of the Medical Research Council in 1946. The Board of Trade proposed to establish factories in South Wales in which men with pneumokoniosis might be employed. Little was known, however, of the employment histories of men who had been certified and who therefore could not work underground but were free to work elsewhere. The sample was chosen from records of men certified by the Silicosis Board kept by the Ministry of Fuel and Power. Two-thirds were working or had worked since certification. Their work experience could be related to the X-ray categorisation of their illness and to the methods they had used to find work. While jobs had mainly been found through employment exchanges 30% of all jobs were taken because nothing else was offered. Twelve per cent of the sample had left their homes, either alone or with their families, in search of work: 35% said they were ready to move and of those 20% said they would move anywhere. The evidence of the survey was that such emigration had been a limited success in the past. The report described the work done, the number of jobs held and how long the jobs had lasted. It also described the financial consequences of the illness and the emotional effects of having to leave mining, and concluded by pointing out the need for an organisation which could 'help men over the difficult period of emotional readjustment and ... to bring to their notice the wide range of jobs which had been done ... this might do much to mitigate the air of hopelessness which many of the Survey's interviewers thought overlay villages hard hit by pneumokoniosis'.

Also in 1946 a survey was designed to help develop recruitment policy for a very different occupation. *Recruitment to the Civil Service* was carried out for the Treasury, which was concerned with the reconstruction of the civil service after the war, particularly the substantial increase in the numbers of executive and clerical officers over those recruited before the war. Samples of non-graduate technical, professional and clerical workers under 30 years were chosen as well as schoolchildren of the appropriate educational level and their parents. Respondents were taken through the various factors they considered important in choosing a career and each of these was then considered with reference to the civil service. The report concluded 'since the main criticisms of work in the Civil Service are that it lacks interest and that promotion is slow it would be desirable for publicity to state clearly what sort of jobs were available and what prospects there are for an individual to rise ... very little is known about working conditions ... since it is however well known that security is an advantage of the Civil Service it seems very little would be gained by emphasising this'.

Similar studies were made to help recruitment to the Royal Air Force (1947), Territorial Army (1948) and other services (1948). The latter study compared the views of volunteer recruits, the relevant sections of the general population and ex-servicemen. It was done at a time of severe economic pressure and the report noted that current emphasis on the importance of some industries and their contribution to exports might have affected response. 'In 1939 there was a war to be won ... in 1948 there is an economic crisis ... the public are generally not convinced of the useful function of the Armed Forces at this time.' The attractions and deterrents of life in the various services and the differences between them were explored. Intelligence test scores devised by the services were used to show how attitudes to such factors varied with intelligence level. It was shown that satisfaction levels dropped as intelligence level increased: 'the higher intelligence groups seek long term satisfaction in the job situation whilst the lower intelligence groups more frequently seek satisfaction in factors incidental to the work itself . . . volunteers to both the Army and the RAF desire or expect to obtain a higher grade civilian job on leaving the Forces but . . . whilst the majority of Army volunteers believe that their prospects of work will not be affected 71% of RAF volunteers consider that their prospects will be improved . . . The attitudes of women towards service life for men must be regarded as one of the more important deterrents to joining'.

This report brought out the differences between volunteer recruits to the Army and the RAF. A later study, *National Service and Enlistment in the Armed Forces*, compared volunteers and conscripts. 'The differences between the social and economic backgrounds of National Servicemen and volunteers within arms are as great as differences between arms.' The report emphasised the relevance of such differences to training programmes and to expectations about living conditions. The conscripts were much less likely to consider themselves usefully employed in the forces, and between a quarter and a third of them said that they thought their employment prospects would be prejudiced by their service. 'Better liaison between services and employers and between employers and young employees seems desirable if the fears of many young conscripts are to be reduced.' It showed that many young men began to think about National Service some years before it happened. Preferences between services changed over time and there were differences in preferences between those with different educational levels.

Most of the recruitment surveys were made before 1951 during the transition to peacetime conditions. The public concern with the economic difficulties experienced in these years and the emphasis on the contribution of some industries provided the stimulus for the surveys described. There were, however, some themes which were taken up repeatedly over much longer periods of time. They mainly concern the changing roles of substantial groups in the population in postwar years, and among these perhaps the most important were women and the elderly.

Women and employment

The high proportion of women in the cotton industry was unusual in the first half of this century – overall the situation was very different. But from 10% of married women in the labour force in 1921 the proportion changed drastically under the pressures of war, and the change persisted until in 1979 nearly half of all married women were economically active. By then 42% of the whole labour force were women and while the number of women employed grew steadily between 1959 and 1979 the number of men employed declined. Such major changes necessarily focused government attention.

In the Survey's work the subject arose naturally during the early years of the war because of the critical importance of women in the war effort, and some of the first Survey studies were about the particular contribution of women. The survey of the Auxiliary Territorial Service (ATS) in 1942 was concerned with an activity which was proving unpopular. Compared with the proportion of women choosing the ATS, four times as many chose the women's airforce or naval services and three times as many chose war work in an office or factory. Those in the ATS believed its general reputation to be much worse than it was in fact. An examination of the reasons given by women and friends or relatives provided some material for a public information campaign designed to develop a more favourable judgment.

In the following year a broader survey, *Women's Registration and Call Up*, for the Ministry of Labour and National Service, investigated the extent to which women under 50 had absorbed the new facts about compulsory registration. About a third either believed they would not have to register or were uncertain about it. Threequarters of all women hoped to be exempt including two-thirds of women without young children. The survey report described what happened during registration and the interview which followed. Most women thought they had been fairly treated and that any special qualifications had been considered, but there was a minority (21%) who believed there were loopholes in the regulations which enabled some women to evade service.

By 1943 some attention had turned to postwar possibilities. The survey *Women at Work* was done for the Minister of Reconstruction. Its prime purpose was to discover what proportion of women intended to carry on working after the war and how this proportion might vary from one industry to another. The report of the survey began with a description of employed women at that time – their education, training and responsibilities, followed by an examination of attitudes – advantages and disadvantages of work as viewed by married and single respondents. The report suggested that based on these attitudes 'The post war labour force of women now 15–59 should be between 20–40% less than in 1943. It should not be greatly altered from before the war so far as marital status of those employed is concerned, but a higher proportion than before the war of women now 35–45 years may be seeking work ... Only a quarter of those who came into industry from their homes propose to go on working after the war. These are principally women over 35 ... work after marriage is condemned by the majority of single women and by a minority of married women'. These predictions turned out to be very far from reality. Clearly they did not and could not take into account the vast changes in industry, standards of living and, above all, expectations after the war.

In 1947 the Ministry of Labour, concerned to increase the recruitment of women to industry, launched an information campaign and a further survey was carried out as part of this effort. This survey, *Women and Industry*, showed that compared with 1943, the peak year of employment during the war, employed women in 1947 were more frequently older married women. The report examined the factors associated with employment and stated 'that it is marriage as such which dissuades women from working and not marriage and children is shown by the fact that of married women without children 32% were in employment compared with 88% of single women who equally have no children ... it appears that it is only children aged 0–4 who exercise any considerable influence on the proportion of married women in employment'. The importance of these demographic factors in various industries and occupations was examined in order to throw light on where possible reserves of labour might be found. The report then looked at attitudes and noted 'the greater part of all women therefore think that women should not work or are dubious about women working for reasons connected with their homes, husbands and children ... it is possible that only 16% of women are positively in favour of women working under any circumstances ... but these ideas are associated with attitudes towards the advantages women see in work and estimates of the difficulties that prevent them taking up work ... this sentiment might be weakened by dealing with the difficulties ... nurseries, shopping, laundering and home helps'. One of the main contributions to the great change that has taken place in women's employment, family planning, does not appear in the discussion. The attitudes of husbands 'would not seem to be of great importance in dissuading women from work' but 20% of employed women spoke of their husbands' disapproval. As with the previous survey, the limitations of the technique employed failed to bring out anything like the full potential for change. Very much more useful were the detailed descriptions of the actual circumstances at the time of individual surveys. The comparisons they made available were better guides to change.

Many economic ups and downs and several changes of government occurred before the *Survey of Women's Employment* was made in 1965. It was still a time of full employment and the new survey showed a continuation of the trends brought out by the two previous ones. In 1943 22% of married women were employed, in 1965 the figures had more than doubled to 45%. The 1965 report noted 'among housewives nearly half were working outside their homes as well as carrying on their household duties ... married women accounted for two-thirds of the female labour force ... One-third of the women who were not working intended to return at some time'. The report went on to look more critically at the nature of women's work. 'Most of the jobs done by women were at a low level in the Registrar General's skills classification ... even those classified as skilled non-manual include very few who could be regarded as skilled in the sense that many male manuals are skilled ... a little over half the working women were very satisfied with their present job ... one woman in ten was seriously thinking of changing but less than half of these had done anything about it.' And there was an echo of the 1947 report in the 'strong evidence that the birth of the first child rather than marriage has now become the most usual occasion for a woman to give up work'. The report investigated who looked after the children and showed that a third of women responsible for children under 16 were working. The proportion for part-time workers was much higher – over 50%. But most of the children were of school age, and most were looked after by relatives when the mother was at work so that for over 70% of mothers of young children there was no cost involved. The report noted that these relatives (grandmothers, middle aged and elderly) had done little or no work since their own marriages. 'With the steadily increasing proportion of women who continued to work after marriage or to return after a few years this reserve available for child care is diminishing.' Apart from children 'one working woman in ten was responsible for the care of at least one elderly or infirm person ... [they were more likely] to be in occupations at the top and bottom of the social scale'. The report examined training, education and qualifications gained in relation to employment, monetary reward and how the money was spent, and concluded with responses to questions about satisfactions, disadvantages, and the views of husbands, which were similar to those asked in the earlier surveys.

In 1980 a fourth survey, *Women and Employment*, was done to bring the picture up to date. By this time the situation was no longer one of full employment and there were many other signs of major changes in the employment situation. These more recent surveys were obviously influenced by the growing interest in equal opportunity and some surveys in later years have been explicitly concerned with situations where equality were thought to be too limited. Legislation aimed at the reduction or limitation of sex discrimination came in 1975, but in 1972 the survey *Fifth Form Girls: Their Hopes for the Future* tried to 'identify conditions and attitudes associated with the failure of some girls to pursue their education as far as their abilities seemed to warrant'. (This survey is described more fully on page 204). In 1973 the Department of Employment asked the Survey to 'find out in what field differences in conditions and opportunities exist between men and women and to define those differences'. The report, *Management Attitudes and Practices towards Women at Work*, noted some sampling difficulties and that response from the establishments approached was much lower than the Survey had come to expect. The design required contact with people at different levels in each establishment, from those responsible for formulating personnel policy to implementers, managers and employees. But the report was 'based almost entirely on answers given by formulators and implementers of personnel policy'. It described the relatively small proportions of those groups who were women: 'In establishments where half or more of employees are women only one-quarter of implementers are women and in establishments with 250 or more employees one-sixth are women. In the engineering industry about 1 in 40 implementers is a woman'. Attitudes towards the 'three important demands – equal pay, more women in senior posts, more training of women for skilled work' were described and views expressed by the respondents on their own behalf were rather more favourable than the views they attributed to their colleagues; 'it appears likely therefore that the attitude of management to equal pay is less favourable than might be assumed from the expressed opinions of respondents'. Substantial proportions claimed that 'women were not career conscious'. The report described attitudes to jobs in which individual women do the same or similar work as men, jobs on which women are never employed and jobs it was said could not be done by the opposite sex. '62% of formulators think there are jobs which no woman could do compared with 14% who think there are jobs no men could do ... the range of jobs named was very much wider for women than for men ... when asked whether jobs could be modified so that they could be done by women in three-quarters of instances formulators said they could not'. The report concluded that 'the application of the principle of equal opportunity is likely to meet with considerable opposition in practice'.

In 1975 the Sex Discrimination Act became law. This focused attention more directly on actual applications and in 1977, at the request of the Equal Opportunities Commission, the Survey studied women and shiftwork. The Act says that the employment opportunities offered to women must not differ from those offered to men. The Factories Acts, however, contain many provisions limiting women's employment – women's hours of work in manufacturing industries and shiftwork. The survey focused on the extent to which women might favour or reject a proposal to change the law on hours of work and the extent to which women might actually work such hours. The survey was to describe and analyse the factors which might influence these attitudes. In order to concentrate the sample efficiently on the most relevant population, a sample of women in wards with high proportions of women 18–59 working in manual occupations and a sub-sample of their husbands were interviewed. Most of the working women in the sample worked locally, spending less than 30 minutes on the journey to work. The report described education and training and noted 'once the qualifications and training of teachers, nurses and a few of the other non-manual occupations are taken into account it may be said that we are interviewing a community of women almost entirely without recognised forms of preparation for work'. The work done was described with special reference to hours worked, starting and finishing times. On shiftworking the report said that 'approval or disapproval are contingent on the domestic situation. Except for night shifts there is fairly widespread approval of single women working shifts; considerably less for married women and widespread disapproval for married women with young children working shifts except for part-time evening shifts'. While respondents very much agreed with the general principle of allowing women to work as much shiftwork as men, fewer approved of the law being changed for specific examples suggested and even fewer were prepared themselves to work such shifts. The report compared the views of husbands and wives on most of the issues examined and noted 'substantial disagreement between wives and husbands on basic issues concerning a woman's role at home and at work ... this includes the issue of shiftwork ... excluding the question of evening shifts at least one-third of couples disagree about changes in the law ... most husbands oppose the prospect of their wives working shifts ... most wives are aware of the opposition but even so many wives would still go ahead and predict no active opposition from husbands'.

Elderly persons and employment

In 1945, the Industrial Health Research Board of the Medical Research Council, acknowledging the growing numbers of elderly people and in the absence of any Census data since 1931, asked the Survey to study the employment of older persons, defined as men and women over the age of 60. The survey was based on a stratified random sample of local rating lists and was one of the earliest examples of the sifting method developed by the Survey to locate particular sections of the population. Households were approached to record ages of members and the older people so located were interviewed. The survey was designed so that comparisons could be made with the 1931 situation. It showed that in mid 1945 28% of all persons over 60 were in employment compared with 34% in 1931 who were either in or seeking employment. In 1931 63% of men were employed compared to 53% in 1945. So there seemed to have been a decline in employment of older persons between the depression year of 1931 and the full-employment year of 1945. The report noted that the number of older persons employed in manufacturing industry increased during the war years and therefore it was possible that if the war years 'halted a decline in the proportion of old people in employment they did no more than act as a break on a long term decline which may continue in the future'. There were quite marked variations in the proportion of over-60 employed males in different regions, greater than corresponding figures for the under 60s. The report showed that men and women over 60 'remain part of a household more frequently when they are in employment than when they are not and as increasing age brings about increasing unemployment so it brings increasing loneliness. It should be remembered that the Supplementary Pension payable to Pensioners in 1945 was subject to an assessment of means which included the incomes of other members of the family'. A comparison of the economic grouping of households with and without old people suggested 'households with old people are more frequently found in the lowest economic group'.

The report investigated occupations, industries and work histories. The majority of men over 60 were either labourers (21%), non-manufacturing operatives (32%) or self-employed (16%). 'Only one person in five worked solely because he or she preferred to do so and a further one in four said they had to work but in any case preferred to do so. Thus one in two did not want to work but had no alternative.' As was expected, the majority of these stressed financial reasons, though 30% of the men and 24% of the women said they had nothing to do at home.

The report warned of the possible effect of wartime dislocation on the results presented, and in 1950 the Ministry of Labour asked for another study of the topic in peacetime conditions, the *Survey of Older Persons and their Employment*. It was based on samples of people aged 55 to 74 and employers. The sample of older people was drawn from local national register files, avoiding the more elaborate and costly sampling method used for the previous survey. Comparison with the earlier surveys showed that 'whilst the proportion of women in full or part-time employment had remained stationary the overall proportion of men in employment was lower than in 1945. The main decline was at ages 65–69, that is roughly at pensionable age. In 1946 44% of male pensioners between 60 and 75 were at work compared with 30% between 60 and 75 today'. In later years these descriptive data would come not only from the Census but also from employment censuses, continuing sample surveys like the General Household

Survey and the regular flow of more extensive departmental statistics. These early surveys provided a convenient supplement to the more exiguous statistics available a generation earlier. The 1950 study showed that more than half the women who at some time had done a fulltime job had given up fulltime work at 44 years or younger. The overall age at which women gave up working was 42, while the overall average for men was 62.

This survey sampled employers as well as employees and covered only firms employing more than 10. Some information about those working in small firms came from the employee sample. Rather more of the workers over 65 worked for smaller firms and the report showed the relationship between retirement age and superannuation schemes in both large and small firms. 'Men working in firms with more than 9 people will give up jobs at 60–65 either because they have no choice or because the inducements to retire are greater than those offered to men working in small firms. In fact about half of those working in or who had worked in firms with a specific retiring age said they would have liked to stay beyond the specific age.' The report described work histories and the attitudes towards retirement of those who at the time of the survey were no longer at work.

There were obvious trends in the results shown by these surveys and they dealt with a growing section of the population. In 1971 the General Household Survey began a new flow of data about the social and economic circumstances of the elderly as part of its multifaceted approach to all age-groups, but it wasn't until 1977 that the detailed *Reasons for Retirement* survey described earlier was done.

Increasing productivity

The central theme of government interest in the period from the economic crises of 1947 through the change of government in 1951 was the need for improved productivity. In part this took the form of concern with the employment of scientists and technicians after graduation and the wider use of scientific and technical information in industry. In 1951 a partial answer to the question on what jobs graduates had taken up and why came from a survey, *The Employment of Science Graduates*, based on samples of London University science graduates who took an honours degree in 1951 (17% of all science graduates) and science graduates who had received a DSIR maintenance grant. It was found that 46% of all the London graduates had taken a research job and a further 7% a teaching job. Of these, 16% were employed in a university, 57% by industry and 20% by the government. Nearly all the DSIR graduates had taken a research job and about half worked for employers in industry. About 58% of the science graduates and 54% of the DSIR graduates had unfavourable views of civil service employment and in particular disliked the practice of central recruitment. In choosing their employment 53% of graduates and 58% of DSIR graduates said the considerations were other than pay or prospects.

In 1958 another aspect of the use of technical information was studied at the request of the Ministry of Education. The 1952 survey of holders of the Higher National Certificate (HNC) was designed to find out who took it and what kind of jobs men obtained as a result of getting it. This qualification was originally intended to enable students to approach, through technical colleges, the standard of a university pass degree. A special feature of the scheme allowed technical colleges to frame syllabuses which included subjects related to the needs of local industry. By 1952 it had become a common way of securing entrance to one of the professional institutions, and three times as many men took it as took a first degree in technology. They were therefore a considerable addition to the country's technical resources, but doubt was felt about the use made of them by industry and the rewards they received. The sample was based on 50% of all the men who passed HNC in 1952 in mechanical, electrical and production engineering. It was thought that by 1958 they would have had time to make a reasonable start to their careers. Only 52% of all the men said that HNC was a necessary condition for their job and at the time of the survey, six years after qualifying, 14% of the men had reached managerial status. Sixty-two per cent were employed in manufacturing industry, mostly in the larger firms, employing 500 or more. Earnings were investigated. The report said 'the possession of HNC appears to have assisted the men in the sample to improve their industrial status but the monetary rewards were not high either in comparison to the effort put into obtaining the qualification or to the pay of tradesmen . . . the majority of the men were not aware of any policy within their firms to promote their interests in future'. This did not stop them from thinking that it had been worth the effort to obtain the qualification mainly because it had helped them to get their present job or they expected that it would help if they wanted to change jobs.

In the summer of 1958 a study was made of response to institutions set up to promote formal training in agriculture, farm colleges and farm institutions. The survey *Formal Training in Agriculture* was designed to find out why response was low. Farmers and farmworkers were interviewed as well as some ex-students of farm institutes. The report showed that 'farmers are, on the whole, in favour of formal training for those who are to hold responsible positions in the industry as farmers or managers. They are much less likely to favour training for those who intend to be farm workers'. Seventy-four per cent of farmers themselves had left school at 15 or less and only a very small proportion had any formal training. There was not much contact between farmers and the training or educational institutions and it seemed that 'most farmers could not give much exact information about training to anyone who sought this'. Most farmers (93%) said they would encourage farmworkers to attend evening classes, 53% said they would be prepared to pay workers for time spent on such classes at times when workers would normally be working and 28% would be prepared to pay for fulltime classes over two or three weeks. Such responses indicating degrees of willingness to facilitate training are related in the report to characteristics of the farmers. Since most farmworkers at the time found their jobs through informal contacts they would not have been given advice about formal training on leaving school. Further, it seemed that ambition to improve their status in the farm industry was limited: '45% of farm workers say they hope to be doing the same job in twenty years time ... even amongst farmers' sons 10% say this ... 90% of workers knew that training opportunities exist but only 42% have had the suggestion made to them that they could take training. 28% had considered the possibility seriously and 6% intend to take training'. But most of the ex-students of farm colleges or institutes seemed sure that such attendance was more useful than just continuing at their jobs, that the balance of instruction was right and on the whole they seemed well pleased with the method of training they had chosen.

Labour Mobility in Great Britain in 1963 described geographical movement 1953–63 and related it to various aspects of employment. The report showed the proportions of movement for different reasons: 'the main reason is to obtain better or more suitable housing. Only 1 in 6 of the moves in the previous ten years was due to work reasons ... however 1 in 4 have moved house because of a job at some time in their life, those with higher education qualifications being more likely to move for work reasons (55% of graduates) than those with lesser qualifications (no qualifications 24%, 'O' level or equivalent 35%)'. Attitudes to movement in different contingencies were examined – 33% of men and 71% of all women said they would not go 'if an employer moves the establishment to another part of the country. 38% of men and 16% of women gave an unqualified "yes"'. The proportions varied with age, qualifications and present region. Forty-six per cent would consider moving if the present job ceased but about the same proportion would rather take a less suitable job. Job histories were described and related to training, the reasons for leaving jobs, occupational status and qualifications. This survey brought up to date a similar study made in 1950 for the Ministry of Labour and the London School of Economics.

These surveys between 1948 and 1962 reflect an increasing concern with the rate of technological change and the state of an industrial organisation in which slow progress was rooted. This disquiet found political expression in a government attempt to stimulate public discussion and three party – employers, workers, government – agreement on industrial change through a new institution, the National Economic Development Council, set up in 1961. This was followed by a political upheaval in which a third of the cabinet was dismissed. The subsequent election brought in a new government pledged to revolutionise the country's technological base. But the realities of under-investment and continuing industrial strife pulled in a different direction, leading to a continuing debate on industrial relations.

Industrial relations

A series of surveys on related themes were made during the ten years 1966–76. The first of these, *Workplace Industrial Relations*, was done for the Royal Commission on Trade Unions and Employers Associations (Donovan Commission) in 1966 and involved studies of shop stewards, trades union officers, works managers, personnel officers and shop-floor workers. The studies were designed jointly by the staff of the royal commission and the Survey and the main results, together with an appraisal of some of their practical implications, were published in a series of research papers. The reports described the background and experience of shop stewards and how they saw their activities, functions and relationships with other parties in the industrial situation. Wherever comparisons could be fairly made the stewards' responses were compared with those of other groups surveyed. This was the first representative data about the parties involved despite the decades of fierce criticism and debate which preceded the commission. In some respects the picture of the main actors which emerged from the survey is very different from the common stereotype.

'Whilst the majority of stewards had wanted the job 40% said they had to be persuaded and more than two-thirds either went through no form of election or were the only candidate ... the average size constituency was 60 members for stewards and 350 for senior stewards ... According to management roughly 13% of stewards were replaced each year mostly because of job changes ... not more than one in seven said the steward was defeated in elections and 3% or less said he was victimized or dismissed.' Thirteen per cent of stewards said they themselves had been victimized. Stewards' description of bargaining and the range of issues covered was reported and also their views on issues which they wanted to settle but which management would not discuss. On some of these matters the views of union members and union officials were compared with those of stewards. Using a series of questions, 'indices of satisfaction' with the system at workshop level were created and where possible used to compare the opinions of the different participants. Opinions among stewards, members and foremen on the influence of stewards on their members were described: 'stewards and officers more often thought stewards were more militant than their members but managers disagreed ... however management agreed by a small majority that *senior* stewards were more militant than ordinary stewards ... Most union members could not see any disadvantages in union membership but one in eight were not satisfied with what their unions did for them. More non-unionists had a favourable than an unfavourable impression of union activities'. Asked whether they found the job rewarding or satisfying 81% of stewards said they did, and the proportion was 88% for those who had represented their members for 10 or more years. Eighty-two per cent of stewards wanted to continue the job.

The report described the role of fulltime officials and the process as seen by stewards. It also gave judgments of officials and analysed their responsibilities: the way they spent their time, the number of stewards involved, visits to plants. The views of managers and personnel officers on the use and growth of agreed procedures were described as well as their experience of strikes and other forms of pressure. Thirty per cent of managers said they had had a strike since taking up their present post, twice as many in large plants as small and twice as many where the use of procedures had increased as where it had remained the same. The report described the views of managers on the activities of stewards. 'Demands made were said to be *always* reasonable by 18%, *usually* reasonable

55%, *sometimes* 21%.' Ninety-six per cent of works managers thought shop stewards were either very or fairly reasonable people. Among those from plants with procedures 29% thought stewards were very reasonable. Contacts of managers with fulltime union officials and their degree of satisfaction with the prevailing system were described, as were their views on possible improvement in work organisation in their plants if they were free to arrange their labour force as they wished. On average they thought that about nine per cent of working hours could be saved and '34% of management thought that trade unionism was a big factor in preventing them from arranging their labour as they wished . . . 40% said there were particular time wasting and inefficient practicies in their plants'.

Industrial relations continued to be a much debated topic with which successive governments were continually preoccupied. In 1971 the Conservative government brought in the Industrial Relations Act. By then it seemed that the information provided in the Donovan Commission was becoming out of date. The Department of Employment asked the Survey to make another study of the same topics and to extend it to some new ones. The concentration was to be on changes in bargaining procedures, relationships between stewards and their members and the way the parties were affected by specific changes in workplaces. A bigger change was in the design of the survey. Whereas the royal commission study had taken samples of individuals, the new survey attempted to study industrial relations situations, defined as 'a work unit within an establishment headed by a person who has responsibility for and deals with the industrial relations for that unit'. In each situation we took 'interlocking samples of individuals: a senior manager, a 'lower' manager, a foreman, three of that foreman's employees, one or more shop stewards, the most senior steward and the fulltime union officials . . . this design allowed the possibility of comparing the answers of the parties in the same situation . . . it permitted a deeper analysis of answers approximating to a series of case studies'. However, it had the disadvantage of severely limiting statistical comparison with the results of the Donovan survey. The sample was selected from all employment exchanges and was stratified to cover the four main industry types from which establishments employing 250 or more persons were chosen. Within the selected establishments industrial relations were sampled. The new method facilitated reporting on how the different parties saw many aspects of the situation examined.

> Very few stewards were dissatisfied with opportunities to contact members but one in three was dissatisfied with the physical facilities for doing their job . . . nearly half of the foremen and 43% of the stewards had taken part in courses run by the firm . . . much more workplace bargaining occurred between managers and shop stewards than between managers and full-time union officers . . . nearly half of the stewards and union officers wanted to extend their range of bargaining but in this survey they were supported by only one in six employees . . . more managers (58%) than stewards. 20% said they had unwritten workplace procedures . . . a majority of senior managers thought stewards were more important, in their system of negotiations, than full-time union officers and lower management were even more convinced by the importance of stewards . . . about two-thirds of senior managers thought the arrangements for dealing with employees' grievances and claims worked well, nearly all

foremen thought they were handled with reasonable speed and two-thirds of employees said the same.

Views on strikes and the circumstances under which they were most likely to occur were examined. In each of the sample workplaces all respondents were asked about one particular 'episode' which had recently affected industrial relations and their responses were analysed by comparing the way different parties saw the process. This was a qualitative analysis written to supplement the quantitative analyses which made up most of the report. In 1973 a further study, *Industrial Relations*, was done rather close on the heels of the 1972 survey 'because it was known that rapid changes had been taking place, especially in connection with actual and impending industrial relations legislation'. It was designed to replicate the 1972 study so as to monitor any changes and the topics covered were the same.

Shortly after that survey, following traumatic economic events such as the three day week, a general election took place in which relationships in industry and their reflection in government policy were a main theme. It was easy to see why in the following years 'industrial democracy' became a major public and political issue, eventually focusing on a Committee of Enquiry chaired by Lord Bullock. The Department of Employment 'against this background had been developing a programme of research designed to monitor and explore a range of options and possibilities amongst the many different interpretations of the scope and function of industrial democracy'. The survey *Company Organization and Worker Participation* in 1976 was designed 'to discover more about existing practices and attitudes, to explore the main forms of industrial democracy currently found, to seek the views held at key levels within companies of employee representation at board level, to find out whether the opinions of individuals at key levels in the same company were the same or different on major questions'. The last two purposes indicated that the design should to some extent follow that used for the last two industrial relations surveys. Samples of industrial establishments with at least 200 employees were selected from a sample of employment exchange areas; 60% of the identified companies cooperated and within these companies individuals in key roles were approached. These included board members, managers, foremen and union representatives. The report described the procedures adopted to identify these different role holders, which was not always easily done within individual establishments. The report described the board style – topics discussed, scope of board meetings and procedures for making decisions. Non-board members' knowledge of these matters was noted. Knowledge of and views on information disclosure, joint consultation machinery and collective bargaining were examined: 'Just over half the sampled companies had joint consultative committees at company-wide level. The sampled managerial levels tended to see current practice and the ideal situation in terms of joint *discussion*; to management ... the issues covered in JCCs tend to overlap with those covered by negotiating machinery ... asked whether any issues were not negotiable the most common answers related to capital investment and, to a lesser extent, new product planning'. Over 70% of the companies had not suffered any strikes in the 12 months before the survey though almost half had faced some form of industrial action like threats of strike (23%), overtime bans (36%) or go slow action (25%).

Responses to questions on whether management or workers' interests were the same (consensus) or different (conflict) permitted a categorisation of attitudes which could be used to throw light on the opinions held on one major suggestion for improving worker participation in the appointment of worker directors. 'The majority of directors were against the introduction of worker directors and three out of five at managerial level were also against . . . at worker representation levels over two-thirds were in favour.' The design of the survey deliberately provided for evidence from different levels in the same company, making it possible to examine the possibility that agreement within a company may reflect a company effect, or vice versa. 'Most of the comparisons between levels which showed an intra company effect related to the more factual questions . . . the vast majority of comparison on opinion questions (particularly those relating to worker directors) showed no clear evidence of an inclination towards intra company agreement or disagreement. So it seems quite possible that answers to such questions may have been influenced far more by their occupational values and status than by the company situation in which they worked. This was also clear in the Industrial Relations survey.' Conclusions were drawn from these analyses about improvements in the design of future surveys on such topics.

During the period in which these surveys were done (1966–76) there were other studies designed to explore working situations or their consequences. They too reflect the concern in this period to ameliorate what was increasingly felt to be an unhappy and economically disastrous situation. This was the period of the creation and disappearance of the Department of Economic Affairs, the negotiations with the International Monetary Fund and the 1967 devaluation. It is characteristic of the period that the rapid turnover of ideas and proposals for economic change led in practice to little change. Two surveys, which were somewhat more narrowly focused, examined working relationships inside the police and fire services at the request of the Home Office. *Some Aspects of Man Management in the Police Service* was done at the end of 1967. A working party on operational efficiency set up by the Police Advisory Board had advised that there was a need for a new training syllabus more relevant to the needs of provincial forces than the existing one which mainly related to the Metropolitan Police District, and that the new syllabus should take account of the views of members of the service. The enquiry was designed in collaboration with the Police Research and Development Branch of the Home Office and was based on a sample of 10% of constables and sergeants and 20% of inspectors and superintendents in all police forces excluding the Metropolitan Police District. Chief constables were visited first in order to explain the survey's purpose and to ask for cooperation, which was given by all. Interviews with other members of the forces were voluntary: 'Officers were told that they were under no compulsion and that if they wished they could stay in the interview room for an hour without answering a single question and no one else would know'. Out of the sample of 3,236 only seven officers refused to answer any questions.

The report described the social background of the officers. 'Most police

Table 26 Whether worker directors would affect managerial authority (1976). Company Organisation and Worker Participation (1976)

Attitude to worker directors	Estab. manager		Industrial relations/personnel manager		Middle manager (production)		Middle manager (white collar)		Foreman	
	Favour	Against	Favour	Against	Favour	Against	Favour	Against	Favour	Against
Base (weighted)	27	48	31	58	60	107	49	73	115	62
	%	%	%	%	%	%	%	%	%	%
Whether worker directors would affect the authority of managers/supervisors:										
Yes	15	31	23	28	5	28	9	19	10	21
No	85	68	77	72	95	72	91	81	90	79
Total	100	100	100	100	100	100	100	100	100	100

Table 27 Informant's view on what worker participation should involve. Company Organisation and Worker Participation (1976)

	Directors				Managers					Employee representatives		
	Managing director	Industrial relations/ personnel director	Finance director	Estab. manager	Industrial relations/ personnel manager	Middle manager (production)	Middle manager (white collar)	Foreman		Most senior rep.	Other senior rep.	Minority union rep.
Base (weighted)	173	93	106	78	91	170	125	178		161	108	84
	%	%	%	%	%	%	%	%		%	%	%
What worker participation should mean:												
A Management alone makes the decisions but keeps workers informed	5	3	5	1	1	3	6	5		0	1	3
B Management makes the decisions but takes account of workers' views	25	17	17	20	6	22	14	16		4	6	7
C Joint discussion and then management makes the decisions	51	55	56	51	42	36	56	31		13	19	16
D Joint decision making between management and workers	13	21	19	25	50	38	23	46		77	70	71
E Workers alone make the decisions	1	—	—	3	0	—	—	0		4	5	2
F None of these	4	3	2	3	—	1	—	1		2	0	0
Not answered, don't know	1	—	1	0	—	—	—	0		0	—	1
Total	100	100	100	100	100	100	100	100		100	100	100

officers left school between 15½ and 16 years of age, approximately equal proportions had attended grammar and secondary modern schools but about two-thirds had some further education and about the same number had passed some external examination ... Between three and four-fifths in all ranks had spent some time in HM Forces ... the majority of wives [almost all officers were married] were reported to like their husbands' jobs ... two-fifths of all constables and sergeants considered the general condition and facilities at their stations to be less than satisfactory.' At the time of the survey two-fifths of inspectors and superintendents had been on courses involving some instruction in man-management; the figure for constables and sergeants was much lower, one in twenty.

Using responses to a group of 34 questions concerned with officers' satisfaction or otherwise with the police service a 'satisfaction score' was devised. '21% had scores of five or less and can be regarded as satisfied with their life in the service. 58% had scores between six and eleven (middle, neutral) and 21% had scores of 12 or over and are here taken as the most dissatisfied group.' These scores were used to identify the circumstances most often associated with dissatisfaction. 'The Scottish City force had the highest proportion of dissatisfied constables and sergeants ... the very dissatisfied group were four times as likely as the middle, neutral group to think they will leave the service before becoming eligible for a pension, they were less likely to have attended a secondary modern school or to have left school at 14 or under, they were very much more likely to have wives who disliked the police service.'

The interviews in the fire service enquiry to some extent overlapped those used in the police service. Here too the main purpose was 'to provide information of relevance to those concerned with man management at the various levels of command in the Fire Service'. The separate samples of junior ranks and senior ranks were selected from 35 sampled brigades in England, Wales and Scotland excluding the then Greater London Council area. As in the police study the report described the social background of the respondents and their reasons for joining. It was shown that about 'one-third of all men now in the Fire Service had seriously considered joining the Police. Half of those or nearly 15% of all men in the Fire Service were not accepted because they did not meet the standards, physical or other'. The men's views on activities during working hours and on the shift system were reviewed. '26% of the junior ranks said they had an outside part-time job either because of the money or out of boredom.' Attitudes towards promotion of both junior and senior ranks were considered. 'Amongst junior ranks from the age of about 25 or after five years service there was a fairly steady decline in interest in promotion ... senior ranks remain ambitious for much longer until they are about 45 or have been in the Fire Service for about 25 years.' The reasons given for not wanting promotion were also very different among junior and senior ranks. 'On average it was about 2½ years since the men interviewed had qualified for promotion by passing the necessary examination for the next rank, many have been waiting much longer ... 57% of the junior ranks and 40% of the senior ranks thought there was something wrong with the promotion system in their Brigade.' Relationships between officers and men were considered. 'Seven out of ten of the junior ranks thought that the running of their station could be improved so as to get the best out of all the men in it . . . a similar proportion of senior ranks thought this.' Opinions on courses which dealt with man management and how they could be improved are described. Leading firemen and ranks above said that they had problems or difficulties in managing ranks below them: 33% of the junior ranks and 40% of the senior agreed. The great majority thought that they got on very well with their immediate superiors but 'about a third of all ranks thought that there were other ranks in their brigade with whom they had insufficient contact'.

The Redundancy Payments Act 1965 'was one of several measures intended to facilitate modernization and change in industry, it was . . . part of an overall manpower policy aimed at securing a greater acceptance by workers of the need for economic and social change and at mitigating the social and economic circumstances of such changes for those workers involved' (From the introduction by W D Ellis and W E J McCarthy to the later Survey report). The central intention was to make changes of job more acceptable in the hope that this would reduce restrictive practices related to workers' fears for the future of their jobs and trades. The Act provided a statutory right to redundancy payments for employees with a minimum period of 104 weeks' continuous employment. The survey *Effects of the Redundancy Payments Act* was intended to contribute to an evaluation of the Act. The report is unusual in that the first part was written by two academics, one of whom had been a government adviser. They drew on the survey and other data for their general evaluation. The second part was written by Survey staff. Samples were taken of employers, workers with and without experience of redundancy, people who had received redundancy payment and their employers, and fulltime union officials. The basis for most of the samples was statistical returns relating to local Department of Employment offices and random samples of households in their areas.

Employers were asked about their experience of redundancy before and after the Act and the criteria they used for selecting workers for redundancy. These responses were related to region, industry, size of establishment, stability of the labour force in sampled establishments and to their statements about the causes of the most recent redundancy. Specific questions about post-Act redundancy produced much the same picture as the unprompted responses given by employers. 'It is clear that hardly any employers thought that strikes were a cause of redundancy even when this was put to them as a possible cause.' The survey report discussed possible effects of the Act on employers' procedures. 'The Act had apparently made no difference to the readiness of employers to put workers on short-time or lay them off . . . the Act appears to have had no influence on manpower planning and very little restrictive effect – compared with Selective Employment Tax on employers' readiness to recruit . . . but had made it easier for many employers to discharge workers largely because it enabled them to dismiss men with an easier conscience and reduce costs and arguments.' The report described the financial circumstances of the redundancy and what was done with the payment received. During the period between redundancy (end of 1967) and interview (April–June 1969) 'one in twelve men were continuously unemployed but on average it was eight weeks before redundant respondents started another job which compares with four weeks for non-redundant respondents ... 11% said the payment helped them to get a better job than one they might have had to take otherwise'.

The responses of redundant employees and their employers on the handling of particular redundancies were compared on a sub-sample. 'They tended to agree quite closely on the reason for redundancy, numbers involved and whether there was a chance of volunteering for redundancy ... but less so on advance warning ... Although more than half of employers claimed to know how employees reacted when first told about their reduncancy the comparative results are more consistent with employers guessing about these reactions.' Fulltime union officials in five unions responded to questions about their experience of redundancy situations. About half of them said that 'at some time they had had difficulty in securing what they regarded as their members' right under the Act ... two-thirds thought the Act had helped their redundant members a lot'. The report compared the views of trade union officials, employers and employees on some issues and in particular on the consequences of the Act.

The Redundancy Payments Act was an attempt to ameliorate the burden of job loss and job change by legislation. Other changes in the law followed the economic crisis of the mid 1960s and the declaration of a prices and incomes policy. In 1967 the National Joint Advisory Council had suggested that the situation of dismissed workers needed public intervention, and one of the recommendations of the Donovan Commission had been that employees complaining of unfair dismissal should have the right of appeal to a statutory independent tribunal. Before implementing these recommendations the Department of Employment felt that more detailed information was needed and turned to the Survey. Whereas in the redundancy payment survey academics had been supplied with tabulations by the Survey for their report alongside the Survey's own commentary, the report *Disciplinary and Dismissal Practices and Procedures* (1969) was produced by the Survey on the basis of fieldwork and analysis specified by the Survey and produced by another survey organisation, Social and Community Planning Research. The Department of Employment wanted to know the nature and extent of existing procedures, what employees who had been dismissed felt about them and what both employers and employees felt about the proposal to allow appeal to independent tribunals.

A sample of establishments was drawn from employment exchange registers and senior managers responsible for disciplinary and dismissal procedures were interviewed. They were also asked to supply case histories of up to eight employees who had left their establishment in the last year. Independently of this, dismissed persons and voluntary leavers were interviewed in employment exchanges. As in the industrial relations surveys the response from employers was considerably lower than was usual in the general run of Survey experience. The report described the labour force in the sampled establishments, turnover and how turnover was made up: '65% of the total sample had to dismiss at least one per cent of their total work force in the last year, 22% had dismissed over

5%. The larger the establishment the more persons proportionally were dismissed', but the highest level of the dismissals were found in firms just below the largest. The employers' information about dismissed persons was described and compared with information given by employees obtained from other sources. The employers were asked to describe the disciplinary procedures – dismissal, transfer, fines and so on – they used. Their responses indicated that firms with high proportions of manual workers were more likely to use such procedures and dismissal was by far the most frequent action. Employees were asked their opinions about various disciplinary procedures. 'Comparison of what employers say and what employees think show that the measure most often used – dismissal – was also the one regarded as most reasonable by employees.'

Fifty-five per cent of employees said they had not received a written notice of their terms of employment (required by the Contract of Employment Act 1963), and many of those who said they had received something could not recall its contents. Five per cent of the sample only knew they had signed a contract of employment. 'Eighty-six per cent of employers said they normally warned employees before dismissal ... in relating case histories they gave evidence suggesting that 65% were warned ... a random sample of these employees provided information suggesting that only 25% had been warned.' There were smaller differences about the reason for dismissal but even so '40% of those who said they had been given a reason felt that it did not represent the truth'.

'It is apparent that comparatively few employees challenge their dismissal but when they do they have often been pre-warned and are prepared to take any openings to do so ... this finding has obvious relevance to any scheme designed to open up opportunities for all employees to air their views.' The effect of trade union intervention was described: 'A majority of union members did not bother to inform their unions'. Workers' opinions on the fairness of their dismissal were examined: 66% thought it was 'unfair' mainly in the belief that needs of the job had not been explained or that actual progress had not been monitored or that advice and help on how it should be done had not been offered. Existing disciplinary procedures were described. They were more likely to be found where the dismissal rate was high, where there was a higher proportion of manual workers where turnover was high and in large firms. '65% of all procedures had been decided upon and instituted unilaterally by management. 52% of all establishments said they had no formal disciplinary procedures and only 22% of the employees had recent experience of an establishment with such a procedure.' The characteristics of establishments which had formal procedures were described. They were more likely to recognise unions, to experience union intervention in cases of 'unfair dismissal' and to have dismissals challenged. They were also less favourable to the various proposals for tribunals. Opinion of the proposed tribunal and interest in using it was examined, but it seemed 'that neither employers nor employees were very knowledgeable about the proposals and those most affected, ie those with highest dismissal rates or with recent experience of dismissal were less well informed'.

The report attempted a definition of unfair dismissal which would be acceptable to both employers and employees. Some forms of personal behaviour (pilfering, endangering safety, persistent absence) were named, employers were asked how often they had occurred in the past year and what disciplinary action had been taken. Similarly, employers were asked what form of disciplinary action might be thought appropriate for six named union or industrial activities, including joining a union, becoming a steward, leading an unofficial strike and joining an official strike. Employees were asked to consider the same forms of behaviour, to say whether they thought disciplinary action was appropriate and dismissal 'fair', and to make judgments about the same union or industrial activities. The report stated:

> There is some form of consensus between employers and employees on what are valid grounds for discipline and what are not ... almost half of each group agreed that unofficial strike activity alone should warrant discipline and dismissal, other 'legitimate' activity should go unfettered. There were different views on various forms of personal behaviour. Nearly all employees saw pilfering and endangering safety as grounds for discipline, whereas to employers persistent absenteeism and lateness are so identified ahead of pilfering. Only a small minority of employers identified endangering safety as basis for discipline. Both sides agreed that 'refusal to do lower grade work' was the least important of the forms of behaviour demanding discipline. For all forms of personal behaviour proportionately *more* employees say they should be disciplined than employers have actually disciplined. For the greater majority of both employers and employees discipline is more or less synonymous with dismissal. Few other forms of discipline are ever considered.

Measuring employment

The years in which concern with working relationships was growing also saw growing concern with unemployment for the first time since the end of the war, and of the attempts to measure and investigate some of its consequences. Growing unemployment focused attention on the adequacies of existing measures which in the United Kingdom were based heavily on registration for work as a condition for receiving unemployment insurance. It was known that many people, particularly women, moved into and out of the labour force without registering. This implied that a more complete picture of movements in the 'gainfully occupied' population required data about all actual and potential members of the labour force. A household survey which recorded employment and desire for employment of all members of the household was a suitable source. Since 1942 the employment and unemployment picture in the United States had been based on a very large continuous household survey carried out by the Bureau of the Census. In 1971 in the UK the General Household Survey, designed to illuminate many of the main economic and social circumstances of the whole population, was started on a much smaller scale and at the request of the Department of Employment a section of it was devoted to questions about participation in the labour force of all members of the sampled households. The 1977 GHS report noted 'the official figures do not include the temporarily sick nor those people who describe themselves in the GHS interview as unemployed but do not register as such ... Between 1974 and 1976 there was an increase in the proportion of the unemployed who were registered although at all times the proportion of unemployed or married women who were registered was below the proportion of men and non-married women. In 1977 the proportion of unemployed men and of non-married women who were registered remained at about the same level as in 1976 but among married women the proportion registered continued to increase so that in 1977 almost half of all unemployed married women were registered'. Such data permit a reconciliation between figures based on registration and other estimates. Since the GHS asked questions

Table 28 Composition of the labour force, 1975 to 1982: economic activity and employment status for males and non-married and married females. General Household Survey (1982)

Economically active persons aged 16 and over (Great Britain)

Economic activity* and employment status	1975	1977	1979	1980	1981	1982
			Percentages			
Males						
Employees †						
-working full time	86	85	82 ⎤ 85	80 ⎤ 83	76 ⎤ 79	73 ⎤ 76
-working part time			3 ⎦	2 ⎦	2 ⎦	2 ⎦
Self-employed †						
-working full time	10	10	9 ⎤ 10	9 ⎤ 10	10 ⎤ 11	11 ⎤ 12
-working part time			1 ⎦	1 ⎦	1 ⎦	1 ⎦
Unemployed	4	5	5	7	10	12
Base = 100 per cent	9,302	8,966	8,486	8,595	8,914	7,409
Non-married females						
Employees †						
-working full time	91	90	72 ⎤ 90	71 ⎤ 88	66 ⎤ 84	65 ⎤ 83
-working part time			17 ⎦	17 ⎦	18 ⎦	17 ⎦
Self employed †						
-working full time	3	2	1 ⎤ 2	1 ⎤ 3	2 ⎤ 2	2 ⎤ 3
-working part time			1 ⎦	1 ⎦	1 ⎦	1 ⎦
Unemployed	5	8	8	9	13	14
Base = 100 per cent	1,843	1,818	1,871	2,003	2,107	1,790
Married females						
Employees †						
-working full time	93	92	39 ⎤ 91	39 ⎤ 91	38 ⎤ 88	37 ⎤ 87
-working part time			52 ⎦	51 ⎦	50 ⎦	51 ⎦
Self employed †						
-working full time	5	5	2 ⎤ 6	2 ⎤ 5	3 ⎤ 6	3 ⎤ 6
-working part time			3 ⎦	3 ⎦	4 ⎦	3 ⎦
Unemployed	3	4	3	4	6	6
Base = 100 per cent	4,318	4,191	3,999	4,082	4,052	3,402

* Full-time students who were working or unemployed in the reference week are classified as economically inactive.
† Totals include a few persons whose hours of work were not known.

about the social circumstances of the employed and unemployed and all the other members of their households it was possible to illustrate the social situation behind the unemployment statistics. Thirty per cent of all men unemployed during the 12 months of the 1977 survey were aged 18–24, compared with 13.9% of the male population who fell in that age group.

> Between 1975 and 1977 about one in seven men who had been unemployed during the twelve months had experienced more than one spell of unemployment and the average length of time that men had been unemployed in total rose from about 19 weeks in 1975 to about 23–24 weeks in 1976 and 1977 ... the data suggest an over representation of coloured men among those who had been unemployed during the twelve month period ... In 1977 two in three of those with experience of unemployment were earning less than £60 a week on average when they were working compared with two in five of those without experience of unemployment ... married men who had been unemployed were twice as likely as those who had not to have three or more dependent children ... this partly reflects the heavier concentration of manual workers amongst those who had been unemployed ... regardless of whether there were dependent children the wives of men who had been unemployed were less likely to be in paid work than were wives of men who had not ... where there were dependent children about one-third of wives of men who had been unemployed were in paid work compared with just over half of wives who had not been.

Household surveys as a source of employment data were also being developed by the statisticians of the EEC and from 1973 onward a biennial *Labour Force Survey* (LFS) was done in all member countries. This survey is partly paid for by the EEC and in 1981 was about seven times as big as the GHS. It was concentrated into one month of the year and special arrangements for interviewing were devised by the Census division of OPCS. The general picture of the labour force emerging from the two surveys is much the same where definitions are comparable, but because of its size much more detailed information is available from the LFS about the various subdivisions of the population, for instance on ethnic origins. The Survey played an active part in the quality control aspects of the Labour Force Survey and in some years did a substantial part of the fieldwork. In 1983 it was decided that a *Continuing Manpower Survey* of which the EEC survey would form part should be carried out by the Survey on behalf of the Department of Employment.

Improving employment services

Alongside legislation in this period there were also attempts to improve the performance of services already in existence. In 1969 people who had gone through the special government training courses were studied in order to find out how their employment histories had been affected and what they felt about the courses they had taken at the centres. *Post Training Courses of Government Training Centre Trainees* was based on interviews attempted with all trainees who completed a course during September to December 1965. The fieldwork was done around three years after the course. A substantial proportion of trainees were either disabled, had been in the armed forces or were unemployed or sick before attending the centres. Forty per cent had been recruited through employment exchanges and two-thirds were able to choose the trade they preferred. The report described their progress through the course, their opinions on it after a lapse of time and experience of working, the process of obtaining a job and their subsequent job histories. The report concluded 'In terms of a selected list of attributes the present jobs of trainees are, taken overall, superior to their pre-GTC jobs. The improvement is not confined to higher wages and opportunities to use skills but also to security and good working conditions . . . 90% of trainees would recommend others to undertake training'.

Reorganisation of the employment service was announced in Department of Employment booklets and in connection with these efforts surveys were made of both employers and actual potential job-seekers. The study *Employers and Employment Services* was done in 1973 by interviewing a sample of people chosen from a representative sample of establishments responsible for recruiting. It dealt separately with the recruitment of manual and non-manual workers and did not cover professional, scientific and technical staff for whom a separate organisation existed. This sample necessarily had large proportions of establishments with under 24 employees and too few larger establishments to give reasonable numbers for analysis, so differential sampling fractions were used and most analyses were related to the size of establishment. It is interesting to note that unlike the industrial relations surveys where response was relatively low, in this study 90% of eligible establishments cooperated. Respondents were asked about methods of recruitment, how successful they were thought to be and how satisfied they were with results. 'Satisfaction with staff from agencies, particularly the Employment Office, was low . . . the two most commonly used methods, local newspaper advertising and personal contact, were rated as best . . . the Employment Office was felt to be the most successful by a fifth of establishments.' After delineating the general situation the report then described the use of all government employment services in the year before interview and then concentrated on those respondents who had used the Adult Employment Office. 'During a year nearly threequarters of all the establishments in the survey had registered a vacancy with part of the government service. A minority, about one-third, had not used the Adult Employment Office and had no intention of doing so . . . But recruitment officers expressed satisfaction with their contacts with office staff . . . some establishments who had used the office reported failures, eg a third of them sometimes had been sent unsuitable candidates.' Contacts between Employment Office staff and recruitment staff are described with opinions on how the service could be improved for employers. The report noted 'Establishments have needs for particular kinds of staff with particular skills but people needing jobs don't always have them . . . the fundamental problem is the discrepancy in the numbers and types of the unemployed and that of vacancies'.

The second survey, *Attitudes to the Employment Service 1973*, sampled the experience and views of people who had been or might be customers of the employment service, 'to describe the methods people used when looking for a job . . . a more detailed look at use of services the Department provided and attitudes towards it . . . knowledge and use of other services provided . . . what sort of changes that might attract more people to use the service'. The sample was restricted to current members of the labour force or those who had recently stopped working, using the 'sift' method. The response rate was 88%. The report described the amount and reasons for job changes and especially the demographic make-up of frequent job changers. 'Nearly one in five of those under 30 had left because they disliked the work or were bored and one in six had left for more money ... those proportions changed with age ... it was the older people, in particular the men, who suffered redundancy.' Sixty-eight per cent of those who could have stayed on had a new job to go to before leaving but only 29% of those who could not have stayed on had jobs arranged. This kind of data helped to assess the nature of the market for employment services, and in particular for the advisory service available for those still in employment. About a third of those who had found a new job said they were not aware of this service. As had become clear from other manpower statistics, women's registration for employment, in particular married women, was relatively low and the reasons for this were explored. Most of those who registered did not rely solely on the service to help them find jobs. Of all the methods people had used, making a direct application to an employer was the most successful. Experience of using the service and the differences between men and women and varying age-groups were described as well as the relationship of this experience with future intentions to use the service. The report described current views on improvements or changes in the service.

In the following years the employment service was reshaped, local offices modernised and job centres began to appear. In 1975 when 45 job centres had been open for at least six months, 70 had opened more recently and a further 105 were planned for the next year, the Survey was asked by the Employment Service Agency to study the market for these services and to find out how their users estimated them. The *Survey of Job Centres* was designed as a pilot study in preparation for a larger survey but the pilot was only just completed when the sponsor found it necessary to make crucial decisions. The limited information available was not on a suitable scale for detailed analysis but was made available and used for what it was worth. The larger main scale survey was not done, losing the opportunity for a comparison with the situation in the 1973 employment service. The indications from the pilot study were that 'four in five respondents knew that their area had a new modernized government employment office ... one in four employers had rejected the Job Centre as a possible supplier of at least one type of worker ... amongst those recruiting manual employees two-thirds had used the job service which was equal in popularity with press advertisements as a method of recruitment ... only a third knew about the information service available'. The proposed survey would have examined responses on the suitability of job centre applicants and why some employers had, so early on, rejected them as a source. It would also have examined the level of satisfaction among users with the kind of employee offered and with the service provided by staff at job centres, together with employment officers' views. The indication from the pilot was that a majority did perceive a difference which was favourable to the job centres.

However, weighing up changes in user experience of the employment service would have been made difficult by the changes in the economic situation since 1973. Many employers who were searching for staff then were laying staff off by the time of the second survey. And in the years that followed the employment services were increasingly involved in a succession of training schemes intended to help individuals develop skills. In 1972 the Training Opportunities Scheme was established and by 1977 over 90,000 people completed courses, of whom half were unemployed when accepted for training. This covered only a small minority of the unemployed and helped even fewer of the increasing numbers of young unemployed. For them the Youth Opportunity Programme was developed, offering work preparation and work experience schemes. The 1981–2 programme provided a quarter of a million places. Towards the end of 1979 the Survey was asked to interview a sample of trainees who had completed their course 18 months previously, and the reporting was done by the Manpower Services Commission. Subsequent studies were done for the Manpower Services Commission on the Youth Opportunity Scheme and other follow-up work on the TOPS programme.

10 Income, expenditure and social security

THERE IS NO SUBJECT in which government is more involved than the incomes of citizens and the living standards they make possible. As government, through taxes and benefits, redistributes large proportions of the national income, it has to respond constantly to pressures and to account for its actions in the name of social justice and economic efficiency. Nevertheless, comprehensive information about the effects on citizens of the ever growing mass of taxes and benefits did not come early: the political rhetoric on the probable effects of new actions ran far ahead of the factual base. Only recently has the Survey's contribution in this subject area become regular and continuing: earlier work was ad hoc with no settled focus.

Early Survey work on income and expenditure

In 1942 at the request of the Board of Trade a study of credit buying was done 'to find to what extent articles other than food are bought on credit by the poorer groups of the population and whether a reduction in credit buying facilities would cause hardship for the lower paid working classes'. The sample was accordingly limited. About a third of the defined groups were 'getting any goods on easy payments'. The poorer they were and the more children they had the greater was the use of credit: over half of the wives of servicemen were using credit and nearly two-thirds of women with more than three children under 14 years of age. The report described how credit was used and what credit systems involved. The poorer people were, the more they paid back each week for credit advanced previously. A majority of those using credit said that without it they would have to give up some articles.

As wartime limitations were slowly overcome governments prepared to meet a world without rationing with little information about the way people might behave. In 1948 the Survey tried to meet Ministry of Fuel and Power wishes to assess what effect decontrol of house coal would have on consumer purchases. The report, *An Estimate of the Demand for Domestic House Coal*, made a rather heroic effort to help the Ministry by examining current methods of heating and opinions on them, helped by earlier Survey work for the Building Research Station. At the time of the survey 'although 93% of householders have either a gas or electricity supply and 66% have both, 96% rely wholly or mainly on solid fuel for space heating ... there has been no significant change in the apparatus to heat dwellings or to cook food since 1942'. But, said the report, 'preferences, habits or economic considerations may have changed' and it went on to examine ways in which such changes might have occurred among the main sample of households drawn from rating lists and a second smaller sample drawn from the more highly rated households, in order to provide a more detailed income group analysis. The report described responses to questions about attitudes and tested responses one against another for consistency. Respondents' estimates of their purchases of coal in a free market at prevailing prices were tested by asking them after the interview to send a prepaid postcard giving a considered judgment. An index was constructed from responses to different questions about future demand and tested against current statistics of consumption.

In an enquiry where respondents are dealing with a topic they know at first hand it is possible to put considerable weight on what they say – but this was not always the case. Following the sharp curtailment of the Survey's activities after the 1951 general election, the Oxford University Institute of Statistics was awarded a Nuffield grant to make a study of personal savings and asked for the Survey's help in designing and carrying it out on a repayment basis. This was a topic in which the Treasury was interested since private savings are an important element in national accounts, so the survey went ahead. The method was to ask very detailed questions about all forms of liquid assets, and three samples were interviewed, in 1952, 1953 and 1954. The responses were compared where possible with other national information on the same items, such as bank balances. The report discussed these comparisons, which offered a means of validating the survey data: they showed that the responses of those who cooperated did not give a valid picture of the national totals. Not surprisingly there had been a marked reluctance to state liquid asset holdings fully, so any interpretation of the detail would have to be very cautious. Nevertheless the survey did show the position at the lower income levels. Thirty-two per cent of income earners had no liquid assets at all; nearly half of all income earners had less than £10. It followed from these figures that a small section of the population held most of the liquid assets. But clearly this was a subject area in which the direct survey method was not very helpful.

The wartime development of a system of national economic accounts was a necessary instrument in the recognised need to control public and private expenditure. There was also a recognition that better information about the movements of consumer expenditure would be necessary to help complete the economic picture. Between 1948 and 1970 a series of ad hoc studies of expenditure on selected commodities and services was done for the Central Statistical Office, which had responsibility for producing the annual national accounts. Topics covered in early surveys included holidays, durable goods, repairs and alterations to property, clothing, medicines and allied pharmaceutical products and betting. Many of these studies served more than one purpose. The betting survey was designed to produce, as well as the expenditure data, information of interest to the Royal Commission on Betting, Lotteries and Gaming. As part of the consumer expenditure work another series of studies were carried out which laid the foundation for an endeavour which has proved of continuing importance and use both in and out of government – the Family Expenditure Survey.

The Family Expenditure Survey

The idea of studying the total budgets of households goes back to the last part of the 19th century where it was seen as providing the basis for two separate lines of enquiry. The first, generally associated with Le Play, tried to use the pattern of expenditure to support a moral interpretation of social life. It was never systematic and used very limited data to support a large theoretical structure. The second was concerned with poverty and its causes. Seebohm Rowntree and A L Bowley may be regarded as the developers of the household budget method as the appropriate instrument for this purpose. Bowley in particular applied systematic sampling methods to give a representative picture of household expenditure and may be regarded as the progenitor of the techniques used today. There was a natural government interest in such studies because changes in price levels led to demands for wage increases or to political pressures for public action to help those most severely affected.

Wartime changes were so widely felt in their effects on patterns of living that in 1946 a new Cost of Living Index Committee was appointed. It recommended that a technical committee should consider the problems of 'instituting budget enquiries to provide the main Committee with information to be used in deciding on a more permanent index'. In December 1950 the advisory committee was brought together and in June 1951 recommended that a new enquiry had become essential; that it should provide the basis for an index for practically all wage earners and moderate salary earners, and that because household budgets provided information for many other purposes the 'new enquiry should take a comprehensive form covering a sample of the whole community'. These recommendations became the foundation stone of the future government household budget studies. The new enquiry was carried out in 1953–4[1] and implemented the recommendations of the advisory committee. It was probably the most carefully controlled budget study done in any country at that time. It was considered large scale, and was technically a great step forward. In considering the results the Cost of Living Advisory Committee recommended that, in future, small scale studies should be conducted at frequent intervals rather than relying on large scale exercises at lengthy intervals. This raised the question, discussed in Part One, of who should carry out such studies.

An eventual decision that the Survey should do the work was made at the end of 1955 and under the aegis of the Central Statistical Office preparations began for a continuing small-scale household budget survey. It was to be continuing rather than intermittent because other government purposes needed annual or quarterly data about consumer expenditure. Detailed information was also to be collected about different types of family so that estimates could be made of the incidence of direct and indirect taxation, subsidies and benefits on different types and on different income and social groups. This implied much greater detail about the make-up of families and about their sources of income than had previously been collected. No decision was made about who should be responsible for the detailed analysis that those purposes would demand until very near the proposed starting date. As the discussions between the departments proceeded it became clear that a very important new source of government information was to be created. Included as a main objective was the Ministry of Labour's responsibility for maintaining a continuous retail price index which would be of critical importance in all negotiations and decisions affected by price movements. The involvement of the Survey in these concerns marked a turning point in its history.

The Family Expenditure Survey, which began in 1957, was only a quarter of the size of the 1953–4 survey. In the first years about 3,000 households cooperated. Budget records or interviews for different segments of expenditure were used but there were many minor aspects of the survey which from the very beginning were subject to critical scrutiny. The first published report noted 'improvements in the interviewing techniques and the design and wording of the questionnaires are made from year to year to reduce the incidence of reporting errors'.[2] Since the results of the survey are used to measure change, comparability between years is of great importance and such alterations need very careful consideration. Throughout the years, experimental testing of the design and proposed changes have therefore been an essential element of the FES. The *Family Expenditure Survey Handbook*[3] describes the procedures in operation in 1980 and the continuing experimental work which underlies the survey, and discusses the acknowledged problem areas.

Since the 1953–4 survey it had been considered essential to attempt to record incomes and with the extending use of the FES for topics where analysis by income and its components are crucial, increasing critical attention has been given to the income data produced by the survey. Except for some clearly identified sections of the population or particular income sources (self-employed persons, investment income), 'On the whole the conclusions regarding the reliability of the FES income data are considerably more favourable than those of some early investigators ... overall our findings lend considerable support to the view that the FES represents a valuable source of data on incomes. But they also indicate the importance of continuing development and refinement particularly in the light of the much wider use of the FES micro data in academic and other research'.[4] The Director of Statistics in the Department of Employment compared FES earnings data with information on employees' earnings derived from earnings surveys completed by employers and found, with some minor exceptions, fairly close agreement.[5]

In the early years of the FES the income schedules were deliberately restricted in length. The 1980 handbook noted 'with increasing experience over the years it became clear that improvements could be made to the clarity of the data by using more elaborate questions, particularly by adding supplementary questions to deal with complex and unusual circumstances ... in 1966 all the interview schedules were reviewed and the opportunity was taken of testing a greatly expanded questionnaire ... this extended schedule was tried out in the last quarter of 1966 ... a 2×2 factorial experimental design was used ... the experiment showed that the subsample using the extended schedule produced a *higher* response rate ... it had in no way led to diminished public cooperation'. From 1968 onwards the income schedules consisted of eight pages – double the size of its predecessor – and on average took about 20 minutes' interviewing time.

The growing importance given to income is significant. It marks the transformation of the traditional expenditure enquiry in which income was simply needed for analysing expenditure into a true multi-purpose study which was more useful for many FES users for its income data than its expenditure information. Such a development was all the more important because experience also showed that in some fields expenditure data provided by the survey was very different from that given by other sources. The best known examples are expenditure on alcohol and tobacco. These known deficiencies can be taken into account in compiling the Retail Price Index, and the handbook describes the experimental work which has been done to improve the methods used. It also describes public response to the survey over the whole period and shows how from a relatively low level of just under 60% it rose to 70% in 1959, and stayed around 71–74% between 1960 and 1967. In 1967 the sample was doubled in size. Given the rotating sample design, this meant that three times as many trained interviewers were needed. From the beginning respondents have been paid for participating in the survey after early experimental work showed the extent to which payment could improve response. Following an increase in payment to counter the effects of inflation the response rate, which was 67% in 1980, jumped to 72.1% in 1981 – a measure of the effect of increasing the financial incentive. The level of cooperation marked by the response rate is high by the standard of international comparison or the early budget surveys, and this, together with the very wide range of information about incomes and expenditure and how they are distributed, has led to the survey becoming one of the most frequently used among all government sources.

Annual reports on the FES are published by the Department of Employment. They provide a wide array of expenditure analyses. Over time they show how patterns of expenditure have changed and since the information flows continuously the patterns are always up to date, and provide the weights for the Retail Price Index. At one time the weights were based on a three year average but since 1975 they have used one year's data. In addition to the general index there have since 1969 been two special quarterly price indices for one person and two person pensioner households, based on three years' expenditure data. The Central Statistical Office uses expenditure data to supplement that from other sources for the national accounts, and produces annually in *Economic Trends* a study of the effects of taxes and benefits on the redistribution of income produced by these government actions. The Treasury has also used this kind of analysis to estimate the effect of budget proposals on different family types. There is a sense in which an acceptable Retail Price Index may be regarded as an instrument designed to facilitate a policy of social justice. It is a measure of changes to which public attention is directed and which therefore cannot be ignored in decisions about public action. Most of these purposes were envisaged during the discussions leading to the inauguration of the FES but as the survey became better known it was seen that other purposes could be served. For example, budget surveys could provide information about the living costs of particular groups such as undergraduates or postgraduates, and could also show other costs associated with student status; this information was very relevant to decisions about student grants.

In 1965 The Allen Committee of Enquiry into the Impact of Rates carried out a detailed and comprehensive study of the relationship between household incomes and local rate payments, and an adaptation of the FES design was used to help. The analysis showed that rate payments were regressive, that is, the higher a household's income the lower the proportion it needed to pay in rates. Following the committee's report a rate rebate scheme was introduced in 1966 which reduced the burden on low-income families. In 1974 the scheme was extended. In 1976 the question of local government finance was reopened in an enquiry conducted by Frank Layfield, and rates and their impact once again came under review. A sample of households who had originally cooperated in the FES were reinterviewed a year later. Over 80% of them cooperated in the new study, enabling the committee to see the impact of changes over the year. As important, however, was the data derived from the income side of the survey. 'We examined the impact of rates using figures for rate payments both gross and net of rate rebated and assistance through supplementary benefits ... we examined the relationship between the number of households eligible for rate rebates and the number who actually claimed them. The number eligible was estimated from the FES.' The data so obtained made it possible for the committee to estimate the position before and after rate rebates were taken into account – to evaluate the effect of all the rate rebate measures which had followed the Allen Committee.

The Department of the Environment makes its own separate analysis of FES housing and incomes information. Other departments, including the DHSS, are supplied with data tapes which contain no information permitting identification of cooperating households, and do their own analysis. The household budget survey, which was originally developed for studying poverty, was not at first used for this purpose although from the beginning it was used for many purposes other than providing patterns of expenditure for the Retail Price Index. The impetus to use the FES for the exploration of poverty came from outside government. Brian Abel Smith and Peter Townsend were contemplating a new survey for this purpose when it was suggested to them that a great deal of relevant information might be already available in the records of the FES. They obtained the cooperation of the Ministry of Labour and produced in 1965 a book, *The Poor and the Poorest*, which effectively reopened the whole issue of poverty in postwar Britain. It used analysis of FES data to make estimates of the numbers of people with income below the adjusted supplementary benefit scale described as 'in poverty'. With other factors including departmental reorganisation and the growing public awareness that postwar economic progress was beginning to limp, it stimulated a more active concern with the large section of the population which seemed not to have participated in the general improvement in standards of living. In 1971 the DHSS produced a report, *Two Parent Families*, which said 'There has for some time been a lack of full and up to date information about the number of characteristics of families with low incomes in relation to their needs ... the Department's Statistics and Research Division has for some time been developing techniques for analysing FES data ... this report (the first in a series) presents the first results of the analysis'. It was based on FES data for 1968–70 and presented estimates of the distribution of 'two parent families with the father normally in full time work by the amount by which their resources are greater or less than their needs calculated on the basis of supplementary benefit practice'. This opening exercise was followed by a series of papers showing increasing sophistication in the handling of material devised from the FES.

One of the early difficulties in using the FES for some of the purposes described was the size of the sample. It was doubled in 1967, and the larger numbers made it possible to tackle those groups of the population in which there was most policy interest. In this way household budget data began to play an important role in public discussion and decisions about low incomes. Even so, given the different kinds of low income groups (single parent families, low-paid employees, pensioner households) the numbers available from the enlarged FES sample which permitted routine examinations were not large enough for the more detailed ad hoc study of particular facets of low income groups which were needed from time to time. The *Family Finances Survey* in 1978–9 used FES techniques to obtain information about a large sample of low income families derived by a specially designed sift process from available records of families receiving child benefit. Tests had shown that postal methods produced an inadequate response, so Survey interviewers called on samples of recipients and went through a carefully designed series of questions to establish whether family incomes were at least 40% above minimum requirements (using levels of requirement in force for supplementary benefit). Resources were regarded as net disposable income minus inescapable housing costs. The results of this interview were summarised by interviewers, and where this summarisation identified families with disposable resources below 140% of the supplementary benefit scale, interviewers returned and sought cooperation in a normal FES study. The Survey's part in this exercise was to identify some families thus defined, enlist them for the FES and then supervise the normal FES procedure of record keeping and interview. A report describing this work and giving descriptive information about the low income families found was produced by the Survey and the intention was that DHSS would produce the more detailed analysis using existing FES computer programmes. Two other features of this study are of special interest. One year after the first round of work all the cooperating families were asked to take part in a follow-up survey in which the same information was sought but the household budget books were not used. Over 80% agreed to help. The intention was to get some measure of change and of the problems of families with continuing low incomes. Secondly, the special nature of the sample was also of interest to the Department of Education which wanted to understand more about the take-up of free school meals by low income families. All eligible families with schoolchildren who could be identified in the *Family Finances Survey* were asked to help. There were some 16,000 children in the families concerned. The survey ascertained eligibility, how much parents knew about eligibility and attitudes towards taking school meals. Both these extra studies were carried by the *Family Finances Survey* but came into the picture only after it was commissioned. The decisions on sample design and field procedures for the survey were crucial for work outside its original scope. Such opportunities must always be considered in an expensive survey, so it is always necessary to ensure that all the technical aspects of such studies are given very close attention.

Notes

[1] Ministry of Labour, *Report of an Enquiry into Household Expenditure*, HMSO 1957.

[2] *Family Expenditure Survey Report 1957–9*, HMSO, 1961.

[3] W F F Kemsley, R U Redpath, M Holmes, *Family Expenditure Survey Handbook*, HMSO, 1980.

[4] A B Atkinson and J Micklewright, 'On the Reliability of Income Data in the FES 1970–1977', *Journal of the Royal Statistical Society*, Vol 146, 1983.

[5] A R Thatcher, 'Distribution of Earnings of Employees', *Journal of the Royal Statistical Society*, Vol 131, 1968.

11 Education, children and the family

Education

IT SEEMS APPROPRIATE THAT the first survey requested by the Ministry of Education should bear the title *Education and the People* (1945). The 1944 Education Act had changed the educational outlook, and embodied much of the thinking of the many committees of enquiry which the ministry had set up. The purpose of the survey was to make some preliminary studies of public attitudes towards various aspects of educational reconstruction and towards some of the provisions of the 1944 Act. The introduction notes the limitations of the survey: 'insufficient attention has been paid to ascertaining how much respondents knew at first hand of the educational process'. But the report nevertheless describes the responses to an interview which was obviously of interest to respondents and manages to cover a fair spread of topics. It is noted that the question 'what do you think are the aims of education?' was repeated at the end of the interview and 'the proportions of respondents making two or three points increased from 27% at the beginning to 52% at the end.

> There was overwhelming support for increased expenditure on education and it appears that the general desire for improvements is related more to dissatisfaction of informants with their own education than to dissatisfaction with their children's education ... about two-thirds thought that some changes were necessary .. much the largest body of opinion was concerned with the need for raising the school leaving age ... next in importance and of much less weight was the desire for improvements in teaching methods or for changes in the curriculum ... the changes suggested in curricula clearly arise out of what people consider to be the needs of everyday life.

However, it is noted 'a large proportion of the population are unaware of the potentialities of the new Act, and in the poorer groups, that is to say the very sections the Act may be expected to benefit most, less than a third know of any of the changes introduced by the Act'.

The 'continuing consultative committee' in the 1944 Act took the form of a Central Advisory Council which reviewed topics chosen by the Minister and had a membership which changed according to the topic. It took one topic at a time, spent two or three years studying it and then published a report. One of the earliest topics examined for the council was concerned with the leisure time interests of schoolchildren and was based on the growing interest in the relationship between school and home. The survey *Children Out of School* (1947) examined the way children used their leisure time in relation to the facilities available. Nearly half of the children surveyed played in the street and it was clear that many mothers were dissatisfied with the lack of suitable facilities and expressed a need for more playgrounds or play centres conveniently and safely located and designed for the age groups concerned. Club membership and cinema going were described: '30% of boys and girls in Grammar schools belonged to hobbies clubs compared with 12% at modern and technical schools ... cinema going was the largest single activity. Grammar school children went less than those at modern and technical schools ... Children are club minded by the age of ten, those organizations which are open to children of all ages were as popular with the 10–12 year olds as with older ones'. In 1948 a more detailed study, *Children and the Cinema*, was done for a Home Office committee.

Over the next ten years only one survey related to education was done – this was the period when the Survey's activities were sharply curtailed. The *Survey of Adolescents* was done in 1950 for a group of departments including the Ministry of Labour, the Ministry of Education and the defence ministries. It was broadly concerned with the movement from school to work and also covered the study of attitudes towards national service described earlier. In 1945 the Ince Committee had made recommendations for a comprehensive youth employment service which would include vocational guidance and placing facilities. Legislation followed and the 1950 survey was designed to study the degree of implementation, related educational and social factors and also the work experience of a sample of 15–20 year-olds drawn from the maintenance registers. The 1944 Act had also provided for the part-time education of young people who were at work in county colleges and the survey also collected information related to the demand for colleges and the social and economic factors which might be related to their activities. It showed how a large proportion of adolescents 'drifted into their first job' in a way which was influenced by the size and social status of the family and their fathers' occupation: 'adolescents frequently leave one employment for another without knowing what the new job involved ... 56% of the whole sample professed ignorance of the nature of their first job and where official agencies were the source of vacancies information 65% professed such ignorance ... vocational guidance was said to have been received by 36% of boys and 31% of girls from the Youth Employment Service'. The report describes first jobs, how satisfied respondents were with them, how long they lasted in relation to how the job was found, and the bearing of all this on the type of information service needed and the ambitions of school leavers. These ambitions, or lack of them, were related to school experience. 'A large proportion of the sample saw no association between school and employment or could recall any subject other than the three basic skills, that seemed to them to have any connection with any work ... those who said they were happy at school were more likely to say they were satisfied with their work ... frequent job changers were less likely to say they were happy at school.' And, referring back to the *Children's Leisure Survey*, it was noted that children with more frequent job changes were more likely to be frequent cinema goers.

Further education

Although some years passed before the Central Advisory Council formally requested more work from the Survey, the survey just described opened up the topic on which a survey was next done – further education, in 1957. The terms of reference remitted to the Council by the Minister included the following: what reasons lead people to decide against embarking on, or continuing in, careers requiring long training after 15? What reasons lead people whose school record seems promising to leave further education halfway through a course? How effective is further education in meeting the needs of those with resource and ambition who did not remain at school and whose jobs preclude part-time day release? How far is the provision of facilities for further education and training a factor in facilitating transfers from one type of employment to another? How far do those who do not use publicly provided further education obtain an equivalent education through private channels? How far do those who lack any contact with further education or the youth service occupy their time sensibly and constructively? How far are the courses provided in schools and further education suitable to the needs of women?

The survey covered only the maintained schools. The sample selected local education authorities and within them grammar or technical schools in correct ratios, and then chose from school registers children who had left in earlier years. Wherever possible, parents of the selected leavers were interviewed; the survey studied home background and factors affecting age of leaving school; the employment record of school leavers, its relation to school attainment and to participation in further education, the effect of employers' attitudes and conditions of work on further education experience and the relationship of further education to leisure activities.

In 1963 two reports were published which dramatically illustrated public concern with the development of a better educational system which would take into account the needs and potentialities of the brightest and the less bright pupils. The Newsam Report, *Half our Future*, was concerned with those of the secondary-school population who did less well. It emphasised the need for more research into relevant teaching methods, more emphasis on personal and social development, the need for a bridge between school and work and more links in school programmes with further education and the youth employment service. These recommendations were essentially concerned with the effect of education's social context, and the early Survey reports described had highlighted this.

The second report, from the Committee on Higher Education chaired by Lord Robbins, was concerned with the higher end of the educational spectrum and the need to expand opportunity for all who could qualify. For this committee the Survey carried out a substantial research programme during 1962 involving interviews with university undergraduates and postgraduates, students at teacher training colleges and at colleges of further education. The surveys' main contribution to the committee was to provide a detailed description of the whole student population – its origins, qualifications, career intentions, courses of study and contact with teachers – plus students' judgments on the relevance of their courses to their career intentions. Undergraduates were asked about their choice of institution and previous advice received on courses chosen, as well as 'Would you have preferred your course to have been more closely related to training for a subsequent occupation or not?' Postgraduates were asked 'Do you consider you are now receiving the right amount of supervision in the conduct of your research or not?' Teacher training students were also asked 'Do you think that taken as a whole your course is too long, too short or about right . . . could you have covered the same ground more quickly or would you have preferred some parts of your course to be cut out?' This kind of descriptive study extended the enquiry beyond what has been called the 'demographic approach' which relates educational progress to social background. It moved the enquiry into the teaching institutions, in parallel with many small-scale research studies concerned with particular methods of teaching or school organisation.

The next study, on primary education, was done for the Central Advisory Council under the chairmanship of Lady Plowden. The Survey's main contribution was the *Survey Among Parents of Primary School Children* (1964). This was based on a random sample of all types of maintained primary schools in England (subsequent work on similar lines was done in Wales). A random sample of children in these schools was selected and their mothers interviewed. Fathers were present at a substantial proportion of these interviews. The interviews covered the background of the families, their social class and incomes, employment of mothers, educational level of parents and educational support given to children, parental aspirations and the physical condition of home. Next, parental attitudes to primary education were explored – preferences for starting age and the reasons for selecting school; parental contact with schools and their level of satisfaction with arrangements for contact and communication, and their views on school organisation and teaching methods.

All this information was collected in its own right, but the committee was also interested to know if such data was also related to children's achievement in schools. To facilitate the necessary analysis the detail just described was summarised with the aid of factor analysis. This produced clusters of items which summed up parental relations with the schools and attitudes to their children's educational welfare. Scores were calculated for all parents on each of six clusters, enabling parental attitudes to be related to achievement. Some years after this enquiry a follow-up study was carried out by the inspector who had been the main statistical adviser of the committee.

The Schools Council

In 1964 the Schools Council emerged as a successor to the Curriculum Study Group which had been set up some years earlier to 'match the development outside the Department'. This referred to the work instigated by the Nuffield

Foundation into desirable changes in school curricula. The intention was to develop such proposals and others and to test them in actual school situations. The Schools Council was described by a permanent secretary of the department as a 'federation of largely teaching interests, local authority interests and the department to offer schools ideas about changes in the curriculum'. The council saw the proposed raising of the school leaving age to 16 in 1970–71 as a major challenge to develop suitable curricula. It enlisted the aid of the Survey in its wide-ranging study of the changes needed if this major step forward in educational reform was to succeed. The terms of reference for the survey *Young School Leavers* (1966) made it clear that the change

> implied keeping in school for a fifth year of secondary education some 60% more of the age group that stayed on voluntarily. The majority of those affected would have an aptitude for scholastic work which is average or below average. Some would come from homes which attached small value to extended schooling. It will be difficult to engage their interest and sense of relevance. Some will actively resent having to stay longer in school.
>
> The success or failure of raising the school leaving age will hinge on the success of the attempt to engage pupils more closely throughout their new five year course. Put at its lowest, the raising of the school leaving age could mean little more than the extension of a struggle between pupils who feel that school has little to offer to them and teachers who feel that they meet little other than boredom and resistance. Schools are, by contrast, likely to be most successful with those pupils who are supported by their parents and whose interest, motivation and sense of relevance are captured by the work they do. The attempt to achieve this can better be undertaken if the schools have more information about the attitudes of those involved. It was for this reason that the Secretary of State for Education and Science commissioned on behalf of the Schools Council an enquiry by the Government Social Survey into the interests and motives of pupils between the ages of 13–16 and their views on the adequacy of their preparation for adult life and work; the teacher's knowledge of what is relevant to their pupils; and the parent's view of their own and the school's role in the education of their children.[1]

The study design accordingly involved sampling pupils and ex-pupils of different ages, parents, teachers and headteachers and studying their attitudes towards longer compulsory education, what they felt the objectives of schooling should be and the values and interests of a range of school subjects. It also examined some aspects of the lives of young people concerned, their personal values and interests, home backgrounds and their experiences of attitudes to school. The survey showed that both 15-year-old leavers and their parents very widely saw the provision of knowledge and skills which would enable young people to obtain the best jobs and careers of which they were capable as one of the main functions that a school should undertake. Teachers, however, very generally rejected the achievement of vocational success as a major objective of education. It was evident therefore that conflict and misunderstanding could arise between the short-term viewpoint of parents and pupils who were concerned with starting work in the immediate future and the long-term objectives of teachers who saw their responsibility as preparing pupils for the whole of their future lives.

There was clear evidence that parents in general were aware that changes were taking place in the schools and they were in favour of the direction of these

Table 29 Comparison of average scores of 15 year old leavers and stayers on dimensions of attitudes to school; school objectives; values, interests and home backgrounds. Young school leavers (1966)

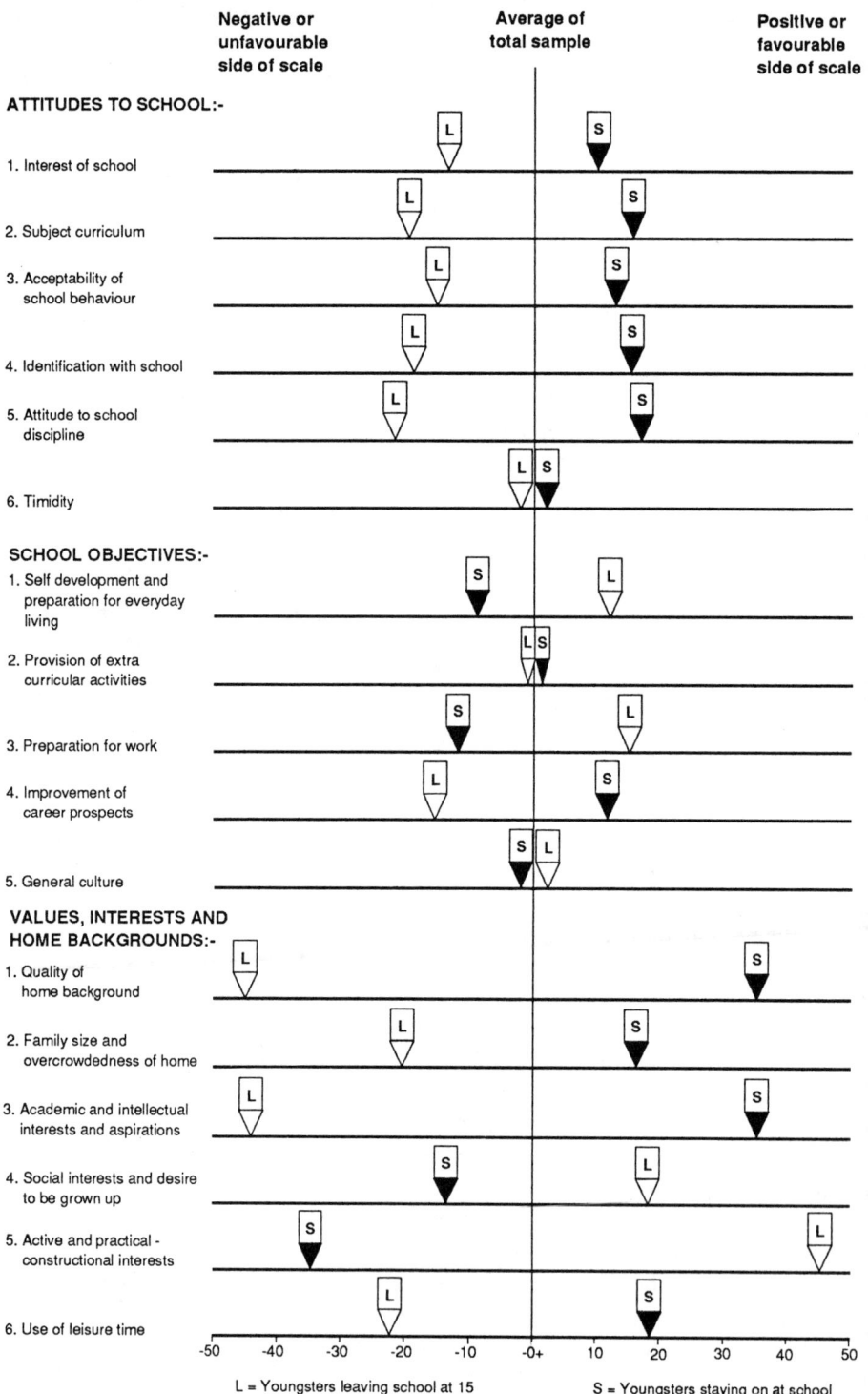

changes. They particularly valued the more interesting and varied curricula offered and the improvements in the standard of work and in the general physical provision for pupils. On the schools' side virtually none of the teachers felt that parents in the main were opposed to what they were trying to achieve. There was, however, much evidence that parents of 15-year-old leavers frequently lacked the active interest and participation in their children's education: teachers were in almost complete agreement over the need to take positive steps to encourage less-interested parents to visit the schools.

The answers of these parents themselves suggested that this apparent lack of interest was not so much an absence of concern about their child's progress at school as the result of three attitudes. First, the delegation of all responsibility for education to the school and, a very important factor, the failure to see the need for any contact unless something was wrong. Second, a very generally held view that they would be interfering if they went to the school uninvited – it was clear that for many this needed to be a very specifically personal invitation indeed. Third, a lack of confidence in being able to have a satisfactory discussion with the teachers if they went. On both parents' and teachers' sides lack of communication between home and school was a matter for concern. Half the parents of 15-year-old leavers were anxious to be told more about how their child was getting on at school and a third felt that teachers should to a greater extent consult them about their child. Very generally teachers considered that they needed to know more about the home backgrounds and lives of these pupils in order to carry out their work satisfactorily.

In the following year the Schools Council showed its interest in the contribution of Survey work to its own activities by asking for studies of a sector of the school population which fell betweeen the students with higher education potential and those covered by the newly raised school leaving age. The 1967 survey *6th Form Pupils and their Teachers* and the parallel study *Students in Full-time Courses in Colleges of Further Education* were designed to help the council develop its work on the curriculum changes called for by the increasing numbers staying at school beyond the official leaving age. The surveys described the courses being taken, the future plans of the pupils and the relationship between them, and then their views on the objectives of sixth-form work and how satisfied they were about the relevance of their courses to these objectives. Teachers were also interviewed on their views of the possible objectives of sixth form work and how pupils adjusted to the move into the sixth form, with special reference to possible disadvantages of some kinds of home background, and also on their views about which pupils should enter the sixth form, and possible alternative organisational arrangements for sixth formers. These surveys of pupils were given extra depth by a further survey of former sixth form pupils from the same schools who had left school approximately two years before interview, and who could assess their sixth form period in the light of their subsequent working experience. The courses they took at school and in particular their examination achievements were related to their occupation and to their judgments.

The sequence of surveys described above covered a large part of the educational population. They were all made as part of the continuing self-appraisal which has been characteristic of postwar educational development. The contribution of the Survey to this process was to apply sampling and interviewing techniques to the various relevant groups to provide representative descriptions of their circumstances, experience and attitudes, which could be used to make judgments about what was happening and how it might be changed for the better. The Survey in these studies always worked in collaboration with those engaged professionally in the subject.

Children and the social context

Alongside these surveys which focused on the education process there were, from early years, surveys concerned with what might be described as the social context in which children developed. The *Children out of School* study (1947) described earlier was the first of these. In 1948 a Home Office committee asked for a survey of children and the cinema and in 1959 the Building Research Station, as part of its postwar housing design programme, asked for a study of the way children's play facilities on housing estates were used and the demand for further provision.

The Youth Service had come into being before the war and as a result of increasing postwar concern with youth problems the Albemarle Committee was asked in 1960 to 'review the contribution which the Youth Service can make in assisting young people to play their part in the life of the community'. The aims of the service, although expressed in worthy terms, were not very clear and above all seemed not to be well rooted in firsthand information about the activities and interests of young people. By 1968 it was felt that a revaluation was needed for which some kind of national study seemed essential, and in 1969 a survey was done to provide such information. By this time interest had focused on narrower objectives than those envisaged by the Albemarle Committee and the survey *The Youth Service and Similar Provision* was mainly concerned with the use of youth clubs and similar facilities. Some of the results seemed to relate to the findings of surveys made to help the work on developing mainstream educational change. Thus attachment to clubs was less likely among those who left school early and it was even less likely among those from less skilled groups. The survey involved interviews with a sample of young people aged 14 to 20 and also their mothers. This made it possible to compare attachments of the young with the attitudes of parents, and particularly any worries or fears parents felt about their children.

Although the school-age period is naturally the concern of the Department of Education, its interests overlap with those of other departments. Thus the Road Research Laboratory, noting the high level of road accidents to children, asked in 1969 for a study of parental awareness of children's activities which might be related to road accidents: 'without this, propaganda and educational efforts directed at parents are unlikely to achieve much'. The survey interviewed the parents of children aged two to eight years and asked where children played.

'Between one-third and one-half were said by mothers to include "the street" amongst usual play places ... 43% of 8 year olds rode bicycles in the road ... only four out of the sample of 1037 who attended school cycled to it ... but three-quarters of all schoolchildren spent some time after school playing away from home, visiting friends or going to a shop.'

Another study related to young children was *Pre-school Children and the Need for Day Care*, done for the DHSS in 1974. Its purpose was to estimate need under various defined headings and then to identify the circumstances under which need might exist. 'The selection of characteristics to describe the sampled children and to distinguish those in need was guided by two considerations which were: they should be administratively visible and, secondly, that other research should have shown or suggested that they were related to specific relevant needs.' In 1968 the DHSS in a guidance note to local authorities had specified particular groups such as children with only one parent or whose home conditions constituted a hazard to their health or welfare (for example because of gross overcrowding). The note indicated the directions in which a more detailed enquiry might be developed. Mothers of a sample of children under five were interviewed, and since no information was sought from doctors or social workers 'the family's and child's state are what the mothers alone perceived them to be and the type of day care used if any is what the mothers believed it to be'. The interview included sections on the child's health, behaviour and development, play experience and use of day care, the mother's health and her desire for and views on day care for the child, and the family's demographic and socioeconomic characteristics. In developing the interview the experience of other researchers on child health and maternal distress was used. A scoring system was devised which collated mothers' experience and types of need so that different degrees of need could be established. These could be related to mothers in different circumstances, and to their desire for some kind of day care provision. The scores could also be used to locate need.

Given the wide range of public educational and social provision for children it is to be expected that administrators will be continually preoccupied with the operational problems thrown up in the maintenance of existing systems. For example, from 1970 the annual growth in school leavers with 'A' levels was consistently less than forecast, in contrast to the 1960s when the numbers of those seeking to enter higher education and with necessary qualifications grew faster than almost every projection that was made. The failure of numbers to grow as expected after 1970 raised questions about the attitudes of 16 and 18-year-old pupils and students towards education and career opportunities. In 1975 the Survey, at the request of the Department of Education, collaborated with academic researchers on a study designed to throw some light on this problem.[2]

The take-up of free school meals presented a rather different aspect of a common problem which arises when provision for specific need does not attract the anticipated numbers. In 1978 the opportunity arose to make supplementary use of a sample designed primarily for a different problem. The *Family Finances Survey* described earlier needed a sample of low income families and the child benefit registers were used for this purpose. Families in that sample with children at school gave information about their financial situation which could be used to estimate eligibility rates for free school meals and to identify families whose income was low in relation to their needs, as defined by DHSS criteria. These families were further interviewed for the *Free School Meals Survey* (1978).

A more long-standing problem concerns the differences between boys' and girls' careers despite the rather small differences in performance at school. In 1972 the Department of Education asked the Survey to design and carry out a project which would 'examine the environmental influences on the attitudes of girls in the 16–18 year age group to their careers including the factors in the home, school and community which have the effect of limiting their ambitions to careers which do not use their full potential'. The survey *5th Form Girls: Their Hopes for the Future* required a sample of girls who completed the fifth form year at a maintained secondary school at the end of academic year 1970–71. A standardised test of ability, the NFER AH Test of general intelligence, was completed, on the basis of which girls were classified into five ability groups. In addition an array of attitude scales was constructed, of which one measuring 'education aspiration' was central to the design. The main thrust of analysis compared

> three groups of girls, one having higher than average education aspiration for their ability, one having average aspirations and one having lower than average. The three groups which together comprised the middle 80% of the sample in their scores on the ability test were equal in size and closely matched for ability so that it was possible to compare girls with low, average and high educational aspirations at all levels of ability ... The three groups were examined in order to see what apart from ability itself distinguished girls who are setting themselves low target of educational achievement from those who are aiming higher.

Some of the findings were to be expected in the light of educational research: 'at all levels of ability home background and school background contributed independently to levels of aspiration ... the girls who were most likely to be aiming low were modern school girls whose parents left school as early as possible and put no pressure on their daughters to remain at school ... the group most likely to have low aspirations for their ability was the small group of bright girls who had been educated in modern schools ... There was little indication that girls had lower aspirations directly because of their parents' financial circumstances ... few girls said they wanted to leave school in order to help their families financially ... low education aspiration was however associated with a desire to earn money and concern about financial security'.

From 1971 onwards the annual chapter on education in the continuing General Household Survey provided current data on some aspects of the education process such as qualifications attained, earnings related to education and schools attended by different social groups. Thus comparisons between 1971 and 1980 show the increase in proportions of men and women with any qualifications at or above GCE 'O' level standard. 'The gross earning differentials between different levels of qualification have diminished in relative terms for both men and women since 1971 ... the average gross earnings of women in

Table 30 Socioeconomic group of father/head of household by type of school attended by age of child. General Household Survey (1973)

Children under 16 and students aged 16–19 not living in institutions (England and Wales – 1973)

	Socioeconomic Group of Father/HOH*							
Type of school	Professional	Employers and managers	Intermediate non-manual	Junior non-manual	Skilled manual and own account non-professional	Semi-skilled manual and personal service	Unskilled	Total
	%	%	%	%	%	%	%	%
Under school age (under 5)								
Not yet started	67	71	72	74	79	79	[59]	76
Day nursery/play group	15	19	22	16	13	9	[6]	14
Nursery school§	18	9	6	10	7	12	[6]	10
Base (=100%)	*141*	*305*	*143*	*204*	*1,011*	*391*	*71*	*2,266*
Primary schooling (5–10)†								
Primary school	82	89	96	97	98	98	94	95
Independent or direct grant school	17	8	4	2	1	1	NIL	3
Other schools	1	3	NIL	1	1	1	6	2
Base (=100%)	*145*	*502*	*167*	*255*	*1,269*	*477*	*109*	*2,924*

Secondary schooling (11–19)†								
Secondary modern school	7	22	20	29	34	40	31	30
Comprehensive (incl. middle) school	38	40	48	47	48	50	58	47
Grammar school	31	21	26	15	12	7	5	14
Independent or direct grant school	22	14	6	7	1	2	1	5
Other schools	2	3	NIL	2	4	2	6	3
Base (=100%)	131	432	145	242	1,016	442	107	2,515
All								
Under school age	34	25	31	29	31	30	25	29
Primary schooling	35	40	37	36	39	36	38	38
Secondary schooling:								
11–15	25	29	27	32	28	31	36	29
16–19	6	6	5	3	2	3	1	3
Base (=100%)								
No.	417	1,239	455	701	3,296	1,310	287	7,705
%	5	16	6	9	43	17	4	100

* For those under 16, the SEG of the head of household (HOH) has been used where the father was not a member of the household.

† Where children were just outside the age group at the time of interview they have been allocated to the age group of the majority (eg primary school children aged 11 are included with the 5–10 group).

§ Including primary and independent school for under 5s, as well as nursery classes in primary schools.

full-time employment have generally improved as measured by comparison with those of similarly qualified men.'

The family

In 1966 the GRO asked the Survey to devise a survey that would provide information different from that on which demographic projections had relied previously – a survey of *expected* ultimate family size which could be used to suggest the trend in family size and which would provide more detailed information on the relation between various demographic, social, economic and attitude measures and family size. The background to the *Family Intentions Survey* was doubt about the interpretation of existing data. While some of the variables which affect the birthrate did not suggest a declining birthrate – for example, women's age at marriage was getting younger – in 1965 for the first time since 1955 the number of children born was fewer than in the previous year. The crude birthrate and the legitimate birthrate also declined in that year and continued to decline until at least 1968. The GRO request presented the Survey with a challenge. Parallel studies had been done successfully in the USA and some academic studies had been launched but not reported in the UK. It would be necessary to collect details of pregnancies and births, views on ideal size of families, information on physical disabilities which might affect fecundity, current contraceptive practice and intentions and other data which the literature suggested might be relevant. Searching pilot studies were made to test acceptability and feasibility of the necessary detailed questions, particularly those related to contraceptive practices.

The report examined the responses and pointed out that the data collected and their interpretation was suggested as a supplement rather than an alternative to projecting past data. In particular it provided direct evidence from the population concerned about their behaviour and attitudes rather than relying on the forecaster's intuition. The study suggested that 'women married since 1959 expect to have on average smaller families than those married during the 1950s ... the decline is particularly significant for women who married before the age of 20 years in the 1960s ... trends in family size based on marriages which took place in the 1940s and early 1950s suggested a continuing increase and the survey directed attention to the point at which the trend was likely to alter and indicated, relatively, the size of the change'. The report discussed the variation in the size of anticipated decline among different groups in the population, the contribution of more reliable methods of contraception and possible changes in the length of intervals between births.

Given the complexity of the study and the sensitive nature of some of the data the report rightly noted the need for a programme of studies which could accumulate experience and improve methodology. While an organised programme did not happen, a series of studies were made between 1966 and 1975 for varying official purposes which profited from the pioneer study. In 1972 a follow-up study, *Families Five Years On*, was made for the Population Statistics

Division of OPCS in order to 'assess the value of women's statements in 1967 about the number of children they expect to have and to investigate fertility behaviour and intentions since the 1967 study'. This was based on recall interviews with some of the women interviewed in the first survey. Continuing contact with all the original sample would have been desirable but was not possible: however, samples of women aged under 30 and those married between 1960 and 1967 were selected and 73% of them were interviewed. The report of the survey examined closely the assumptions on which the methods used in both the 1967 and 1972 studies were based. 'Evidence from this study suggests that predictions made early on in marriage are subject to considerable variation and that half of the women married less than five years in 1967 had different expectations when interviewed in 1972.' The report draws the conclusion 'the use of number of children expected would be more effective after five years of marriage ... a series (so based) would indicate changes in women's thinking and this together with number of children actually born within five years would provide additional information on which to base further projections'. In 1971 and 1975 the two surveys *Family Planning Services* and *Family Planning Services Changes and Effects* described earlier were made for the policy divisions in the DHSS. It is obvious that the experience gained in the earlier surveys was used in their design and that the analysis of the later surveys has continued to contribute to the comprehensive background needed to improve the design of demographic enquiries.

The continuing concern with population movements led to the setting up of an Official Committee on Population which recommended a programme of research leading to the Demographic Review of 1977. There was also at this time discussion of a United Nations' programme of worldwide demographic research – a world fertility survey. This comprised sample surveys in many countries with the twin objectives of encouraging research into population matters and accumulating data from which wider generalisations might be made about world population. The design of these surveys, it was hoped, would be a cooperative undertaking so that some control could be exercised over design, operation and analysis to maintain comparability between countries.

These events stimulated a request for another survey from the Population Statistics branch of OPCS, *Family Formation 1976*. The aim of this study was to examine 'the family formation histories of a sample of women'. Despite criticism of studies which excluded men the survey was limited to women, mainly because registration data and previous surveys were based on women and it was important to maintain comparability. Unlike the early surveys single women were included; the family planning surveys had shown that this was feasible and an increasing proportion of conceptions and live births had occurred to single women. So the sample covered all women between 16 and 49 years. A postal sift was devised and 85% of women in the eligible age-groups identified in this sift cooperated in the survey. Although some of the subject matter of previous surveys was deliberately repeated the scope of the interview was in some respects more searching. Family formation histories were recorded giving dates of marriage, dates of all pregnancies, live births, stillbirths and spontaneous or induced abortion. The period before marriage was also considered and those factors which may have affected premarital pregnancies and the timing of marriage – marriage was therefore treated as an event in the family formation process. Other topics investigated were women's attitudes and opinions on family formation, views on sex before marriage, abortion, sterilisation, exposure to risk of pregnancy at different times and the use of contraception, periods of employment, husband's employment, housing and, finally, expectations and intentions not only for children but also for level of living indicators.

The report describes the extent of premarital relationship by date of marriage: 'the date of marriage increasingly has to be regarded as an arbitrary point in a couple's relationship. It no longer coincides with the beginning of sexual relations for the majority of couples'. Premarital births and abortions could be compared with registration data and were clearly under-reported. 'It is clear from the survey that women who marry young and/or are pregnant at marriage also start the family building cycle of their lives in relatively deprived circumstances – less education, lower status occupations, many have to share homes and already have lower expectations for material goods and their ability to plan or control their lives.'

The surveys described above relate to some central aspects of family life. Significant other aspects, such as financial circumstances, are covered in the *Family Expenditure Survey*. The *General Household Survey* provides continuing information about the changes in some areas described in the surveys about families as well as more detailed information about conditions and circumstances, so that some of the main conclusions reached can be regularly updated and trends in the statistics noted. Some ad hoc surveys done in response to particular policy pressures have also contributed to statistical knowledge about families and their problems. *The Survey of Adoption in Great Britain* (1967) for the Home Office is one example. It seemed that no comprehensive data was available about adoptions arranged through agencies or privately and the way in which the adoption procedure worked in practice. A new departmental committee to consider the law, policy and procedure on the adoption of children was in prospect and more information was necessary. A stratified random sample of all the courts considering applications in 1966 was drawn and the court files used as a source. Survey interviewers visited the courts and extracted information recorded on standard forms about the children, applicants and the parents of children as well as the decisions made. The data was analysed and reported by the Survey and the Home Office Research Unit, and the report was published as *Home Office Research Study 10*[3].

The Finer Committee, appointed in 1969 to consider one-parent families, also asked for help from the Survey, and the survey *Families and Their Needs* was done in 1970. It was designed to produce information which would permit comparisons between one-parent and two-parent families. There were at that time relatively few one-parent families and a national sample was thought to be a rather wasteful procedure. So the decision was made to attempt intensive studies of five areas with different social circumstances and within them to collect much more detailed information about relationships with local services and other sources of help than would have been possible with a national sample. Five area studies were done and no attempt was made to produce national estimates, although attention was drawn to 'a number of findings which are common to all areas and which can therefore be regarded as giving an indication of the national position in qualitative though not necessarily quantitative terms'. Since this survey the numbers of one-parent families have grown and three-yearly moving averages are given by the *General Household Survey* of numbers and many of the circumstances of these families.

Notes

[1] *Young School Leavers*, report of an enquiry carried out for the Schools Council, HMSO, 1966.
[2] DES Reports on Education, No 86, July 1976.
[3] *Home Office Research Study 10*, HMSO, 1968.

12 Criminal justice and law

GIVEN THE VARIED NATURE of Home Office responsibilities it was to be expected that Survey activities on its behalf would be similarly varied. But the largest proportion of Home Office surveys done over a span of 30 years relates to some aspect of criminal justice or the legal system, and as in so many fields there was one particular study which seemed to act as point of entry.

T S Lodge, a former Director of Statistics at the Home Office Research Unit, in an account of its founding[1] has noted that prior to 1948 very little official interest was shown in research despite the urging of noted reformers like Margery Fry. In 1948 during the passage of the Criminal Justice Bill through Parliament an amendment was accepted giving the Home Secretary power to make resources available for research purposes. At about the same time a greater interest in improving criminal statistics manifested itself and in 1949 a Home Office Statistical Adviser was appointed. One of the growing concerns of the period was with juvenile delinquency. The work of Dr Herman Mannheim at Cambridge University on a pilot prediction study of Borstal boys was funded by the Home Office, and at its request a senior research officer of the Survey was assigned to help. Lodge comments 'Wilkins' enthusiasm and ability had far reaching consequences for this study and eventually for criminological research as a whole'. Some years later, following the publication of the report on this work,[2] the Home Office Research Committee recommended that Wilkins should be invited to join the Home Office and he was appointed Deputy Statistical Adviser in 1956. Lodge says 'in practice though not yet formally this was the beginning of the Home Office Research Unit'. In 1957 during a parliamentary debate the Home Secretary said he intended to give first priority to expanding the research programme.

The Borstal prediction study did not use customary field sampling techniques, nor did it follow the best known American models which had the same objective – to devise a system of identifying characteristics of offenders which would enable a prediction to be made of the chances that after release they would reappear for a further term. The English researchers obtained their data by 'interviewing the files'. That is, they identified a standard set of recorded characteristics and, using multiple regression, reduced a large number of variables to about half a dozen on which they based a system of scoring which gave a reasonable prediction of the chance of reconviction within three years of discharge. Such an approach could be used on other kinds of offenders and implicitly shows whether a particular form of treatment gives rise to high rates of recidivism. The project was carried out as a Survey study and Survey interviewers extracted the data from the relevant Borstal files.

In 1954 a similar project was done on approved schools and in 1960 the *Young Offenders Survey* was done in collaboration with psychologists at University College, London and the Prison Commission. It was designed to provide information about the social and family background of young people who were serving prison sentences. The reports emerging from these two studies were not the responsibility of the Survey, whose contribution was to advise on a suitable sampling method and then to carry out the fieldwork required. Given the particular population involved this was sometimes onerous. For example, the young offenders study required very lengthy interviews with the mothers of young prisoners.

A rather different aspect of the social context of prisoners was the survey *Offenders as Employees* (1960), one of the projects arising out of the Home Office support to researchers at Cambridge University's Institute of Criminology. It was concerned with the employment situation of former prisoners and involved surveys of samples of employers and prisoners. Its aim was to ascertain the attitudes and practices of employers towards engaging men previously convicted, and of men already in employment who were suspected or convicted of committing criminal offences, and to relate this to information about the firm. The method employed was not to ask hypothetical questions about intentions but rather to concentrate on employers' actual experience; the employers were a sample of all employers in Reading. The Survey participated in the design of the study, making a special contribution to the sampling and the questionnaire, carried out fieldwork and tabulated the responses. The reporting was done by the Cambridge Institute.

A third study in 1960 moved from offenders to the other end of the spectrum. Increasing concern with the work of the police had led to the setting up of the Royal Commission on the Police (Willink). Among its terms of reference the commission was required to consider 'the relationship of the police with the public and the means of ensuring that complaints by the public against the police are effectively dealt with', and it felt that it would be useful to assess the attitudes of the two groups in relation to each other. So in addition to inviting organisations and individuals to say what they thought, the commission also asked the Survey to speak to representative samples of the police and public about their relations with each other. Questions were asked about the most recent occasions on which there had been some kind of direct contact; what were the most unsatisfactory experiences of contact within a recent period and whether the public had any direct experience of some of the forms of police behaviour which it was alleged were unsatisfactory. The answers to some of these questions were used to divide informants into two groups, one consisting of those who on one or more occasions had had some personal contact with the police in which, in the informant's own opinion, the behaviour of the police was considered to be incorrect or unsatisfactory in some way, and the other of those

Table 31 Comparison between proportions in different sections of the population who had had some unsatisfactory experience with the police. The Police and the public (1960)

Classification of informants		Personal experience of police conduct		Total	
		Satisfactory No experience	Unsatisfactory experience		No.
Type of district in which informant lived					
Large town	%	70	30	100	1,374
Other urban	%	69	31	100	702
Rural	%	75	25	100	529
Social Class					
Professional, managerial (I and III)	%	67	33	100	547
Skilled – manual and clerical (III)	%	70	30	100	1,331
Semi-skilled, labouring (IV and V)	%	76	24	100	564
(Unclassified, eg Housewife, No answer)	%	(77.9)	(22.1)	(100	163)
Age					
21 and under	%	59	41	100	113
22–25	%	64	36	100	195
26–35	%	69	31	100	499
36–45	%	70	30	100	605
46–65	%	75	25	100	1,193
Motoring experience					
Motorists	%	56	44	100	772
Non-motorists	%	77	23	100	1,833
Sex					
Men	%	62	38	100	1,261
Women	%	80	20	100	1,344
All informants	%	71	29	100	2,605

Note: When considering the proportion of informants who have had some unsatisfactory experience with the police, it should be borne in mind that these include *people who have had only one unsatisfactory experience* which may have occurred a long time ago. The primary object of these comparisons is to indicate which groups are more liable than others to be sensitive in their relations with the police.

who were satisfied with police behaviour in all personal contacts with them and those who had had no personal contact with the police. It must be emphasised that this was the informant's own assessment of police conduct – but dissatisfaction or annoyance felt by the informant was real irrespective of the justification for it.

It was specially relevant in this enquiry to compare the attitudes of different sections of the population and to find whether there was any special sense of grievance among such groups as motorists and teenagers. Above all it was found interesting and illuminating to compare the public's view of the police in the performance of their duties against the view the police had of public attitudes towards them. There was found to be a great deal of discrepancy on the public image of the police, who imagined themselves to be much worse thought of by the public than turned out to be the case. Over two-thirds of the police interviewed thought that the general public's opinion of them had changed for the worse in the past 10 years, but over 86% of the public interviewed said that their feelings towards the police had not changed during that time. Teenagers and to a lesser extent motorists were thought by the public to be more resentful of the police than formerly and the police agreed with these views. Perhaps most useful in this study were the views of the police on how relations with the public might be improved.

Deterrents

Given the particular difficulties with teenagers which the report just described emphasises and the increase in the numbers of youths convicted annually, it was clearly becoming important to know more about their relation to the law and law enforcement. In 1963 the Home Office asked the Survey to design and carry out a study, *Deterrents and Incentives to Crime amongst boys and young men aged 15–21*, to throw some light on the influences restraining young males from offending against the law and their effectiveness. Since minors were involved it was felt necessary to make the enquiry known to parents before an interview was attempted and this affected the response rate to some extent. Nevertheless over 70% of the set sample gave long interviews of about two hours, and most of these were made with only the respondent and interviewer present. Respondents were asked about offences they might have committed including some trivial and some more serious, and the familiarity with the courts as a defendant or otherwise. The latter proportions ranged 'from 6% at age 15 to 27% at age 21. One-fifth had appeared in court by the age of 19 ... For all but eight of those offences for which anyone in the sample had appeared in court the number of offences per court appearance exceeded 20'. Respondents were asked to rate offences according to how serious they thought them to be and what they would feel should any friends commit them. The responses permitted the construction of a 'permissiveness' scale, and it was shown that 'there was consistency between the number of offences the respondents admitted and the number they rated at the extremes of the permissiveness scales'.

Respondents were asked to rank eight things which might worry an offender who had been found out by the police. The three most important were 'what the family would think', 'the chances of losing my job' and 'the shame or publicity of having to appear in court'. Punishment ranked *below* these. This was consistent with the high proportion of cases where parents never got to know about their sons' offences – less likely when court appearances were involved. An attempt was made to measure the effect of 'conscience' against the chances of police detection. Over half said they were most put off breaking the law by the feeling that it was wrong, and the proportion varied inversely and systematically with numbers of offences admitted. Respondents were asked of a group of nine offences how they rated their chances of 'getting away with it'. In five out of the nine the average estimate favoured the offender but estimates varied greatly with the particular offence. These estimates could be related to the number of offences respondents admitted. 'Over 20% of those with the worst actual offence records also tended to rate highly their chances of getting away with it for five or more of the nine listed offences ... over half of those with the worst personal offence record were also more likely to feel that their chances of detection were more important than their feeling that it was wrong to break the law.'

Respondents' reactions to various current penalties were noted, with their estimate of the worst penalty somebody of their own age might suffer for a list of offences. A substantial proportion claimed not to have heard of at least one type of penalty and it appeared that opinion was 'rather muddled' about the worst possible penalty. Respondents were also asked for their views on the police. 'There was very widespread general sympathy for the individual policeman and recognition of the difficulties of his job ... few had reached the stage of regarding the police as enemies or rejecting them outright ... Despite these generalized indications of goodwill there were very few who had no specific criticisms' and the report examines these beliefs in detail. It was shown that such criticisms were associated directly with the number of personal offences admitted.

The next survey in the series concerned with people and the law related to crime had a peculiar history. A Royal Commission on the Penal System had been set up, a research secretary appointed and a research programme had begun to develop when the government decided to disband the commission. However, the Home Office decided that the study results would be valuable, so the survey *Crime, Criminals and the Law* went ahead as planned in 1966, on behalf of the Home Office. Its purpose was to give guidance on the state of public knowledge about crime and criminal procedures and to provide a basis for judging whether existing penal concepts reflected public opinion, and to what extent public attitudes were based on any sound knowledge of offenders and the crimes they commit. The sample was of individuals aged 21 to 69. The survey attempted to cover a lot of ground, and to reduce the burden on respondents the sample was divided into three parts. The questions put to each part were arranged so that the number of people asked any given question approximated to two-thirds of the total. The three parts of the sample were demographically equivalent but it appeared from subsequent analysis that in some cases responses to individual questions were affected by the fact that not all the questions were put to all individuals. An appendix in the report illustrates these effects, which do not seem to have prejudiced the general representativeness of the results.

The report began with a discussion of respondents' personal experience of courts and how it related to knowledge of differences between courts; 14% had appeared as defendants, 20% as witnesses, only 3% as jurors, and just under half had ever attended any court. Many more had attended magistrates courts (36%) than higher courts (14%) but it seemed that most people were not aware of major differences between judges and magistrates. Twenty-eight per cent believed that magistrates were given defendants' previous records before evidence was heard and those who had attended higher courts were less likely than those who had not to know the actual situation. The report described how much people knew and what impressions they had about what happens to someone charged with an offence – the position on legal aid or the effect of a plea of guilty on the trial or possible sentence. About seven out of ten people and even more of the better educated thought (wrongly) that most defendants in higher courts pleaded not guilty. Almost half the sample thought that someone with money would stand a better chance of having someone defend him but about eight out of ten thought judges would give the same treatment to rich and poor offenders. Opinion on magistrates was less favourable. Respondents were asked how representative magistrates were, or should be, how much legal training they were thought to get and what they needed apart from training in law to help them pass the right sentences. Forty per cent thought that magistrates were 'nearly all well off'. The report then discussed judgments of and opinions about prisons and prison life. 'In general people were not well informed about what goes on behind prison walls. They have a number of misconceptions most of which indicate that they do not think it too onerous an existence ... the majority simply acquiesce in what they *believe* is official policy ... nevertheless nearly half feel that prisons are in general not severe enough.' These opinions were analysed by whether respondents had had contact with prisoners.

Respondents were asked to rate the degree of seriousness of an array of offences. Their responses fell into three groups of declining seriousness: offences against the person, offences against property and other indictable offences. They were then asked what they thought was the frequency with which people were accused of these offences: this gave a rating which could be compared with the actual frequency of these offences. This comparison showed that robbery with violence, factory and housebreaking and cruelty to children were relatively overrated by respondents while deliberate damage to property and fraud were underrated. These differences varied with the socioeconomic status of respondents as did respondents' judgments of whether particular offences had 'increased quite a bit' in recent years. Following these questions were others seeking opinion on possible ways of reducing crime, and then the report examined opinions on the causes of crime, the characteristics of habitual offenders, why people believe they become such and what would need to be done to induce them to give up breaking the law. 'The two measures thought by a majority of respondents, 54% and 51%, as likely to affect the majority of offenders favourably were: if prisoners were trained during their sentence for a job they wanted to do when they came out; and if prison life were made harder.'

The final section of the report was concerned with victims. This is of special interest since it was the first time this aspect of crime had been examined. Later the topic was explored in the General Household Survey (1972, 1973, 1979, 1980) and in 1982 the Home Office mounted a sample survey wholly devoted to the topic, on about the same scale as the General Household Survey but not carried out by the Survey. The topic was approached cautiously in the survey described here because within a very long interview relatively little time could be given; it was known that memory very seriously affected recall of such events, and the numbers required to record useful incidence data for many crimes were much larger than the sample size available. Nevertheless, given the subsequent interest it was a useful trial run: it indicated what proportion of events of victimisation were reported to the police and thus what might be the size of the so-called 'black figure' of unreported crime, and how this varied for different kinds of crime, different areas and different sections of the population.

As frequently happened with Survey studies unplanned secondary interest developed a few years later when the Advisory Council on the Penal System, the standing committee of the Home Office on penal matters, began a review of the treatment of young offenders. They were of course interested in the objectives of the penal system and the constraints presented by public opinion on the aims of sentencing. Papers based on surveys described above were prepared as evidence for the committee. These surveys took place over the period 1950–66. During this time the Home Office research interest grew steadily. By 1959 the research unit had developed a programme in several areas including nine further prediction studies and was supporting research inside academic centres. By 1967 the research programme included more than 50 projects, the research unit had been separated from the statistical department of the Home Office and a wide community of academic researchers had been funded to develop the new discipline of criminology. The nature of Survey work related to law and the penal system was inevitably affected by this growth of other research resources, and it began to move towards helping with the examination of legal institutions.

Legal institutions

The Survey had explored and made known the use of the Electoral Register for sampling purposes. The Departmental Committee on Jury Service, considering future qualifications for jury service in 1964, needed to know how many jurors there were under the existing system and asked the Survey to help. As the Electoral Register indicates those eligible it was possible to examine it and give some reliable estimates. It was also possible to illustrate an array of anomalies which indicated that the number of people in different areas marked as eligible in the register varied in ways which could not be explained by the known criteria for eligibility. Thus the proportion of electors marked as jurors ranged from 2% in Gateshead to 42% in some parts of Birmingham. The proportion of females marked as eligible varied even more widely. It was clear that the authorities responsible were carrying out their responsibilities in preparing the register very differently in different areas. In 1981 and 1982 further studies of the Electoral Register were made for the Home Office which shed more light on the coverage of all eligible persons.

In 1967 the Departmental Committee on Death Certification and Coroners was undertaking a wide review of the relevant law and practice. It needed information about the way the coroner system was working and asked for the *Survey of Attitudes of Relatives of Deceased Persons towards the Coroner System.* 'The committee attaches considerable importance to an investigation of this kind which might demonstrate the attitude to the coroner of members of the public who have not been concerned with him and, more important, the attitude of persons who have been involved in a death reported to the coroner. In the latter category it would be desirable to find out whether the relatives considered that the inquest was satisfactory, whether they felt they had been sympathetically dealt with, whether they had any questions which they felt had been left unanswered, whether they had any complaints about the procedure, and similar matters.'

The sample covered two types of cases – those in which an inquest was held and those in which a post-mortem was carried out but no inquest was held, and cases were selected from coroners' or registrars' certificates in 40 coroners' districts. An attempt was made to interview those closest to the deceased who had been sufficiently involved in the enquiry to provide the information required. The survey showed that, contrary to the impression given by some newspaper accounts, 'in general relatives were well satisfied with the manner in which enquiries were conducted'. But that was not to say that relatives suffered no distress. 'In 20% of inquest cases and 5% of all post-mortems relatives had been upset by delays in the funeral', although the survey showed that a large majority of funerals took place within seven days of death. 'In 23% of inquests and 22% of all post-mortems relatives had been upset by the fact of post-mortem and the proportion was higher when deceased was a young person ... one-fifth of respondents in inquest cases were not entirely satisfied with the results of the inquest ... 43% of respondents in inquest cases said they had to wait until the inquest before learning details of the cause of death ... 20% of inquest cases with post-mortems and 12% of post-mortems took place before respondents had been informed of it.' However, 'complaints against the coroner himself were rare and usually came from people who were dissatisfied with the outcome of the inquest, mainly in road accident cases'. Only 5% of respondents who had given evidence or been present when it was given thought that coroners had been unkind or lacked consideration. While the majority of respondents in inquest cases had no strong objection to newspaper reports, in 27% of cases they would have preferred to avoid the publicity and 12% of respondents in inquest cases complained quite strongly that newspaper reports were inaccurate or misleading.

In 1974, prompted partly by the substantial increases in the amount of business done by the courts, the James Committee, which had been appointed jointly by the Home Office and the Lord Chancellor, was investigating the distribution of cases between crown courts and magistrates' courts. One of the committee's tasks was to review the criteria which determine at which kind of court cases might be held, and they felt that as well as hearing the views of those with professional interests they should also know why some defendants, given the right to choose, made the choices they did. The Survey was asked to design and carry out an appropriate study. *The James Committee Survey of Defendants* required a sample of defendants who had exercised this option and they were found by choosing from court records defendants whose cases included an eligible criminal offence. The sample was selected so that comparisons could be made between those choosing to be tried either in magistrates' or crown courts. Just under 70% of those chosen were interviewed but predictably, quite a few of those selected could not be found at the address recorded. The report noted the proportion who denied having a choice and examined the probable reasons. Defendants' stated reasons for choice of different courts were examined and showed that the choice was greatly affected by the distribution of guilty or not guilty pleas: 88% of those choosing magistrates' courts pleaded guilty while 69% of those choosing crown courts pleaded not guilty to all charges. The main reasons for choosing crown courts related to what was seen as improved chances of acquittal, while at magistrates' courts the main reasons related to having the case finished in the shortest time with the minimum penalty and expense. The report showed that defendants' previous convictions influenced the choice. At the end of the interview defendants were asked whether if they could go back and choose again they would make the same decision: 20% of those choosing crown courts said that if they had known how long they would have to wait they would have preferred a magistrates' court, but over 30% of those choosing either court would have made the same decision. The interview asked about advice received before the choice was made from solicitors or police, defendants' previous experience of courts, how they had learnt abut the possibility of being able to choose the venue and what they knew about the differences between the courts. It seemed that very few defendants would have changed their decision had they been informed, but given the opportunity to agree or disagree with two series of statements expressing favourable and unfavourable attitudes toward the courts, considerable proportions disagreed with the favourable comments and the majority of defendants, regardless of the venue chosen for their trial, expressed agreement with statements commenting unfavourably on the court system.

In 1978 the Scottish Courts Administration, acting on behalf of the Scottish Law Commission, asked for the *Survey of Defenders in Debt Actions in Scotland*. The commission, in its second programme of law reform, was examining law and practice on the subject of 'diligence' – action approved by the courts in Scotland to enforce decrees for payment and other forms of recovery of debts. They were particularly concerned with the social aspects of this legal procedure: 'Default and decree debt is increasingly becoming recognized as a problem as economic circumstances, unemployment, inflation, impinge on people's financial situations. It is estimated that some 150,000 actions may be awarded in a single year of which there are up to 35,000 cases of final diligence executed'. What was wanted was a study of the characteristics and circumstances of people who had court action taken against them, to ask them how the debt was incurred and what they knew about the debt recovery process, and to examine the circumstances in which the debt was settled. The sample of debt actions was drawn from sheriff court records and summary warrant records and covered all courts with more than 35 cases per month. A high proportion of debtors were young males. A fifth were unemployed at a time when 5% of men in Scotland were unemployed and 45% were in fulltime employment when court action started. Forty-one per cent were in households where the main income was likely to be state benefits and they were more likely than other Scottish households to have dependant children.

> Those sued for arrears of rates were rather different – older, more likely to be in fulltime employment and with a higher income ... The overwhelming majority of debtors had when taking on the commitment been confident about ability to pay ... of those without means to settle over half said their difficulties resulted from lost or reduced income ... Just over one in three debtors sued for non-payment of rent or other accommodation charges said they had been taken to court previously for another debt by the same creditor ... Nearly half said they had not been warned by the creditor that court action was going to be taken ... about half of the debtors sued in payment actions had exercised their option of returning part of the summons mostly in order to make a formal offer to settle the debt outright or by instalments ... and informal settlements had also been reached by half of those who did not return the summons. Overall about two-thirds of debtors had just offered to settle at or before the first calling of their case.

The survey report identified four main stages at which settlement by payment was first agreed, what kind of debtor was involved and how the money was raised. The report examined debtors' knowledge and awareness of the court process and suggested that 'there are aspects of the court process where improving debtors' awareness of their situation or action open to them might encourage early settlement'.

The law commissions in Scotland, England and Wales have a mission to reform and a concomitant obligation to enquire into existing circumstances to see where changes might be beneficial. They are permanent bodies and work to a programme, largely on areas where there has developed an acknowledged need for change. In 1970 the Law Commission in England, turning to family property law requested help from the Survey: 'The present legal values concerning the acquisition and ownership of property by married persons have given rise to much litigation ... one problem which has arisen is that we have no detailed information about the present pattern of acquisition and ownership ... as a result it is difficult to assess the extent of the present defects in the law and the possible impact of any changes we may propose'. What was needed was a study of the way in which married people managed their financial affairs. The survey *Matrimonial Property* was based on married and formerly married persons found in a sample of over 3,000 addresses selected from the Electoral Register. The report dealt first with the matrimonial home and in whose name it was, then recorded which bank accounts or other assets were held jointly or in one name and what had been the contribution of wives to major items of matrimonial property. The attitudes of couples to joint ownership or responsibility were examined with particular reference to occasions such as breakdown of marriage or death, when decisions are needed on inheritance, and to knowledge of the laws of intestacy. The latter was very relevant since 76% of husbands and 90% of wives had made no will. 'Only three persons in the sample were able to state correctly what were the laws of intestacy.' The report noted that 'for many couples the law relating to property must seem very remote since they themselves own little property of great value ... 23% of couples said that excluding the house or current bank account the total value of other assets was less than £100'. At the time of the survey most did not own their homes. Some years later a similar study was requested by the Scottish Courts Administration on behalf of the Scottish Law Commission. The report, *Family Property in Scotland* (1978), covered much the same ground as the English study.

Other Home Office surveys

The Survey also made contributions to other disparate responsibilities of the Home Office. The study of *Betting* (1950), part of the series of expenditure surveys, was extended at the request of the Home Office to help the Royal Commission on Betting, Lotteries and Gambling, and further work was commissioned in 1965. The 1970 survey *Public Attitudes to British Standard Time* collected information for a Home Office review of changes introduced on an experimental basis in order to test reactions. The sample design was arranged so that comparisons could be made between sections of the population living at different latitudes and therefore with different degrees of exposure to the effects of change, as well as the more usual demographic comparisons between families with schoolchildren who might be going to school or returning at times when daylight was limited by some of the proposed hours. Two other 1970 surveys were tackled within the framework of one sample and both were done for the Home Office and the Scottish Home and Health Department.

The Shopping Habits Survey was designed to describe attitudes to current restrictions on shopping hours at a time when marked changes had occurred in the numbers of shops of different type and ownership since the 1950 Shops Act and also in the employment of women. The report described arrangements for household shopping, when and by whom it was done, the mode of access to shops and how convenient all this was. Two-thirds of household shoppers were 'very satisfied' with existing shop hours: 55% were in favour of shopkeepers themselves deciding what their hours should be and 43% said they would favour later closing in the evening. The report paid special attention to the views of working housewives and to opinion about the law on Sunday trading. Over half felt that it was illogical and outdated, but over a third favoured existing restrictions.

The *Public Attitudes to Liquor Licensing Law in Great Britain* survey had a background going back to 1958. At that time there was concern with increases in convictions for drunkenness, particularly among young people, and an awareness that the convictions statistics gave only a limited insight into the problem. However, it was not felt at the time that enquiries into drinking habits should be undertaken, and a first study confined to police officers and designed to draw out their experience was envisaged. *The Survey of Public Behaviour under the Influence of Alcohol* (1955–59) was based on a representative sample of police districts with probability of selection proportional to the size of police forces. Within these districts the actual areas to be covered were to be selected at random and officers were chosen by two methods, one giving weight to officers with special qualifications to speak about drunkenness in their town, the other comprising a nominal roll of the force excluding only officers with less than five years' experience. Contrary to the evidence of the drunkenness conviction statistics, very few of the police officers interviewed had noticed any change in the amount of drunkenness or drink-associated behaviour that required their intervention. It seemed clear that the annual statistics gave only an incomplete indication of the amount of police effort involved and there was a considerable difference between the ability and/or disposition of different officers to deal with incidents of drunkenness in such a way that no charge resulted. It followed that the annual conviction numbers might be appreciably affected by the ability or willingness of new recruits to deal with incidents without taking any one in charge. The report also notes that during the period immediately preceding the enquiry the upward trend in convictions was reversed and consequently the generally favourable trend noted in the views of police officers might reflect this short-term improvement.

The favourable trend in the statistics did not continue and by 1963 the Home Office once again approached the Survey to design studies which would 'throw light on the nature of the behaviour leading to convictions of drunkenness and the characteristics of the people involved, the extent to which increase in conviction may be attributable to changes, known to the police, in types of behaviour amongst particular groups; and to enquire into other factors such as changes in police practice which may have led to an increase in convictions'. These terms of reference obviously relate to the analyses and conclusions of the previous study which had therefore, despite the sampling limitations, served as an illuminating pilot study. Once again however the emphasis was on information which could be obtained from police officers. In its proposals for this survey the Survey had emphasised that 'it will be desirable ultimately in order to understand what the drunkenness statistics imply in terms of drinking habits, and of wider social trends, to extend enquiries to samples of the general public'. And in view of the Survey's work for the Royal Commission on the Police it seemed that more information was specifically needed about and from younger people.

The report of the survey *The Drunken Offender in Britain* noted wryly that, as before, no sooner was the study launched then the statistics once again changed trend and from 1963 to 1966 the number of drunken offences proved in the courts declined each year. However, for this study the sample design was implemented in full and the report showed that the data obtained was representative of the most nearly comparable national figures for drunkenness offences and for all parts of the country. The method used was to get chosen police officers to complete a form designed by the Survey in respect of each person charged during a period of 18 months. The form recorded when and where an incident took place, details of the officer who first intervened, a description of the incident behaviour, the charge made and other information about the offender. The survey was carried out in Scotland on the same lines. The survey report showed that about two-fifths of all offences of drunkenness in England Wales happened in the Metropolitan Police District, and the characteristics of these London offenders were compared with those in the rest of the country.

Changing public comment on the social aspects of alcohol consumption in the next few years gradually changed official views on the administrative feasibility of studies of wider groups of the population. Pressure was building up for a general review of the licensing laws and the evidence given by the National Consumer Council to the Monopolies Commission on what might be called restrictive practices in the sale of alcohol lent extra force to the public comment, as did a Monopolies Commission enquiry into the supply of beer. It was a period when restrictions on personal freedom were becoming unfashionable. This was the background to the appointment of a Home Office Departmental Committee on Liquor Licensing (Erroll Committee) and for the Survey study. The population sample approached was asked questions for the *Shopping Habits Survey* described earlier and also about drinking, public houses and restrictions on the sale of alcohol. The general questions about shopping hours came first and provided a convenient entrée for the more specialised topic. The survey report first described drinking habits among different social groups and where alcohol was consumed and then analysed respondents' views on current restrictions on the sale of alcohol. Overall only 14% thought it was too restricted and almost as many that it was not restricted enough; among the more highly educated 31% thought it was too restricted compared with 10% of the less educated. The report then turned to direct questions about licensing hours and noted that just under a quarter thought public houses should stay open all day. Again the better educated were more likely to favour relaxation. Respondents were asked about services and commodities provided in public houses and were substantially in favour of facilities like play gardens for children and background music. Ninety-seven per cent still thought that there should be a minimum age at which young people could consume alcohol in licensed premises: two-thirds thought it should be 18 years. There was a great deal of support for the concept of a place rather different from present licensed premises where 'the whole family could sit down together', not necessarily involving the use of alcohol.

The Erroll Committee report recommended many changes. While still seeing a need for statutory controls it advocated greater flexibility in hours at which drink could be sold and other changes which would make possible the introduction of premises catering for the whole family. A different committee considered the situation in Scotland where there had been a much greater concern with alcoholism. It was therefore not surprising that a full scale survey was launched in Scotland in 1972 which examined drinking habits in much greater detail than was needed for the study just described. This and subsequent surveys of drinking habits in England and Wales were described earlier in the context of health education. This may seem a rather different concern from the early Home Office worries about the fluctuating drunkenness conviction statistics but there are several points at which the different concerns come together and where studies designed to meet these joint interests are suggested by some of the findings described. For example, the 1967-8 study of Scottish Licensing Laws was designed to monitor the effects of changes in the laws after the 1973 Clayson Report. It was felt that apprehensions about the effect of relaxing the licensing laws could be tested by using the techniques developed in the drinking habits surveys. The study was initially designed to examine the effects of extending evening closing time to 11 pm but subsequently it was extended to cover the Sunday opening of public houses. By converting seven days' consumption of different quantities and types of alcoholic beverage by a sample of the whole Scottish population into standard units of equivalent alcohol content, and comparing these measurements for the population in the period just before the 11 pm extension and six months later, and just before the Sunday changes and 18 months later, some assessment could be made of the actual changes in consumption which followed the changes in the law. Such evidence could be related to descriptions of who drank, where and when and to opinions on the changes in the law after they had been put into effect. It would not have been too great a step forward to integrate this kind of information with that collected and analysed in the study of police actions.

Notes

[1] T S Lodge in R Hood (ed), *Crime, Criminology and Public Policy*, 1974.
[2] Dr H Mannheim and Leslie T Wilkins, *Prediction Methods in Relation to Borstal Training*, HMSO, 1955.

13 Operational surveys

IN PREVIOUS CHAPTERS surveys done at different times and for different sponsors have been brought together under broad subject headings to show their contribution to some major policy concerns of government. Among the studies discussed are some that were less concerned with changing policy than with providing information useful for attempts to implement and evaluate it – information about the efficacy of actions taken. This information was described as operational. There is no clear dividing line between these studies and others: a serious review of policy with the intention of reform must necessarily build on reliable descriptions of what is currently happening. During the first half of the period covered in this account the emphasis of much of the work was on helping officials to perform existing functions in a more informed way. In the war years this was of course the first priority, but later, as the work of the Survey became better known, wider sections of the administration wanted increasingly to use survey research to describe current situations and evaluate past decisions.

During the first ten years of its existence and especially in the war years surveys related to current operations were a major part of Survey work. Immediate problems were put to the Survey within the first few weeks of its existence, connected with the administration of the wartime rationing system and with the efforts made by the information services to brief the population on the problems and progress of the war effort, and to enlist participation in the national cooperative effort. Food rationing and supply problems were tackled during the first months. The Ministry of Food's audience for its regular 'Kitchen Front' radio programme was examined and its reactions to the programmes recorded; the work and eating habits of young workers were studied, and a series of short studies were made of national wheatmeal bread, egg and milk consumption and the distribution of oranges. The Board of Trade needed to know how different features of its clothes rationing scheme were working and in the September of this first year, 1941, posed a rather unusual problem: the supply of steel was pre-empted for war purposes and therefore not available as stiffenings for ladies foundation garments – estimates of demand were needed. Studies were also made of some of the Ministry of Information's efforts in film making.

In the following year similar studies were done on the use of manufactured foodstuffs, cooking habits, shopping problems and the use of canteens, and the Board of Trade had special problems with the allocation of coupons for occupational clothing, stocks of pottery, the problem of working women and credit buying. Also in 1942 the Ministry of Health asked for work on its new diphtheria immunisation campaign; the Ministry of Supply wanted to know about the public reaction to its salvage campaign; the Ministry of Employment needed help in connection with the registration and call-up of women, and the Ministry of Agriculture asked for a study of its 'Dig for Victory' campaign. Clearly there were officials in many branches of government who could see how the Survey and the methods it was developing could be of use to them in their day to day activities.

But even in 1942 not all the work was related to immediate problems. Some thinking had already begun on postwar concerns, notably on postwar housing. This was also the year in which the Beveridge Report was first presented publicly. The pattern of work during the remaining years of the war was set at this time – a mixture of immediate concerns about shortages and rationing, help with information campaigns on the wide variety of topics on which departments needed to communicate with the public, and surveys to help these officials thinking about the problems of postwar reconstruction. Most of the Survey's work on rationing and shortages finished with the ending of the war although rationing of some goods continued. One of the last clothes rationing surveys had to do with the way demobilised men and women were using the coupons issued to them. By September 1945 over 400,000 people had been demobilised and very large numbers of coupons were coming onto a market which was only slowly changing from wartime limitations. It was therefore necessary to find out the rate at which coupons were being spent, on what clothing and how many were spent not by demobilised people but by their relatives.

Information surveys

The Ministry of Information after the war became the Central Office of Information and the main agent for official information activities using a wide range of media. As described earlier, the Survey became a division of the COI and surveys related to public information activities therefore continued for some years after the war. They included the work on nursing recruitment, the anti-venereal diseases campaign described earlier and the economic information surveys done for the Treasury Information Unit, as well as studies designed to examine the effectiveness of some of the media used by the COI, such as films and exhibitions. A series of surveys was made between 1952 and 1954 of overseas visitors to the annual British Industry Fair, at the request of the Board of Trade. Visitors were sampled as they entered or left the fair and questions asked to identify their country and interests and the impact made on them by the fair. The reports showed that the majority of visitors came from non-Commonwealth countries: only 19% of firms represented were regular visitors and about a third represented manufacturing firms. But two-thirds had made a special and sometimes a long journey to visit the fair and therefore needed to know about the arrangements well in advance. The importance of an official invitation in encouraging visitors and the value of advance publicity were noted. In 1953 overseas buyers were asked about various factors such as price, delivery dates and class of market which in their opinion affected the competitiveness of British products, which countries were thought to be the main competitors and what reasons they had for buying or not buying British goods. Another exhibition with rather different objectives was intended as a contribution of Parliament to the Festival of Britain. The exhibition *Parliament Past and Present* was mounted in the Grand Committee Room near Westminster Hall in the autumn of 1951 and proved very popular with visitors from all over the country. The audience and its reactions to the contents and arrangement of the exhibition were studied in order to add to knowledge of the use of exhibitions for public information purposes. People leaving the exhibition were asked questions to find out what they had learned; the time they said they had spent in different sections was compared with observations made of a sample of visitors, and the length of the visit was analysed by a range of factors.

This group of surveys ceased after 1953 following the major economies in the information services decreed by the government. The only exceptions were surveys related to efforts to recruit to the armed services, some of which have been described in Chapter 9. The information surveys were quite important in the Survey's development during its first decade. They were requested because departments were undertaking new responsibilities: innovative administrative procedures were needed and many people had come into government from backgrounds different from those of pre-war civil servants. The newcomers were more familiar with methods and resources used outside the civil service like sample survey research for business, some academic research and BBC audience research. Their use of the Survey helped to open doors and make its contribution more widespread.

The Post Office surveys

Between 1951 and 1962 a series of studies was made for the General Post Office, which functioned then as a government department and was trying in the spirit of the times to modernise its services. One of the earliest studies developed out of a problem typical of the period – the need to reduce government consumption of paper. Telephone directories use a lot of paper and much labour especially since they are often updated and reissued. In 1951 the GPO asked the Survey to find out for how long a new London telephone directory could be withheld without causing inconvenience to subscribers or increasing the costs of Directory Enquiries to such an extent that it offset the saving in directory printing costs. Samples of subscribers throughout the area covered by the directory were taken. The purpose of the survey was broadly explained to them and they were asked to keep records for over two weeks of all outgoing telephone calls and to record for each the day on which it was made, the time it was made, the source of the telephone number, the exchange called and the recipient. This material made it possible to draw a very close picture of telephone habits with particular reference to the use of the telephone directory. It seemed that it was playing a relatively minor role as the source of telephone numbers and in the London postal area less than one call in eight appeared to be based on the actual use of the telephone directory. The data collected made it possible to construct an estimate of the ratio of numbers obtained through Directory Enquiries as a proportion of all telephone calls made.

The report of the study then used the following reasoning pattern. Even if new directories were not issued subscribers would still have their out-of-date issues. It was possible to estimate from other Survey work the extent to which normal movement of the population would be likely to result in changes of addresses, and hence an increase in the proportion of wrong addresses in the out-of-date directories held by the subscribers. To this had to be added the telephone numbers of new subscribers after the directory had ceased to be issued and whose numbers would not therefore be available to subscribers. Further, small proportions of entries in out-of-date directories would be misleading due to the deaths of subscribers or original mistakes in compilation. It was possible to calculate what those figures would be on the basis of factual data collected from different sources. From this information estimates were made of the extent to which not reprinting would impose extra demands on the Directory Enquiries service. The general answer reached was that at most 1.3% of all calls from subscribers would involve an extra wasted reference (in the sense that the numbers were wrong) to the London directory and consequently would lead to increased use of Directory Enquiries: in the Outer London area the figure was likely to be less than half of one per cent. Following the survey new issues of the London telephone directory were withheld and in the first year the total saving in directory costs was around £270,000. From the technical point of view it is interesting to note that in the eight months following the withholding of the first directory due, only 56 subscribers (out of 250,000) enquired why it had not been issued and only nine asked for copies to be sent to them.

Surveys examined public reaction to other changes the Post Office were considering to cut costs, such as address coding, two-tier delivery schemes and more restricted delivery services. The address coding study not only sought opinions, especially from business customers, but also devised some experiments to test public willingness and capacity to use address codes. The survey report *Postal Services and the Business User* (1960) found that 'most firms would be willing to cooperate' but examined also the attitudes opposed to the introduction of address coding. The parallel report *Postal Services and the General Public* (1960) estimated the proportion of inland mail originated by private individuals and says 'It is estimated that 60% of this fraction will bear an address code on the envelope once the scheme has become reasonably established provided the public are kept up to the mark by a persistent publicity campaign, not so much to persuade people as to remind them ... the principal group who will have difficulty with the scheme are the elderly'. A more limited enquiry in 1962 looked at customers' reasons for using post office counters when stamp machines were available. Shortly after this survey the Post Office ceased to be a government department and decided no longer to use the services of the COI. It asked the Survey to continue working with it, but it was decided that if other divisions of the COI were not to be involved neither should the Survey be, and the series of studies was brought to an end.

Road safety surveys

Between 1945 and 1959 a series of surveys related to road safety were made for the Ministry of Transport. The early ones were interview studies designed to find out something about the impact of road safety campaigns run by the ministry, but even the first of these surveys also incorporated observation of actual road behaviour at different dates as a harder test of effect. In 1948 some of the earlier work was repeated in order to measure the durability of the earlier results but more searching questions were asked to test the impact of particular messages or devices used. It was found, for example, that by far the most effective attention-securing device was the 'Black Widow' – a drawing of a woman in mourning for a road accident victim. It was, however, withdrawn as an improper device for a public information campaign. This survey extended the range of observations of road behaviour and this time related behaviour to response to the advertising campaign. 'The seriousness with which people regard the problem of[road accidents appears to bear little relation to their actual behaviour on the roads ... while few people rate the chances of their being involved in an accident very high, the enquiry among careful and careless pedestrians shows that attitudes in this matter bear no relation to good and bad behaviour on the road.'

Such results eventually led to the conclusion of road research experts that publicity alone could probably not achieve very much more and that actual road arrangements must be such as to reduce the possibility of unsafe behaviour. A further impetus was given to work on this topic by the report of the 1950 Select Committee on Estimates which examined the government information services and recommended 'a social survey should be undertaken immediately to find out how far road users have been affected by road safety publicity ... if there has been little or no effect further money should not be spent on publicity but the Ministry of Transport should concentrate their activity on administrative action'. Some months later the ministry asked for such a study to be made. The report, *Effects of a Local Road Safety Campaign on Behaviour of Road Users* (1951) concluded from systematic observations and interviews: 'There was no indication that behaviour had improved after the campaign ... the interviews support the observations indicating that the campaign in this city had no measurable effects'. But the report also expresses some doubt about 'the particular nature of this local campaign' and suggests that attention should be given to a 'model' campaign 'designed to utilize to the best advantage all the resources which could be mustered'. Further work was done along the lines suggested in Slough, where knowledge and behaviour were measured over a two-year period during which many things were done to improve safety. The report *The Slough Experiment on Road Safety* notes the effects of their durability (1955–9).

Other operational surveys

The studies described so far in this chapter had a certain continuity. Because a series of surveys was done it was possible to develop appropriate methodology as knowledge and experience of the subject matter developed. There were, however, other operational surveys where the subject matter was very heterogeneous. They have occurred throughout the Survey's history and were prompted by increasing awareness of the record of the Survey throughout the government and by the willingness of Survey staff to put their accumulating experience to work wherever there was a useful government purpose to serve.

In 1946 an interdepartmental committee was investigating the postwar demand for holidays and in particular the relationship between demand and available accommodation. It needed information about holiday habits and preferences. Given the changes produced by the war it was doubtful if reliable information about habits could be produced, but it was possible to assess existing sentiments, probable plans for the year ahead and preferences for different times of the year and types of facility. It is indicative of the changes since those years that only a very small minority referred to holidays abroad. The report *The Demand for Holidays in 1946 and 1947* noted that '50% more people wanted holidays in 1947 than had them in 1946; ... holiday makers might be better pleased if the summer season could be extended from the beginning of June until the middle of September'. The customer committee among its recommendations proposed a British Tourist and Holidays Board which took responsibility for further research. It was not until 14 years later that more work was requested on this topic. This later report, *Motives in the Timing of Holidays* (1960), done for a Committee on the Extension of the Holiday Season, focused on a narrower problem. In effect, it was a somewhat delayed confirmation of the earlier study.

In 1946 the Home Office was charged with the distribution of a medal to be awarded for service within the United Kingdom. The Survey was asked to make an estimate of the likely number of applications. The report of the survey *The Defence Medal* (1946) noted that the survey results heavily overestimated the number of applications and made some sharply critical comments on the methods used. This was a trial run for a more detailed study, *Prediction of the Demand for Campaign Stars and Medals,* in 1947 which was much more successful. The report to the Treasury committee on the grant of honours and medals described the methods. A more detailed interview was made, the responses were combined in an 'attitude score' which measured the degree of interest in receiving the medal and, perhaps most important, a practical test was made of willingness to take some action in order to receive medals. A section of the sample (which was drawn from the appropriate section of the Maintenance Register) was asked to send a postcard indicating interest in receiving details of awards and application procedures. The attitude scores could be related to this evidence of interest and a cut-off point selected which indicated the attitude level at which action might be expected. Since attitude scores were available for the whole sample some estimate could be made of likely demand overall for medals and for differing levels of demand for different medals and from different services. The predicted proportion of all medals for which service personnel were eligible and would apply was between 30% and 40%. According to *Hansard* (Vol 466, June 1949) applications were received from 34%. The proportions of eligible applications from different services and for particular campaign medals were also fairly close. These results became widely known and when interest in improving criminal justice statistics and procedures strengthened in the next few years some of those who knew of American prediction studies in this field began to ask if a British effort at applying prediction methods could be attempted. The Survey research officer responsible for the campaign medals study was invited to participate and the first prediction study sponsored by the Home Office, the *Borstal Survey*, was in fact carried out as a Survey project.

In 1950, following a general election which made little mention of civil defence, the Home Office and the Scottish Office asked for a study 'to measure the awareness of the public to recent Civil Defence publicity' and to discover why the response to recruiting appeals had been so poor. Two surveys were organised, one before the campaign and the second a year later to measure its effects. The first survey, *Recruitment to Civil Defence* (1950) examined attitudes towards the possibility of war and defence, the atom bomb ('the best way of preserving peace') willingness to take part in civil defence and previous service. The questions were chosen and analysed to indicate likelihood of participating. The responses were examined by factor analysis to identify groups of responses: thus informants could be divided into groups of which the first had some likelihood of joining, the second little likelihood of joining and the third no likelihood of joining. At this stage of course such a subdivision of the population was somewhat hypothetical, resting entirely on their responses to questions. It was necessary to provide some crucial test of this subdivision into groups.

At the same time as the attitude surveys were being made a survey was also being taken of those members of the public who had responded to the first appeal and had already become members of the civil defence service. It was possible to relate the answers given to the attitude questions by those already in the civil defence service with the answers obtained from the general population sample. By appropriate analysis it was possible to show that in almost all the questions used in the enquiry the responses of those who had been categorised as having 'some likelihood' of joining fell between those who had actually joined and those categorised as having little or no likelihood of joining. It was also shown to what extent the four groups were already members of other voluntary organisations and held responsibility in them at any level. This material indicated that the grouping of the population was consistent with other data collected in the course of the enquiry and it was possible to proceed to the next stage. It was asked in what ways the group of the population shown to have some likelihood of joining differed from the rest of the population, and what its social and psychological characteristics were. The results indicated which sections of the population would be most likely to respond to appeals to join and where they could be most easily found.

Following the campaign a sample of those interviewed in the first survey were interviewed again. The report *Recruitment to the Civil Defence Service II* noted that 'the eligible sample interviewed in 1951 were no better informed [about civil defence] than those interviewed in 1950 ... few of the recruits were well informed about the allied services ... it seemed therefore that accurate and comprehensive information about eligibility and the various branches of Civil Defence was not an essential pre-requisite of joining ... There had been little change in general attitude to Civil Defence between the surveys ... 84% thought it a good idea to have Civil Defence Forces in peacetime but only 4% said they intended to join and three-quarters said they could not spare sufficient time to join ... Nearly half thought Atom bombs likely to be used in a future war but two-thirds thought some protection existed or would be developed ... from 1950 to 1951 the population as a whole had been forced to believe that Civil Defence was necessary ... but ... most people in 1951 seemed to find it necessary to have a reason for not joining'. As part of this study people were asked by letter if they would like a local recruiting officer to call. One per cent asked for such a call and one half of these did join. The conclusion was drawn that 'unless the situation became markedly different not more than a further 1% of the eligible population would join and these only if the appeal was made to them directly and strongly'.

The great contribution made by British farmers during the war years had involved closer participation by officials than before the war, and postwar economic difficulties emphasised the continuing public interest in stimulating productivity and the use of new techniques. In Britain the National Agricultural Advisory Service had been involved in innovation research and had begun to consider the possible contribution of evaluation studies to its work. In 1957 the Ministry of Agriculture, Fisheries and Food asked for a study which 'might give some guidance on the extent and the manner in which technical developments in agriculture are being disseminated, and in particular, how far these developments are being achieved through the Ministry's advisory services'. They had done much work on grassland improvement and therefore proposed that 'the enquiry should be centred on grassland ... to throw light on farmers' attitudes to technical change and the ways in which we can use our limited advisory staffs to the best advantage'.

The survey was organised rather differently from most Survey work. Clusters of farmers were sampled in many different parts of the country and were interviewed on their farming practices and their knowledge of various sources of information as well as their contact with the official advisory service. They were then asked which of the farmers in their own immediate district they would regard as technically advanced. The farmers indicated in this way were also interviewed when possible to compare their characteristics in terms of experience, training and education with those of other farmers in the same district. On this data it was possible to isolate the outstanding characteristics of farmers who would be recognised as technically advanced by other farmers. It was thought that such leading farmers would be likely to have influence on the activities and practices of surrounding farmers. Information which would make it possible for the advisory service to identify men capable of giving such potential technical leadership clearly would be of practical utility and the data was analysed with this in mind. The report *A Survey among Grassland Farmers* (1957) described the penetration of a selection of new methods and the sources of information available to farmers, including seeking advice from other farmers. 'Farmers were reasonably aware of what other farmers were doing in their neighbourhood ... there is evidence that such knowledge does influence farmers to take up new practices and the suggestion is made that an effective and economical way of influencing farmers would be through 'leader' farmers.'

The DHSS asked the Survey in 1974, as part of a general review of local office organisation, to speak to the customers of one local social security office about their views on the service and to describe their experience when obtaining benefits. The study was designed to provide

> indepth qualitative information about the range of views and opinions held by different groups of claimants. It was carried out in one local office and so provided an opportunity for the staff of that office to become involved in the research ... as the main aim was to explore rather than quantify claimants' views it was important that the interviews should be sufficiently flexible to give individuals the opportunity to raise topics which were of particular concern to them. It was therefore decided that a relatively unstructured and non-directive form of interview should be used [a form which allows the respondent a certain freedom in the issues which are discussed]. The questionnaire consisted almost entirely of open questions and throughout the interview the respondents were encouraged to talk as much as they wished.

Different groups of claimants were selected from the main range of the office's work. The office notified all the people selected for interview that the survey was to be done and that participation was voluntary. 3% said they did not wish to be interviewed.

The report *Social Security Claimants* (1979) was published some years after the survey was done. 'On the whole customers were more impressed by the pleasant, helpful and understanding approach of the staff than by any other feature and most critical of the amount of time they had to wait and the general atmosphere that prevailed ... generally speaking there was a mixed reaction to home visits ... pensioners were in favour but non-pensioners mentioned more unfavourable aspects ... customers preferred face to face contact ... found it difficult to explain in writing or over the phone and thought that staff could not or would not sort things out through a telephone contact. They suggested many ways in which contacting the office could be improved ... most expressed some degree of sympathy or concern for the unpleasant or difficult situations staff had to cope with.' Attitudes towards claiming social security benefits were explored. 'Around one in seven people thought they might be entitled to benefits, pensions or payments other than those they were receiving. The main reasons for not applying were that they were too unsure about entitlement, that previous claims had been refused or because of difficulties involved in making a claim ... It is clear from the interviews that the local service and the system are inseparably linked in customers' minds. The majority said they were generally satisfied with the service they had received, a quarter said they were very satisfied and approximately one in six were dissatisfied. A much larger proportion of supplementary allowance than other claimants said they were generally dissatisfied'. The interviews with dissatisfied people were carefully studied in order to extract the main causes of discontent, either perceived or real.

Voting rights practically depend upon inclusion in the Electoral Register, which is updated each year: it is therefore of great importance to the democratic process in Britain. Changes in population led to some doubts about the utility of the register and in 1981 the home departments and OPCS joined in sponsoring an examination of the coverage and quality of the register together with a study of the registration process. To measure the accuracy of the register it was necessary to have a sample of individuals which was independent of it. This became available at the time of the 1981 Census when a Post Enumeration Survey was carried out to test the coverage and quality of the Census. The interviewing that was required for the Electoral Register check was incorporated within the Census quality check interview during which the Census form filler was interviewed about the household composition. Any members of the household who had been erroneously excluded from the Census were interviewed as part of the quality check and also added to the Electoral Register check sample. The technique then was simply to ascertain how many people so identified and eligible were not included in the register. The first report of the study *Electoral Registration in 1981* noted:

> It is estimated that overall 6.5% of eligible people in Great Britain were not included in the 1981 register of electors ... In 1966 between 3.4% and 4% were not registered ... some of the increase in non-registration is due to the lowering of the minimum voting age ... however there is an increase of non-registration rate of the older groups ... Wales had the highest non-registration rate (9.2%), England 6.5% and Scotland 5.3% ... Inner London 14.4% ... between 11% and 17% of eligible people in their late teens and twenties are not registered ... of people who move during the six months either side of the qualifying date 27% are not registered ... New Commonwealth citizens have a particularly high non-registration rate of 21%.

Twenty-three per cent of respondents asked about the non-registration of eligible people 'were unsure that persons concerned were eligible and about 40% did not remember receiving the relevant form'. These results imply that for some purposes the Electoral Register is deficient as a sampling frame. Since it was early Survey work that established its use for this purpose it seems very appropriate that with changing circumstances it was a Survey report that described its limitations.

The second report *The Electoral Registration Process in the United Kingdom* was based on a survey of the registration officers and examined the methods they used in carrying out their duties, in particular what they do when the appropriate registration document is not returned. The return varied from 95% in 70% of non-metropolitan districts to only 20% in the London boroughs. In most areas if there is no response at this stage the names are carried forward from the previous register. 'In a separate study carried out in five wards in England it is estimated that 40% of the names carried forward on this basis would be ineligible and that without it 37% of eligible adults at the addresses from which there had been no response would be omitted.' The right to make claims for inclusion is rarely exercised. The resources available to registration officers were examined and they were asked which were the groups of electors who caused problems for them and what were their views on ways of improving the register. The results of these surveys were discussed in the 1982-3 session of the Home Office Committee of the House of Commons and recommendations made for changes in the registration documents, improved coverage and the work and procedures followed by registration officers.

A very different survey was requested in 1954 by the Ministry of Agriculture, Fisheries and Food. Regular agricultural censuses provided the ministry's basic statistics but they were related to farms. There were also some smallholdings (under one acre) where information was available through the feeding stuffs rationing procedure, but it was known that quantities of pigs and poultry were kept by people not covered by such registered data and it was thought that they contributed substantially to national stocks. Other information available to the Survey suggested a sampling scheme whereby addresses in strata with different probabilities of poultry keeping could be sampled differentially and approached through the post. The incidence of poultry and pig keeping was likely to be low, so a substantial sample would be needed – 10,000 addresses. Although pilot studies showed that there was a fair chance of a satisfactory return there was some doubt about non-response bias, so for half of the sample interviewers followed up the non-responders. This exercise worked quite well and some information was obtained from nearly all the addresses. The information required was very simple – just whether or not poultry was kept and how many were chicks, and how many pigs were kept if any, and how many were breeding. The information was needed for three years, with an indication of whether or not the smallholder got feeding stuffs through the rationing system. The report *Domestic Pig and Poultry Keeping* notes that about 11 million birds were found in this way, all outside the normal statistics. The survey was repeated in 1956 and was done completely through the post. In 1958 the ministry asked for another repeat. A similar sampling scheme was used but this time with a total sample of 18,765 addresses, distributed in four separate waves over a year. The response rate to a questionnaire, which this time included a question on eggs sold and the use of battery cages, was 89.8%; this time rather more poultry was found.

In 1974 a Royal Commission on Civil Liability and Compensation for Personal Injury was set up to consider the possibilities for a compensation scheme which would rely on a central fund rather than the existing legal procedures. The commission needed to produce some notional picture of the sums of money involved, which could be approached by getting estimates of the number of people injured in a year who might be eligible for this different method of compensation. The Survey was asked to help. The purpose of the survey was to estimate the number of people per year injured seriously enough to receive treatment from a doctor or hospital and to be incapacitated for work and/or other normal activities for at least four days; to estimate the cost of these injuries and the extent to which it was offset by the various types of compensation then available, and to examine the conditions under which people who have been injured consider claiming damages in court and how far and how successfully such claims are pursued. The Survey required a two-fold interviewing process. An initial interview was carried out on a sample of 40,000 households to identify individuals in the eligible groups to allow incidence rates to be calculated. More detailed interviews were then done with people injured in 1973 or suffering from illness during 1973 which they attributed to their work, and with people who had taken steps towards recovering damages for injuries received during the previous seven years. There were many problems in meeting these needs and an account of the survey published in the second volume of the royal commission's report (1978) described its operation and the limitations on the results.

Statistical self appraisal

Criticism by statisticians of their own methods has long been part of the statistical tradition in Britain. Survey research has been among the means used to check the validity of the output of statistical enterprises or to test a proposed method. This contribution could only grow as familiarity with Social Survey work became more widespread, so it wasn't until 1966 that the Survey was first asked by the GRO to carry out a post-enumeration check on a population census. The 1966 Census was the first sample census and the first to be done in mid-decade, and the survey *A Quality Check on the 1966 Ten Per Cent Sample Census* was the first examination of a Census carried out by an organisation outside the Census Office. Five years later the Survey and GRO were brought together in the Office of Population Censuses and Surveys, and no doubt the work done on the 1966 Census contributed to that development. The report describes the Survey's approach to the problem of carrying out the required check: 'we considered that the main aim of a quality check should be to take the classifications which appear in the published Census tables and measure the total error associated with them. Such a measurement would involve comparing the final version in the Census table with what we believed to be the correct version. But we wished to go further. We considered it equally important to find out how, why and at what stage any census error arose; for in this lies the hope of improving future censuses'. The quality check was to be done on a sample of the sample Census. One hundred Census districts were taken as first-stage units selected with probability proportionate to the number of enumerator workloads in a Census district, and addresses were sampled from the selected enumerator workload. Photocopies of the enumerator record books were given to Survey interviewers with the selected addresses marked, with photocopies of the relevant completed Census forms. Interview schedules were not the same as original Census questions; the test questions were different and more detailed, but from them the Census classifications could be derived. It was the comparison of these classifications with the original Census schedule classifications that provided the basis for the check on the quality of the Census.

The report on the survey deals in detail with all the main classifications and estimates 'misclassification rates' for them together with a suggested 'correcting factor'. It records the view that 'too much has come to be expected from the census which is designed to produce population statistics and simple information for local areas'. The report drew attention to difficulties arising out of the failure to pretest some questions and urged the importance of pretesting the Census questions. Post-enumeration surveys have been done on all subsequent censuses and the Survey has been involved in the pretesting of questions.

Ethnic origin

One topic on which a great deal of work was done by the Survey was ethnic origin. A 1978 White Paper announced its belief in the 'need for authoritative and reliable information about the main ethnic minorities ... in order that the Government and Local Authorities could carry out their responsibilities under the Race Relations Act and develop effective social policies'. The White Paper noted that the registrars general were considering possible forms of a direct Census question on ethnic origin: this work was started as a special study and from 1972 was done as part of the Census pre-testing studies. It was clear that a question about country of birth did not give clear-cut answers and was likely to give progressively less useful information as bigger proportions of immigrants' children were born in the UK. The series of tests with different formulations tried out many variants for feasibility and acceptability. Some of the early results were published in the OPCS periodical *Population Trends 13* in 1978 and a final field test in a London borough was arranged for April 1979. An organised campaign in the borough urged people to refuse to answer questions on ethnic origin arguing that the results would be used to change the nationality laws, and cooperation on the test was severely affected. In March 1980, following the election of Margaret Thatcher's conservative government, it was announced that the 1981 Census would not contain questions on ethnic origin, parents' country of birth or nationality. In the second report of the House of Commons Home Affairs Committee for the session 1982–3 a recommendation was made that 'questions on ethnic or racial origin should be asked in future censuses subject to adequate reassurances on confidentiality and the unequivocally stated objective being to improve existing programmes against racial discrimination. This objective should be set out on the question form itself'.

However, since 1971 some information about the size of the coloured population in the UK and their circumstances has been collected in the General Household Survey and published annually without any agitation. The GHS information relates to colour, not race, and records the observations of interviewers. Similarly, the International Passenger Survey has provided annual data since 1962 on population movements into and out of the UK, analysed by country of last or next residence. These and other continuing surveys have over many years been the major contribution of Survey research to government migration statistics.

General Household Survey

The *General Household Survey* has been referred to many times in the preceding pages. This is because it is designed as a multipurpose survey and contributes to the statistical needs of many sections of government. The primary purpose of the survey is to serve as a vehicle for collecting information, at the request of many departments, in the course of the annual sample survey designed to represent the whole population over a whole year. The first chapter of the first introductory report in 1971 describes in some detail how the survey developed. It emphasises

> the obvious utility of multi-purpose surveys in many countries; the time gaps between decennial population censuses; the growing need for more information than was available from administrative statistics on many aspects of public policies and services in this country; and a readily available means of examining relationships between some of the main areas of social statistics.
>
> The central objective then was to use household sample survey methods to make available a substantially improved flow of social statistics. A continuing survey, it was clear, would have to be rooted in the needs of public services and would also have to take into account the possibilities and practicabilities of survey research in the United Kingdom. It would have to draw on available skills and experience and its scope and scale would have to be related to the resources available at the time ... In the event, during the first year, the GHS provided information on some aspects of housing, employment, education, health and social services, transport, population and social security.

Since the survey was to be a service to departments it was thought to be important to involve them as closely as possible in the design of the work. Emphasis was put on getting results of the first year's work back to the customer departments as soon as possible so that through joint discussion agreement could be reached on amendments, changes to definition and the balance of the content of the interview. The intention was to conduct the survey as a kind of cooperative government research activity in which the information collected was related as closely as possible to needs of departments, as they saw them. A study of households rather than individuals seemed most relevant and a combination of questions, some to be repeated year by year, some to appear periodically and some only infrequently. A large scale pilot survey was done in February 1970 and the full survey was launched in October with an annual sample of around 15,000 households, in which all adults were interviewed. This was about one-sixth the size proposed in early discussions but the interviews included questions in five subject areas as well as details of income. The pattern of the survey has been maintained since its inception, although there has been a substantial change in its content over the years in response to changes in departmental interest, as was originally intended. The total span of subject matter since 1971 is therefore very large, and Appendix D gives a summary of main topics included in the period 1971–81.

The sample design followed the usual principles established over many years by the Survey. The sample in Scotland was twice the size required for representation in order to provide adequate numbers for Scottish analyses; the weighted national figures, of course, correct for this. The response was described in detail in the first report, including two innovations: three response rates were given according to the degree of cooperation obtained, and sampling errors related to the multi-stage stratified design were given for many variables rather than the usual procedure which assumes a simple random sample. The central response rate was 'the proportion of the eligible sample from whom all or nearly all the information required was obtained'. Between 1971 and 1982 this varied between 81% and 84%.

Following the Rayner review of the statistical services the CSO in 1981 conducted a review of how the GHS was used by departments. It confirmed what was already known from continuing experience, that many departments used the survey and in many fields of public interest it provided the only detailed information available. Nevertheless, the sample was reduced by 15%, although other features of the survey's design and operation were not altered.

The Labour Force Survey

The *Labour Force Survey*, the fifth continuous survey for which the Survey is responsible is very new, but the combination of circumstances from which it originated is familiar. Pressed on the possibility of improving its employment statistics by the Estimates Committee (session 1966–7), the Ministry of Labour preferred to continue its existing procedures: it had good sources which it could control and great experience in handling them, and at a time of financial pressure it was unlikely that the staff required for new systems would be readily forthcoming. So despite pressures from inside and outside government the procedures used in other countries were not adopted and it was expected that some of the gaps in knowledge could be filled by the General Household Survey from 1971 onwards. But events were taking place which eventually forced a change. By 1973, by which time the United Kingdom had joined the Community, the EEC decreed that a labour force survey based on a sample of households should be done every two years in all member countries, an obligation sweetened to some extent by repayment of some of the costs involved. Changes in national insurance procedures deprived the ministry of some of its most important data about employment and from 1979 it became clear that changes in registration for employment would render this source of information much less useful. The growing problem of unemployment was forcing attention on the need for more comprehensive information about the whole labour force, and the biennial EEC surveys demonstrated what could come out of a household survey.

In June 1983 the Secretary of State for Employment, Norman Tebbit, announced in the House of Commons his intention to 'improve the statistics of the labour force so as to provide a more comprehensive, accurate and up to date picture. I am arranging for the Labour Force Survey hitherto conducted every few years to be replaced by a more frequent survey'. The new survey was to 'provide annual data and indications of trends in the course of the year for broad groups within the labour force . . . an improved indication of trends in self employment, a check on trends in the number of employees – between triennial censuses of employment – a more up to date guide to trends in the overall labour force and activity rates and more frequent survey type information on the unemployed'.[1] The Social Survey was asked to design and carry out the new survey. A parallel statement in the *Employment Gazette* in July 1983 recorded the installation of a new Employment Market Research Unit 'to coordinate and analyse all research about the labour market for employment policy purposes'. This was to be directed by a senior economic adviser and would have six economists and other social scientists.

The new survey was a major challenge to Survey staff. It is based on panels of households. The selected households are to be interviewed five times over a period of about one year. This should reveal changes in people's circumstances. Five thousand households will be sampled each month. In any month one-fifth of the sample will be contacted for the first time, one-fifth for the second time, one-fifth for the third time and so on. The first interview would be a normal face to face interview at which respondents after the employment related interview are asked if they agree to further interviews, and if agreeable, whether these further interviews can be done by telephone. If there is no available telephone number repeat interviews would be done by personal visits. The use of telephones for up to four-fifths of interviews would result in major economies in fieldwork. During three months of the year an enlarged sample would be taken to meet EEC requirements for its international Labour Force Survey.

Analyses of results would be expected each quarter within six weeks of the completion of fieldwork. To meet this timescale new procedures have been devised which eliminate much paper handling at headquarters. The Postcode Address File, which is the Post Office list of addresses, is used as a sampling frame and address lists for interviewers are generated from the file by computer. Interviewers work to tightly controlled time schedules and code responses according to detailed coding instructions. The coded interview schedules are passed very quickly directly to the computer for analysis. There is clearly heavy reliance on the computer for achieving the timing objectives but the basic data will still come from the direct contact of a trained interviewer. The use of the telephone for the follow-up interviews was a new departure for the Survey but was already being used for some market research and public opinion polling. In accordance with its history the Social Survey has responded in an innovative way to an opportunity.

Note

[1] *Hansard*, 29 June 1983.

14 Institutions and scrutiny

WHEN EXISTING PROCEDURES for the conduct of public business or the discharge of public responsibilities are criticised or become less acceptable, the legal or customary framework within which they work comes under scrutiny. Generally in Britain, changes in such procedures follow public discussion, sometimes preceded by public enquiry, sometimes following private examination of past experience. The general purpose of public enquiry through departmental committee or appointed committees or commissions is to ensure that where the performance of some public function is in question evidence is invited from all quarters and no relevant experience is excluded. Over the years methods of enquiry have become more systematic – it is now expected that statistical evidence will be more organised and more likely to be based on available stocks of data – and survey research has become increasingly used to make available evidence of the behaviour, circumstances and attitudes of all the affected sections of the population. This chapter looks at ways in which the Survey has contributed to enquiries concerned with assessing the structure or functioning of existing procedures in the public domain, or the relations between officials and public.

Local government

In the years between 1965 and 1975 local government came under review. The Committee on the Management of Local Government, chaired by Sir John Maude, was concerned with management in local government and with its personnel. For this committee the Survey organised two studies in 1965, one of councillors and the other of local government electors. *The Local Government Elector* examined 'the public's knowledge of and contact with their local councils and councillors, and some of their attitudes towards the local government system as at present constituted ... we have tried to get some measure of the pool of potential councillors and to discover why these people are not at present participating more fully in local affairs'. The report noted the degree of ignorance about local services: '20% of our informants were unable to name a single service provided by their councils ... people living in country boroughs were better informed than the rest of the electorate ... older people appear less informed than younger people about almost every aspect of council activity touched in the survey'. But 26% had had some contact with the local town hall or council offices in the last year; they were more likely to be younger, educated people in higher socio-economic groups. Six per cent claimed to have contacted a councillor in the last year. The limited contact did not prevent over three-quarters believing their councils 'run things very well or fairly well'. About 20% expressed positive attitudes towards voting in local elections but about half were negative or tending that way, and about half were either uninterested in local affairs or did not believe that they could influence their council. Nevertheless, 65% said they had voted compared with an actual turnout for 1964 of 42%. The report describes the 'community conscious elector'.

The *Local Government Councillor* is 'an account of some of the people in local government, who they are, how they spend their time and how they feel about some aspects of council work'. The survey was based on a postal sample and two interview samples which all interlocked. The postal sample was addressed to one in ten councillors in 200 local authority areas and secured responses from 88%. The interview samples with councillors and ex-councillors were much smaller, but 92% of councillors contacted were interviewed. The report showed how councillors compared demographically with the general population. They were much older, and only a small proportion were women. 'The proportion who were employers and managers of small businesses or farmers was four times that of these groups in the general population ... they were somewhat better educated ... many councillors had only short experience of council work and many with over three years experience were over 55 years ... 38% of all councillors had been returned unopposed ... in rural districts 69% were returned unopposed ... nearly half said they did not know much about the work of a councillor when they first stood.' The report described how councillors spend their time and on how many committees, and showed how the meeting times of committees related to the kind of councillor who attended. Councillors' satisfactions and frustrations with the work were described: 'Councillors' main satisfactions arise out of particular council activities amongst which housing and old people's welfare were prominent ... frustrations arise mainly out of the way the machinery of local government works ... there are discrepancies between what councillors feel about the work of the council and their own part in it'. The report described the views of councillors on the part played by party politics in the work of councils and what they felt about their relationships with the public. Using data from both surveys the report compared the views of electors and councillors on priorities for 'the next year or so'. There were big differences between the opinions of councillors and the more interested sections of the public on what kinds of council work had been of most help to people or on what problems most needed council attention.

These were the views of the generation of councillors before the 1972–4 reorganisation of local government. Two years later a royal commission was set up 'to consider the structure of local government in relation to its existing functions and to make recommendations ... for functions ... having regard to size and character of areas in which these can be most effectively organised ... and the need to sustain a viable system of local democracy'. It felt that for this

Table 32 'Looking back on the time you have so far spent as a councillor what one thing did you find most frustrating or unsatisfactory?' – by council type. Committee on the Management of Local Government (1965)

	All councils	Counties	County boroughs	Metropolitan boroughs	Municipal boroughs & urban districts	Rural districts
	%	%	%	%	%	%
Administrative efficiency:	(48)	(51)	(45)	(45)	(55)	(46)
Relations with central Govt/County Council	18	9	10	13	25	20
Delays/slowness/inability to get things done	16	18	21	13	18	15
Difficulty of obtaining finance	9	17	11	15	8	7
Relations with officials	3	5	3	4	—	3
Committee system	2	2	—	—	4	1
Relations with other councillors:	(16)	(22)	(23)	(20)	(17)	(14)
Ignorance/apathy/hostility of council members	8	13	8	7	4	9
Party politics/group opposition	8	9	15	13	13	5
Particular council activities:	(10)	(2)	(14)	(17)	(6)	(11)
Housing	8	1	13	17	4	8
Traffic/roads	2	1	1	—	2	3
Attitude of public	4	1	3	—	4	5
Other answers	10	12	11	9	7	10
No comment/not answered	12	12	4	9	11	14
Total	100	100	100	100	100	100
(Numbers)	(1,235)	(152)	(134)	(46)	(483)	(420)

purpose it needed a better picture of the nature of electors' attachment to their communities and the accessibility of representatives. The *Community Attitudes Survey* was based on a sample of electors. It described the degree of attachment felt to a 'home' community area. Generally this was smaller than a local authority area and in urban areas threequarters of the sample defined their home area as something smaller than a ward. Those living closer to the centre of their local authority area were more likely than others to think of their home area as comprising the whole of that local authority area. Forty-one per cent said they would be very sorry and a further 24% quite sorry to leave the home area; 62% had lived in the home area for more than 10 years, just over half had adult relatives and/or in-laws living within 10 minutes walk of their home and about four in 10 (or 66% of all employed) were employed within their own local authority area. Interest in 'what goes on in the home area' was positively related to the size of the home area. Where this was small – part of a ward – only 47% said they were very or quite interested; where it was large, bigger than a town or city, 80% said they were very or quite interested. The views of electors on the consequences of council areas becoming larger or smaller were described and 40% thought it would make no difference. 'Electors' opinions on the optimum size of their local authority show a marked preference for the status quo.' The nearer electors' homes were to the town hall the more likely they were to think that it should be fairly near, but a majority did not care where it was. The report described electors' contacts with officials and representatives and how satisfactory electors found the contact, and views on local services are noted.

Devolution

In 1970 a Royal Commission on the Constitution, chaired by Geoffrey Crowther, was set up to consider the wider question of devolution. The commission was interested in attitudes on participation (whether people feel shut out of government and play no part in it); nationalism (were sentiments stronger in Wales or Scotland and how many in those countries would want independence even if they would be economically worse off); and devolution (if there was a demand for it, what forms did it take). The brief for the survey in fact constituted a long-term research programme, but this was not possible given the commission's timetable. The imminence of a general election meant that the survey had to be designed very quickly and avoid questions to which responses might be heavily influenced by electioneering activities. The election came sooner than expected: the fieldwork had to be postponed and was not completed until six months later, by which time the commission needed some results. These facts affected the design of the survey and the report, and only part of the brief could be dealt with. The sample had extra numbers in all the main regions so that response could be analysed by region, particularly in Scotland and Wales: 6,400 people in all were interviewed.

The report, *Devolution and Other Aspects of Government*, was rather cautiously worded and drew attention to how opinion on public issues may change over time. 'The report is not a prediction of how people might feel at some future time regardless of changes in institutions and circumstances which might have intervened meanwhile.' It was a description of current attitudes. It noted 'some general feeling of dissatisfaction with the way Britain is run at present but general attitudes towards some of the public services are in the main positive . . . only 14% feel that a great deal of improvement is needed in the way things are run'. There was no evidence that 'dissatisfaction with things as they are at present is associated with interest and involvement in political and community affairs. Only about one-quarter show any marked degree of active interest in affairs of this kind. And they are not significantly more dissatisfied than the remainder of the population'.

A scale of 'confidence in political capability' based on questions about the job of a local councillor was used to assess the extent to which people themselves felt capable of dealing with the issues with which local government deals. 'Just less than a quarter have any measure of confidence.' This suggested that most people felt that those in government were rather different from the 'ordinary man'. Further support for this idea came from a scale based on questions which indicated a common dimension, described as a feeling of 'powerlessness in the face of government'. Questions included 'should the council pay more attention to the views of people?', 'how willing are MPs to listen to people's views?', 'does local or central government tell people enough about what they are doing'. About a quarter did feel very powerless, and expressed an extreme position on five out of six separate questions. Over half had some feeling of powerlessness. 'Among the questions on this scale those which indicated a felt lack of communication between government and governed received the most emphatic responses.' Within each region it was widely felt that things would improve 'if government took more trouble to understand the region's special needs . . . if MPs had stronger regional ties and had more influence over what the government does in the region.' Respondents were asked what they had done about any past grievances against a number of organisations. Those most dissatisfied 'with the ways things are run' were, as expected, most likely to have grievances, but 'they were no more likely than the satisfied to have actually complained'. Similarly, those who felt 'powerless in the face of government' were 'more likely to have grievances but were less likely to have actually complained than those who did not feel powerless'.

'The concept of a "region" appeared comprehensible and acceptable to the majority. Regional identification is fairly strong throughout the country. Though particularly strong in Scotland and Wales, it is almost as marked in the South West and Yorkshire.' These sentiments of attachment to a region were examined in some detail. Most thought that the government understood the needs of their region to about the same extent as for other regions. Of the major regions Scotland, Wales and the north were seen by their inhabitants as being less well understood than other regions. The regions closest to the centre of government, Greater London and the south east, tended to feel that their needs were better understood. The idea of regional self-determination as a way of improving things in the area appeared to be more in the forefront of the minds of those in

Scotland and Wales than elsewhere: 20% in Scotland and 9% in Wales spontaneously mentioned this when asked what improvements they would like to see in their region, compared with only one per cent in English regions. The report noted 'There is widespread interest in some change to more regional responsibility for running things but the indication is towards a *greater* say for the region in running their own affairs not for *complete* regional responsibility'. It was apparent that interest in complete regional responsibility in Scotland was not much more widespread than in some English regions and in Wales it was no stronger than in Britain as a whole. 'A combination of dissatisfaction with how things are run at present and feeling strongly that the ordinary man's needs and problems are not taken into account by government is particularly strongly associated with favouring more devolution ... it would give the ordinary man more say in deciding what is done in the region.'

This survey was carried out by a combination of resources from the Survey and an independent research organisation. This device, used from time to time, helped to spread available Survey staff and technical skills in sampling and interviewing over a wider range of studies than would otherwise have been possible. The procedure generally used was for the Survey to take responsibility for overseeing the whole survey, to supply Survey staff who could be made available, to invite tenders and contract for other necessary services, and then to ensure that a satisfactory report to the commissioning body was presented. This procedure was used to carry out another survey concerned with an aspect of local government the Layfield Committee work described in Chapter 10. The committee was considering the rating system as a method of local government finance. The survey had two parts: one part examined how much was known and understood about the existing system and what views were held about possible alternatives; the other involved reinterviewing an FES sample a year later in order to measure the impact in the rates levied.

All these local government studies were ad hoc and separated by some years, but there is considerable overlap in their subjects, and local government was sufficiently prominent in public discussion during the period in which the surveys took place to have benefited from a more organised programme than was feasible in the circumstances. The early intention to keep education under continuing surveillance was implemented in the procession of well-known reports which focused public attention over several generations. The work of the National Advisory Council, in its different incarnations, and the Schools Council, provided the mechanism for organising much of this work and sustained the principles of continuing intellectual scrutiny of this major public service. This acceptance, until recent years, of the principle of self-scrutiny by a public service seems important, and within that tradition the Survey found a chance to contribute for over 20 years. There has, perhaps, been more continuity in this work than in most other subject areas.

The purpose of the law commissions is also to scrutinise with a view to reform, specifically, by revision of laws. The work done in connection with the review of matrimonial property law and defenders in debt actions falls into this category, as well as the surveys for committees considering the licensing laws and shop closing hours. Similar scrutinies have been made not specifically with a view to changing law (although that may sometimes follow) but to examine the way in which institutions and existing procedures are working. Survey research has been able to contribute to many such scrutinies, such as the various commissions which have considered the police, and particularly relations between the police and the public; the work of the James Committee on the distribution of business between magistrates' and crown courts; the study of local social security offices; the operation of electoral registration, or the experience of relatives of deceased persons involved in coroners' enquiries. These were all ad hoc enquiries. Many were concerned with topics which only become public business at long intervals. The National Health Service, on the other hand, is perhaps the institution of most concern to a larger proportion of the population than any other. Here too, the contribution of the Survey has mainly been ad hoc, and the array of health and social services is so wide that Survey work-programmes have included more separate surveys on topics related to them than any other subject area.

It is appropriate to finish this chapter with reference to a survey of an institution which has been involved with all the studies described – the civil service. The survey was requested by the committee chaired by Lord Fulton which was set up following a recommendation of the Estimates Committee (the Bray Committee on Government Statistical Services) in 1965. Perhaps the Fulton Committee may be seen as part of the wave of 'modernisation' announced in the programme of the government elected in 1964. It was 'to examine the structure, recruitment and management' of the civil service. Two academics were asked to make an appropriate study, and saw their brief as follows: 'the Committee had in mind that such a survey might provide a sociological portrait of this group of professions and occupations and might serve to integrate other enquiries'.[1] The survey, which was developed in cooperation with Survey staff, was therefore designed to provide information about the social background of civil servants. The committee's timetable made anything other than a postal survey impossible, and this decision limited the subject matter and the questions which could be asked. The sample provided data for 26 separate groups in 10 main classes in each of which over 200 persons were selected from the Central Staff Record. The information required covered social origin, education, family, social activities and newspapers and periodicals read. Income could be derived from the records. The survey data, collected January–February 1967, was analysed by the Survey to provide tabulations specified by the academic researchers.

Their report obviously reflected many of the issues raised in public discussions about the civil service and examined the relevant data in some detail. 'The pattern of classes in the Service reflects the pattern of the country's educational system . . . it tends to follow that the pattern of classes in the Service also to some extent matches the pattern of social classes in the community . . . The administrative class is more exclusively educated than either the scientific class or the professional works group. 56% of the administrative class were educated in the private sector (ie direct grant, public and other fee paying schools) compared with 36% of both professional works group and the scientific officer class but as many as 67% of the legal class ... two-thirds of graduates in the administrative class came from Oxford or Cambridge, only 17% of the scientific officer class and 13% of graduates in the professional works group'. Some of the survey results were compared with similar data from other countries. 'There is no doubt that promotion widens the educational and social base of the administrative and scientific officer classes and the professional works group. Its impact is most marked on the administrative class ... between 34% and 46% of all promotions to all these classes are of working class origin. Similarly, a large proportion of the promotees were educated at state schools ... The main trend in recruitment of direct entrants has *not* been towards recruiting from steadily widening social background. Overall it has been static. Thus our sample shows that 85% of those directly recruited between 1961 and 1965 were middle class in background.' The report examined changes in 'quality' of recruits by considering the class of degree they attained: 'There has certainly been a decline in the proportion of direct entrants with firsts recruited both to the administrative and scientific officer class'.

Note

[1] A H Halsey and I M Crewe, *Social Survey of the Civil Service*, (Fulton Committee Report), HMSO, 1969.

15 An appraisal

THE SURVEY'S HISTORY EVOLVED during a period of great national change. It would be misleading to suggest very direct connections between all these changes and the twists and turns in the Survey's fortunes. But the Survey was certainly affected by some of the changes and it is therefore appropriate to note those movements on the larger stage which provides the background to its work.

There were some officials who perceived at a very early stage that a more adequate public service in the future would require a better understanding of the lives and problems of the population. By 1946, when the decision was made to retain the Survey in peacetime, these views predominated. This decision did not include any final judgment on the scope of the Survey, any written terms of reference or indeed any agreement on exactly where it should be located. This indecision was not unusual at a time when many procedures were in flux, but in the case of the Survey the indecision lasted for over 20 years. During this time it was freely recognised that the Survey was wrongly located in the COI and that the consequent classification of its staff was inappropriate. So it has turned out that the Survey's de facto terms of reference have been shaped by what it did and does. The Survey's place in government and its contribution are the result of the responses of its staff to the opportunities it found to render service.

The survey method is highly elastic and the description of surveys done shows that there are very few public interests to which some kind of contribution cannot be made. If the Survey had been firmly located in a department with responsibilities in a limited field its work would probably have covered a much smaller span. It would also probably have enjoyed less freedom to innovate methods which would have to fit in with the procedures of a more limited parent body or for which that body would have to take responsibility. In the event the Survey had great technical freedom and the record shows that it was able to respond to a very wide spectrum of government interests.

Over the whole period, even during times when the future looked problematical, the work proceeded. New subjects were tackled and technical innovation continued. The Survey has probably worked on a wider range of issues than any other public social research unit and every study, from the beginning, has followed an administrative decision that it would be helpful and relevant to the work of officials charged with promoting or assessing decisions about departmental responsibilities. In this sense all the work was policy related. More than this, since the survey method, by definition, is a means of communicating with large numbers of people, a decision to make a government survey is a public decision which accepts the possibility of public discussion or criticism of the policies under review. It is noteworthy that the great majority of Survey reports have been published as written by the Survey researchers concerned.

The implications of this are that the work methods and public acceptability of the Survey were known to the officials asking for the work, that the Survey had available the resources needed, and that its staff were ready to work to departmental briefs and to develop whatever methods seemed likely to enable departmental needs to be met. None of this could have happened without the energetic efforts of the Survey's changing personnel and their commitment to facilitating their customers' work. It was their contribution which gradually turned a small, rather isolated unit into a government institution firmly located in the public apparatus and capable of withstanding the political onslaughts which inevitably accompany public financing.

Public acceptability had to be demonstrated. This did not mean avoiding topics wrongly thought to be too delicate for government departments. A successful campaign against venereal diseases required assessments of public knowledge and acceptance of publicity on the topic, and for this very direct questioning was needed. Useful information about consumer expenditure also needed rather detailed information about household incomes, and for an appraisal of programmes designed to help develop local family planning services it was necessary to devise searching interviews. The necessary interviewing methods had to be developed and officials convinced that they could be addressed to quite large numbers of people without any consequent embarrassment to ministers. Such topics were increasingly entrusted to the Survey as it became known that it would do its utmost to safeguard the public position of departments while pressing the work to all feasible limits. The confidence thus created was indispensable for the growth of the Survey as an accepted part of government. A willing response to expressed needs was essential for this development, but this did not mean that the Survey was a mere willing instrument. Surveys were designed in active cooperation with responsible officials knowledgeable about the topics under review, and the growing experience of the Survey staff was invaluable in the discussion.

Of course, in the early days interest in the use of survey research for public purposes was far from universal. At different times for reasons of public policy particular groups of people in the public service called on the Survey to help, and these 'gatekeepers' provided the opportunities for response. Early on during the war, officials concerned with information work, especially as related to wartime controls, the use of manpower and particularly woman power, were more likely than most pre-war officials to have become acquainted with sample survey methods and to need direct information about public reaction to their work, and they willingly called on the Survey for help. The decision in 1957 to give the Survey responsibility for the Family Expenditure Survey marked the reversal of the long period of difficulty following the major cutback of 1951. As well as meeting its primary purpose, to provide weights for the Retail Price

Index, the FES also provided a continuing flow of information for government economists and statisticians. These groups of social scientists had become strongly entrenched in government, and their interest in the FES also helped to strengthen the position of the Survey throughout government. Later, it was the personal interest in and experience of survey research of a new head of the Government Statistical Service which led to the creation of the OPCS and the solution of a long-standing problem – the appropriate location of the Survey in the machinery of government.

While some parts of government thus played an important role in opening up opportunities for the Survey to demonstrate its contribution, this was not enough to protect it from all the political winds. As was shown in 1951 and 1981 the scope of the Survey might be arbitrarily and seriously curtailed as a result of a general government policy, such as cutting the size of the civil service. On neither occasion was there full consideration of all sides of the Survey's work; hard-won experience in working on particular problem areas was lost and major discontinuities in subject expertise ensued. The abolition of the Survey of Sickness in 1952 is a good example of how a developing field of great potential importance could be abolished at short notice.

So the political climate was of critical importance, and it was regularly shaken by economic crises. The social reforms of the postwar decades developed against this background. With changes of government came changes in ideology and different emphases on policy or even the structure of government. The 1951 government made early decisions leading to a 10-year freeze in the location and staffing of the Survey. The decisions accompanied firm statements that the Survey's work would continue but there would be less of it. Similar statements were made 30 years later. But the reality of the 1951 cuts was that the Survey had to struggle to survive. The decisions in both cases seemed to reflect not critical views of the method but unwillingness to have part of the government apparatus approaching the public on behalf of another part to examine the effectiveness of policies or reactions to them. It was accepted in principle that the apparatus should include the skills needed for such forms of social intelligence but the staff and budgets required were sharply reduced.

The 1951 government, however, had a populist streak embodied in the speeches of Harold Macmillan on housing. The apparent success on this front led to growing confidence in the possibility of radical changes on housing policy and there followed the 1957 Rent Act. The Survey, called in to evaluate the effects of the Act, showed that the limited information on which the reforms were based could be greatly extended by the survey method and the Ministry of Housing subsequently turned to the Survey for continuing help. Together with the decision on the FES in 1957 this work restored the Survey's position and made it possible to think more positively about new fields of work and an appropriate structure for the organisation.

The 1960s also saw, several years after the postwar expansion of economic statistics, the development of statistical work in the social departments. Growing expenditure on health services and particularly on hospitals prompted some of the changes, and further stimulus came from changes in education. In some of these areas the Survey made contributions which helped to show departments the range of possibilities the survey method made available, and the spread of statisticians into the social arena seemed to offer opportunities for professional collaboration. Perhaps even greater potential for long-term development came from the changes suggested in 1962 by the new ideas on more rational and systematic public expenditure crystallised in the Plowden Report. This seemed to offer quite far-reaching changes in the way departments controlled their expenditure. Almost as important was the Plowden emphasis on a more quantitative manner of assessing the results of public expenditure – Survey methods seemed to offer something here.

The Macmillan era also crumbled under economic pressure. It was followed by a new populism – the 'modernisation' of many aspects of life in Britain. The emphasis was on improving technology, but the history of the Ministry of Economic Affairs showed how important was the parallel development of economic information and planning techniques. Consciousness of the need for radical economic improvement was evident on all sides, not least because of the continuing pressure for social improvement and higher standards of living. So together with the regular economic perturbation came further change and its usual consequence – renewed interest in the possibilities of better social intelligence, reflected in an increased demand for help from the Survey. Gradually the Survey's staff increased to match it, and at about this time three developments responding to the urge for social reform offered alternative possibilities for increased public support for social research.

First, the Ministry of Health began to shape ideas on health service related research under the guidance of a former senior member of staff at the Medical Research Council. Not surprisingly what emerged was strongly influenced by MRC patterns, although it was the limited attention given to health services by the MRC as opposed to basic research which provided much of the impetus for the Ministry of Health's efforts to develop its own research network. Second, in 1964 a parliamentary committee chaired by Dr Jeremy Bray investigated government statistics. It seemed that the committee regarded the Survey and its capabilities as part of the statistical service. The organisers of the Ministry of Health research plans, too, apparently thought of the Survey simply as part of the official apparatus and in some way distinct from the research council type network it was developing. There was some confusion here about the nature, contribution and appropriate location for research. So the Survey was called in by the ministry when an administrative or policy interest seemed to require the kind of study with which officials were familiar, such as the survey of dental health, or the major study of the handicapped, or the evaluation of the home-help service, none of which arose out of procedures used by the new research network. And, thirdly, the appointment in 1963 of the Heyworth Committee to 'review social research in government and outside it and to advise if changes are needed in arrangements for support and coordinating this work' was a major indicator of the turn in the tide for social research. The Survey was to be included in this review. The activities of the committee added stimulus to departmental interest in social research and may have prompted some of the growth in departmental research expenditure. The committee's recommendations did not lead to any lasting change in the Survey's organisation, though its advice to take the Survey out of the COI led to the Survey being made responsible in 1967 directly to the Treasury as a kind of sub-department for a short interim period. Neither the committee nor the Treasury seemed to take into account the changes in government social statistics which were in the making.

Within a few years the OPCS was set up and the Survey found within it a settled and appropriate location. The Heyworth Committee's main contribution to social research was outside government – the establishment of a Social Science Research Council with funds for academic research. There were no feasible suggestions for better coordination of research inside government. Indeed, the committee not only rejected the idea of an interdepartmental mechanism which might help to make better use of resources going into work sponsored by departments, it even rejected the suggestion that social research units could be set up inside some departments to foster and facilitate social research.

The new OPCS incorporated the office of the Registrar General whose function, established many years ago, was to survey aspects of the social scene and to publish the results. The new survey techniques formally took their place alongside the traditional Census methods and analyses of registration data and considerably widened the range of topics which the office could describe and publish. The Survey had officially become part of the Government Statistical Service. It had, however, been agreed that it would still carry out the ad hoc surveys which had become very well known. This research contribution would therefore supplement the work on continuing surveys which met the needs mainly of departments' various statistical sections.

Early efforts, following the Plowden Report, to control, analyse and systematise public expenditure accompanied the attempt to improve management practices. Some of these efforts, if widely implemented, might have provided the framework for a more profitable use of government research activities. They would at some point have needed appraisal of the outcome of public expenditure, and appraisals of major continuing government programmes would have called for the kind of descriptive accounts which the Survey had shown were possible. It has been suggested that this did not happen because some of the recommended methods were presented as 'standardized schemes that had to be adopted and complied with rather than as techniques which could be adapted to different departments, types of work . . . the marked degree of centralized prescription tended to alienate those with management responsibility for large executive functions'.[1] This comment by an experienced Deputy Secretary notes the reaction of a public administrator to methods adapted, it was claimed, from techniques with proven success in business administration. The Heath Government of 1970 pressed forward attempts to improve the structure of government, to make more businesslike decisions and to measure more systematically the effects of government expenditure. But the political climate often made more efficient policy decisions difficult or impossible; policy decisions were thus not made at the appropriate time and any later attempts at decisions became all the more difficult.

In due course what had come to be expected as a usual economic crisis occurred, but this time it was different from its predecessors. In 1976 a dramatic and symbolic action publicly acknowledged that the government needed international help to solve the financial and economic problems which confronted it. The approach to the IMF marked the end of a period of expansion in government, and the change was emphasised in the rhetoric of the government which followed the general election of 1979. As in all periods of contraction in government there followed decisions to curtail publicly funded social research. It seems that a public climate of social change and hope of improvement fosters research which describes the circumstances requiring change, explores obstructions to change or helps to organise change. The early 19th century social statisticians, who had invented the idea of social surveys and created professional societies as forums for discussing the results of their studies, had shared these sentiments. The social surveyors at the turn of the century, too, were concerned with the need for social amelioration. But the Survey's experience over a generation shows that when the public climate, or at least its parliamentary manifestation, changes and governments set out to limit social expansion, part of this process is an attempt to limit social investigation.

This experience raises questions about the rationale of the procedures used to assess the effects of public expenditure. The Programme and Analysis Review (PAR) technique introduced by the business management advisers of the Heath Government was regarded as critical to the improved management of public expenditure. It did not however flourish. In the 1983 Reith lectures Sir Douglas Wass noted the need for methods

> to give Ministers a sounder basis than they have at present for exercising choice about where to expand and where to contract and to help them away from the inefficient and indiscriminate approach where cuts have to be made uniformly and across the board ... I would like to see regular evaluating of the expenditure incurred on each programme against the objectives it was designed to achieve ... in the science of politics we know very little a priori about the likely results of a radical policy development ... it is surely right that policies should be rigorously evaluated ... dependent as they are on a public perception of their competence and resolve it may be hard for governments to admit they have been wrong. But without the strength of moral purpose to make such an admission they may in the long run expose themselves and the country to risks and dangers which far exceed the costs of policy change.[2]

These comments were made some years after the 1979 government had formally announced the end of the PAR system. There had followed a series of decisions about policies and public expenditure which presumably were made without the 'sounder basis'. And, in fact, the contraction in the statistical service discussed earlier seemed to indicate little sympathy with any such move. Commenting on an earlier proposal to publish more of the policy studies of government, or at least more of the background material collected and analysed for policy purposes, Sir Douglas noted 'I have seen a certain amount of departmental analysis which has not fully supported government policy or government statements about the effects of policy. A quiet decision not to publish has been the easy way out ... Ministers are far more apprehensive than their official advisers about the threat to policy that the publication of damaging or unsupportive material can pose'. Since officials have to work with ministers Sir Douglas also noted the possibility, if publication of such material were obligatory, that 'departments which feared that some evidence would be inconsistent with policy might be tempted not to collect it. Ministers might expressly forbid the carrying out of certain research'. These comments illustrate well the general climate in which the Rayner review could advance the opinion 'it is doubtful if the government has so large a requirement for its own operation as the OPCS capacity indicates'.

The fortunes of the Survey were greatly affected by the fluctuating political climate, but there were other long-term problems that conditioned growth. The accident of location in the COI made it possible for the Survey to offer its services across the whole gamut of government interests. In principle it could have grown steadily and gradually as departments became familiar with its potential: in fact, growth was uneven. Table 33 shows the number of Survey staff employed and in post 1946–83. Over most of the period the numbers of research staff are separately noted but the total column includes them with all other staff. In accordance with the Survey approach to organisation many of the research posts included officers responsible for guiding and developing the technical sections concerned with sampling, fieldwork, primary analysis and computing. The total column refers only to headquarters' staff, and does not include interviewers, whose much larger number reflected the total work programme.

The first few years show steady growth. From 1948 the bumpy economic climate did not inhibit change but made it more uneven. The harsh effects of the 1951 cutbacks persisted until 1957, then came, with the general research expansion, continued growth which by 1967 almost trebled the total headquarters' staff. These changes do not include the changing totals of interviewers, strongly affected by the 1957 FES sample size increase, and the change in headquarters' staff was mirrored in the field force. Part of the headquarters staff was of course permanently occupied with the recruitment, training and overseeing of interviewers.

The increase in numbers during this period of growth also involved developing ideas on the most appropriate internal organisation for the kind of work programmes tackled. These ideas arose directly out of growing experience, and once again location in the COI played its part. Since most of its activities bore little or no relation to what the Survey was doing the senior staff of COI did not have any firm ideas on a suitable structure for a social research unit. They were therefore able to accept strongly expressed proposals from the Survey and to put them forward as the agreed views of the COI to the controlling authorities. Here, however, things were not so easy. What the Survey was doing was not usual within the civil service and those concerned centrally with staffing matters had some difficulty reconciling current practice with the Survey's convictions on the best way to do its particular kind of work. Staff inspectors could not help a great deal. They were experienced in assessing work against criteria developed

Table 33 Government Social Survey: Staff in post 1946–1983

	Information or survey research	Total headquarters	Fulltime interviewers
1941–2		12	56
1942–3		35	56
1943–4		36	55
1944–5		42	51
1945–6	13	64	51
1946–7	14	64	46
1.4.47		87	
1.4.48		70½	
1.4.49		93	
1.4.50	43	85½	
1.4.51	43	91½	
1.4.52	34	82	
Oct 52		59	
1.4.53	23	56	
Oct 53		52	
1.4.54	21	54	
Oct 54		53	
1.4.55	21	52	
Oct 55		50	
1.4.56	23	51	
1.4.57	24	54	
1.4.58	24	65	
1.4.59	22	59½	
1.4.60	28	68	
1.4.61	32	69	
1.4.62	42	90½	
1.4.63	44	101	
Oct 63	46	104	
1.4.64	44	94	
1.4.65	52	122½	
1.4.66	66	143	
Oct 66	66	150	
1.4.67	72	158	
1.4.68	84	189	
4.9.69	101	213	
1.6.70	107	204	
1.6.71	111	177	
1.4.72	107	181	
1.4.73	124½	198½	
1.4.74	132½	207	
1.4.75	120	210½	
1.4.76	119	218	
1.4.77	117	209	
1.4.78	111½	202½	
1.4.79	46	204½	
1.4.80	50	203½	
1.4.81	49	199½	
1.4.82	44	172	
1.10.82	38	152	
1.4.83	39	151½	
1.4.84	42	175	

for the large blocks of normal departmental functions and of course looked for the minimum levels of staffing which, by these criteria, could be entrusted with such closely defined functions. But the Survey work ethic was strongly influenced by its conviction that contributions were needed and forthcoming at all levels, and that elasticity in the use of whatever staff were available was the only way to cope with tackling new topics and shaping new methods. To this central principle was added the further conviction, also rooted in practice, of the useful division of labour and specialisation in the technical aspects of surveys. The permitted number of staff in different grades had to be argued in terms of workload, so staff only increased after it could be shown that more work was in prospect or, frequently, already being done. Increases then usually occurred only after the work situation had already changed, and there was further delay while agreed numbers were being recruited. During this period of expansion there was always great pressure on available staff to organise and carry out work.

After 1967 when, following the Heyworth recommendations, the Treasury became directly responsible, the new Government Social Survey Department took over responsibility for financial and staff control, and payment of interviewers and other part-time staff. Part of the increase in numbers between 1967 and 1970 reflects the change. Similarly, when the Survey became part of the OPCS, these administrative functions were taken over by a new central administration. The table reflects these changes between 1969 and 1971, not a decline in the numbers involved in running surveys. Between 1971 and 1976 the staff so involved grew again, but these increases also include staff working on the new continuing General Household Survey from 1970 onwards. The number of ad hoc surveys did not change, but some of the surveys done were major efforts. In 1976 the Survey's computing section was merged with the OPCS Computer Division, and this change too is reflected in the changing numbers of the Survey headquarters' staff. Taking all these changes into account the Survey reached its peak staff numbers around 1978–9. From then until 1983 the numbers declined as the policy of reducing the civil service was followed ever more stringently. In 1984 the Department of Employment transferred staff to the Survey so that the new continuing Labour Force Survey could be carried out, thereby increasing staff numbers. Apart from these changes, the change of classification in 1979 moved many of the staff concerned with the technical stages of survey work out of the common class they shared with research staff. This made a sharp change in what was described earlier as the work ethic of the Survey. It is probably a change which would have been approved by the staff inspectors with whom so many early arguments took place about the relevant organisation and use of available staff.

The most useful expression of available financial resources is given by the annual Vote, the figure agreed with Treasury each year and formally approved by Parliament. This only very infrequently involves parliamentary discussion but, nevertheless, it is the public acknowledgement of the legitimacy of the organisation. The Vote provides resources for headquarters' staff, salaries, interviewers' pay and expenses, and also for such expenditures as payments to respondents for recording household expenditures or payments to contractors.

In a period of inflationary change real resources can be seen only if account is taken of cost inflation. Civil service salary changes for the executive and clerical grades in equal proportions were used to compile an index of civil service pay. This index was used to deflate the annual Vote so as to yield a measure of change in real financial resources, shown in Table 34.

In any year the available staff and finance resulted from the settlements with the central control agencies. These settlements were always shaped by proposed work programmes and strongly influenced by the political weight of the particular surveys proposed, yet a settled appropriate structure was vital to the Survey's planning for any year if best use was to be made of resources, customers' needs were to be met, new staff to be trained or new technical methods developed. New large projects like the IPS in 1961 or the GHS in 1970 played a major role in deciding annual votes and, usually sometime later, in adapting staff numbers and organisation. Some of the major ad hoc studies affected the Vote in particular years, clearly because they provided information on which substantial financial decisions were to be made. The large continuing surveys gradually came to provide continuity which certainly helped to settle the organisation.

The internal structure of the Survey, reflecting experience in designing and carrying out a very large and mixed range of studies, came to be based on ideas about the need for some kind of division of labour which, it was believed, could accumulate expertise in sampling, fieldwork organisation, coding and so on. The economic base for this structure was a large enough output to keep the technical sections continuously occupied. The size of the work programme thus influenced the internal structure – as the Vote grew so could internal specialisation. Permanent specialist sections not only guaranteed the quality of work done at all stages of a survey, they also provided opportunity for newcomers to learn. This ensured the technical continuity of the organisation. Agreement on these arrangements came slowly. Progress was marked only in the third phase of rapid growth and consolidated only when it became clear that government social statistics would have political support and that the Survey was becoming a permanent contributor. The eventual large work programme which justified these decisions could only come from a wide array of customers located in many different parts of the government.

It was not sufficient to get agreement on complements – people had to be recruited and trained to fill the posts. The periodic cutbacks did not help. After 1952, 1976 and at other times of retreat, trained experienced staff left the Survey. Human resources accumulated over years could be disbursed at such times and replaced, when the tide turned, only with difficulty. It was not surprising therefore if from time to time the Vote provided money for studies on particular topics for which Survey staff were not available. When existing tested techniques could be applied under supervision, the appropriate solution was to contract-out work to survey agencies. There had been provision in the Survey's Vote for contracting out from very early days and apart from other advantages it made possible a rather more selective programme for existing Survey staff.

Table 34 Survey vote, actual and deflated, 1941-2 to 1981-2

Financial year	Vote £	Index of civil service pay	Deflated vote £	Index of real growth
1941-42	41,800	100	41,800	
42-3	46,360	100	46,360	100
43-4	47,750	100	47,750	103
44-5	73,819	100	73,819	159
45-6	63,000	107	58,879	127
46-7	63,000	120	52,500	113
47-8	70,059	125	56,047	121
48-9	106,500	127	83,858	181
49-50	124,021	127	97,654	211
50-51	127,700	131	97,481	210
51-2	133,600	142	94,085	203
52-3	112,300	153	73,399	158
53-4	89,000	158	56,329	122
54-5	107,200	163	65,767	142
55-6	110,500	172	64,244	139
56-7	113,500	195	58,205	126
57-8	127,500	205	62,195	134
58-9	136,503	214	63,785	138
59-60	170,000	222	76,577	165
60-61	190,000	227	83,700	181
61-2	256,500	234	109.615	236
62-3	315,000	243	129,630	280
63-4	418,000	256	163,281	353
64-5	500,000	274	182,482	394
65-6	710,000	283	256,883	554
66-7	761,250	288	264,323	570
67-8	850,000	296	287,162	619
68-9	900,000	314	286,620	618
69-70	1,061,000	333	318,619	687
70-71	1,220,000	374	326,203	704
71-2	1,098,000	408	269,118	580
72-3	1,504,000	431	348,956	753
73-4	1,636,000	483	338,716	731
74-5	2,125,000	589	360,781	778
75-6	2,380,000	714	333,333	719
76-7	2,382,000	735	324,082	699
77-8	2,686,000	735	365,442	788
78-9	2,833,000	930	304,623	657
79-80	3,379,000	1,076	314,033	677
80-81	4,428,000	1,342	329,955	712
81-2	4,990,000	1,461	341,547	737

When a new technique had to be developed or the subject matter seemed to require strong official backing it was generally desirable that the Survey should take direct responsibility. The fieldstaff trained to apply an array of interviewing and recording techniques were particularly likely to expand and contract with changes in the Survey's fortunes. Contraction not only affected the work on ad hoc studies, it also impinged on the results of the continuing surveys. In most of the reviews made throughout the Survey's history, particularly the most recent, the Rayner review, there seemed to be little awareness of the way the different Survey functions interlock. When they advised the elimination or curtailment of ad hoc surveys there were consequences for most of the techniques making up the Survey's repertoire of methods.

The Survey's working methods have always been adapted to subjects and to the technical problems presented by particular topics and the relevant populations. Behind the varied approaches, however, lie some principles worked out during the early years and applied throughout the whole range of work done. Representative, probability, samples have been used for nearly all Survey projects since 1950. Although face to face interviews have been the most common technique for securing responses, Willcock showed how observation methods could be used in road safety surveys and in studying the work of hospital nurses. Contrary to the misleading indications of many textbooks the Survey has used postal enquiries successfully, with responses up to 85%. Recently telephone interviewing has been used for the large scale continuing Labour Force Survey and for some ad hoc studies. Decisions on the appropriate method were made with judgment based on past experience and tested always by preliminary pilot studies. Interviewers must always be chosen carefully: most of the applicants are not found suitable after testing. A special study of the period 1958–62 showed that only five or six per cent of applicants were accepted for training: of these about half survived field training, and recent experience is similar. These cautious methods are judged necessary since all interviews are done on behalf of a department whose Minister is answerable and may be questioned about the survey. A self-critical approach to the methods employed is in the tradition of earlier statisticians like Bowley and is certainly appropriate, even essential, for an organisation whose work is open to critical review from many quarters and likely to be used for secondary analysis long after its initial publication.

Survey studies have been designed to provide representative, quantitative data from direct contact with individual members of relevant populations. Thus defined, the subject matter and methods of the Survey do not fall strictly within the scope of sociological research as far as this is concerned with theories about social structure and social change. Nevertheless, the subject matter of much survey research is obviously relevant to sociological speculation or enquiry and is often used for these purposes. Many major academic sociological projects since the war have employed methods not very different from those developed by the Survey, and on some of them, as noted earlier, the Survey has collaborated. Recently, however, survey research has fallen out of favour with some sections of the sociology world. For these critics all survey research is categorised as 'positivist', that is, based on an assumption that human behaviour can be studied in such a way that statistical regularities can be observed and described.

The criticism focuses on the use of techniques described earlier which are designed to produce quantitative descriptions of circumstances, behaviour or attitudes. The critics suggest that responses to standardised observations or interviews are contradictory and biased: therefore, it is argued, the outcomes of such procedures are misleading.[3] The conclusion of these critics is that survey methods should be abandoned. This takes no account of the mass of experimental work done on question design, nor of the pilot and validating studies done before most professional survey research is launched to ensure that survey instruments are comprehensible to and sympathetically received by respondents. Professor Philip Abrams, in a much quoted paper to the British Association in 1981, said of the period following Sociology's expansion in 1960–70:

> Many of the complaints made about the turbulence, incoherence, mystification and of course uselessness of the subject lose their force when one remembers that sociology as a nationally established discipline is still in its first twenty years ... the first few years of large scale sociological work were really bound to be years of apparent intellectual fragmentation, of vehement debate, the excited discovery of red herrings, the zealous denial of orthodoxies, the over-emphatic proclamations of new options, dichotomies, polarities, repudiations, manifestos.

So if the Survey had needed to base its designs on some appropriate theories it would clearly not have been altogether easy to decide which to choose.

But the prime purpose of the Survey is not and never has been the promotion of academic study. Perhaps it is more relevant to describe the Survey as part of the response of government to the social environment of the times. Simply put, the survey method amplifies available knowledge of the circumstances, behaviour and attitudes of the population and of groups within it. It thereby helps to extend the contribution of other professionals such as administrators, to make their advice or decisions better grounded and to put in perspective the representations of special-interest groups. 'Bureaucracy' as a term of abuse becomes less effective if administration can be shown to be in contact with and conscious of the social situations with which it purports to deal. The onus for refusal to acknowledge these situations then rests more clearly on the political component of government. The early surveyors embodied the public conscience about living conditions. As they moved into public service they gradually legitimised public enquiry as a preface to public action, and it might be argued that to the extent that this kind of professional social intelligence was permitted to influence policy decisions, it helped to amplify the conscious, rational component in public administration. The Survey's history shows that, over time, as survey research demonstrated its potential contribution, governments came to make more general use of it. It is no longer possible to plead ignorance of social situations which it has been shown can be studied effectively. However, the will to use the method is also necessary. This is subject to political decision and, ultimately, to some concept of the legitimate role of government or public action.

A somewhat paradoxical situation has developed. While the work of the Survey has played a large part in legitimising the survey method throughout government, the actual work programmes in recent years have become weighted towards helping the statistical function. So the idea of the Survey as a cooperative body serving the needs of all professional groups inside government has given way to its position as part of the government statistical service, and for decisions on its funding to be decided accordingly.

There are other paradoxes. Both the Rayner and Merchant reports accepted government's need for survey research and both underlined the necessity for some kind of advisory, coordinating centre. Little thought was given to how the necessary expertise and experience for such a function could accumulate and be maintained. For this to happen it seems necessary to enable the Survey to act as a cooperative body working with all the sections of government whose work could be aided by the use of survey research. It has been argued earlier that the maintenance of the Survey's specialist division of labour, which is an essential part of its expertise, depends on annual budgets which permit the Survey to carry out a suitable work programme. If these fall below the adequate levels or if available resources are concentrated on only some parts of the spectrum of government needs then it will be difficult, if not impossible, for the Survey to sustain the all-round technical competence which comes from experience and practice.

In the longer term the Survey can only realise its full potential if the opportunities to make its particular contribution become available. This depends not only on its ability to survive periods of pressure on research but also on the survival of the more self-conscious and self-critical appraisal of public policy and action which has developed over the last 20 years or so. These are the notions embodied in the 1962 Plowden Report, the reforms of the 1970s with Programme and Analysis Review and the thoughts expressed in the 1983 Reith Lectures by Sir Douglas Wass. In principle, these views bring up to date the sentiments of many of the early social surveyors. Here were the roots of the survey method. Perhaps its greatest contribution has still to be made.

Notes

[1] John Delafons, 'Working in Whitehall', *Public Administration*, Autumn 1982.
[2] *The Listener*, 24 November 1984.
[3] AV Cicoural (1964) is often quoted in this connection.

APPENDIX A

 Paper for Estimates Committee, March 1966

Origination of Government Social Survey Projects

THE GOVERNMENT SOCIAL SURVEY is only permitted to engage in work which has some *administrative relevance*. Some public body must ask for the work and a government department must sponsor it. After this the Treasury must give authorisation before any money can be spent in those cases where the total costs of the enquiry are to be repaid by an outside body. These conditions ensure that no work can be done by the Social Survey unless there is a very clear-cut Government interest. The Government interest must relate to policy as defined by the normal political process and as interpreted by civil servants. It follows from this that only work will be done which is compatible with the general system of public control and accountability to which the Civil Service is subject. As with any other part of the Government apparatus, what the Social Survey does must be politically defensible; this is to say Ministers must be willing to answer questions about it. The subjects investigated and the methods of work must be such that they can at any time be publicly discussed and defended. All work which has so far been done has had to be carried out in such a way as to meet these necessary conditions.

The staff of Social Survey consequently works in very close cooperation with those who ask for the work to be done. It is for the Departments, when policy decisions seem to require a study of a social or an economic situation, to put the issue to the Social Survey; or when the request for data comes from an outside body it is with the departments that this request must in the first instance be discussed. The practical possibility of collecting relevant information is then a matter for joint discussion to which Social Survey staff bring their experience of research methods, field organisation and knowledge of the subject derived from previous work. The design and scope of any Social Survey study is therefore a cooperative undertaking in which Social Survey research workers combine their knowledge with that of a department's officers or advisers. When a decision has been made on what kind of data is needed and how it is to be got, it is for the Social Survey then to carry out the study and produce it. Any final report is a product of a combination of skills, technical knowledge and departmental awareness of policy implications and, since public departments will have to take public responsibility for any study which is carried out, there is a very special relationship between the Social Survey and the public departments. Departmental interests are very much shaped by policy requirements and political possibilities. On the other hand the Social Survey has to be concerned with shaping its enquiries so that specified and agreed objectives can be achieved.

Much of the work of the Social Survey is done for the statistical divisions of departments and is designed to help complete the official statistical framework which over the years had slowly been build up by means of census, regular statistical returns and special departmental enquiry. Departments call for this kind of assistance when data is needed which they cannot themselves conveniently collect and analyse or which can be better organised by a sample survey unit or where the methods of survey research provide the most appropriate techniques for the particular information required.

Another very large group of government officials who are interested in the work described above are the many professional groups engaged on a wide range of specialist activities inside the Government apparatus; doctors who are concerned for example with nutrition or older people; inspectors in the Children's Department of the Home Office who are interested in the organisation and working of the children's home or boarding out; inspectors in the Ministry of Education who are interested in aspects of social or community life which affect the efficient functioning of the educational system; technical officers of the National Agricultural Advisory Service who are interested in ways in which farmers can be encouraged to make more use of new methods; scientists in the many government research stations who need social and economic data to ensure the practical development of their enquiries; Government economists concerned with the analysis of economic change who are interested in consumer expenditure, changes in the labour force and price movements. For all these people survey research offers one way of extending and deepening the range of their knowledge and awareness of what goes on in the community and particularly in those parts of the community which it is their professional business to study.

If information collected by the Social Survey is to be useful to these people it must have regard to criteria which they find acceptable. The data provided must seem sufficiently valid to be useful and not available from any other more convenient source. Their active participation in the development of survey research enquiries working in cooperation with the Survey's own research and technical staff is the best guarantee that what is done can be used.

When advisory committees, departmental committees of enquiry or Royal Commissions are set up, their expected function is to assemble and crystallise existing knowledge using for this purpose all the resources of the government apparatus. Over the years they have turned increasingly to the Social Survey as a means for providing material which they find they need to complete their studies and which is not available from other parts of the government apparatus.

Amongst government employees perhaps most important of all is the attitude taken by administrators to the use of survey research. This is because under the British system of government administrators are the guardians of policy. Because the Government Social Survey is outside the main Government Departments and exists as a central service it is called in only when the departmental apparatus cannot itself meet the needs of the Department. An extension of any department's function is then involved when the Social Survey is invited to help. Furthermore any Social Survey enquiry may involve contact with thousands of members of the public. By its very nature the research done by the methods of sample survey is a public activity and may well lead to Parliamentary questioning. It is clear then that a survey research apparatus can only continue to exist and function efficiently if administrators find it useful and politically safe. Experience over the years has shown that there are very many ways in which administrators have thought it useful to employ the methods of survey research, to extend and amplify the apparatus of their own departments and in this way to put to work, for government benefit, some of the methods of Social Science.

There is no standard shape or form to survey studies, the Family Expenditure Survey goes on continuously; some studies may run two or three years; 250,000 people may be involved or only a few hundred. Sometimes it may be found possible to cover the needs of three or four departments within the scope of one study. Sometimes a series of studies alone will suffice for one subject. Some of the work is for very immediate purposes, some for relatively long-term purposes. Short-term studies are likely to be those needed for direct operational decision. Long-term studies begin to approximate to academic research and many of them have originated in academic interest as was the case with the Oxford Savings Surveys, the first Labour Mobility Survey carried out in 1948 or the study of the Economic and Social Circumstances of Older People. So at one end of the range Social Survey work is at times closely related to an immediate departmental concern. At the other end of the range, working with academic researchers, Social Survey has helped to add to the corpus of social science knowledge and in this way to play a part in shaping the social and economic atmosphere within the decision-making apparatus of society and government operates.

Although as explained above most of the studies of the Social Survey, whatever shape they take, are designed to meet a special need there are many fields in which over the years ad hoc social surveys have gradually accumulated much detailed information. These separate pieces of work do not form a coherent or integrated body of data, they represent rather an unplanned de facto programme of work than a designed and coherent group of studies. Nevertheless in their own way such de facto programmes help to show how survey research methods can be deployed on very many different aspects of some major problems.

It may then be said in summary that the work of the Social Survey over the years led to an accumulation of knowledge on those aspects of particular social or economic issues where survey research has been thought to be politically possible and administratively relevant. It follows from this that although work has been done over a wide area there has been an emphasis on selective aspects of the subjects investigated. This is an inevitable condition of any government research. However it also follows that as government interest changes so can the range and depth of government survey research. The record of work done shows that already in many fields the scope of government survey research in the United Kingdom is as wide as that of academic enquiry and that at different times a very wide range of detailed investigation has been covered.

If administrative relevance has been politically necessary for the continuance of the Social Survey as a government organisation then equally *technical relevance* has been essential for adequate performance of the survey's role inside the government apparatus. It is clear that a very wide range of work has been attempted. It necessarily follows from this that an equally wide range of techniques has been implied. There are unfortunately many to whom this conclusion may come rather as a surprise. Sample survey work has a public 'image' which in the minds of many derives from the work of public opinion polls. The methods used by the Social Survey are in no way unique. Comparable work is done by business and industrial organisations in order to guide their own decision making. And independent academic researchers make use of similar techniques for their purposes. Public opinion polls are however a very special case of the application of sample survey research methods. They are designed to provide features for newspapers and if they are to suit current newspaper techniques they must deal with simplified issues and produce results which can be presented in equally simplified form. Such methods are clearly not suited for most of the enquiries which the Social Survey is asked to carry out. If information is to be of operational value and capable of providing a basis for decisions about future actions then the techniques employed must be appropriate. Perhaps the essential feature of the techniques employed by the Social Survey is that they are tailored to fit the subject matter. There is no common technique which is adequate for all research purposes. Indeed, since there is continual change in the focus of Government interests and, consequently, the Social Survey is continually faced with new subjects, there is a need for continual adaptation of method.

APPENDIX B

 # Government Social Survey Department

Note by the Treasury

Introduction

In answer to a question in the House of Commons on 17th February, 1967 the Financial Secretary to the Treasury announced that, as from 1st April, 1967, the Social Survey would become a separate Department reporting to Treasury Ministers in accordance with the recommendations of the Heyworth Committee (Report of the Committee on Social Studies Cmnd. 2660 Rec. XXIV). On that date the Social Survey ceased to be part of the Central Office of Information and became the Government Social Survey Department. For convenience the new Department is referred to in the remainder of this note as 'the Survey'.

2. The Heyworth Committee also recommended that an interdepartmental Committee, composed of the representatives of the main user departments and of the Social Science Research Council, under treasury chairmanship, should determine the Social Survey's programme. This Committee was set up in January, 1966 'to review the role of the Social Survey; and then annually to advise the Treasury on the total resources to be made available for the Survey and to determine how these resources should be allocated'. Its first Report was submitted to the Treasury in March, 1967.

3. This note defines the future role of the Survey and sets out the relationship between the Survey and user Departments that has been proposed by the Social Survey Programme Committee and accepted by the Treasury.

Future Role

4. The role of the Survey will be to act as the central co-ordinating body for all Government survey research. It will continue to conduct direct surveys, not least because it is important that it should in this way have first-hand experience of all appropriate techniques, as they develop, and of the practical problems of managing surveys. It is not, however, intended that all Government survey work should be completely centralised: Departments with specialised facilities will continue to use them where appropriate. The Survey will provide a technical and managerial advisory service, as required by Departments, across the whole range of Government survey research.

Future Programme

5. The future research field of the Survey may be expected to include social, as well as economic, matters. The extent to which one or the other predominates will depend in part on the nature of Departments' requirements and in part on the extend of the Survey's own resources and the availability of alternative facilities.

6. In order to concentrate the Survey's work on the subjects for which it is best suited, future programmes will be compiled to give greater prominence to Departments' long-term and continuing needs for data. The programme will include a sufficient proportion of projects, requiring interpretative skills, which the Survey itself will carry through to the report stage. There should be a general presumption in favour of allowing the Survey to carry each project as far as possible in the light of the balance of expertise in the subject matter of the project between the Survey and the sponsoring Department.

Relationship with Departments

7. If the Survey is to discharge its function effectively, Departments must consult it before undertaking or contracting out any work within its competence. As a general rule they should consult the Survey before commissioning survey research about the circumstances, behaviour and attitudes of individuals, including cases where such research is part of a wider project. Departments canvassing large institutions, representative organisations and business undertakings need not generally consult the Survey, though in some cases they may wish to do so. The generality of social research undertaken by Departments and not based on survey techniques of the type employed by the Survey should not be referred to the Survey.

8. The new concept will be an essentially co-operative enterprise, in which Departments and the Survey each contribute what they may best provide, and Departments are therefore requested to consult the Survey at the earliest possible stage in planning future surveys. From that point Departments' survey plans will be formed in a process of continuing joint discussion. It is recognised that this process may call for adaptations in the internal organisation of some Departments and will therefore need to be implemented progressively. Its pace is bound to be affected by the extent of the Survey's own manpower, especially at directing level, available from time to time.

9. The new system should lead to more long-term planning of the Survey's programmes based on close cooperation at all stages between the Survey and user Departments under the general eye of the Social Survey Programme Committee. It is also envisaged that joint planning involving several Departments will become a regular feature. The programme will emerge from a three-stage process:-

(a) regular annual bilateral discussions between Departments and the Survey, aimed at rolling forward long-term survey research programmes and at finalising requirements for the next financial year;

(b) general review of draft programmes by the Social Survey Programme

Committee, who may call for adjustments to rectify distortions or undesirable trends in the shape and balance of programmes; and
(c) submission by the Committee to the Treasury, in time for the Estimates review, of its recommendations for the next financial year based on the draft programme.

It is expected that this new system will enhance the Survey's direct and indirect contribution to Government survey research without derogating from Departments' ultimate responsibility for obtaining whatever survey material is needed for the formulation and execution of their policies.

APPENDIX C

 Statement by senior staff on the announcement of the new office

The Head of the Office of Population Censuses and Surveys

Following on the announcement of the inauguration of the new Department we thought it might be useful to you to have on record the views of the senior staff of the GSS.

1. We understand that the main purpose in setting up the new Office is to strengthen Government social statistics and social research so that a better contribution can be made to the public interest. We can readily understand that some strengthening of official work in these spheres might be expected from better co-ordination of the work done by the General Register Office and the Government Social Survey which are the two leading organisations in this field at the present moment. We hope that the new organisation will in fact make possible such a development in all forms of official statistics and enquiries on matters of social interest. Indeed this has been the main incentive for the work in which all of us have participated over the past years and it is with this purpose in mind that the Government Social Survey has developed its unique team of research workers and specialists which has now made for itself an international reputation.

2. We are sure that it is realised by all concerned that the Government Social Survey, which is not a very large organisation, has only been able to make its contribution over the past years by acting as an integrated team. It is fundamental to the design and operation of all forms of survey research that those in our specialist sections who have various specialist skills to contribute should work closely at each stage of the work with research staff who have overall responsibility for specific projects. We would like to emphasise our conviction that this internal exchange of ideas is indispensable for efficient survey research. It is the means whereby the accumulated experience of all of us is made

available and we are convinced that we shall be able to make the best contribution to the work of the new organisation if ways can be found to ensure that the specialist and research staff of the GSS section continue to work thus closely together. This would require both organisational and physical contact without which team work becomes difficult if not impossible.

3. As the new office comes into being and staff begin to work together we would of course expect developments in its organisation. But the work which is now being done and which we are committed to in the immediate future does require the continuation of the present Government Social Survey procedures which have been worked out over many years and this is all the more important in view of the very unsettling period of past history through which we have just passed.

4. A great deal of goodwill has been built up round the name of the Government Social Survey. This is known all over the world and in Great Britain it is familiar to local authorities, research workers in many fields, sources of information, the newspapers and the general population. The name is associated with high standards of work and the contribution made to Government in Britain by survey research methods. In our view it would be wise to do everything possible to retain this goodwill and the name over the immediate future, possibly as a divisional title as was the case in the COI.

5. We are sure that in the long run the new organisation will come to be widely recognised for its contribution to the public service and the general welfare of the population. We look forward to making our own specific contribution to the work.

APPENDIX D

 Summary of main topics included in the GHS questionnaires 1971 to 1981

BURGLARIES AND THEFTS FROM PRIVATE HOUSEHOLDS
                                            1972–73, 1979–80
Incidence of burglaries in the 12 months before interview
Value of stolen goods and whether insured
Whether incident was reported to the police
Reasons for not reporting to the police

CAREER OPPORTUNITIES   **1972**
Attitudes towards careers in the Armed Forces and the Police Force
Whether ever been in one of the Armed Forces

CAR OWNERSHIP
Number of cars or vans, if any, available to the household for
   private use   **1971–81**
In whose name (person or firm) each car/van was registered   **1980**

Driving licences and private motoring   **1980**
Whether held current licence for driving a car or van, and for
   how long full licence held
Whether non-licence holders (aged 17–70) intended to apply for a
   licence (again), and reasons for not having done so or for not
   intending to do so
Frequency of use, for private motoring, of car/van available to the
   household
If household car/van not available, or not used for private
   motoring in the year before interview:
   – whether used any car/van for private motoring in that year
   – whether drove a car, van, lorry, or bus in the course of work
      in that year

COLOUR AND COUNTRY OF BIRTH
Colour, assessment of persons seen* 1971–81
Country of birth
  of adults and their parents 1971–81
  of children 1979–81
Year of entry to UK
  adults 1971–81
  children 1979–81

DRINKING 1978, 1980
Personal rating of own drinking behaviour
Rating of drinking behaviour according to quantity-frequency (QF) index based on reported alcohol consumption in the 12 months before interview
Whether think drinking/smoking can damage health

EDUCATION
Current education
Current education status 1971–81
Type of educational establishment currently attented
– by adults aged under 50 1971–81
– by children aged 5–15 1971–77
Qualification/examination aimed at 1971, 1974–76
Expected date of completion of full-time education
Whether intend to do any paid work while still in full-time education, and if so when } 1971–76
Whether currently attending any leisure or recreation classes 1973–78, 1981

Past education
Age on leaving school 1971–81
Age on leaving last place of full-time education
Type of educational establishment last attended full-time
Qualifications obtained } 1971–81

Pre-school children (aged under 5)
Whether currently attending nursery/primary school, day nursery, playgroup, creche etc 1971–79
Frequency of attendance 1979
Whether received regular day care from person other than parents, and for how many hours per week
Whether working mothers would have to stop work if existing arrangements for the care of their children were no longer available, or whether they could make other care arrangements } 1979

Job training
Whether currently doing a trade apprenticeship 1971–81

* Including children.

Identification of persons seriously thinking of taking a course of
training or education for a particular type of job, with some
details of the course and the source of any financial support   **1973–74**

Students in institutional accommodation   **1981**
Estimate of numbers of full-time students at university or college
living away from home in institutional accommodation, and
therefore excluded from the GHS sample

EMPLOYMENT
Those currently working
Main job   – occupation and industry
           – employee/self employed   **1971–81**

Subsidiary – occupation and industry
job   – employee/self employed   **1971–78, 1980–81**

Journey time to work   **1971–76, 1978**
Usual number of hours worked per week (excluding overtime)   **1971–81**
Hours of paid/unpaid-overtime usually worked per week   **1973–81**
Usual number of days worked per week   **1973, 1979–81**
Number of days worked in reference week   **1977–78**
Length of time with present employer/of present spell of self-employment
                                                                        1971–81
Number of changes of employer in 12 months before interview
                                                                        1971–76, 1979–81
Number of new employee jobs started in 12 months before interview
                                                                        1977–78
Source of hearing about present job started in 12 months before interview
                                                                        1971–77, 1980–81
Source of hearing about all jobs started in 12 months before interview
                                                                        1974–77, 1980–81
Whether paid by employer when sick   **1971–76, 1979–81**
Whether covered by employer's pension scheme, whether the
  scheme is contributory, reasons for not belonging to
  the scheme   **1971–76, 1979**
Whether retained any pension rights from any previous
  employer
Type of National Insurance contribution paid by:
– married and widowed women
    aged 16 and over   **1972–79**
    aged 16–59   **1980**
– married, widowed, and separated women aged 16–59   **1981**
Level of satisfaction with present job as a whole   **1971–81**
Level of satisfaction with specific aspects of present job   **1974–81**
Whether thinking of leaving present employer, and if so why   **1971–76**
Absence from work in the reference week
– reasons for absence   **1971–72, 1974–81**

– length of period of absence	**1971–72, 1974–80**
– number of working days off last week	**1981**
– whether absent because of illness or accident, and length of absence	**1973**
– whether in receipt of National Insurance sickness benefit (and supplementary allowance) for this absence	**1971–76**
Sickness absence in the 4 weeks before interview	**1981**
Whether registered as unemployed in the reference week (if had worked less than full week)	**1977–81**
Unemployment experience in 12 months before interview	**1975–77**
Economic activity status 12 months before interview and, if economically inactive then, reasons for (re-)entering the labour force	**1979–81**

Usual job of father
– of all persons aged 16 and over	**1971–76**
– of persons aged 16–19 in full-time or part-time education	**1977–78**
– of all persons aged 16–49	**1979–81**

Those currently employed

Most recent job – occupation and industry	
– employee/self-employed	
Whether registered as unemployed in the reference week	**1971–81**
Methods of seeking work in the reference week	
For those who in the reference week were waiting to take up a new job already obtained:	
– would they have started that job in the reference week if it had been available then, or would they have chosen to wait	**1977–81**
– when was the new job obtained and when did they expect to start it	**1979**
Whether paid unemployment benefit (and supplementary allowance) for reference week	**1971–74**
When last worked and reasons for stopping work	**1971–73, 1974–79**
Reasons for leaving last job	**1981**
Length of current spell of unemployment	**1974–81**
Unemployment experience in 12 months before interview	**1975–77**
Economic activity status 12 months before interview and, if economically inactive then, reasons for (re-)entering the labour force	**1979–81**
Number of new employee jobs started in 12 months before interview	
Source of hearing about all jobs started in 12 months before interview	**1977**
Whether retained any pension rights from any previous employer	**1971–76, 1979**
Usual job of father	
– of all persons aged 16 and over	**1971–76**

– of all persons aged 16–49 in full-time or part-time education	**1977–78**
– of all persons aged 16–49	**1979–81**

The economically inactive

Major activity in the reference week	
Last job – occupation and industry	**1971–81**
– employee/self-employed	
Usual job (of retired persons)	
– occupation and industry	**1973–76, 1979–81**
– employee/self-employed	
When finished last job	**1971–73, 1977–78**
Reasons for stopping work	**1971–73, 1978–81**
Whether registered as unemployed in the reference week	**1972–81**
Whether paid unemployment benefit (and supplementary allowance) for reference week	**1972–74**
Unemployment experience in 12 months before interview	**1975–77**
Economic activity status 12 months before interview (persons aged 16–69)	**1980–81**
Number of new jobs started in 12 months before interview	
Source of hearing about all jobs started in 12 months before interview	**1977**
Whether retained any pension rights from any previous employer	**1971–76, 1979**
Future intentions, including whether would seek work earlier if satisfactory arrangements could be made for looking after children	**1971–76**
Usual job of father	
– of all persons aged 16 and over	**1971–76**
– of persons aged 16–49 in full-time or part-time education	**1977–78**
– of all persons aged 16–49	**1979–81**

FAMILY INFORMATION/FERTILITY
Married women aged under 45

Date of present marriage	**1971–78**
Whether first marriage	**1974–78**
Expected family size:	
at time of present marriage	
at time of interview	
Whether woman thinks she has completed her family	**1971–78**
Age when most recent baby was born	
Age when expects to have last baby	
Date of birth and sex of each child born in present marriage	

Ever married women aged 16–49, and single women aged 18–49

Marital history	**1979–81**
Current cohabitation	**1979–81**

Cohabitation before current or most recent marriage	**1979, 1981**
Date of birth and sex of all liveborn children and whether they live with mother	**1979–81**
Where children under 16, not living with mother, are currently living	**1979**
Date of birth of step, foster, and adopted children living in the household, and how long they have lived there	**1979–81**
Whether women (under 45) think they will have any (more) children, how many in all, and age at which they think they will have their first/next baby	**1979–81**

HEALTH
Chronic sickness (long-standing illness or disability)

Prevalence of long-standing illness or disability*	**1971–76, 1979–81**
Causes of the illness or disability*	**1971–75**
When the illness of disability started*	**1971**
Prevalence of limiting long-standing illness or disability*	**1972–76, 1979–81**
When it started to limit activities and whether housebound or bedfast because of it*	**1972–76**

Acute sickness (restricted activity in a two-week reference period)

Prevalence and duration of restricted activity*	**1971–76, 1979–81**
Causes of restricted activity*	**1971–75**
Number of days in a bed and number of days of (certificated) absence from work/school*	**1971–76**
Help from people outside household with housework or shopping	**1971–74**

Health in general in the 12 months before interview   **1977–81**
Chronic health problems   **1977–78**

Prevalence of chronic health problems

Constant effects of chronic health problems (eg taking things easy, using prescribed/non-prescribed medication, watching diet, taking account of weather)

Contact with health services in 12 months before interview because of chronic health problems

Effects of chronic health problems in the 14 days before interview (eg resting more than usual, using prescribed/non-prescribed medication, changing eating or drinking habits, cutting down on activities, consulting GP, seeking advice from other persons)

Short-term health problems (in the 14 days before interview)
1977–78

Prevalence of short-term health problems

Effects of short-term health problems in the 14 days before interview (see examples above)

* *Including children.*

GP consultations

Consultations in the two weeks before interview:
- number of consultations*
- NHS or private*
- type of doctor*
- site of consultation*   **1971–81**
- cause of consultation*   **1971–75**
- whether consulted because something was the matter, or for some other reason*
- whether was given a prescription or a National Insurance medical certificate*   **1981**
- whether was referred to a hospital*

Access to GPs: **1977**
- whether own doctor worked alone or with other doctors
- whether could usually see doctor of own choice at surgery
- most recent consultation at surgery:
  – when it took place
  – NHS or private
  – by appointment or not
  – how far ahead appointment made
  – time spent waiting at surgery
  – attitudes towards waiting time for appointment, waiting at surgery, and length of consultation

Outpatient (OP) attendances

Attendances at hospital OP departments in a three-month reference period:
- number of attendances*   **1971–81**
- NHS or private*   **1973–76**
- nature of complaint causing attendance*   **1974–76**

Appointments with OP departments: **1973–76**
- whether had (or was waiting for) an appointment*
- how long ago since told an appointment would be made*

Inpatient spells

Spells in hospital as an inpatient in a three-month reference period:
- number and length of spells*   **1971–76**
- NHS or private patient*   **1973–75**

Whether on waiting list for admission to hospital and length of time on list*   **1973–76**

Accidents at home   **1981**

Accidents at home, in a three-month reference period, that resulted in seeing a GP or going to a hospital:

* Including children.

whether saw GP or went to hospital or did both and, in the last case, which first*

whether went to hospital A&E Department (Casualty) or other part of hospital*

Health and personal social services
Use of various services:
- by adults and children — **1971–76**
- by persons aged 60 and over — **1979**
- by persons aged 65 and over — **1980–81**

Elderly persons
Persons aged 60 and over living alone, whether any relatives living nearby — **1979–80**

Persons aged 65 and over:
- whether need help in getting about inside the house and outside, and with a range of personal and household tasks, and, if help is needed, who usually helps
- frequency of social contacts with relatives and friends

1980

Sight and hearing
Difficulty with sight and whether wears glasses or contact lenses:
- persons aged 16 and over — **1977–79, 1981**
- persons aged 65 and over — **1980**

Difficulty with hearing and whether wears an aid:
- persons aged 16 and over — **1977–79, 1981**
- persons aged 65 and over — **1980**

Types of hearing aid worn, and whether obtained through NHS or privately

Reasons for not wearing an aid

1979

Tinnitus (sensation of noise in the ears or head)
Prevalence of tinnitus, frequency and duration of symptoms, whether ever consulted a doctor about it — **1981**

Medicine taking — **4th qtr 1972, 1973**
Medicines taken in the seven days before interview:
- categories of medicine
- patterns of consumption of analgesics

HOUSEHOLD COMPOSITION
Age*, sex*, marital status of household members
Relationship to head of household*
Family unit(s)

1971–81

Housewife — **1971–80**

* *Including children.*

HOUSING (see also MIGRATION)
Present accommodation: amenities

Length of residence at present address* ⎤	
Age of building	
Type of accommodation	
Number of rooms and number of bedrooms ⎬	**1971–81**
Whether have separate kitchen	
Bath/WC sole use, shared, none	
WC: inside or outside the accommodation ⎦	
Installation/replacement of bath or WC ⎤	
Cost of improvements made to the accommodation ⎦	**1971–76**
Floor level of main accommodation ⎤	
Whether there is a lift ⎦	**1973–81**

Tenure

Whether present home is owned or rented	**1971–81**
Whether in co-ownership housing association scheme	**1981**
Owner occupiers:	
– in whose name the property is owned	**1978–81**
– how outright owners originally acquired their home and source of any mortgage or loan	**1978–80**
– whether currently using present home as security for a (second) mortgage or loan of any kind	**1980–81**
– whether recent owner occupiers had previously rented this accommodation and, if so from whom and for how long	**1981**
Renters:	
– from whom the accommodation is rented	**1971–81**
– whether landlord lives in the same building	**1971–72, 1975–76, 1979–81**
– whether have considered buying present home and, if not, why not	**1980–81**

Housing costs

Gross value ⎤	
Net rateable value ⎦	**1971–81**
Yearly rate poundage	**1972–81**
Type of mortgage, and current mortgage payments ⎤	
Current rent ⎬	**1972–77, 1979, 1981**
Amount of any rent rebate/allowance and/or rate rebate received ⎦	

Central heating and fuel use

Whether have central heating	**1971–81**
Type of fuel used for central heating ⎤	
Type of fuel mainly used for room heating in winter ⎦	**1978–81**

* Including children.

Consumer durables
Possession of selected consumer durables   **1972–76, 1978–81**
Possession of a telephone   **1972–76, 1979–81**

HOUSING SATISFACTION   **1978**
Overall level of satisfaction with present accommodation
Reasons for dissatisfaction
Satisfaction with specified aspects of accommodation
Troublesome features
Housing preferences

INCOME
Income over 12 months before interview
Gross earnings as employee, from self-employment
Income from state benefits, investments, and other sources   **1971–78**
Number of weeks for which income received from each source
Whether currently receiving income from each source   **1974–78**

Current income   **1979–81**
Current earnings (gross, take-home, usual) as employee, from self-employment, and from second or occasional jobs
Current income from state benefits, occupational pensions, rents, savings and investments, and any other regular sources

LEISURE   **1973, 1977, 1980**
Holidays away from home in the four weeks before interview:
  length of holiday
  countries visited (in UK)
Leisure activities in the four weeks before interview:
  types of activity
  number of days on which engaged in each country
  whether activity done while away on holiday

LONG-DISTANCE TRAVEL   **1971–72**
Number of long-distance journeys made in the 14 days before interview
Starting and finishing points of journeys
Type of transport used for longest part of jouneys
Main purpose of journeys
Number of people travelled with

Migration
Past movement
Length of residence at previous address*   **1971–77**

* *Including children.*

Previous accommodation:
- tenure 1971–73, 1978–80
- household composition
- number of rooms 1971–73
- bath/WC: sole use, shared, none
- WC: inside or outside accommodation
Reasons for moving from previous address 1971–77
Number of moves in last five years* 1971–77, 1979–81

Potential movement
Identification of households containing persons who are currently thinking of moving*
Whether will be moving as whole household or splitting up* 1971–78, 1980–81
Size of future household* 1971–76, 1980–81
Reasons for moving 1971–76, 1978, 1980–81
Proposed future tenure 1980–81
Actions taken to find somewhere to live 1971–76, 1980–81
Whether had experienced difficulties
- in finding somewhere else to live 1980–81
- in raising a mortgage/loan or in finding a deposit

Frustrated potential movement
Identification of households containing persons who, though not currently thinking of moving, had seriously thought of doing so in the two years before interview*
Whether would have moved as whole household or would have split up* 1974–76, 1980
Proposed tenure
Reasons for deciding not to move 1974–76, 1980
Whether decision not to move was connected with rise in house prices

Whether had experienced difficulties in raising a mortgage/loan or in finding a deposit 1980

SMOKING
Cigarette smoking
Prevalence of cigarette-smoking 1972–76, 1978, 1980
Current cigarette smokers
  number of cigarettes smoked per day
  type of cigarette smoked mainly 1972–76, 1978, 1980
regular cigarette smokers:
  - age when started smoking cigarettes regularly 1972–73

* *Including children.*

occasional cigarette smokers:	
– whether ever smoked cigarettes regularly	
– age when started to smoke cigarettes regularly	1972–73
– number smoked per day when smoking regularly	
– how long ago stopped smoking cigarettes regularly	
Current non-smokers	
whether ever smoked cigarettes regularly	**1972–76, 1978, 1980**
age when started to smoke cigarettes regularly	
number smoked per day when smoking regularly	**1972–73, 1980**
how long ago stopped smoking cigarettes regularly	

Cigar-smoking

Prevalence of cigar-smoking	**1972–76, 1978, 1980**
Current cigar smokers	
number of cigars smoked per month	**1972–73**
type of cigar smoked	
age when started to smoke cigars regularly	
Current non-smokers	
whether ever smoked cigars regularly	**1972–76, 1978, 1980**
age when started to smoke cigars regularly	**1972**
how long ago stopped smoking cigars regularly	

Pipe-smoking

Prevalence of pipe-smoking among males	**1972–76, 1978**
Current pipe smokers	
amount of tobacco smoked per week	**1972–73**
age when started to smoke a pipe regularly	**1972**
Current non-smokers	
whether ever smoked a pipe regularly	**1972–76, 1978**
age when started to smoke a pipe regularly	**1972**
how long ago stopped smoking a pipe regularly	

VOLUNTARY WORK **1981**

Whether did any voluntary work in the 12 months before inteview
  and, if so:
- what kind of work, whether any organisation was involved, who mainly benefited from the work
- whether the work was done regularly or from time to time, and on how many days in the preceding month

Index

A

A.T.S. (Auxiliary Territorial Service) 5, 169
adolescents 21, 202
  offenders 218, 220–221
  smoking and 135–6
adoption 215
agriculture 28, 238–9, 241
  training in 175
alcohol consumption 81, 104, 136–7, 197, 227–30
armed forces 5, 167–8, 233
Association of Market Survey Organisations (AMSO) 103–4
Atkinson, Jean 63

B

betting 195, 227
Board of Trade 2, 6, 8, 11, 20, 32, 126, 231–2
  see also Department of Trade and Industry
Boreham, John 79, 96, 100, 101, 103
Borstal training 28, 32, 217–18, 237
Box, Kathleen 5, 11, 17, 18
breastfeeding 133–4
British Sociological Association 23
British Standard Time 63, 227
Brooks, Helen 5
Building Research Station 8, 109, 110–11, 124, 194
Business Statistics Office 61, 70, 72
Bynner, John 63

C

Census of Population 49, 50, 71, 80, 82–3, 90, 113, 114, 119, 173, 240, 242–3, 259
Central Advisory Committee for Education 37, 49, 201, 203, 204, 252
Central Office of Information (COI) 14, 15, 19–21, 30, 232, 255, 259, 261
  see also Ministry of Information
Central Policy Review Staff (CPRS) 75 et seq, 84
Central Statistical Office 19, 30, 32, 59 et seq, 72–3, 79, 95, 97, 126, 194, 195, 197, 245
Chapman, Dennis 5
children: day care 209
  dental health 159–60
  immunisation 135, 232
  leisure 201–2, 208
  nutrition 37
  play areas 111, 208–9
  smoking 136–7
  see also: schoolchildren
children's homes 153–4
Civil Defence 237–8
Civil Service 49, 59, 60, 66, 253–4
  recruitment 167, 174
Civil Service Department (CSD) 61, 89
coalmining 112, 165–7
coding methods and techniques 29, 85

Committee on Higher Education
(Robbins) 43, 203–4
Committee on Medical Aspects of
Food Policy 133
Committee on Social Science
Research (CSSR) 50, 51
community care 156
computing 87, 263
construction industry: labour in 80
consumer expenditure surveys 18
et seq, 32, 194–6, 256
consumer needs and shortages 11,
231–2
contracting out 12, 15, 252
'Cooper's snoopers', 3, 6
Corlett, Tom 17, 22, 23, 28, 44
coroners 224, 253
courts 104, 224–5, 253
credit 193, 232
crime: deterrents and incentives 43,
220–1
public attitudes and knowledge
221–3
victims of 222–3
criminal justice surveys 217–30, 237
customers 5–6, 7–8, 11, 256
outside government 15, 28, 33
see also individual organisations

D

day care 209
deafness 18, 140–1
debt actions: Scotland 225–6, 252
dental surveys 63, 81, 159–60, 252
dentists: pay 37, 154–5, 160
Department of Education and
Science 50, 78, 82, 84, 200, 208
see also Ministry of Education
Department of Employment 63, 80,
93, 99, 105, 145, 154, 171, 178,
185, 187, 188, 190, 196, 263
see also Ministry of Labour
Department of Health and Social
Security 76 *et seq*, 104, 109, 133,
145, 151, 198, 199, 209, 210, 239
see also Ministry of Health

Department of Scientific and
Industrial Research (DSIR) 8,
29–30, 32, 44–5, 47, 50, 111,
174
Department of the Environment 76,
78, 111, 119, 121, 124, 198
see also Ministry of Housing,
Ministry of Works
Department of Trade and Industry
126
see also Board of Trade
Department of Transport 104–5
see also Ministry of Transport
devolution 63, 250–2
diphtheria 135, 232
doctors: GPs 158–9, 162–3
hospital 161–2
pay 37, 154–5
disability 63, 81, 104, 141, 144,
148–51, 258
drinking 81, 104, 136–7, 197, 227–30
Durant, Mary 64

E

education surveys 43, 49, 63, 82,
201–8, 252
egg consumption 128, 130
elderly persons 81, 141–7
disability 150
employment 172–4
housing needs 111
work and retirement 80, 142, 145,
147, 174
Electoral Register 22, 85, 90, 104,
109, 145, 223, 226, 240–1, 253
electricity 109, 194
employment services 188–92
employment surveys 91, 164–92
art college leavers 63
ex-offenders 218
pneumokoniosis sufferers 18
young persons 202
empty housing 80, 121
Equal Opportunities Commission 172
ethnic origin 83, 91, 243
Evans, Glyn 21, 23

expenditure: Social Survey Vote and budget 8–9, 23, 24, 27, 30–31, 38–9, 40, 47, 50, 53 *et seq*, 65, 67–70, 85–6, 95, 263–5
expenditure surveys 30, 36, 124, 126, 193–200

F

fairs and exhibitions 232–3
Family Expenditure Survey 28, 36–7, 40, 43, 49, 50, 55, 63, 64, 66, 71, 72, 82, 91, 93, 97–8, 99, 131, 195–200, 252, 256–7
Family Finances Survey 199, 200, 209–10
family intentions and formation 49, 83, 213–15
family planning 63, 81, 104, 137–40, 214, 256
farming 28, 238–9, 241
  training in 175
fieldforce *see* interviewers
Fife Clark, T 20, 34–5
fire service 183–4
flats: access 111
follow-up surveys 198, 199–200, 204, 213
food and nutrition 5, 11, 32, 37, 104, 127–34
Fothergill, Jack 17, 29, 37
foundation garments 231
Franklin, W E 5
free school meals 82, 200, 209–10
Fulton Committee on the Civil Service 49, 59, 60, 66, 253
further education 203–4, 207, 209

G

General Household Survey 65, 67, 71, 74, 80, 81 *et seq*, 93, 97, 99, 119, 136, 159, 160, 173–4, 187, 188, 189, 210–13, 216, 243, 244–5, 263, 279–90
General Register Office 9, 19, 33, 42, 50, 51, 70, 71, 72, 73, 82, 126, 157, 158, 213, 242, 259

  see also Office of Population Censuses and Surveys
Ginsberg, David 18, 21
Government Social Survey Department 58–9, 70, 91, 273–5
  origination of projects 269–72
Government Statistical Service 79, 100, 259
Gray, Percy 17, 18, 21, 22, 23, 28, 37, 43, 44, 47, 93

H

Handbook for interviewers 22–3, 35, 63
Handicapped and impaired in Great Britain 63, 104, 148–51, 258
Harris, Amelia 18, 29, 43
Harris, Muriel 17, 21, 22, 28, 35
health education surveys 8, 11, 134–5
health surveys 127–63, 253
hearing aids 18, 37, 81, 140–1, 142
heating 109, 110, 193–4
Heyworth Committee 45 *et seq*, 58, 70, 91, 258–9, 263
Higher National Certificate 175
holidays 236
home help service 63, 145, 156, 258
Home Office 3, 28, 32, 43, 49, 50, 62, 78, 83, 84, 100, 104, 136, 153, 180, 217, 220, 223, 224, 227–30, 236, 237, 240
hospitals 63, 84, 160
household budget surveys 2, 23, 36, 85, 195–6
household surveys 61–2, 63–5, 113
Housing Survey 43, 49, 115–17
housing surveys 38, 43, 49, 63, 80, 82, 84, 109–21, 232, 257
Howard League 28, 33
Human Sciences Committee 44–5
Huchinson, Bertram 18, 21

I

immunisation 135, 232
income surveys 82, 84, 193–5, 196–200, 256

industrial democracy 80, 179–80, 181, 182
industrial relations 49–50, 80, 176–87
infant feeding 133–4
Institution of Professional Civil Servants (IPCS) 10, 71, 89, 92
International Passenger Survey 43, 44, 69, 93, 97, 99, 124–6, 243
interviewing methods and techniques 28, 221, 241, 246, 266
IPS 126

J
J-index 23
job centres 191
jury service 22–3

K
Kemsley, Bill 18, 21, 22, 36, 37, 43, 47, 63, 93
Kingdom, T R 57, 65

L
Labour Force Survey 80, 85, 90, 105, 188, 245–6, 263
labour force surveys 43, 64, 80, 84, 121, 176
Lambeth, Dennis 18
Law Commissions 226, 252
Lewisham Survey 143
licensing laws 63, 227–8, 229–30, 252
living standards 193, 195, 198–9, 215–16
local government 49, 247–50, 252
London School of Economics (LSE) 3, 21, 176
London Transport Executive 28, 33, 124

M
McKennell, Aubrey 43–4, 63
Manpower Services Commission 192
Market Research Society 29
matrimonial property 226–7, 252
meals on wheels 142, 156

Medical Research Council (MRC) 15, 16, 60, 62, 131, 258
Medresco hearing aids 37, 140–1, 142
mentally handicapped 155–6
Merchant review 100–104, 268
methodological work 85, 94
migration 124–6
milk consumption 127, 128, 129, 133
mining communities 112, 165–7
Ministry of Agriculture 28, 33, 232, 238, 241
Ministry of Education 175, 201, 202
  see also Department of Education and Science
Ministry of Food 5, 6, 8, 11, 20, 23, 32, 121, 127, 128, 231
Ministry of Fuel and Power 193
Ministry of Health 8, 9, 11, 20, 24, 28, 32, 42, 60, 62–3, 128, 131, 134, 135, 137, 143, 148, 157, 158, 232, 258
  see also Department of Health and Social Security
Ministry of Housing 20, 43, 114, 115, 148, 257
  see also Department of the Environment
Ministry of Information 3–4, 6–7, 9, 13, 14, 15, 231
  see also Central Office of Information
Ministry of Labour, 2, 3, 6, 8, 32, 36, 55, 169, 173, 176, 196, 198, 202, 245
  see also Department of Employment
Ministry of National Insurance 28, 33, 142
Ministry of Social Security 50, 148
  see also Department of Health and Social Security
Ministry of Transport 34, 43, 124, 235
  see also Department of Transport
Ministry of Works 8
  see also Department of the Environment

mobility 28, 43, 80, 113–16, 124, 147
  labour 21, 43, 176
Monsky, Selma 43
morbidity 9–10, 12, 16, 18, 19, 20,
  24, 27, 33, 71, 151, 157–9, 257
Morton-Williams, Roma 43, 92
Moser, Claus 51, 59, 61 *et seq*, 70,
  100–102
Moss, Louis 3, 4, 5, 13, 23, 29, 37,
  64–5, 73–4, 92
motoring 43, 124

N

National Agricultural Advisory
  Service 37, 238
National Corporation for the Care of
  Old People (NCCOP) 142, 143
National Dwelling and Housing Survey
  119, 121
National Food Survey 23, 27, 30, 32,
  47, 93, 97–8, 99, 105, 131
National Health Service 10, 27, 42,
  81, 83, 84, 127, 138, 140, 151,
  152, 156 *et seq*
National Institute for Economic and
  Social Research (NIESR) 3–4
National Travel Surveys 47, 49, 80, 124
new towns 63, 111, 112
noise 43–4, 80, 109, 110, 121–3
nursing 28, 32, 80, 84, 151–3, 155–7,
  161–2
nutrition surveys 11, 37, 49, 104,
  127–34

O

offenders 218
  drink and 43, 228–9
  young 218, 220–1
Office of Manpower Economics
  (OME) 154–5
Office of Population Censuses and
  Surveys 72–4, 79, 84, 85, 90, 91,
  95, 97, 100, 103, 126, 188, 214,
  240, 242, 257, 259, 277–8
one-parent families 215–16
One Per Cent Survey 90–91, 93

operational surveys 231–46
orange juice 132–3
Oxford Institute of Statistics 28, 33,
  194

P

pedestrians, people as 80
pensions 28, 33
personal injury 241–2
pig- and poultry-keeping 28, 33, 241
pilot studies 37, 213, 244, 266
Plowden Report 42, 45–6, 48, 60, 75,
  76, 258, 259, 268
pneumokoniosis 18, 166–7
Political and Economic Planning
  (PEP) 15, 33
police 180, 181, 218–20, 228, 253
Post Enumeration Survey 49, 50,
  104, 240, 242–3
Post Office 43, 233–5
postal services 234
postal survey methods 28, 37, 44, 50,
  85, 133–4, 199, 214, 241, 248,
  253, 266
postcodes 234
  sampling 85, 246
poverty 198–9
primary health care 81, 162–3
prison staff 104
productivity 174–6
Programme Committee 50 *et seq*, 57,
  59–60, 64, 67–8, 70
property letting 43, 80, 82, 117–19,
  120
publication of reports 7, 18–19, 256

Q

qualifications 210–13
quota sampling 8, 22

R

random sampling 8, 9, 22
rates 82, 198, 252
Rayner review 96–104, 245, 261,
  266, 268

recruitment: armed forces 21, 167–8
  Civil Service 167
  coalmining 21, 165–6
  cotton industry 21, 164–5
  nursing 151–2
Redundancy Payments Act: effects 63, 184–5
refusals 6
Regulations for the Organization of Individual Surveys 7
Rent Act 37–8, 114–15, 117–19, 257
rented accommodation 43, 80, 82, 117–19, 120
repayment 21, 28, 33–4, 56–7, 95, 98–9, 102, 103, 104
residential care 43, 153, 155
respondents 6, 197
response 6
  FES 197
  GHS 244–5
  IPS 126
  non-response 22, 241
Retail Price Index 28, 36, 82, 98, 99, 114, 196, 197, 198, 257
retirement 28, 80, 142, 145, 147, 174
Road Research Laboratory 208
road safety 28, 34, 37, 208–9, 235, 266
road traffic 123
Royal Commission on Civil Liability and Personal Injury 241–2
Royal Commission on the Distribution of Income and Wealth 82
Royal Commission on the National Health Service 81, 83, 160
Royal Commission on the Remuneration of Doctors and Dentists 37, 154–5
Royal Commission on Trade Unions and Employers' Associations 49–50, 176–7, 178
Royal Commissions 1–2
Royal Statistical Society 2, 11, 22, 100–101
rural depopulation 113

S
sampling: FES 199
  GHS 244, 245
  IPS 126
  LFS 246
  methods and techniques 2, 8, 9, 22, 28, 85, 94, 104, 215, 217–18, 227, 238–9, 240, 241, 266–7
savings (personal) 28, 33, 194
school children: careers 49, 80, 82, 202 *et seq*
  fifth form girls 80, 82, 171, 210
  leisure 201–2, 208
  nutrition 82, 104
  primary schools 206
  sixth formers 49, 63, 207
  smoking 104
school meals 82, 104, 128, 200, 209–10
Schools Council 204–8, 252
science graduates 176
Scientific Advisory committee 11, 15
Scotland: alcohol consumption 137
  debt actions 225–6, 252
  devolution 251, 252
  family law 83, 227
  housing survey 8, 119
  licensing laws 229
  mining 112–13
  new towns 111, 112
  rural depopulation 113
  small firms 34
Scott, Christopher 44
Scottish Home and Health Department 111, 112, 113, 227
Scottish Council 34
Scottish Office 8, 33
Select Committee on National Expenditure 6–7, 10, 15
Sendall, Bernard 13
shopping hours 63, 227, 229, 252–3
sift method 149, 214
sixth formers 63, 207
smoking 49, 63, 81, 104, 135–6, 137, 197
Social and Community Planning Research 185

Social Science Research Council 47, 48, 60, 101, 259
social security 82, 83, 253
   claimants 83, 239–40
Social Survey: location in government 6–7, 14–15, 16, 29–30, 40, 48–9, 57–8, 62, 70–74, 255, 257, 259
   staff 261–3, 264–6
      1942–46 7, 11, 12
      1946–69 16–17, 19–20, 22, 23, 24, 30–31, 38–9, 40, 47, 57, 65–6, 69
      1970–81 73–4, 85–7, 91–4, 95, 99, 103
      gradings 14, 15, 21, 34, 54–5, 66, 70, 86, 87–90, 255, 263
      part timers 31, 34, 38, 41
      recruitment 66–7
      structure 35, 40–41, 54–5
Stocks, Percy 9, 157, 158
students 203–4
   income and expenditure 82
Survey of Sickness 9–10, 12, 16, 18, 19, 20, 24, 27, 33, 71, 151, 157–9, 257

T
Taylor, Stephen 4, 7, 11–12
telephones: directories 233–4
   interviewing 246, 266
Thomas, Geoffrey 5, 11, 17, 21, 28, 37, 44, 47, 74, 92, 93, 94
tourism 124
town and country planning 21, 109, 111–13
trade unions 49–50, 176–9, 186, 187
   see also Institution of Professional Civil Servants
training 189–90, 192
Treasury 14–15, 17, 18, 24, 27, 29, 31, 34, 36, 37, 42, 47 *et seq*, 59 *et seq*, 65, 66, 67, 70, 82, 99, 107, 167, 194, 259, 263

U
unemployed 104, 187, 188
unfair dismissal 185–7

V
venereal disease 134, 256

W
Wagner, Gertrude 17
waiting lists (housing) 20, 113–14
Wales: devolution 251, 252
war medals 21, 256–7
water heating 109, 110
welfare foods 37, 128, 132–3
wheelchairs 81
Whitehead, Frank 92, 93–4
Wilkins, Leslie 17, 18, 21, 28, 29, 217
Willcock, Bob 17, 18, 23, 28, 37, 43, 47, 266
Witzenfeld, Sam 41, 67
women and employment 8, 21, 80, 168–72, 232
   attitudes to 171–2
   shiftwork 80, 172
worker participation 80, 179–80, 181, 182
Workplace Industrial Relations 49–50, 80, 178–9

Y
youth employment 49, 80, 82, 202 *et seq*
Youth Service 208